DOMINANCE AND DECLINE

14-10-2015   09:10:47

DOMINANCE AND DECLINE

THE ANC IN THE TIME OF ZUMA

SUSAN BOOYSEN

WITS UNIVERSITY PRESS

Published in South Africa by:

Wits University Press
1 Jan Smuts Avenue
Johannesburg, 2001
www.witspress.co.za

First published 2015

978-1-86814-884-4 (print)
978-1-86814-887-5 (PDF)
978-1-86814-885-1 (EPUB: North America, South America, China)
978-1-86814-886-8 (EPUB: Rest of World)

Edited by Monica Seeber
Proofread by Lisa Compton
Index by Sanet le Roux
Original cover concept by Susan Booysen
Cover design by Hybrid Creative, South Africa
Typeset by MPS Limited, Chennai, India
Printed and bound by Paarl Media

CONTENTS

LIST OF FIGURES AND TABLES

PREFACE

As President Jacob Zuma starts his exit from formal state and party power, I realised that it was time to take stock of what has been happening to the African National Congress (ANC) as well as the government and people of South Africa 'in the time of Zuma'. Capturing trends meant taking aim at a moving target. Even if the analysis followed a fairly predictable track, it was going to be, in ANC language, a 'challenging' task to capture the infamous epoch. Events unfolded as my research and writing took shape. Projects accumulated to build Zuma's legacy, explain or reinterpret the consequences of the period, and there was fervour from within for the post-Zuma era to resemble the Zuma era. Despite new developments, the fundamentals of the era had been cast; the trends presented themselves for capture into a book, *this* book.

Dominance and Decline follows in the footsteps of my earlier book, *The African National Congress and the Regeneration of Political Power. Dominance and Decline* is not a doomsday analysis – it recognises the ANC's strengths and accomplishments amidst the havoc sown by the Zuma-ist ANC, which has also become *the* ANC of the time. The central questions the book answers are: How much damage has been wreaked and how permanent is it likely to be? My analysis also casts light on the question: What kind of ANC after Zuma?

The time of Zuma has turned out to be one of many turning points – away from unambiguous moral high ground, from idealised leaders, from the hope that policies brought by the extensive and expensive state will anchor continuous liberation. The time of Zuma has been one of persistent ANC dominance yet also of appalling decline. It is the entanglement of glory and irony. There is little doubt that South Africa – perhaps also the ANC – will glance back and contemplate what went awry, at what exact point in time, amidst what pieces of countervailing information. This book is intended to take stock and analyse, to map and interpret the unfolding trends.

It was never going to be easy to execute a study of this period. While the analysis gives credit where credit is due, it is also consistently critical of the party-movement that has epitomised much of South Africa's liberation struggle. The task is particularly precarious given that the organisation has immersed itself in the project of recreating patriotism and nationalist understandings of the infancy of the economic and political struggle. Publicly it expects ongoing recognition that the liberation struggle is only just beginning. The researcher or analyst dissecting the contradictions is but a small spoke in the wheel of history, but a guaranteed large thorn in the ANC's flesh. The most tangible indicator of this climate is the frequent question, when I get stopped in public places, 'Are you not afraid to say what you do?' So far, my answer is 'No', largely because my critiques are widely shared. I know this from my research interviews, including many that come from the heart of the ANC.

The idea for a follow-up book to *Regeneration* first came from Wits University Press's publisher, Veronica Klipp, at the 2013 African Studies Association meeting in Baltimore. When I started planning my 2014–2015 sabbatical, a second edition of *Regeneration* quickly metamorphosed into a sequel: a study of a remarkable period in South African and ANC history – one in which the enigma of Zuma and the contradictions of an ANC that selected and stayed with a tragic president (who brought some gains yet also damaged the ANC) were on graphic display. This book profiles an ANC that has remained strong but could ill afford the Zuma imprint at a time when the liberation stamp has started to fade.

I wish I had a research team to thank. Instead, I draw on my extensive personal research, ongoing since the *Regeneration* ink went dry. Wits University sponsored segments of my research. A selection of cited, albeit often not by name, research informants helped me draw the contours of the Zuma landscape: my thanks to those in the core of the movement and of state power who made the time to talk to me; news media that extended my observations to where I could not be personally; the anonymous reviewers who said 'Publish!'; David Moore, who read my first draft and gave valuable comments; Monica Seeber, who understood my project and used her great editing skills to fine-tune my copy; many friends who supported me through the process; and, above all, to the Wits University Press team who brought the project to fruition.

Susan Booysen
September 2015

INTRODUCTION

As the African National Congress (ANC) enters South Africa's third decade of democracy, it is strong but flawed, and increasingly frayed. It is far from defeated, but is toiling to prevent itself from falling below the waterline that separates exceptionalism from ordinariness. It is on the borderline where famed-liberation-movement-turned-political-party could become an ordinary contestant in a multiparty democracy or – worse – a predatory strongman.[1] The ANC leads with substantial margins over its political rivals. It is in charge of a state that holds powerful apparatuses. This is still the time of ANC dominance and hegemony,[2] although symptoms of declining power speak of a tumultuous twenty years in government that have gone well for the party but hardly as well as expected. Hegemony is being eroded. The liberation movement that had moved into democratic state power is making space for a new, reinvented, modern ANC. Its moral leadership is questioned, often.

It is a time of major contradictions for the ANC. The contemporary ANC has the inner organs and the nostalgic aura of the former liberation movement; it has the framework of a constitutional state and multiparty democracy, and lifeblood that blends high morality with corruption and self-humiliation – it wears the coat of a developmental state mired in patronage. It is hard work for this transformed ANC to build and maintain its power, and its methods do not always do justice to the lore of the former liberation movement. But the ANC does what it takes to defend its edge – within the parameters of its own rules and the political system in the time of President Jacob Zuma. The ANC of 2015–2016 is forging its way into continuous power, but is not regenerating at replacement levels.

Twenty-five years ago the enemy was external and the contest easily defined. Now, the ANC mostly battles enemies within. Many citizens still identify deeply with the ANC, but they also see the avarice and attempted delusion perpetrated by leaders. This dissonance fuels opposition parties and adds to citizens' disappointment with transformation. The state malfunctions and underperforms, and at times the ANC barely controls it. The state is in courtship-partnership with black business and in tolerant coexistence with white business that plays by the ANC state's black economic empowerment (BEE) rules. The ANC is pliable when it comes to political class interests. Confirmed characteristics of the emerging new ANC include the contented coexistence of corruption and threatened clampdowns to correct the rot. The ANC knows how best to be the people's movement, but believes that it retains enough sway with the people to do it the leaders' way. Near-absolute presidential power in the Zuma heyday blends into state patronage, and a factional cadre reward system nurtures the ANC government's power structure.

This contemporary ANC does not take kindly to the minority parties. Demonising and undermining them are a *sine qua non* for the ANC that still aspires to resurrect its former electoral majorities. Constructing the public agenda through extensive media influence, and ensuring that state delivery carries an ANC-specific label are simply part of helping the ANC to build sustained hegemony.

Dominance and Decline analyses this moment in South Africa's political history – the time of Jacob Zuma – as the ANC's liberation dividend is wearing thin and a new generation becomes the electorate; as opposition parties grow and reposition; as state institutions are hollowed out through patronage – and as South Africa urbanises and post-liberation issues start to dominate.

THE FOUR FACES OF ANC POWER IN THE TIME OF ZUMA

This ANC is the embodiment of fragility amid considerable strength distributed across four faces of power: its interface with the people; electoral contests; operations in state and government; and the ANC organisationally. The ANC's first two decades in power have demonstrated its ability to pull itself together and out of trouble, even if by denying, ignoring and deferring issues or by sending them down the path of legal process – until civil society and opposition parties grow tired. Such evasive actions have often carried the consent of a large proportion of the people who support ANC action on its enemies of choice: opposition parties, the media, 'third forces' or intra-state critics.

Dominance and Decline builds on the base of my theory of the four faces of ANC power in my 2011 book, *The African National Congress and the Regeneration of Political Power. Dominance and Decline*, a period study, explores the ANC's hold on political power, specifically during Jacob Zuma's dual presidencies of the ANC and South Africa. The scope and significance of events from 2011 to 2015 warrant a specific analysis. The developments have changed the character and status of the ANC: it remains predominant but is no longer omnipotent.

The book assesses and interprets events, statements, interviews, speeches, surveys and other sources to analyse the ANC's double act of decay and continuous dominance. It offers an interpretative analysis. It extracts trends to show the fault lines of the present and the future that are unfolding for the ANC as party-movement and government. It builds on a continuous, multifaceted research project on the ANC. It uses primary research (including interviews, public opinion surveys, qualitative content analyses and observation) along with a range of documents and media reports that help relate the events that the study interprets. It dissects the words of political actors, and assesses plans, strategies and programmes. Formal statements and events in the life of party and government converge with denials and contradictory behaviour to constitute *de facto* policies, political actions that matter and *de facto* trends. Strategies for the maintenance, recovery and regeneration of political power are manifested by both design and default – and the study extracts these strategies from deliberately intended and serendipitous sources.

The ANC remains secure in its national electoral power, albeit with disconcerting fractures springing up. The ANC was hurt in Election 2014. A result of 62 per cent of the national vote was remarkably good, but for the first time since it took power in 1994 trajectories solidified along which it could eventually lose power. There is a gradual attrition of trust in the ANC as the party that corrects problems. Its unambiguous credibility has lapsed. The rise of a 'left' opposition, in particular the Economic Freedom Fighters (EFF) and, tentatively, a post-election new workers' party (associated with the National Union of Metalworkers of South Africa [Numsa] and the United Front), has marked the era. Gauteng province is the ANC's Achilles heel, and the metros that exclude rural bases are the second major electoral weak spot.

The EFF, Democratic Alliance (DA) and the 'new opposition' alliances have focused on weaknesses in ANC governance and revealed an ANC in state institutions and policy that is in power but not always in command. Perhaps this is convenient for the ANC – organisationally it would stand to benefit from

3

the use of state resources to nurture the patriotic bourgeoisie and keep middle-class 'tenderpreneurs' contented and civil servants politically loyal, whereas an efficient and capable state would give it less leeway. But, instead, corrupt and mismanaging politicians and bureaucrats have often run amok while security, legal and essential service institutions are hard at work, although sometimes deviously and with reduced control of their functions.

ANC power is entrenched in the state. Party and state are thoroughly fused. The ANC uses its command over the state not merely to strengthen itself but also to protect its president – for which purpose, a 2015 snapshot reveals, a range of public institutions are serially disgraced. The ANC reassures South Africans that it is turning corners in infrastructure, industrialisation and small business development. It influences (but cannot control) the media, devises sophisticated communication strategies to manufacture a president that does not really exist, and refines counter-information through the public and private (or semi-private) sympathetic media.

The ANC has become Janus-faced in its relationship to the people. It shows weakness when it proclaims closeness. 'The people' remain largely in the ANC camp, but nowadays ask questions to which only uncomfortable answers are forthcoming. Public attitudes are becoming more critical, affected by lapses in leadership.[3] South Africans, irrespective of political orientation, live under command of a government that allows the lawless and corrupt in its ranks. This is the new, post-liberation ANC, comfortable with living a double life of left-speaking while right-pleasing big business's interests. Patronage and patrimony feed the middle-class game while the social wage and grants signify caring for the underclasses. Millions of South Africans reward the ANC by voting for it.

South Africans are not disinheriting their ANC, but are less forgiving than they were a decade ago. They are far more critical and cynical of their ANC 'parent' and liberator and ongoing political home. In many ways, the people have changed as much in their political and social culture in the first two decades of democracy as has their ANC and their ANC government.

The ANC claims sole ownership of the liberation victory. There is no rival organisation that can count on as much of the liberation dividend as it can. The struggle against the legacies of apartheid will possibly never be over and the ANC will have perpetual grounds to relive the conquest. Organisationally, the party has changed. Factional control is entrenched and from 2007 onwards the Zuma faction has gradually become accepted as *the* ANC. This Zuma-ANC was challenged in internal elections, but only half-heartedly, given the

Zuma-ists' tight control. Many of the adverse signals were evident in the days of former president Thabo Mbeki, some even in the time of Nelson Mandela's presidency. The Zuma era added serial scandals and embarrassments and the prevailing leadership might one day have to account for letting the movement change to this extent, and explain why it sacrificed so much for the protection of one person.

The ANC is throwing everything into the mix in order to stay on the commanding heights. It has thoroughly learned its lessons from its fellow liberation-movement/governing-parties, especially of Zimbabwe, Namibia, Botswana and Mozambique.[4] It understands that its majorities are likely to fray further, but knows that preventative measures must be taken to ensure it will not (as in Zimbabwe) have to rely on violence on its own citizens in order to retain power. It also understands that (as in Namibia) overwhelming majorities can be resurrected as long as opposition parties cannot win over the people. Most of all, the ANC has learned to take preventative action to maximise – within legal and constitutional parameters – its control over information. This is the new post-*Regeneration* world that *Dominance and Decline* dissects.

CRISIS – THE ANC'S OPERATING PROCEDURE

'The time of Zuma' has been a time of change for the ANC. The party retains a reservoir of support, a buffer that gives it a substantial edge over its closest political rivals. There remains an ample amount of goodwill, even in the face of public outcries (including from its own supporters). It may very well be in power for some time to come, but it is on the defensive, and working hard to halt the decline before it reaches critical levels.

The ANC circa 2014–2015 has sustained power amid frequent crises, both organisational and in government. Scandals at the top level of political leadership (notably at presidential level, but for which the president has not assumed responsibility) have blown up almost routinely. Enclaves of state institutions and governance processes have fallen apart even as the president has described them as well-functioning.[5] Old scandals have neither been resolved nor faded, but were just eclipsed by passing time (every so often they have come home to roost). The ANC lives a contradiction. In the frank between-election periods its followers criticise it – before closing ranks and reaffirming the ANC in power at the point of the next contest for voters' allegiance.

5

At presidential and top-ANC political class level the series of crises reads like a string of dishonour – Nkandlagate, Guptagate, arms deal, spy tapes, tolerance of corruption in upper government, dysfunctionality in security institutions, inability to contain malfunction at the lower end of the state, clampdowns at Parliament – and some added the great escape of Omar al-Bashir to the roll. In the ANC government, the failure to create (or stimulate the creation of) enough jobs to match and exceed labour force growth,[6] the poor and erratic quality of services delivered, the inability of local government to discipline and improve itself, and the efforts to escape top-level responsibility for the Marikana killings stand out as thorns of incapacity, disgrace and arrogance. South Africa's democratic institutions have suffered and the ANC government's moral authority has been eroded. The ANC in Parliament pleads respect for the institution and its majority, while the majority elevates the interests of the president above scrutiny (in some instances the courts have restored trust).

The ANC has over-interpreted its 2014 electoral endorsement, equating it with the people pardoning the president and condoning accumulation by the ruling class, and it defensively uses its electoral majority to carry unpopular parliamentary decisions – for example, using the *dicta* 'no charges, no findings' to shield the president, or 'innocent until proven guilty' to dismiss suspicions of his abuse of power and his personal enrichment.

The name of the primary political game during Zuma's time at the ANC helm has been the advancement and protection of the interests of the powerful ANC ruling class – the class, as noted by Karl Marx,[7] 'which is the ruling material force of society [and] is at the same time its ruling intellectual force'. Governance has taken second place, although symbiotically linked to the elite's power prerogatives. The political class in government has ensured there would always be enough evidence of delivery and transformation to indulge themselves, either privately (moonlighting, or piggybacking on public positions, associated tenders and other deals) or through direct lucrative public sector and political employment. It has nurtured extensive bonds for benefactor business and small business patronage circles, and ploughed business opportunities into private hands – and resources into party pockets.

Corruption itself, along with half-hearted, partial and inconsequential action against it, has become a crisis for the ANC. There has been much 'going softly and slowly' on corrective and disciplinary action against cadres generally – and politically deployed cadres specifically. Intra-ANC factional interests are

6

a prime consideration. Decisive action still has to be mediated by the level of influence of those prone to corruption,[8] and by possible repercussions for the politically ambitious on the privileged insider track in the next round of branch, regional and provincial ANC elections.

The crises overall have been of such magnitude that by most general (and many expert) impressions South Africa is in an unfolding fully-fledged crunch. However, the crises coexist with an ANC that remains electorally strong and thoroughly entrenched in state power. Contemporary writing offers insights as to the unfolding condition of the ANC, with book titles reflecting the nature of the changing polity, the recognisable crises and scholars' perspectives on the balance between crisis and continuity of ANC power.[9] Veering between class, race and neopatrimonial interpretations, published books and articles explore the 'fall of the ANC' and the possibility that South Africa is 'on the verge of a failed state' and in a 'looming crisis'. 'The Zuma years' are affecting South Africa in an unprecedented way, 'the arrogance of power' pulling the ANC down even as it remains electorally in charge. The ANC remains determined to see its revolution, even if by now a revolution in name only and with ownership contested by the EFF. The 'revolution was deferred', 'the revolution was suspended', but 'the revolution was coming', albeit some way off and conditional on left parties almost miraculously developing staying power in the face of an ANC that was 'just singing and dancing' to sabotage and fend off opposition party onslaughts. 'Zuma was exposed', but in the land of advanced patronage there was always something 'left to steal'. The ANC ticked on, 'regenerating power' in ways sufficient to sustain itself.

'Could anyone vote DA?' was a crunch question for many South Africans who continued celebrating the dawn of democracy, in effect desperately 'holding onto a dream', even if Thabo Mbeki's dream was 'deferred'. 'The founders', imperfect themselves, might wish to distance themselves, yet ANC leaders threaten disaffected voters with the spirits of the founders should they dare to endorse an opposition party, even one increasingly under young, black and credible leadership. Critical voices appear out of ANC trenches, heads just 'above the parapet', but strictly *only* once they have exited from the heart of the ANC power works and moved into retired (or more neutral) post-peak ANC-related deployment. Come election time, it remains – largely but slowly decreasing – the time to remember 1994. 'Remember not to forget' the past, the ANC tells the voters. When the titles in the literature carried the dismal message of the revolution locked into a time capsule, a 'rumour of spring' brought a positive spin (albeit only in the title, not the content), confirming that the political reality is in many ways that of a revolution aborted by a ruling class firmly entrenched in power and contented with gradual socioeconomic change amid far-reaching deficits in transformation.

Few authors in this body of literature, no matter how gloomy their prognoses, write off the ANC. The authors of the epoch – myself included – are (at least in part) products of a past that we struggled to defeat. Struggle against injustice is ingrained, and we do not want to forget it – even if a sometimes loathsome ANC reminds us of its limited liability for the incompleteness of the transformation, at least up to 2015. The period of anti-apartheid struggle and its immediate aftermath was a 'kind of magic' in many ways, with the ANC relentlessly remaking itself and reinventing the onslaughts. In the first couple of democratic decades, robust opposition politics became referred to as the destabilisation of ANC and government – the struggle was not complete, especially not in party-speak. The opposition, the media, at times the courts or other state institutions (especially the public protector) were continually being convicted, in the court of the ANC, of 'betraying the revolution'. It will take a very long view to complement the 'long walk to freedom' on this route.

It is these complexities of the ANC at the time of entering the third decade of democracy that *Dominance and Decline* explores. It tests the findings of *Regeneration* in the particular period of the ANC under President Jacob Zuma. *Dominance and Decline* details how the ANC's changing identity affects its hold on political power – as it unfolds organisationally, in relation to the people, in electoral dominance over other parties and in its control over and use of state power. The 2011 book *Regeneration* stands as a work of reference presenting the core arguments and their research substantiation. It covered the ANC's first eighteen years in political power and captured the earlier phases of the dynamics currently unfolding around the ANC – the complex and often self-contradictory story of a weakening yet thoroughly entrenched ANC.[10]

Dominance and Decline is an applied sequel, an in-depth study of the ANC in power in the Zuma era. It is not a comparison of liberation movement governments or one-party dominant systems, and nor is it about transitions to (or relapses from) democracy. The analysis occasionally refers to other former southern African liberation movements in power, but avoids positioning the study in relation to the diverse and only partially relevant bodies of literature. The ANC never quite fits the mould of these generalisations.[11]

CONTOURS OF THE ZUMA ERA

Two decades of being in power and celebrating achievements – while finding ways to live with compromised liberation ideals and feeding frenzies at the trough – have rendered the ANC a thoroughly changed organisation, straddling the divides between noble and compromised, between grassroots caring and elite greed, and between democracy and control to try to reverse negative perceptions.

Organisationally, the ANC is the 'former' liberation movement more than the 'liberation movement in power'. It works hard to nourish the liberation links that have suffered through failures in government. Contemporary ANC leaders still conceptualise praxis as an ongoing struggle against the dark forces of the apartheid and colonial past. As the ANC settles into its third decade in power, it is well beyond its centenary celebrations, but keeps the flame of history alive as struggle heroes are proclaimed and honoured (and occasionally created) and 'twenty year' narratives continue to permeate speeches on national radio and television to find their way into South Africans' political consciousness.

The ANC has lost the innocence of the newly-in-power liberation movement learning the ropes, keeping its followers assured that it is acting in their interests with consistency and planning, and not just as a coincidental side-effect of its leaders' self-interest. It has to do this well enough for people to remain trusting that the ANC is their best chance of a better life and to be persuaded that the better life, adapted to contemporary expectations and changing demands, is a practical possibility. Satisfaction with the governing party is not guaranteed through once-off delivery. Economic liberation, for example, is not achieved through a social wage, a social grant and a reconstruction and development (RDP) house when the middle class has grown impressively and the ruling class has achieved wealth. The poor see the gap as getting wider; they do not see how precarious is the hold of the middle class on the good life with its high debt, no savings and compulsive consumerism.

The people compare themselves to their political leaders – and see many an ANC leader flounder. They do not lead by example; they place themselves in front of delivery queues; they see ethics and honesty as negotiable. This form of leadership includes ample application of state resources for self-advancement. The people resent this tangibly but their feeling is often based on resentment of leaders looking after themselves better than their followers. Moral condemnation of unethical behaviour often follows, tentatively.

While the ANC's electoral support has gone into decline, the party has been relying more on state power, massaging its image as guardian of liberation politics, and utilising scare tactics. The 2014 victory came on the back of the effusive use of state power – at worst the blatant redirection of public resources to aid its election campaign, at best the skilful synchronisation of state delivery with electoral cycles, spiced with reminders of the public benefits that accrue to citizens through ANC policies. In 2014 the ANC had the benefit of celebrating two decades of democracy, and this resource could also have staying power: Election 2019, after all, will coincide with campaigns celebrating a quarter of a century in power, and 2024 will mark thirty years of democracy.

Many communities have been content to continue combining electoral support for their ANC with protest at poor living conditions and life opportunities. Communities compete with one another for attention to problems, aspiring to getting at least what neighbouring communities have received. In most cases community protests have been about services, living conditions (ranging from mild deprivation to squalor) and better representation. In some instances the protests have been severe, resembling localised revolts of the poor. Repeated xenophobic attacks have highlighted the need of deprived citizens to vent their anger and to do so against available and powerless targets – often foreign citizens in their own areas.

In this time, the force of the democratic institutions has weakened as the ANC as organisation has increasingly fused with the state and imposed its internal politics onto government. Parliament and municipal councils alike have earned citizen disrespect, if not disdain. State-owned enterprises have fallen like dominoes as presidentially driven deployment initiatives took their toll.

In many respects, the ANC in government has upheld constitutionalism and the rule of law, or respected freedom of expression and freedom of the media. In other instances, however, these fundamental principles of South Africa's constitutional democracy have prevailed only after extensive civil society and opposition party mobilisation, court cases that ended up in the high courts or Constitutional Court, and crude policy initiatives and legislation that had to be appealed and then aborted or suspended. The ANC excels at double-speak. Upon the 2014 launch of the media working group, for example, President Zuma praised the contribution of the media to South Africa's liberation, along with the values of 'the right of the public to information' without allusion to the pressures the government has placed on the media to rally behind the good story *sans* public and political sector corruption. In 2015, the ANC proclaimed that it does not get involved in operational matters in government, but is contradicted by the ruling of the Eastern Cape High Court that a former Nelson Mandela Bay municipal manager could not do her work for political meddling.[12]

South Africans, both by virtue of political culture and by eager pursuit of the example of their leaders, have become an exuberantly lawless and noisy nation and community protest action is but one example. There is also general tolerance of petty to modest crime, with the line drawn at personal violence and violation. Blue-collar crime is seen as not too bad; citizens turn a blind eye to acquiring stolen or pirated goods, and corruption could be 'harmless' because there are no immediate victims.[13] The e-toll saga highlighted the corrosion of government authority, and even with the 2015 amendments citizens dug into their non-payment trenches. In other cases, the judicial system fails citizens and they take the law into their own hands.

This is a weakened political order, yet it is possible that this post-Polokwane ANC will remain standing for some time. It has to demonstrate visibly that it has the interest of its followers at heart. Leadership needs to strike a calculated balance to be seen as in control of the corruptible modern-day cadres, and project that it can still steer government towards achieving the greater national good. The ANC has epitomised factional battles for control since its 2007 Polokwane elective conference. The Mbeki faction (without Mbeki) became the Congress of the People (Cope); many returned to the ANC; others scattered. Mangaung 2012 saw another pro-Zuma factional victory, a costly victory. The Zuma camp ensured that the delegate list was unassailable. In the process, the ANC lost some of its character as an organisation of the people, structured bottom-up through branches, becoming instead a top-down and a semi-consultative structure (the lower rungs organising to get seniors' approval and elevation into important party and public positions).

With Zuma-ists firmly entrenched in party and government at national, provincial and local levels, positioning for the post-Zuma era turned out to be alternative slates emerging from within the Zuma faction, with 'little ANCs' spawned in the ranks of those out of favour or temporarily alienated.[14] There is sufficient forgiveness of the aberrant ones, and incorporation of varying factions by the Zuma-ANC, to enable it to maintain a coherent centre.

This paints a picture of an ANC in control and popularly anchored but it is not nearly as strongly settled as it was two decades earlier; nor as strongly as it was one decade ago. In late 2014, Zuma acknowledged publicly that the ANC was 'in trouble'.[15] The strongest redeeming factor for the ANC is that growing disillusionment, cynicism and disaffection are not being converted straight into support for opposition parties – although the opposition is at its strongest in the more than twenty years of democracy. On the ANC's right the DA is growing incrementally. Although handicapped by internal contradictions, it is the most consistently growing political party in South Africa, arguably with enhanced electoral appeal under the leadership of Mmusi Maimane, and it is capturing a portion of the patriotic bourgeoisie from the ANC. South Africans are nowadays less hostile towards the DA, although the ANC projects it as racially biased and colonially inspired.

The ANC's standing was also being dented from the left. The economically deprived 'children' of the democratic era increasingly had new options. Much of the EFF's legitimacy comes from being within the ANC 'kraal', associated with resistance and liberation. Voters and traditional ANC supporters could support this party and not feel treasonous about it. The left-of-the-ANC at times was a new hive of action. No ANC dissidence to date has had the potential to speak to the grievances of the underclasses and the un- or under-employed left behind in the race for middle-class status. This rise of the EFF as a left flag-bearer stood in the context of the failure of the Tripartite Alliance. The Congress of South African Trade Unions (Cosatu) was fracturing. Along with the South African Communist Party (SACP), the Alliance had been a left-leaning clearing house for the ANC's policy stances, especially in the immediate aftermath of Zuma's election at Polokwane. Over time, the SACP fused into the ANC, with minimal policy differentiation and few notably left alternatives to mainstream ANC policy decisions.

Perhaps the Cosatu fractures illustrate the contradictions of the ANC Alliance more than any other – and they are excessively personalised to boot. The Zwelinzima Vavi feud and subsequent expulsion were triggered by Vavi's outspokenness on the ANC and Zuma's flaws (and fuelled by suspect personal judgement in terms of office affairs). The intent of the National Union of Metalworkers of South Africa (Numsa) to form a left political party spurred Cosatu's ongoing but staggered process of crumbling. The ANC stepped in to prevent Cosatu's fracturing before Election 2014, and urged the mid-2015 summit to resolve discontent and retain Cosatu (but always on the conditions set by the Zuma-ists, with Cyril Ramaphosa's task team nominally trying to patch things up). Numsa commenced the United Front initiative, a social movement project to feed into the launch of a workers' party, also referred to as the Movement for Socialism. The EFF had a significant head start in channelling left sentiment into parliamentary politics. The Marikana killings widened the distance between the ANC and the left. They revealed an ANC that is not just anti-militant-worker, but a party that would go to some lengths not to assume responsibility at the level of the political executive.

In 2015 forces opposing the ANC were gaining in scope and momentum. The centre of the organisation was holding but now it was more fragile and contested than at any preceding point in democratic South Africa. The ANC was attempting to prevent these forces from reaching the electoral arena. Simultaneously, ANC attention was increasingly required to hold together and improve its operations in government. The ANC in government had to find the answer to cadre deployment running out of credibility when it had no alternative strategy for being in control of the state and keeping patronage going. State-party predicaments came to a peak at the exact time that the ANC was starting to run short of time to make good on more of the promises for a state that would fill in the voids of poverty, unemployment and inequality – or simply for a state that was not seen as a dispensary for cadre privileges.

This was an ambiguous period for the ANC. The two plates of the ANC's life were crossing: the ANC, in many eyes a noble liberation movement; and the ANC as a compromised and modern governing party, stumbling on through the minefield of managing a state while being more and more deeply imbricated in it. Perhaps most of all, the ANC under the tutelage of Jacob Zuma was characterised by the defence of denying wrongdoing and lapses.

THE ANC'S REGENERATION SHOW SAILS ON

The chapters of *Dominance and Decline* offer details to the broad contours outlined in this Introduction, spelling out how, by both design and default, the ANC circa 2015 continues to regenerate power, amid the struggles of the Zuma epoch. For the ANC to maintain itself in power over time, it needs to regenerate across the four faces of political power (Figure 1.1) and do so sufficiently to counter or neutralise its losses.

Regenerative actions will be scrutinised, identifying the mechanisms created and used by the ANC to build real or imagined power.[16] The book's statements about regeneration are conditioned by questions of extent, proportion and scale of decline. Nonetheless, the words that often preface statements about the extent of the ANC's continuous project for the regeneration of its political power are 'overwhelmingly', 'largely', 'mostly' and 'regularly'. The mechanisms explain how the ANC keeps its head above water during Jacob Zuma's time.

Figure 1.1: Trends in ANC power into the current conjuncture: Interpretation of empirical data

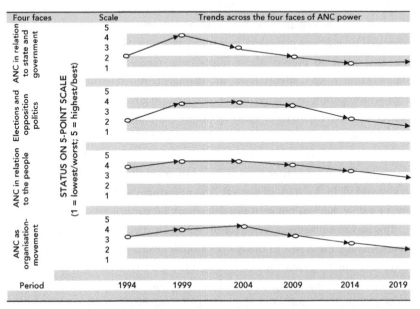

Note: *The African National Congress and the Regeneration of Political Power* ended this graph at 2009 and projected trends towards 2014. *Dominance and Decline* captures the subsequent period and projects trends towards 2019.

Primary mechanisms are upfront, in clear and overt manifestations and specifically designed and used to produce power. *Secondary mechanisms* may very well be by explicit design, but may also be manifested *de facto* – they are not planned interventions but emerge as unintended by-products of policies and actions. Jointly the operation of the mechanisms tells the tale of an oddly anarchistic and often lawless society, led by dubious examples but that at the end of the day hangs together, endorses the ANC, and largely works … even if in the presence of crime, corruption, failures in multiple public institutions, and the tolerance of these transgressions by citizens and government alike. Most of these mechanisms operate in a way that preserves ANC power. They are activated not because the ANC is under immediate threat, but in order to forestall and fend off further attacks and to prevent criticisms from eroding the outer layers of ANC power.

People

The ANC's bond with the people remains strong, even if it often seems an irrational attachment as between elections voters censure the ANC yet at election time they tend to re-endorse their party, flaws, misdemeanours and all. These are the main mechanisms for power regeneration in the domain of the people:

- *Nurture, replenish and reinvent the ANC's close association with the political liberation of South Africa.*

  The ANC's association with struggle and liberation is constantly cultivated in the public mind. The momentum it generated in its hundredth anniversary year and the twenty years of democracy celebration continues unabated – for example, it uses every opportunity to bring the past into the present, big occasions and speeches drawing out the links. Official hero ('giants of liberation') and statesperson funerals are carefully designed to reinvigorate the link to the struggle past; 'hidden histories' of struggle figures are uncovered; reburials have been arranged to fit the profiling of current government and the rekindling of memory. Patriotism and nationalism are carefully nurtured around the ANC as principal agent.

- *Work to have the ANC always accepted as the legitimate struggle parent figure, as well as contemporary gatekeeper to economic survival and well-being.*

  The ANC and ANC-as-government are often seen as the caring parent who will be 'bringing food home tonight'. Increasingly the 'children-citizens' also inverse this role, talking about the ANC as the aberrant child who will come around, mend its ways, and again choose better, more ethical leaders. The parent has in fact brought much food home, even if not in sufficient amounts or as much as the leaders ensure for themselves.

- *Govern and deliver to foster loyalty to the ANC.*

  The ANC has evolved: from getting popular support (largely courtesy of its status as liberator) to getting popular backing (courtesy of its hold over state power and its status as dispenser of services, social support and jobs). The change might not be as much as expected – but the ANC has an automatic winning position: comparing its delivery with that of the apartheid past. In a new and modern manner, prevalent among the youth, the ANC is supported as the party to a transaction, dispenser of patronage with control over who gets a job, the other side of the transaction being favour at election time.

- *Tolerate and tread carefully on community protest.*
  The ANC benefits from the ongoing twinning of protest and electoral support. Protesters are often citizens who have benefited from ANC rule.[17] The party recognises that protest is a vent, releasing anger, enabling voters to reaffirm it. Protest has largely become integrated in the mechanism of representation – it can require extreme action, including violent protest, to get representatives to attend to needs. Community protest has not, however, become integrated across communities to constitute a national revolt, partly because government treats protesters with kid gloves. Protesters get arrested occasionally but charges are brought rarely and it is exceptional to see convictions (beyond minimal admissions of guilt) in the courts. Operation Fiela of 2015 served in some respects to preserve this privileged ANC-protester relationship by trying to remove criminal elements that can stir up or exploit the 'standard' protests.

Organisation

No other party has captured citizens' pro-ANC sentiment or rivalled its bond with the people. The prominent opposition parties have largely lacked liberation or authentic anti-apartheid struggle credentials. The ANC and its networks remain a family to a great extent, bound at first by the liberation struggle and subsequently by the control over and dispensing of state resources for public, private and ANC-organisational good. Several mechanisms serve the ANC, especially:

- *Accept factional control and reward loyalists and returnees.*
  Factional governance of the organisation has become the affirmed and tolerated practice. There is an understanding that there will be a circulation of elites, and that those out of current favour either have to wait their turn or accept statuses as members of 'fringe ANCs' – who might enjoy the benefits of positions or professional-business opportunities, as long as they have not affronted the in-faction. The likelihood of splits in the core has subsided as it has become accepted for the ANC to be ruled by a faction, with the little ANCs on the fringes. These ANC fragments, perhaps marginalised from power and immediate enrichment, maintain a revolving door to eventually returning to the main ANC, where they hope to be rewarded for not having gone public with their insights into the movement's scandals and leadership lapses.

- *Exercise internal discipline and prevent dissidence in the style of the ANC Youth League (ANCYL).*

  The ANC under Zuma acts more decisively on internal dissidence than on public and representative sector corruption and mismanagement, strong in its assertion that its faction's control is in the best interest of the ANC. There is limited room for experimentation with internal criticism, especially when it came in the form of Julius Malema-style criticism of the top leadership. By expelling Malema and dissolving the ANCYL, the Zuma ANC was emphatic that it does not tolerate internal 'uprisings'. The 'disciplined cadre' is the submissive and preferred role model. When the Zuma faction suspected that the follow-up ANCYL might become an anti-Zuma platform (or just see itself as a kingmaker body), it intervened to convert an elective conference into a national consultative congress.[18] In the wake of this conversion, the 2015 ANCYL conference elected a compliant youth leadership, who spoke the language of the main body's masters.

- *Promulgate and exploit the rule of no 'premature' campaigning for ANC positions.*

  This rule means not campaigning for ANC top positions in particular (as in campaigning for the Mangaung elective conference), but when convenient it has been more widely applied. No premature campaigning equalled no campaigning at all while the prime candidate – that is, Zuma in the Mangaung run-up – used official ANC and government events to campaign abundantly. A replay unfolded in the run-up to the 2015 National General Council (NGC) meeting and the 2017 elective conference: amid some early succession slates within the Zuma faction, many adhered to the *dictum* of no premature campaigning, and in essence waited for Zuma to pronounce his preference and anoint a successor. This process became evident when the Women's League in August 2015 (after having been prompted by Zuma a year earlier) announced that it would back a women's candidate for ANC and South African president.

- *Manufacture substitute institutions for the bleeding Tripartite Alliance and Cosatu, or reconstitute Cosatu on parent-body terms.*

  The ANC has lost Cosatu as unambiguous Alliance and elections partner. Cosatu has formed the Liberated Metalworkers Union of South Africa (Limusa) to substitute for the controversially expelled Numsa – it decided to have a small Cosatu rather than a Cosatu that includes Numsa and Zwelinzima Vavi. In 2015, Zuma proposed renewed peacemaking in Cosatu (despite Zuma himself having been *much of the cause* of the Cosatu collapse) and in mid-2015 talks again unfolded. The SACP, despite growth in membership, became ineffectual as internal opposition voice but the Zuma ANC preferred this to internal contest. The ANC started its mass volunteers contingent, reasonably effectual for election campaigning. The divided MK Veterans' League became the troubleshooters and 'grey shirts'. The ANC Women's League remained the loyal chorus, while the ANC kept on hoping that it would sprout more inspirational action. Its 2015 conference saw the flame flickering again.

Elections and opposition

The ANC constructed the easy-win 'good story' as its 2014-going-into-2016 election narrative. It reported the progress of transformation over twenty years of democracy in broadly statistical terms. Few voters would even attempt to contradict the story of things being better in 2014 (thanks to the ANC) than in the apartheid past. All had experienced tangible benefits in the first two decades of democracy. Even opposition parties were forced by voter sentiment to incorporate themes like 'good success until the time of Jacob Zuma' into campaigns. The ANC trounced the 2014 opposition. Nevertheless, given its record of delivery in the time of democratic government, the association with Nelson Mandela, and the all-encompassing national celebrations of twenty years of democracy, it had hoped for better. With the 2016 local elections around the corner the ANC appears insecure, working hard to find ways to retain the metros in which it has been slipping. The ANC's mechanisms include:

- *Rekindle and maintain the memory of 1994.*
  The ANC is masterful at constantly reminding South Africans not to forget the miracle moment of the 1994 elections and the liberation. Public radio and television have a big role in the daily teaching of the history lessons. The 2014 election followed six months after the passing of Nelson Mandela. Had it been legally allowed, the ANC would have inserted Mandela's face on the ballot paper. Zuma was only prominent at high-profile and controlled events, and ANC posters moderated his appearances (Zuma's face was only a small part of the busy design).
- *Let state resources converge with ANC programmes.*
  The ANC has the benefit of *de facto* bottomless advertising resources, especially when it comes to celebrating twenty years of democracy. Many

government departments under ANC national and provincial control plunge resources into advertising their achievements. A multitude of departments, public agencies, and state enterprises ensure that delivery budgets and cycles articulate with ANC campaign needs.

- *Minimise chances for business to align with opposition parties to provide funding.*
  Business has limited space to sponsor or forge bonds with opposition parties. For example, in early 2013 First National Bank (FNB) ran a high-profile media campaign to celebrate South African greatness, but it came across as criticism of the ANC. The ANC's Keith Khoza asked when an advert sells a product and when it calls for the removal of a government. FNB amended its campaign.[19] This type of sensitivity cautioned business to say nice things about the ANC or to be quiet.
- *Delegitimise, undermine and even sabotage opposition parties.*
  This is a natural part of party politics. A Community Agency for Social Enquiry (Case) report demonstrated the extent to which ANC election campaigning spans the whole spectrum, from legitimate to illegal.[20] If the ANC can undermine an opposition party's expansion, it will.

State and government

The ANC has tight control over the delivery levers of state power – this is the party's biggest and potentially most effective instrument for constant renewal. However, there are inherent weaknesses. On the one hand, the ANC controls the bulk of public resources, allocations and deployment. On the other hand, many state operations are failing (policing, justice, local government, state security and intelligence agencies, substandard public education and health systems). These miscarriages hold severe implications for the longer-term credibility of the government. Parliament, as the core representative institution, has on occasion become a laughing stock, with the majority party's dedication to protecting the president's interests. Such popular disdain for the highest office in the land makes it essential for the reputation of the institutional side of government to be redeemed – however, the Cabinet's accomplishment in this realm (among others) has been questionable. The following mechanisms emerge as central to ANC power in the domain of state and government:

- *Reinvent the ANC government as 'pristine'.*
  This mechanism was evident in the aftermath of Election 2014 and has continued unabated. Elections in South Africa are used to invent clean slates

and present a starting-from-afresh ANC to the people after the election. The ANC then suggests that the voters have accepted and pardoned whatever disgrace or misdemeanour had gone before. In 2014, the 'new government', spurred on by a new popular mandate, revved into action, leaders promising new attention to demands that were about twenty years old.

- *Reward loyalty.*

  The ANC's incumbency has a self-regenerative effect. Aspiring dissidents know – from observing the fate of breakaway parties before them (for example, the Congress of the People [Cope]) – that career prospects beyond party politics, as well as financial fortunes, suffer when individuals fall out and move away from the ANC circle. President Zuma explicitly reminded businesses donating to the ANC that they would 'prosper'.[21]

- *Exercise control with the help of compromised underlings.*

  The top ANC leaders who have never put to rest the corruption allegations swirling around them benefit from having compromised leadership in, for example, the police and the National Prosecuting Authority (NPA), where continued deployment in high positions depends on not acting, or blocking action, against equally (or more) compromised leaders.

- *Continuously shuffle responsibilities, change deployments.*

  Crucial deployees often do not stay in jobs long enough to be subjected to systematic scrutiny against job performance criteria. When these criteria do feature, they are often vague. Political deployees remain largely unaccountable, but generally offer their political bosses both protection and loyal, unquestioning service.

- *Construct the image of active correction of public sector corruption.*

  The ANC ensures that it records anti-corruption pronouncements, but its application to the incumbents is insufficient. The ANC has become largely unaccountable for the high levels of corruption (revealed in multiple government sources, including the reports by the public protector and the auditor general). The ANC's purported corrective actions fall short of reversing corruption. To illustrate: ANC spokesperson Zizi Kodwa issues a statement about how much the ANC reveres the work of public protector Thuli Madonsela. Soon thereafter, however, President Zuma's response on the Nkandla report follows and he subverts the public protector's recommendations,[22] and in addition the bulk of the recommended steps would be in the hands of ministers who owe loyalty to Zuma. Then, Zuma

20

proclaims how no one in the ANC leadership is above the law, and cites as example the interrogation of Deputy President Cyril Ramaphosa in the Farlam Commission of Inquiry into the Marikana mass killings of mineworkers. A mere two days later Zuma issues his response to the public protector's Nkandla report, bearing overwhelming evidence of Zuma placing himself above the law and above rulings of a Chapter Nine institution.

- *Use procedures, institutions, commissions and legal appeals as extension of executive rule.*

'Zuma's pattern of ruling [is] by obfuscation, silence, denials and indefinite delays.'[23] This was evident in Zuma's delayed response to the public protector's Nkandla report, and his defence of 'no case against me' in Parliament. Then there is the arms deal scandal and the appointment of the Seriti Commission once the ANC government was forced to do so by parliamentary procedure. Its prolonged work revealed frustrated investigations, and agendas to keep the ANC and Zuma safe. By the time the commission had run its course it was seen as a farce. Judge Willie Seriti disallowed evidence of which the witnesses, including experts, were not the authors, even if the documents were significant.[24] The commission itself failed to analyse and use thousands of relevant documents. The Marikana inquiry worked to defuse the charges of police shooting and killing the miners, and soften impressions of the ANC government's refusal to assume responsibility. The ANC also used the mechanism in cases of leadership's legal predicaments and government scandals. At a lower order, government used task teams and interministerial committees (evidence of which was rife in Zuma's 2014 post-election State of the Nation address) to defer problems.[25] Manifold complex tasks in government are given the 'solution' of interministerial committees. The ANC is forever ready to present evidence that it is working on the nation's problems.

- *Subjugate institutions of democracy in order to protect the executive from embarrassment and losses of power.*

Parliament serves as the prime example of the subjugation of institutions that do not serve the interests of the executive. The ANC caucus stands under firm party political rule. There is no freedom of conscience on contentious matters. Parliamentarians Ben Turok[26] and Gloria Borman and their opposition to the first version of the Protection of State Information Bill (the 'Secrecy Bill') are a case in point. More enduring subjugation was evident in the ANC's Gwede Mantashe instructing Parliament to protect the president (after the ANC's August 2014 National Executive Committee [NEC] meeting). Subsequent to that, the 'Pay back the money' disciplinary hearing of EFF MPs took force and the president was, first, relieved of obligation to answer questions in person in Parliament, and then entirely exonerated by the ANC, but eventually, under multi-opposition party assault, obliged to answer questions. Nevertheless, evasiveness remained his bottom line.[27]

- *Optimise control over information and analysis.*
  Such control was fine-tuned (but had originated earlier, especially through threats of controlling the media through a tribunal) when the ANC came under pressure around 2012–2013. The controversial Secrecy Bill came under this mechanism. By 2015 the amended and softened yet contentious legislation remained in the president's inbox. The parliamentary cellphone signal-jamming scandal of February 2015 brought crude evidence of attempted control. The ANC was also on a continuous quest to co-opt critics, opening up and offering briefing opportunities to influential journalists and analysts. The media landscape changed shape as some media companies became somewhat more sympathetic or were lured simply by revenue through state advertising. A further aspect of this mechanism is the proclamation of 'threats' to democracy (read 'to the ANC') posed by opposition and critics and the mobilisation of state security agencies to deal with such threats.

- *Position presidential and executive rule within the parliamentary democracy.*
  The ANC played an intricate game with the executive (over which the president rules supreme) as the overarching government in South Africa. Rather than Zuma as president simply accepting the responsibility as commander of the Cabinet, he has a compliant 'appointed by the president and loyal to the president' Cabinet that would act, even without being requested, to oblige and shelter him. One such instance concerned the president and his family benefiting personally from Nkandla's upgrades. Cabinet members were expected to come to the president's defence, while Zuma pretended to defer to them.

Both individually and collectively, this repertoire of mechanisms illuminates how the ANC, despite severe governance and organisational problems, maintains itself in power in the third decade since liberation.

CONCLUSION: THE 'MIRACLE' OF SUSTAINED ANC POWER

It is not a coincidence that the ANC has remained powerful. The ANC works hard at maintaining every bit of its strength, across the four pillars or faces of power. The 'miracle' of the ANC sustaining such power, against the odds and despite its own self-defeating actions, can be attributed to a toolbox of mechanisms and the miracle is by now thoroughly manufactured, even though it draws on a sustained connection to the liberation struggle. Delivery on policy undertakings and further socioeconomic transformation, along with powerful information and communication access and control, bring home the message to supporters, both strong and wavering. If these two are synchronised, the ANC will be constantly condoned and endorsed.

Corruption and elite enrichment, the mask of neoliberal policies, ungovernable government, and lawlessness in state and society are markers of this era in which the ANC continues to rule supreme, despite the clear and dangerous signals of decay. The ANC runs against itself in many contests, except at election time, when supporters and leaders close ranks behind it. It is often almost incomprehensible that the ANC retains and regenerates as much power as it does, given all the wrongs that pile up.[28] This book will attempt to clarify the almost incomprehensible.

NOTES

1   Drew Hinshaw and Patrick McGroarty, 5 December 2014, 'The return of Africa's strongmen', *Wall Street Journal*, http://www.wsj.com/articles/the-return-of-africas-strongmen-1417798993?mod=WSJ_hppMIDDLENexttoWhatsNews, accessed 7 December 2014.
2   'Hegemony' refers to the dominant class successfully positioning its view of reality in order to get subordinated groups to accept it as the most suitable way of seeing the world. Hegemony is exercised through the combination of force and consent: subordinated groups consent to the domination, which they believe is in their best interest. Acceptance of moral leadership is central to hegemony. Antonio Gramsci, 1971, 'Hegemony, intellectuals and the state', in John Storey (ed.), 1994, *Cultural Theory and Popular Culture: A Reader*, New York: Harvester Wheatsheaf, pp. 215–221.
3   See my article of 22 March 2015, 'Zuma isn't exactly Mr Popular', *The Sunday Independent*, http://www.iol.co.za/sundayindependent/zuma-isn-t-exactly-mr-popular-1.1835410, accessed 2 April 2015.
4   Gwede Mantashe, December 2014, ANC National Working Committee Report to the National Executive Committee, reported in Mmanaledi Mataboge, 19 December 2014, 'Gwede Mantashe admits ANC could lose power', http://mg.co

.za/article/2014-12-18-gwede-mantashe-admits-anc-could-lose-power, accessed 4 January 2015.

5 Jacob Zuma, 11 March 2015, Answers to parliamentary questions, Parliament of South Africa, Cape Town.

6 See, for example, *Annual Labour Market Bulletin*, 2014, reporting that South Africa's labour absorption rate remained stagnant at approximately 42.8 per cent. Of the 607 227 new job seekers in 2013/14, only 2.5 per cent found jobs in that period.

7 Karl Marx, 1845–46, published 1932, 'The illusion of the epoch', in *The German Ideology*, https://www.marxists.org/archive/marx/works/1845/german-ideology/ch01b.htm, accessed 2 September 2013, denotes: 'The ideas of the ruling class are in every epoch the ruling ideas ... The class which has the means of material production at its disposal, has control at the same time over the means of mental production ...'

8 To illustrate, see Mcebisi Ndletyana, 1 March 2015, 'No way is Zuma seriously fighting corruption', *The Sunday Independent*, p. 16.

9 See, in the sequence in which the title is alluded to (in inverted commas in the text): Prince Mashele and Mzukisi Qobo, 2013, *The Fall of the ANC: What Next?* Johannesburg: Picador Africa; Alex Boraine, 2014, *What's Gone Wrong? On the Brink of a Failed State*, Johannesburg and Cape Town: Jonathan Ball; RW Johnson, 2015, *How Long Will South Africa Survive? The Looming Crisis*, Johannesburg and Cape Town: Jonathan Ball; Richard Calland, 2013, *The Zuma Years: South Africa's Changing Face of Power*, Cape Town: Zebra; Martin J Murray, 1994, *The Revolution Deferred*, London: Verso; Adam Habib, 2013, *South Africa's Suspended Revolution*, Johannesburg: Wits University Press; Xolela Mangcu, 2014, *The Arrogance of Power: South Africa's Leadership Meltdown*, Cape Town: Tafelberg; Adriaan Basson, 2012, *Zuma Exposed*, Johannesburg: Jonathan Ball; Mzilikazi wa Afrika, 2014, *Nothing Left to Steal: Jailed for Telling the Truth*, Johannesburg: Penguin; Susan Booysen, 2011, *The African National Congress and the Regeneration of Political Power*, Johannesburg: Wits University Press; Community Agency for Social Enquiry (Case), 2014, *Just Singing and Dancing*; Eusebius McKaiser, 2013, *Could I Vote DA? A Voter's Dilemma*, Johannesburg: Bookstorm; Donwald Pressly, 2014, *Owning the Future: Lindiwe Mazibuko and the Changing Face of the DA*, Cape Town: NB Publishers/Kwela; Abebe Zegeye and Julia Maxted, 2002, *Our Dream Deferred: The Poor in South Africa*, Pretoria: South African History Online (Saho) and Unisa Press; Mark Gevisser, 2007, *Thabo Mbeki: The Dream Deferred*, Johannesburg and Cape Town: Jonathan Ball; André Odendaal, 2012, *The Founders: The Origins of the ANC and the Struggle for Democracy in South Africa*, Auckland Park: Jacana; Ben Turok, 2014, *With My Head Above the Parapet: An Insider Account of the ANC in Power*, Auckland Park: Jacana; Max du Preez, 2013, *A Rumour of Spring: South Africa After 20 Years of Democracy*, Cape Town: Zebra; Rushil Ranchod, 2013, *A Kind of Magic: The Political Marketing of the ANC*, Auckland Park: Jacana; JP Landman, 2013, *The Long View: Getting Beyond the Drama of South Africa's Headlines*, Auckland Park: Jacana/Stonebridge; Nelson Mandela, 1995, *Long Walk to Freedom*, New York: Little Brown.

10 Tom Lodge, 2013, book review: *The African National Congress and the Regeneration of Political Power*, *Journal of Contemporary African Studies*, vol. 31 (2), pp. 325–327, highlights the theoretical base that *Regeneration* sets out.

11 Roger Southall, 2008, *Liberation Movements in Power: Party and State in Southern Africa*, Woodbridge and Scottsville: James Currey and UKZN Press, offers an illustration of this literature.

12 See *Cape Times*, 20 October 2014, 'President launches media working group', p. 5; Setumo Stone, 20 May 2015, 'Mayor "interfered" with metro boss, court says', *Business Day*, p. 3.

13 Susan Booysen, 2013, *Twenty Years of South African Democracy: Citizen Views of Human Rights, Governance and the Political System*, research report, Johannesburg and Washington DC: Freedom House; Charl du Plessis and Carien du Plessis, 12 October 2014, 'Zuma wanted charges dropped because corruption is a Western thing', *City Press*, http://www.citypress.co.za/politics/corruption-western-thing, accessed 1 March 2015.

14 James Ngcakula, seminar at Nelson Mandela Metropolitan University, June 2012.

15 See Greg Nicolson, 27 November 2014, 'Zuma and the nightmare of Malema's past', *Daily Maverick*, http://www.dailymaverick.co.za/article/2014-11-27-zuma-and-the-nightmare-of-malemas-past/, accessed 28 November 2014.

16 Imagined power results when the ANC so delegitimises criticism and opposition that reluctance to express such 'negativity' results, and a false sense of power spreads in the ruling class.

17 Jacob Zuma, 2014, in interview with Kevin Ritchie, 14 August 2014, 'Zuma – leaner, and confident that SA is on the right track', *Cape Times*, p. 10.

18 See Jacob Zuma, 27 March 2015, 'Political overview by president to the meeting of the ANC National Executive Committee', Cape Town, e-mail from ANC media.

19 Interview with Bernice Samuels, FNB chief marketing officer, and ANC spokesperson Keith Khoza with Xolani Gwala, SABC-SAFM, 21 January 2013.

20 Case, 2014, *Just Singing and Dancing*, research report, Johannesburg.

21 Sapa, 13 January 2013, 'Zuma: Business which backs ANC will prosper', *Fin24*, http://www.fin24.com/Economy/Zuma-Business-who-backs-ANC-will-prosper-20130113, accessed 1 April 2014.

22 President of the Republic of South Africa, 14 August 2014, *Report to the Speaker of the National Assembly Regarding the Security Upgrades at the Nkandla Private Residence of His Excellency President Jacob G Zuma*, http://www.citypress.co.za/politics/nkandla-jacob-zuma-responds-thuli-madonselas-report/, accessed 12 September 2014.

23 Ranjeni Munusamy, 15 August 2014, 'Blurred lines: Zuma's non-response to Nkandla report', *Daily Maverick*, http://www.dailymaverick.co.za/article/2014-08-15-blurred-lines-zumas-non-response-to-nkandla-report/#.U-3iZWN6joQ, accessed 16 August 2014.

24 Several witnesses – Andrew Feinstein, Paul Holden and Hennie van Vuuren – refused to testify, citing the loss of public faith in the proceedings. The Seriti ruling led to the exclusion of available evidence and limited admissible evidence to writings by those who had been corrupted, according to legal argument for Van Vuuren. See *The New Age*/Sapa, 21 October 2014, 'Arms deal critics refuse to testify at inquiry', p. 4.

25 Jacob Zuma, 17 June 2014, State of the Nation address, joint sitting of Parliament, Cape Town, http://www.thepresidency.gov.za/pebble.asp?relid=17570, accessed 18 June 2014.

26 Ben Turok, 2014, op. cit.

27 ANC spokesperson Zizi Kodwa originally noted that the 'president cannot go to Parliament when that Parliament is a circus' (while parliamentary rules require the president to answer questions in Parliament four times a year). Then presidential spokesperson Mac Maharaj remarked that the elections had shortened available time, and that the president continues answering written questions. See *The New Age*, 20 October 2014, '*Times* lies about Zuma', p. 4. The 2015 reversal followed on 11 March 2015. See YouTube, 'Zuma answers questions in Parliament', www.youtube.com/watch?v=V3xrgkgolBg, accessed 11 March 2015.

28 Prince Mashele and Qobo Mzukisi, 2013, *The Fall of the ANC: What Next?* Johannesburg: Picador Africa.

1

THE ANC'S FUSED PARTY-STATE

Jacob Zuma's years in command of the ANC have irrevocably changed the party as organisation – and the South African state. The ANC is captured as a tide gradually receding towards a point that marks the end of its hegemony,[1] its fate linked to, but not solely determined by, President Zuma. The power of Zuma is formidable, but also contested. While factions are battling out the succession, the damages that the Zuma era has inflicted on the ANC pose two questions. Would the ANC recover from the wounds inflicted by Zuma? Could the ANC reposition itself to rise above the party that installed, retained and protected Zuma?

Some of the changes to the ANC organisationally in the course of Zuma's two presidential terms have resulted specifically from his presidency, his style of leadership and the way in which he rules over the ANC and the government. Other organisational changes might have materialised no matter which ANC leader was in power – many were due to the organisation's own continuous metamorphosis from liberation movement to a powerful majoritarian and dominant party that fused with the state. It was a particular type of organisation that allowed Zuma to become and to remain its president for two terms. But Zuma and those close to him in the organisation also have agency – they shape events rather than experience them passively. They fostered the ANC's integration with the state and they allowed an ANC in which the president rules. As a result, there is more emphasis on a party that sees state institutions as personal (and, occasionally, organisational) fiefdoms. Under this tutelage the ANC has become even more of an organisation that readily submits to the top leadership, plays extensively in succession politics and excels at factional mobilisation. In such an orgy of power there is little time to contemplate accountability to the public who had put the party in power – except in the narrow sense of reporting to ANC structures and events and roughly abiding by state-institutional processes.

The intra-ANC wrangle is about the extent to which the Zuma band of leaders – forcefully but ambiguously because of uncertain succession outcomes – will create openings for a post-Zuma order that will dare to diverge from the dictates of the Zuma era. Zuma-ists might be steering the ANC towards Zuma-cloning, extended presidential protection and continuous subjugation of institutions of democracy to the will of a commanding leader. The next round in the succession game has become fraught, as the most likely choices are between those candidates made *by* Zuma, and those who *made him* and facilitated his incumbency. A further likelihood is that a succession project run by this core group (anchored by Zuma and Secretary General Gwede Mantashe, before evidence grew of schisms between the two) will fracture and open a new game. Two prime layers of contestation are at stake: the contest to succeed Zuma as ANC president, and the contest to become ANC deputy president and best positioned for the next round.

This chapter considers aspects of the ANC as organisation in the time of Zuma along the lines of the subjugation of the ANC to the travails of the leader, while allowing for strains of organisational autonomy to prevail as well. It focuses on changes that the ANC underwent in the time of Zuma, often *because of* Zuma. It explores how the ANC in the time of Zuma related to the people and how the ANC branches mediated this relationship. It spells out the 'rules' by which the contemporary ANC operated. This ANC is inseparable from personalised power and from the fusion of organisation and state.

FUSED WITH THE STATE

Well into its third decade in office, the ANC is a mass of contradictions. Above all, the synthesis of state and party has grown in leaps and bounds from the already substantial conflation under Thabo Mbeki. Zuma has 'perfected' the mix and in his reign the ANC has received the ultimate gift of power: it is now inseparable and often indistinguishable from the state.

The ANC has become an organisation boosted (if not sustained) by drawing on the state and its resources. It has almost undisputed control, a reality that is also evident from the state mechanisms through which the ANC regenerates its power. Given the ANC's power and resources in relation to the state it is almost inconceivable that it could be defeated by any opposition party. Yet at the same time as the ANC has become firmly ensconced in state power it has also suffered organisational weakening in some respects.

The weaknesses are evident in daily displays and in longer-term trends. Demonstrations of factions and splits within factions are significant, especially at ANC nomination and election times. As the provinces usually constitute important ANC national conference blocs, and the provinces comprise regions, many of the regional elections and emerging affiliations to top leadership con-tests carry weight. In the run-up to Mangaung a few ANC figures lost their lives and many more their political lives; in KwaZulu-Natal in 2015, bribery and manipulation of regional elections appeared the order of the day. In the Western Cape, factions effectively hijacked several regional conferences, stepping roughshod over rules and procedures to install predetermined office bearers. The Eastern Cape was plagued by gatekeeping – the practice of ANC factions barring members who support rival factions from branch general meetings.

Factions are common to political parties, so what is the problem with factions in the ANC? It is hardly more factional than other parties, as Pallo Jordan once observed. It is problematic, however, in the sense that ANC contests and their repercussions are directly transferred into the state when the fear of antagonis-ing leaders triggers inaction and paralysis in the public sector. Top-level polit-ical deployees change frequently, as political executive appointments change,[2] and their loyalty amid paranoia – for fear of being set up for failure or brought to book for malfeasance – needs constant massaging. The ANC deploys to influential positions people with uneven or suspect professional and personal records knowing that these persons would be dependent on their principals to be retained and rewarded. This has far-reaching implications for governance and the fiscus. They have to protect their executive political handlers – keeping them out of court, shielding them from uncomfortable questions, moderating succession contests. In this way, the state and the ANC's governance project are in many respects subjugated to narrow interests. Moreover, the state security services are frequent participants in the internal manoeuvres. Further down

29

the state hierarchy, in the provinces and municipalities, the game is replicated around lesser principals.

There are privileges in enclaves beyond the formal rules of the state for those who operate on the right side of the ANC president, especially (but not necessarily) if they have helped to protect him over time, even back in exile days, but even more so if they have been following through consistently. The saga of lieutenant general Richard Mdluli is one example: a former head of police intelligence, suspended (ongoing by 2015) and appearing in court on a charge of a 1999 murder in a love triangle, his rumoured bond to the presidential protection circle is an intelligence report in which he cautioned the president against political enemies. Others point out that he regularly produces such reports. Serial revelations of Mdluli living the high life off crime intelligence funds and appointing cronies to intelligence jobs did not clip his wings. Mdluli was brought to task because Mxolisi Nxasana, embattled and, from June 2015, *former* national director of public prosecutions (NDPP), had reinstated the withdrawn charges as part of a raging National Prosecuting Authority (NPA) war. In 2015, the non-governmental organisation Freedom under Law won a Supreme Court of Appeal ruling to reinstate charges. The existence of a Special Operations Unit within the South African Revenue Service (Sars) 'geared to enrichment and fighting political battles' was revealed,[3] leading to the exposé of yet another inner state organ geared to serving high-level political agendas. State institutional misuse in the security sector is rife, and entangled in top-level ANC party politics.

The party has gained the 'right' over time, and in parallel operations not covered in the Constitution and state-operational legislation and regulations, to intervene and direct strategic state decisions. When high-level interests are at stake the ANC does so at will. Examples abound. Vusi Pikoli recalls that despite the Ginwala Commission's finding that he was fit to hold the NDPP office, provincial leaders of the ANC, a businessman from KwaZulu-Natal, and a member of the Johannesburg Bar warned him to resign or they would let the ANC overrule the Ginwala recommendation to Parliament.[4] In similar vein were the 2014 revelations that the president intervened to fire senior intelligence officials on suspicion that they had remained loyal to their redeployed former minister. The redeployed staff said they were being moved into ambassadorial posts by (rather than being fired from) the State Security Agency (SSA) owing to top-level fears that they might turn into enemies, as were former intelligence agency boss Billy Masetlha and his two senior chiefs, Bob Mhlanga and Gibson

Njenje, in the time of Mbeki.[5] Beyond the security sector, the political determination of public sector and political appointments continued.

Through weakness at the top of the ANC, combined with fusion between party and state, the ANC government is struggling to pull together its governance project. It declares – after more than two decades in government – that 'now is the time for implementation'.[6] Despite such acknowledgements and undertakings to clamp down, civil servants and politicians in all spheres of government continue to conduct business with the state and to trade on their public positions.[7] This corruption spreads into the police service and legal system, giving the green light to criminally inclined citizens to go about their business with impunity. At the same time, the ANC in the elected institutions suffers – yet defends – the corrupt practices in the name of the president (a president who has earned himself the nickname of 'there is no case against me')[8] and a range of other party principals. In local government, corruption and dysfunctionality are common, despite multiple strategic interventions. It is only in occasional internal ANC and government reports that the truths of these failures are mentioned. The Tripartite Alliance notes that 'subversion of internal democratic processes through the manipulation of membership through gatekeeping and the use of money to advance individual ambitions and factions based on patronage and nepotism' alienates people from leadership.[9]

Before factions started spreading their wings tentatively to prepare for a post-Zuma order, this space was highly controlled: little was left to chance because chance might have brought results most unpalatable to ANC incumbents. The ruling party became a highly structured, measured mass party under factional leadership, the president and his regiments of loyalists exercising control through commanding the branches and regions. Add to that the continuation of the prevailing economic order, executive rule over the state and sophisticated operations to curb expressions of discontent, and continued control seems to be on track, for now.

Under Jacob Zuma, the ANC's liberation dividend continued to be its great insurance for retaining high popular standing. The liberation struggle link remains, and its conventional identity of 'parent-party' merges with 'patronage-broker'. During its first fifteen years in power prior to Zuma's rule, the ANC had already metamorphosed into an organisation that leverages state power to build the fortunes of the governing party.[10] This happened both directly by delivering goods and indirectly through control over resources and information to build the ANC image.

31

It became the state information apparatus's function to drive home the message of the link between liberation status and present-day deliverer. The apparatus includes privately owned media that have started moving into closer relationships with the governing party, through personal friendships, increased government investment, and transfers from the state to these media by way of advertising or events. Cases in point are *The New Age* media, Independent Media and Hosken Consolidated Investment and e.tv (some more consistently and better trusted than others by the ANC). The South African Broadcasting Corporation (SABC) was already in a close relationship.

The ANC, expertly so in the time of Zuma, never lets an opportunity slip to connect its present to the self-sacrificing past to ensure that South Africans *will not forget* to link liberation to the ANC. In the government report on twenty years of democracy,[11] the point of comparison remained the apartheid order, rather than the ANC's original goals. In comparison, even modest ANC achievements came across as outstanding. Continuous reinvigoration is possible, given figureheads such as Nelson Mandela and the selection of glorious liberation struggle moments which can be exhibited, at least for another generation.

The fusion of state and party is at the heart of the ANC's regeneration of its political power. The impression by 2015 is that as the ANC becomes weaker electorally, it becomes more firmly entrenched in state power. It remains the first 'port of call' for the elite, the gateway for the politically and economically ambitious to advance – and this has spilled over into much of society. Before people start disaffecting openly they consider the near certainty of ongoing ANC incumbency. Political elites largely only break from the ANC, or become severely critical, if they have alternative careers in place, or when retirement benefits are secured, or when they have little to lose. The ANC is the keyholder to state power and opportunity.

IN SYNC, AT ODDS – THE PEOPLE AND THE NEW ANC

The ANC is as strong as its bond with the people of South Africa. This is where the final endorsements are vested, even if the contemporary ANC often acts as if it is autonomous and the leaders a force of their own. The people are famed for their patience with *their* ANC. They acknowledge that 'Rome was not built in a day'. They recognise the enormity of the task of recovery from the legacies of apartheid and colonialism.[12] They know their leaders face enormous challenges, by far not all of their own making. Yet there are signs that the patience and tolerance are running thin.

Damage is still limited. The new character of the ANC as an elite beneficiation machine with patronage as a big component did inflict electoral damage but it was far less than the disappointment and discontent expressed in pre-election periods. As demonstrated in *Regeneration,* the problems and grievances about the ANC and ANC-in-government are largely not carried into elections.[13] Issues with the party and its leaders are often forgiven, but displeasure is simply suspended. Despite this general trend, the 2014 election, more than any preceding post-1994 election, was used as a point of reckoning (as judged by the ANC's decline nationally and in several provinces). In 2015, the ANC viewed with loathing the possibility that 2016 local elections would register another bar in its consistently dropping popular support. Public polls of 2015 showed that ANC support continued declining across most provinces.

While the ANC was slipping in relation to the electorate (*and* while many citizens do not bother to vote or do not care who governs, because they argue it is unlikely to make much of a difference to their lives) the ANC was further fostering its powerful alternative power base – one of patronage and strengthening of the middle class, with notable albeit insufficient care also taken of the lower classes. The ANC was in a complex double bind: beyond the political elite many in the middle classes felt free to leave the ANC while increasingly volatile underclasses were in the ANC's political and security net. For example, the total spent on all social grants in 2013–2014 was R109.1bn and rising: there were 16 242 196 grant beneficiaries at the end of June 2014, compared with 15 932 473 at the 2013 count (70 per cent of them received child support grants; R39.6bn was paid out on child support grants during 2013–2014).[14] The elite project was developing expertly; the 'only' ANC problem was to keep the discontent away from the electoral verdicts. There was an underclass, mostly of young people, who might be better off than before but who see no hope of escaping from township or informal settlement conditions and were nowhere in line to benefit from the ANC's patronage. The 2015 outbreak of xenophobia simultaneously highlighted the dismal living conditions of the poor and the bleak reality of young people with nothing to lose except their last hope of finding a job. These glimpses of South Africa's dark underbelly were light years away from the ANC's good story of splendid delivery. Its campaign of telling the good story (both in Election 2014 and beyond) had been designed to help set the terms for its ongoing reinvention but it was hard to reconcile the good story and the squalor.

Apart from this strained delivery-linked approach, the ANC continues nurturing its direct appeals to, and direct bonds with, the people. For many, this continues to work. Many still see the ANC as their political 'family', and feel powerful in relation to the ANC as parent figure, but in some respects they are becoming less available for this direct and powerful relationship. In other ways they remain accessible, albeit in differently defined relationships – for example, as state-business partners or as unemployed or rural citizens who live the life of the social wage.

The people have also been changing. Corruption and mismanagement among the leaders are matched by a largely (but by far not only) harmless lawlessness among the people. Citizens have not been witnessing effective application of the law by the president, government departments, the state's security apparatuses, the courts or the local police. People ignore e-tolls, break traffic laws, evade taxation, pull all possible state benefits, take an RDP house but sell it and find a way to claim another, or defraud the system of social grants and public servant salaries. They use corrupt contacts to get more of anything (in exchange for sharing in the spoils). They take the law into their own hands and dispense justice. Much of this culture relates to the failure of state institutions: police who have become corrupted and act unevenly against criminals; the judicial system that cannot be trusted to mete out justice; and MPs, MPLs and councillors who have little concern for their constituents.

The ANC has also survived its modern-day excesses because it has become the predominant post-liberation party of aspiration. The elite largely associates with the ANC, whether it is by now peopled by the established rich, active in the black economic empowerment (BEE), or by those who still aspire to join it. They are a core motive force for the ANC[15] which leads by example: the good life is the ANC life![16] The aspiring classes hope to graduate into affluent businesses; for many of them political life revolves around public declaration and demonstrations of pro-ANC sentiment – admission tickets into the goodwill of the ANC family. This new ANC is a thoroughly post-liberation party, but also an organisation that feeds off the history of oppression and apartheid. For leaders and followers alike there is a seamless transition from suffering and injustice to the expectation of publicly funded benefits and opportunities as compensation.

For those ANC followers less accepting of the right of the leaders to feast while followers drink water,[17] the leadership narratives reveal how the ANC sees the threat of dissent. ANC leaders steer close to the 2009 narratives of a God-sent party attuned to the 'return of Jesus'.[18] By the time of Election 2014 the trend was more about suppressing displeasure and putting angry supporters, critical of campaign promises and absentee representation, in their place. When the ANC leaders surfaced on the campaign trail, they were confronted by citizens who would only, later, on election day, suspend their anger and again vote ANC. In the face of this anger, ANC leaders ran out of rational arguments and appealed to base and traditional instincts, including insults and the obstruction of opposition. A previous Gauteng premier told protesters in Bekkersdal that the ANC did not need their 'dirty votes'; the ANC's head of elections said the DA is a 'party of demons'; a Cabinet member averred that the Western Cape is 'run by witches' (with reference to DA leaders) and that 'tokoloshes' had to come and run the DA provincial government out of power; the ANC national chairperson said 'the struggle spirits' are watching and would deal with disloyal voters; and the president and ANC deputy president warned voters that their ancestors would turn on voters if they fail to vote ANC.[19]

People know that they have *relative freedom* to criticise the ANC and its leaders, as long as they do not default by associating with an opposition party, criticising the president, or forget to preface criticism with references to the struggle. This freedom has helped to create legitimacy for the ANC, but is also a double-edged sword: there will be tolerance as long as they still vote ANC (*and* proclaim it publicly), thus demonstrating a belief in the ongoing ability of the ANC to self-correct. Freedom of speech applies as long as no-go areas determined by democratic centralism are respected. Foremost is that the president shall not be criticised. Those who withdraw in desperation or disgust from the main ANC often find their shelters in their own alternative political homes,[20] a political shelter until the wheel turns and it is time to return to active ANC life, probably in the time of new leadership. 'Discipline' is the core of this project. The overwhelming experience is that it is cold outside the ANC – and Cosatu.

Many among the youth – the born-frees who were first-time voters in 2014 – are little enamoured with both the old and the new ANC. They are often rebellious, disillusioned with the post-liberation ANC, or have started disbelieving ANC promises and the propaganda of the nirvana awaiting them when ANC finishes defeating the apartheid enemy. Some former ANC Youth Leaguers who left with Julius Malema and his group saw gaping holes in the ANC's world of ideological concessions, unimplemented policies and compromised leadership. This new generation is no longer automatically an ANC generation. The most tangible evidence of this alienation between the ANC and young people is in the form of more than one million young people who gave their 2014 national vote to the EFF. The EFF estimates that roughly 85 per cent of its 1.1 million 2014 national votes were from voters up to thirty-five years of age. With more than half of the 2014 electorate already younger than forty, the ANC's battle to maintain its bond with the people is on.[21]

THE CENTRE IS HOLDING

The Zuma ANC had become *the* ANC. It was only after Election 2014 that some opposing ANC voices started emerging, veiled and haltingly, and a modest shift towards a post-Zuma era became evident. However, implored by Luthuli House to protect the president against 'enemies' who wanted to 'destabilise' the ANC and South Africa, potential new leaders had to watch their step. Internal opposition voices only started cohering gradually in the post-Mangaung deliberations on leadership succession. The moves were overwhelmingly clandestine, significant for the fact that Zuma's own followers were starting to mobilise against Zuma's equally veiled but increasingly apparent own initiatives. Hence, the Zuma camp was fracturing – not in terms of retaining Zuma, but for his succession.

These aspects of succession politics are crucial to the character of the ANC as organisation in the time of Zuma. Much of ANC organisational politics was subsumed in strategising for position and eventual succession. The nature of the ANC of the time becomes clearer through a consideration of the contests since Polokwane.

The ANC's 2012 Mangaung leadership contest illustrated important prevailing dynamics of the time: Zuma dictates the rules of the contest, besides having a strong hand in positioning a successor. At Mangaung the indications were that the ANC's new and reduced centre was holding, despite problems; it was a succession battle in the time of tight control by the Zuma-ists. Former ANC and South African deputy president Kgalema Motlanthe's ANC presidential campaign was half-hearted, while Zuma's incumbent campaign was full-throttle. The *dicta* of the Zuma campaign were to 'fight for continuity' and 'give Zuma a second chance'. At no time did Motlanthe's campaign give the impression of believing that victory was possible; it was self-censored to avoid Polokwane-like party-wide destabilisation. Motlanthe foot soldiers made sacrifices by going publicly anti-Zuma.

The Motlanthe campaign put forward a compromise position (originally mooted by the Zuma kitchen cabinet at a meeting in late September 2012 and subsequently disseminated through the branches): Zuma for ANC president and Motlanthe for president of South Africa from Election 2014 onwards. Zuma would remain as ANC president until 2017 and Motlanthe step in as number one on the ANC's national proportional representation list and hence become its candidate for the national presidency.[22] In another attempted compromise repeated at Mangaung, Motlanthe was offered the deputy presidency position under Zuma on the Zuma slate. He declined. Cyril Ramaphosa accepted after Motlanthe assured him that he was unavailable. Ramaphosa became ANC deputy president, and deputy president of South Africa. He was, however, an 'invitee' of the Zuma group and not automatically on any privileged insider track to become the ANC's anointed 2017 presidential candidate. Ramaphosa nevertheless campaigned diligently: he carefully bolstered and defended the president, allowed the president to take the bow for work Ramaphosa had done, and did not show overt presidential ambition. In the run-up to the 2015 National General Council (NGC) this appeared to have borne fruit – some Zuma-ists argued that 'it will be impossible to keep Ramaphosa out; it will be easier to give him one term'.[23] Others reckoned the thrust of a 'woman for president' might prevail.

The Mangaung campaign was exceptional in that Zuma pitched himself against the ANCYL and subsequently expelled ANCYL president Malema. The anti-ANCYL battle cry endured until Luthuli House officially allowed campaigning, from October 2012. Malema's ANCYL had Motlanthe as its Mangaung presidential candidate. For an extended time in the run-up to Mangaung, the ANCYL was the only intra-ANC entity that spoke openly about the compromised Zuma's determination to cling to power. Malema became the Zuma ANC's prime target, with attack forces largely led by Secretary General Mantashe on behalf of Zuma. In September–October 2012 the Hawks Special Investigating Unit (SIU) moved in on some of Malema's associates, and Sars and the public protector brought action and investigations against Malema. Malema, the ANCYL and the new Friends of the Youth League faded as general Mangaung campaigning took off. The diffusion of ideas associated with the league – for example, 'generational change' – only resurfaced in the subsequent ANC branch nominations. The Malema-ist ANCYL exemplified youth frustration, desperation with not making progress, not finding jobs, and bearing the brunt of social exclusion. Malema's expulsion from the ANC and ANCYL did not exorcise his impact: it fed directly into the formation of, and electoral support for, the EFF.

A reduced and disciplined ANC centre prevailed, despite this split. A tight in-group around the secretary general helped to control processes and give preferred emerging leaders an inside track. For example, places on the ANC's top-thirty list of 2014 national election candidates were a stepping stone;[24] leadership of NEC subcommittees or of parliamentary caucus study groups were useful accelerators. Appointment into senior or significant Cabinet positions is the next step. Once in Cabinet this next cohort of leaders gains *gravitas* that few others can match. Even factional change would find it difficult to undo most of the tracks into leadership survival that are established in these ways – short of a clean sweep of a tranche of leaders, as had happened at Polokwane and in post-Polokwane deployment.

Zuma had started his ultimately successful campaign to surmount the corruption charges against him in 2003. It involved the co-option of multiple organisations and divisions of state, party and Tripartite Alliance. At the time, Bulelani Ngcuka had decided to charge Schabir Shaik and Jacob Zuma on corruption and related charges separately.[25] The struggle to let Zuma succeed into the ANC presidency in 2009, and again in 2014 plus into the South African presidency, refocused subsequent politics. The explicit phase of this project started in 2005 at NGC, but Zuma's rise through ANC ranks had commenced much earlier (see Table 1.1).

In the first five years of the Zuma presidency the ANC in government elected and installed loyalists who would protect him against the onslaughts linked to his and his government's scandals (appointments were also frequently used to reward those who had been personally close to the president). There were, to be sure, some meritorious appointments across the state institutions, but because of the scope of the controversies that surrounded President Zuma, and the continued addition of new ones, in subsequent years substantial state forces were directed at further helping to safeguard Zuma's years in power. Through the Nkandla saga this safeguarding became linked more than ever to the president's personal enrichment through the use of state resources, and protection in general became focused on protection of the president in particular. Much of the thinking about post-Zuma succession was tainted by 'what would be good for Zuma', equating the good of Zuma with the good of the ANC.

The next question was what form of contest would be possible from 2015 to 2017 and what it would tell us about the ANC's centre. The 2015 NGC was set to be another suppression of leadership contest, to contain ambitions until the top leaders were ready to publicly endorse their 'anointed ones'. The enforcement of disciplinary action in the name of the ANC as 'disciplined movement' came to characterise a movement that resembled a personal Zuma fiefdom. Malema's ousting, for example, was portrayed as protecting the 'dignity of the

Table 1.1: ANC top elected officials, 1991–2014, highlighting Zuma's rise and staying power

Position	1991	1994	1997	2002	2007	2012
President	Nelson Mandela	Nelson Mandela	Thabo Mbeki	Thabo Mbeki	Jacob Zuma	Jacob Zuma
Deputy president	Walter Sisulu	Thabo Mbeki	Jacob Zuma	Jacob Zuma	Kgalema Motlanthe	Cyril Ramaphosa
National chairperson	Oliver Tambo	Jacob Zuma	Mosiuoa Lekota	Mosiuoa Lekota	Baleka Mbete	Baleka Mbete
Secretary general	Cyril Ramaphosa	Cyril Ramaphosa	Kgalema Motlanthe	Kgalema Motlanthe	Gwede Mantashe	Gwede Mantashe
Deputy secretary general	Jacob Zuma	Cheryl Carolus	Thenjiwe Mtintso	Sankie Mthembi-Mahanyele	Thandi Modise	Jessie Duarte
Treasurer general	Thomas Nkobi	Makhenkesi Stofile	Menzi Msimang	Menzi Msimang	Mathews Phosa	Zweli Mkhize

Source: www.anc.org.za, various windows, accessed 12 September 2009; 2 June 2015.

president' in the face of being unfavourably compared to Mbeki and the latter's record as an African statesman. In due course, in Parliament, the 'dignity of the president' also became equated with his right to benefit from public money. Equally, the split in Cosatu was linked to the Zuma-ists' (assisted by the SACP) determination to forge an unquestioning – even if numerically reduced and intellectually emasculated – post-liberation pro-Zuma-centrist movement.

Thus factional domination in the ANC was effective up to at least 2015. It was, however, an already weakened ANC that was exercising it, besides the fact that the contests were unlikely ever to be as controlled again. The post-Mangaung and post-Election 2014 ANC is possibly a stronger party than it was in the trauma years of 2003–2009, but only in the sense that there was no split pending and control was strong. To conclude that the ANC is organisationally sturdy depends on accepting that it has become a reduced and factional party from which many critics and independent thinkers have withdrawn. It remains a broad church but suffers suppressed dialogue and leadership contests. The centre is holding because dissent has become unaffordable, forced into scattered ANC enclaves. As Zuma's exit came closer South Africa was holding its collective breath to see whether the trend would persist or if his departure would cause his faction to fall and a group of challengers to rise.

BRANCHES – RULED BY THE CENTRE

ANC branch membership and branch organisation are significant because they contribute the bulk of the members of the electoral college responsible for electing the ANC NEC and the top six officials of the party, besides anchoring the ANC at grassroots level into communities. They also constitute the prime building blocks of succession slates. The leagues' delegates offer most of the balance of voting delegates at elective conferences (Table 1.2). The branches thus elect the president of the ANC and, indirectly, the president of South Africa. They are gatekeepers and kingmakers, albeit thoroughly subjected to manipulation by or instructions from party principals.

The number of ANC branches has increased as ANC membership has grown. At the time of the ANC's 2012 centenary it had truly become a mass membership, with more than one million members. Secretary General Mantashe targeted 2.5 million. Amid leaders' preoccupation with organisational politics, however, there were signs by 2015 that not only might this target be missed, but that numbers might decline. The ANC's 2007 organ-isational report recorded that 2 669 branches (or 69 per cent of 'potential' branches) were in good standing and could be counted formally as real branches entitled to be represented at the Polokwane conference. The num-ber of represented branches grew to 3 687 at Mangaung in 2012. A further 14 per cent of the branches at this time (620) were not in good standing. The organisational report stressed that this was a high figure. However, propor-tionately it was lower than at Polokwane.[26]

It was a wildcard membership, given that political education was a paper policy, except for variable branch inductions and new members following the example of leaders. By 2014–2015 there was renewed emphasis on the branches,

Table 1.2: Branch delegate allocations at the ANC's Polokwane and Mangaung conferences

PROVINCE	ALLOCATED NUMBER OF BRANCH DELEGATES PER PROVINCE	
	Polokwane 2007	Mangaung 2012
Eastern Cape	906	676
Free State	363	324 (disallowed)
Gauteng	354	500
KwaZulu-Natal	608	974
Limpopo	400	574
Mpumalanga	325	467
North West	280	234
Northern Cape	220	176
Western Cape	219	178
TOTAL	3 675*	4 103**

Source: ANC updates on preparations for the ANC 52nd national conference, 11 October 2007; ANC's 53rd national conference, 6 October 2012.
Notes: * Ongoing changes in branch credentials resulted in an adjusted 3 983 ballots being issued on Polokwane voting day.
** 91.2% of the voting delegates from branches; rest: ANCWL, ANCYL and MK Veterans' League each 45 voting delegates; NEC 82 and nine PECs 20 each – for an additional 397 delegates (8.8% of total).

with the ANC recognising that it would have to renew branch connections to avert future defeat in national elections. In some instances, branches had started evolving into street-level cell-like structures that were often connected via cellphones and social media.[27]

The ANCYL has traditionally been known to act as kingmakers, pushing delegates into elective conferences via the league's allocated quota and mobilising to get in through standard branch allocations. This capacity took knocks when the Malema-ists departed, and again in late 2014 when the National Working Committee (NWC) demobilised the emerging post-Malema ANCYL.[28] It is precisely because the ANC branches have this dual importance of elective and mobilisational power that the ANC's headquarters at Chief Albert Luthuli House leave branch mobilisation and membership to as little chance as possible. Luthuli House (largely, secretary general plus deputy secretary general) control is not absolute, but it went a long way toward determining the outcomes of the Polokwane and Mangaung national elective conferences, and in provincial and regional equivalents. It is widely known that Luthuli House carefully maps and audits the branches.[29] In actions that fed into the 2017 succession stakes, Mantashe had to rule over the legality of procedures at the ANC's 2014 and 2015 eThekwini regional conferences. Although organisationally sound, his actions undermined his own standing in the race at the time.[30] Cooperation is frequently compliant – sub-national structures collaborate consensually, eager to be in the good books of the in-faction. This mode changed as the post-Zuma succession battle started taking shape. Both branch leadership and Luthuli House know the importance of excluding unwanted competitors or troublemakers across the organisational tiers, even if the 2015 Alliance summit statement pronounced against it.

The ANC's Mangaung elective conference provides pointers into how branches operate in times of organised contest. Control over the delegations was the key to realising Zuma's dream of a second term. There were reports of ghost branches and parallel branch structures, manufactured with the encouragement, complicity or consent of Luthuli House – all in aid of building Zuma's Mangaung majority.[31] Opponents came from the grouping that had hoped to see Motlanthe, then deputy ANC president, replace Zuma as president. Under the watchful eye of Luthuli House, and in particular Jessie Duarte, the ANC branches were audited in the run-up to Mangaung. Fake branches were reportedly rooted out – but the stories about manufactured branches that got their delegate quotas would not subside.

In the course of the pre-Mangaung branch audits it had become clear that record-keeping of membership in the branches had often been problematic. Secretary General Mantashe remarked:

> … [A] lot of the membership is falling through the cracks, either as a result of gatekeeping or mere inefficiency in capturing of membership … members of the ANC are deliberately excluded from processes. This is most glaring when we go to conferences when comrades try to have more members who are likely to support them in the elections and seek to marginalise those who are likely to support a different candidate. [32]

Mantashe criticised the existence of 'paper members', noting that they do not believe in the ANC but in the person who had bought their membership.[33] Further examples of alleged vote-buying included the 2014 ANCYL lobbying for the elective (subsequently collapsed) conference, the ANCWL'S 2015 conference and the 2015 eThekwini regional elections that were rerun repeatedly. Given the huge membership of roughly 75 000 (although down by about a quarter since its 2012 high), its location in the KwaZulu-Natal ANC heartland, and factional alignments with alternative succession slates, eThekwini was an early pointer to the 2017 succession.

The 2012 project of monitoring the branches had paid off, amid several court battles over who were to be designated as the Mangaung delegates. Several killings, including assassinations among rival and aspiring delegate groupings, were part of the mix in Zuma's Mangaung re-election. Some Free State delegates took court action concerning the legality of the Free State elective conference.[34] In the end the final Mangaung counts disallowed the Free State ballots (a different-colour ballot was used to distinguish the 324 Free State voting forms). Given the practice of slate-voting and the predominance of the Zuma camp, the Free State factor did not change the overall result. When eventually the contested Free State ANC conference was rerun, the steam had gone out of the contest; the rebels had moved on.

At the same time the NEC had been deliberating the exact formula for delegate numbers to Mangaung. In the end the number of branch delegates was not in direct relation to branch membership figures (although it still played an important role). A direct relation would have knocked many branches out of conference delegate status (Table 1.2). Rather it was determined that each branch should have at least one delegate, as the ANC constitution indicates.

This reduced the total number of KwaZulu-Natal delegates from potentially over a thousand to 974 (up from 608 in 2007).[35] The dispute around possible supplementary delegates granted to mega-branches (that featured, for example, in KwaZulu-Natal) was resolved and the Eastern Cape, originally punished in the delegate stakes for reported organisational problems, retrieved some of its expected branch recognitions.

A breakdown of the 2012 ANC membership figures, which informed delegate numbers, reveals much about the ANC in the time of Zuma: 2012 was a dramatic year. The Mangaung membership registration drive followed on the ANC having reached its centenary target of one million members. By the time of the 8 January 2012 anniversary date the one million mark was exceeded. By mid-2012, as branches were readying themselves to elect their delegates, Luthuli House released updated and revised membership figures. There were further huge increases in the provinces that had already expressed themselves in favour of Zuma's candidacy: KwaZulu-Natal (approximately 87 000 added), Mpumalanga (34 000 added) and Free State (around 45 000 added). This was an additional 166 000 ANC members in these three provinces alone (Table 1.3). The voting branch delegates in 2012 were 4 103, compared with 3 675 in 2007. KwaZulu-Natal's proportion rose from 18 to 24 per cent – close to one-quarter of all branch delegates – and crowned it as a pivotal voting bloc. It was at this level that Zuma won his Battle of Mangaung.

In *Regeneration* it is noted that the Polokwane conference had helped strengthen the ANC organisationally, reinvigorating it, revitalising its relationship with the people, and contributing to an enhanced lease on life. This dynamic had run a full circle by the time Mangaung ended. Mangaung was an easy win for Zuma but took a toll on the organisation. It was a tough battle with no room for defeat for the Zuma slate (Table 1.4). There was none of the Polokwane euphoria, and promises for the second-term magic for a Zuma regime deflated as the conference doors shut. In many respects the Mangaung moment was the antithesis of Polokwane.

The ANC changed in the five years from Polokwane to Mangaung. The branches lost their fervour. The Polokwane delegates' war cries for a reconnected organisation turned out to be hollow. The Polokwane dream was to turn the ANC into the vehicle to launch an alternative set of leaders into power, and the new incumbents knew their power games and how to entrench themselves. As Mangaung's dominant grouping, the Zuma-ists also demonstrated that they knew how to use power, even occasionally reconciling with 'exiled' internal

44

Table 1.3: ANC membership figures, 2007–2012

Province	December 2007	%	September 2010	%	January 2012	%	2007–2012*	June 2012**
Eastern Cape	153 164	24.7	161 161	21.5	225 597	22	–2.7%	187 585
Free State	61 310	9.9	41 627	5.6	76 334	7.4	–2.5%	121 074
Gauteng	59 909	9.7	70 305	9.4	121 223	11.8	+2.1%	134 909
KwaZulu-Natal	102 742	16.6	192 618	25.7	244 900	23.8	+7.2%	331 820
Limpopo	67 632	10.9	101 971	13.6	114 385	11.1	+0.2%	161 868
Mpumalanga	54 913	8.8	46 405	6.2	98 892	9.6	+0.8%	132 729
North West	47 353	7.6	57 911	7.7	60 139	5.9	–1.7%	75 145
Northern Cape	37 262	6.0	37 122	5.0	42 342	4.1	–1.9%	34 428
Western Cape	36 497	5.9	40 427	5.4	43 397	4.2	–1.7%	38 499
TOTAL	620 782	100	749 547	100	1 027 209	100	–	1 218 057

Source: ANC, 2012, *Organisational Report*, p. 38.
Notes: * Figures in this column: percentage points.
** Figures in this column: audited membership numbers, December 2012. At the ANC's October National General Council meeting it was announced that membership numbers had declined to 769, 870; a figure just above that of September 2010.

Table 1.4:   Polokwane and Mangaung election results for the top-six-official slates, 2007 and 2012

Conference: Position	2007				2012			
	Zuma slate		Mbeki slate		Zuma slate		Motlanthe slate	
President	Jacob Zuma	2 329 (62%)	Thabo Mbeki	1 505 (38%)	Jacob Zuma	2 983 (75%)	Kgalema Motlanthe	991 (25%)
Deputy president	Kgalema Motlanthe	2 346 (62%)	Nkosazana Dlamini-Zuma	1 444 (38%)	Cyril Ramaphosa	3 018 (76%)	Mathews Phosa, Tokyo Sexwale	470 (12%) 463 (12%)
National chairperson	Baleka Mbete	2 326 (61%)	Joel Netshitenzhe	1 475 (39%)	Baleka Mbete	3 010 (76%)	Thandi Modise	939 (24%)
Secretary general	Gwede Mantashe	2 378 (62%)	Mosiuoa Lekota	1 432 (38%)	Gwede Mantashe	3 058 (77%)	Fikile Mbalula	901 (23%)
Deputy secretary general	Thandi Modise	2 304 (61%)	Thoko Didiza	1 455 (39%)	Jessie Duarte	Unopposed	–	–
Treasurer general	Mathews Phosa	2 328 (63%)	Phumzile Mlambo-Ngcuka	1 374 (37%)	Zweli Mkhize	2 988 (76%)	Paul Mashatile	961 (24%)

Source: Polokwane and Mangaung conference announcements, 18 December 2007; 19 December 2012.

opponents. This was the new ANC: to make progress and gain access to power and privilege, cadres had to be on the good side of this grouping.

FACTIONALISM, CAREERISM, PRESIDENTIAL PROTECTIONISM

Factionalism became a strident feature of the ANC, despite the fact that its constitution outlaws it. Upon joining, each member must take an oath to 'defend the unity and integrity of the organisation and its principles, and combat any tendency towards disruption and factionalism', as then secretary general Motlanthe reminded the delegates to the 2007 Polokwane national elective conference.[36] Two-term ANC secretary general Mantashe took this message into the ANC's 2012 organisational report. At Mangaung he bemoaned the scourge of factionalism across provinces like the North West, Free State, Northern Cape, Eastern Cape and Western Cape; even the young SACP members saw themselves as a faction within the ANC. Mantashe's avalanche of words described the practice:

> The new signs of divisions and factionalism are a source of worry and concern. The determination by some members of our movement to destabilise the organisation and disrupt meetings with the objective of achieving their goals in conferences or any other structure of the movement are clear signs of a revolutionary movement that is being infiltrated …
>
> The ANC is severely compromised by the leaking of documents, detailed briefing of journalists and spinning of information in favour of factional positions.
>
> Factionalism seems to have become institutionalised. We are seeing more boldness in the provinces, where factions even give themselves formal names. This kills objectivity, with comrades supporting or opposing each other not on the merits of ideas or strength of arguments but on the basis of who makes the proposal. This is extremely harmful to the ANC … Factionalism has also led to the virtual collapse of discipline in the structures of the ANC. The disruption of ANC meetings and gatherings is becoming a norm …
>
> Elections based on slates have introduced a new dynamic into conference politics, that of every faction losing the elections appealing the

outcomes as a group. When comrades are made aware that the organisation cannot institutionalise factions, branches are made to sign a letter typed with the same font, from the same machine, using the same language and thus flood the SGO [secretary general's office] with these letters of appeal. This is one challenge that the new NEC will have to pay attention to, as it constitutes a threat to the unity and cohesion of the movement. [37]

The report is silent on Mantashe being regarded as a leader of Mangaung's *über*-faction, in being on a slate that he advanced from the then unassailable platform of Luthuli House, and that Luthuli House polices the *de facto* enforcement of factional rule. The Tripartite Alliance's 2015 summit declaration (continuing the laments of the previous years) refers to those who are 'guilty of funding factions' and 'guilty of accepting money for these purposes' – and confirms that factionalism was persisting.

The vibrancy of contest was one of the greatest losses that the ANC Tripartite Alliance has been suffering in the Zuma era. It has been under stress since the Mbeki days, but up to at least the latter phases of Zuma rule it is stopping short of disintegration. The SACP is intact but feeble in these days of the Zuma ANC because at top level it is integrated into the Zuma faction, continuously rewarding Zuma for bringing the SACP in from the cold marginalisation of Mbeki days. The party has been accepting high-level appointments in the legislatures (national and provincial) and the executive (Cabinet, deputy ministers and premiers). By 2015, the SACP had 230 000 members compared with the 160 000 of just two years earlier (the 2013 figure had already represented a tripling of membership since 2008). The SACP became a booking-in point for a career track into the ANC and public sector; a high ranking in SACP leadership structures elevated that candidate in ANC leadership contests. In the latter phases of Zuma's presidency the SACP has started reflecting on the damage that its unquestioning support for Zuma had inflicted. Its 2015 congress discussion document illustrated the turmoil that emerged in the wake of the SACP's close association with Zuma.[38]

The SACP has had free rein to polish its ideological interpretations of Zuma government policy for compatibility with a 'communist party'.[39] Its policy contributions to government have been modest and not distinctly socialist although not without social-welfarist and developmental content. On the major issue of the Marikana police mass-killings, the SACP concentrated its condemnations on Lonmin and the Association of Mineworkers and Construction Union (Amcu) and was silent on the role of the police.[40] It was frequently also SACP members who took the intra-Cosatu lead in mobilising against then Cosatu general secretary Zwelinzima Vavi in the factionalist battle for control of Cosatu. The intention was to force Cosatu to support Zuma uncritically – even if the ANC itself reported that the pro-Zuma Cosatu faction also went against the ANC task team instruction to be more conciliatory and retain unity. Vavi was one of the highest-profile and most critical figures in the battle for influence in and over the ANC.

Cosatu was splitting (through disunity, with some unions operating half-in-half-out of the federation) because of ANC factional rule transposed onto the Tripartite Alliance. The bid to capture Cosatu and thwart the Numsa attempt to sway the trade union federation as a whole in its favour has been one of the signature moves of the ANC in Jacob Zuma's time.[41] Much of the antagonism came from the Zuma-ists (including in the SACP) and the efforts of Cosatu president S'dumo Dlamini to draw Cosatu wholly into the circle of presidential adoration. The problems were also linked to Numsa's more leftward ideological positions; to antipathy towards several Cosatu policy compromises with the ANC on anti-workerist policies; and to Vavi's outspokenness against the Zuma-ist ANC and its association with corruption. Numsa was at odds with a mainstream Cosatu that was following the new *dictum* of the Zuma decade – sing the praises, please the president, and gain opportunities and privileged deployment.

The ANC was deeply involved in the Cosatu wars, including through the task team[42] under Deputy President Ramaphosa and Deputy Secretary General Duarte, who remarked to a peace meeting between the Cosatu factions that their decision would be as important as the outcome of the popular vote in the (then) pending 2014 election.[43] The ANC first stalled a Cosatu split before the election. Afterwards it worked to forge a superficial holding operation. A Numsa breakaway was averted at the earlier stage so that the ANC could enter the election without being *actively opposed* by the biggest and most left-leaning of Cosatu's affiliate unions. When Numsa was expelled in November 2014 there were many public laments on how detrimental the split was, not least from Mantashe:[44]

> We reaffirm our position that the expulsion of Numsa from the Federation is bad for the Cosatu itself, it is bad for the ANC, bad for the Alliance, the progressive forces as well as for society in general.

Numsa's Castro Ngobese pointed out that it has been a long-standing project of SACP general secretary Blade Nzimande to deal with Numsa, because it had 'failed' to support Zuma and had not supported the ANC in the 2014 election. The charge sheet against Numsa confirmed this: at the top of the list was Numsa's special national congress (December 2013) decision not to support the ANC in Election 2014, its call for Cosatu to break from the Tripartite Alliance, and the resolution to explore a movement for socialism.[45] Subsequently, more attention switched to Numsa's resolution to do cross-sectoral membership recruitment (a common trade union practice, as Numsa pointed out).[46]

No one wanted to bear the weight of splitting Cosatu, especially at the approach of its thirty-year celebrations of 2015. Ramaphosa's statement 'the ANC's preference is that Cosatu should remain united'[47] and the task team's later lament that the Cosatu acrimony had extended into disregard of task team wishes coexisted with the decision of the Cosatu main body to shed Numsa, Vavi and several other unions. It was also determined to stay with that decision and, in due course, win back at least parts of the dissident unions. The SACP and the pro-Zuma faction in Cosatu placed the blame for the split on Numsa. For the SACP it was about vindication and celebration. Seeing itself as the real vanguard of the working class, it declared that Cosatu's Central Executive Committee (CEC) '... was left with no option but to take the drastic and unpleasant step of expelling Numsa from its ranks ...'[48]

Cosatu had already become paralysed in leadership and decision making, and often ineffectual in representing worker issues, but it would be worse to have an officially fractured labour union that released resources for anti-ANC mobilisation. From Numsa's side it was about leaving an organisation which it could capture – if it could successfully steer it through a national elective Cosatu congress. In mid-2015 a set of pro-Numsa Cosatu unions turned to the courts to get formalisation of the plans for a special national conference – besides Numsa, the Food and Allied Workers' Union (Fawu), South African Football Players' Union (Safpu), South African Municipal Workers' Union (Samwu), Democratic Nursing Organisation of South Africa (Denosa), Communication Workers' Union (CWU), South African Commercial Catering and Allied Workers' Union (Saccawu) and South African State and Allied Workers' Union (Sasawu). Numsa had already gone ahead to initiate United Front structures tentatively, in an effort to align it with community struggles.[49] The United Front was set to be the precursor for the anticipated Numsa political party, the Movement for Socialism.[50] The United Front's launch was repeatedly delayed owing to a lack of funds.

From Cosatu's side the exit of a substantial portion of Numsa members, along with notable numbers from other unions supporting Numsa, and the associated loss of revenue, were drastic.[51] The biggest issue, however, was that this Cosatu and this ANC under Zuma would go down in history as the forces that moved for the dissolution of the Tripartite Alliance and ANC as we have known it. Cosatu's historical mission had not yet been achieved, yet its political contradictions, which had little to do with attainment of socialist objectives, had overtaken it. One of the greatest ironies of the 'takeover' was that Numsa's financial contributions had been subsidising the non-rent-paying SACP in Cosatu House, Johannesburg.

The Numsa-Cosatu battle suggested one possible trajectory into the ANC's further decline. The broader movement could no longer move ahead, even if it understood perfectly the necessity of retaining unity and reclaiming the days of unified struggle glory – the days before Cosatu had traded a chunk of its soul for the political expediency of being integrated into the ANC's vehicle of state power.

CONCLUSION: THE NEW ANC INTO THE FUTURE

This chapter sketched the outline of the ANC as it has evolved in the time of Zuma into a compromised and weakened organisation hanging on to its liberation credentials. At the same time, and ironically, this ANC has remained powerful. The ANC and the Tripartite Alliance partners are wracked with self-serving factions. The ultimate feat for a faction has been to get on the president's side, with little consideration of the implications for the post-Zuma order. Factionists win fame and fortune, but insiders know that the wars are never definitively won. Unless the ANC president still needs the comrade's future favour, past loyalty will not count for much.

As political time starts running out for Jacob Zuma, much of political life in and around the ANC remains absorbed by Zuma the survivor, the seemingly master strategist for whom the ultimate achievement is miraculous personal survival rather than the reputation of the organisation, or the government, or the greater good of a once-great liberation movement in power. The ANC in these years *became* Zuma.

ANC succession politics have provided the first set of indicators of the road ahead. For much of 2014–2015 Zuma and his loyalists have been fighting for his security as South African president, largely through control over the ANC, and attempted domination of other parties in Parliament. They have been ensuring that followers are continuously positioned in a protective presidential cordon, especially in the security services; and also ensuring that his proxies enter favourable positions for succession. A shortlist of ANC presidential successor candidates is evolving, and a set of next-round, perhaps next-generation candidates are assuming positions to await the completion of the rotation act. All is set for a battle between Cyril Ramaphosa, Zweli Mkhize and Nkosazana Dlamini-Zuma,[52] with Gwede Mantashe as a powerful 'dark horse' outsider candidate and the other hopefuls Baleka Mbete and Jeff Radebe. Some were aiming at the ANC presidency, others positioning for the deputy presidency.

Factors like incumbency and grassroots popularity, closeness to the president who still needed protection, the (infamous and often-abused) gender card, the finishing school of African Union service, the right province (read KwaZulu-Natal followed by Gauteng and the Eastern Cape), power over the provinces and branch organisation, the ANC staring into the face of popular decay – all these came up for consideration, as branches, and particularly Luthuli House, are preparing for the next round. There are many contradictory signals as to the state of Zuma's ultimate power over succession. Signs of shrinkage were evident in the appointment of the May 2014 Cabinet. Zuma ceded a large say in the appointments, directly to the ANC and specifically to Mantashe. However, the way in which all the ANC national structures rose and closed ranks in September 2014 to protect Zuma against public protector Thuli Madonsela suggested that his power was holding. Parliament's question time in March and August 2015 confirmed that Zuma loyalists tolerate presidential denialism and partial truths about the non-security, state-sponsored upgrades to the president's Nkandla residence. The outcomes of the 2015 Tripartite Alliance summit, and the special national congresses of the SACP and Cosatu recorded the early signs of change in Zuma's power, but Zuma was still far from 'out'.

The next concrete signals of ANC succession directions are to emerge around the time of the 2015 NGC meeting of the ANC. It is an event where ANC governance and policy are reviewed, but in the run-up many within the party will start speaking succession and responsibility for policy change and implementation beyond the Zuma age. Crown princes or princesses will legitimately, through policy debate, start strutting their leadership abilities. Three mini-scenarios are possible as the ANC moves towards 2019. In *the first*, Zuma steps down as ANC president in 2017, and gradually scales down for the new ANC president to ease into the job and lead the ANC as presidential candidate into the national elections. In *scenario two*, once the ANC has elected a new president in December 2017, Zuma declares two centres of power to be undesirable, taking his lead from the 2007 ANC resolution. He then steps down early in 2018, based on real or ostensible health (or other) considerations. A newly elected ANC president takes over as president of South Africa and provides strong, exemplary leadership to help the ANC move into Election 2019. A *third scenario* is the prolonging of Zuma's say over the ANC and an eighteen-month extension of Zuma's ANC term so that ANC and government presidential terms will coincide. The latter is the best 'Zuma protector' but will minimise new momentum and hope for a reinvigorated ANC in 2019. Much of South Africa might be so relieved, and so hopeful that a dark phase in South African politics is passing, that the ANC might be disproportionately rewarded for a change in leadership.

NOTES

1   Based on a quotation from an ANC intellectual, informal communication, 2011, IEC Elections Centre, Tshwane, 19 May 2011, cited in Susan Booysen, 2011, *The African National Congress and the Regeneration of Political Power*, Johannesburg: Wits University Press, chapter 13.

2   See Verashni Pillay and Laura Grant, 26 September 2014, 'Exiled DGs held in government's "Siberia"', *Mail & Guardian*, http://mg.co.za/article/2014-09-25-life-is-peachy-in-siberia, accessed 26 September 2014.

3   Jacques Pauw, 10 August 2014, 'Sex, Sars and rogue spies', *City Press*, http://www.citypress.co.za/news/sex-sars-rogue-spies/, accessed 12 August 2014; Ferial Haffajee, 17 August 2014, 'Don't allow Mzansi to become Thugsville', *City Press*, p. 3.

4   Vusi Pikoli with Mandy Wiener, 2013, *My Second Initiation: The Memoir of Vusi Pikoli*, Johannesburg: Picador Africa.

5   Qaanitah Hunter, 5–11 September 2014, 'Paranoid president axes more top spooks', *Mail & Guardian*, pp. 2–3.

6   Minister of Finance Nonhlanhla Nene, in radio interview, SABC-SAFM, 20 October 2014. This statement has appeared in multiple variations, in at least the period from 2011 onward.

7   Auditor general of South Africa, 30 July 2014, *Consolidated General Report on the Audit Outcomes of Local Government 2012–13*, http://www.agsa.co.za/Documents/Auditreports/MFMAgeneralreportsnational.aspx, accessed 2 August 2014.

8   Jacob Zuma, 11 March 2015 and 21 August 2014, questions to the president in Parliament, Cape Town, responding to questions from the EFF and DA.

9   Alliance Summit Declaration, 1 July 2015.

10 Also see Susan Booysen, 2013, 'The ANC circa 2012: Colossus in decline, no lethal crisis lurking', in John Daniel, Prishani Naidoo et al. (eds), *New South Africa Review 3*, Johannesburg: Wits University Press; Susan Booysen, 2012, 'Regeneration of ANC political power, from the 1994 electoral victory to the 2012 centenary', in Arianna Lissoni, Jon Soske et al. (eds), *One Hundred Years of the ANC*, Johannesburg: Wits University Press.

11   The Presidency, *Twenty Year Review: South Africa 1994–2014*, http://www.the presidency-dpme.gov.za/news/Pages/20-Year-Review.aspx, accessed 20 August 2014.

12   Susan Booysen, 2013, *Twenty Years of South African Democracy: Citizen Views of Human Rights, Governance and the Political System*, research report, Johannesburg and Washington DC: Freedom House.

13   Susan Booysen, 2011, op. cit.

14   These details were offered by the minister of social welfare in response to a parliamentary question, October 2014. See Sapa, http://citizen.co.za/261153/16m-social-grants-cost-r109bn-minister/, accessed 23 October 2014. Social grants were expected to reach 17.3 million people by 2017–18; National Treasury, Medium Term Budget Policy Statement of October 2014.

15   ANC, 2000, 'Tasks of the NDR and the mobilisation of the motive forces', NGC discussion document, http://www.anc.org.za/show.php?id=2356, accessed 12 September 2014.

16   Richard Poplak, 2014, 'Fantasia', in *Until Julius Comes*, Cape Town: Tafelberg, pp. 152–156, sketches the details of the culture of this new phenomenon.

17   Quotation from senior ANC leader, 5 February 2015, interview, Johannesburg.

18   Jacob Zuma, in Sabelo Ndlangisa, 10 April 2011, 'Vote ANC, vote for God', *City Press*, p. 1; ANC, 6 February 2011, 'President Jacob Zuma's figurative expression amounts to no blasphemy', statement, Johannesburg, 6 February 2011.

19   See, for example, *The Star*, 20 April 2014, p. 4; *City Press*, 13 April 2014, p. 3; *The Sunday Independent*, 14 April 2014, p. 4.

20   James Ngcakula, in Political Studies colloquium, 24 April 2012, 'The ANC and its 2012 phase in the regeneration of political power', Nelson Mandela Metropolitan University.

21   National Youth Summit, Electoral Commission, 9–12 September 2014, The Lakes Hotel, Benoni, http://www.elections.org.za/content/, accessed 1 March 2015.

22   Susan Booysen, 2012, *The ANC's Battle of Mangaung*, Cape Town: Tafelberg Shorts e-Book series.

23   Interview, 19 May 2015, NEC member from KwaZulu-Natal, Johannesburg.

24   The list was, in descending order: Jacob Zuma, Cyril Ramaphosa, Malusi Gigaba, Naledi Pandor, Jeff Radebe, Fikile Mbalula, Blade Nzimande, Bathabile Dlamini, Lindiwe Sisulu, Collins Chabane, Angie Motshekga, Nathi Mthethwa, Pravin Gordhan, Nosiviwe Mapisa-Nqakula, Thoko Didiza, Aaron Motsoaledi, Nkosazana Dlamini-Zuma, Derek Hanekom, Max Sisulu, Baleka Mbete, Thulas Nxesi, Maite Nkoana-Mashabane, Kgalema Motlanthe, Zizi Kodwa, S'bu Ndebele, Jeremy Cronin, Edna Molewa, Buti Manamela, Lulu Johnson and Jackson Mthembu. See Piet Rampedi and Baldwin Ndaba, 29 January 2014, 'Trusted Zuma allies top ANC election list', http://www.iol.co.za/news/politics/trusted-zuma-allies-top-anc-election-list-1.1638510#.VGp7Z8l6inq, accessed 30 January 2014.

25   See Mzilikazi wa Afrika, 2014, *Nothing Left to Steal: Jailed for Telling the Truth*, Johannesburg: Penguin.

26   ANC, 2007 and 2012, *Organisational Report*, http://www.anc.org.za/show .php?id=2539; http://www.anc.org.za/docs/reps/2012/organisational_reportk.pdf; accessed 4 October 2014.

27   Interview, ANC organiser in North West province, 27 September 2014.

28   Sibongakonke Shoba, 30 November 2014, 'Besieged Zuma "fears coup by youth league"', *Sunday Times*, p. 4; also see Introduction.

29   ANC senior leader, interview, Luthuli House, Johannesburg, 5 February 2012.

30   For an overview of some of these dynamics, see Nathi Olifant and Sibongakonke Shoba, 10 May 2015, 'Trouble at the top …', *Sunday Times Review*, p. 2.

31   Interview on condition of anonymity with senior ANC delegate with close connections to ANC guests at Mangaung conference, 20 December 2012, Mangaung.

32   Gwede Mantashe, 2012, interview with *Mail & Guardian*, http://mg.co.za/article/2012-12-17-anc-membership-numbers-soar/, accessed 21 August 2014.

33   Ibid.

34   See Greg Nicolson, 18 December 2012, 'ConCourt slams ANC Free State, but clears delegates for participation in Mangaung', *Daily Maverick*, http://www.dailymaverick.co.za/article/2012-12-18-concourt-slams-anc-free-state-but-clears-delegates-for-participation-in-mangaung/#.VE4O_xZ6joQ, accessed 18 January 2013.

35   ANC media releases and briefings, June–December 2012.

36   ANC Secretary General Kgalema Motlanthe, 2007, Polokwane, ANC *Organisational Report*.

37   ANC Secretary General Gwede Mantashe, 2012, ANC *Organisational Report*, pp. 3, 10, 12–13.

38   SACP, July 2015, Meeting the challenges facing the trade union movement, Discussion document, Third Special National Congress, http://cdn.mg.co.za/content/documents/2015/06/28/meetingthechallengesfacingthetradeunionmovement-sacp3rdsnc2015.pdf, accessed 13 July 2015.

39   See, for example, SACP, 15 July 2012, Declaration of the 13th national congress of the SACP, http://www.sacp.org.za/main.php?ID=3679, accessed 20 August 2014.

40   See SACP Central Committee, Statement, 19 August 2012, http://www.politicsweb.co.za/politicsweb/view/politicsweb/en/page71654?oid=320124&sn=Detail&pid=71616, accessed 1 June 2014.

41   Vavi was suspended when caught in a love tryst with a Cosatu employee. Dlamini thwarted Numsa's push for a general Cosatu conference to reconsider the suspension by an irregularly constituted central executive committee (Vavi became reinstated through a courtroom victory). The price Vavi paid was to be effectively silenced and subjugated to Zuma-ist Cosatu president Dlamini.

42   Amy Musgrave, 13 August 2014, 'ANC needs more time to mediate Cosatu peace deal', *Cape Times*, p. 4; Natasha Marrian, 8 August 2014, 'Cosatu's influence over the ANC is often overstated', *Business Day*, p. 8; Matuma Letsoalo, 22 May 2015, 'Cosatu "ignored" ANC advice on healing rift', http://mg.co.za/article/2015-05-21-cosatu-ignored-anc-advice-on-healing-rift?utm_source=Mail+%26+Guardian&utm, accessed 22 May 2015.

43   Jessie Duarte, quotation in SABC-TV3 news clip, 1 May 2014.

44   ANC statement in reaction to the developments in Cosatu, 10 November 2014; Gwede Mantashe, 10 November 2014, ANC media briefing, Johannesburg. The SACP took on a divisive role, then turned to a somewhat moderated position. See, for example, Castro Ngobese (Numsa national spokesperson), 16 November 2014, 'The SACP's divisive role in the fracas', *The Sunday Independent*, p. 14.

45   Castro Ngobese, 16 November 2014, op. cit.

46 Interview with Numsa national treasurer Mphumzi Maqungo, *Forum at 8*, SABC-SAFM, 9 March 2015.

47 Cyril Ramaphosa, 22 October 2014, media briefing at Parliament, Cape Town, noting that the expulsion of Numsa 'is not one of the ANC's preferences. The ANC's preference is that Cosatu should remain united.'

48 SACP Political Bureau, 11 November 2014, Statement on developments in Cosatu, http://www.sacp.org.za/main.php?ID=4549, accessed 15 November 2014.

49 Numsa, 30 January 2014, Resolutions adopted at Numsa Special National Congress, December16–202013,http://www.numsa.org.za/article/resolutions-adopted-numsa-special-national-congress-december-16-20-2013/, accessed 2 February 2014.

50 As background, see Luyolo Mkentane, 20 October 2014, 'Pushing a United Front', *The New Age*, p. 20, drawing on an interview with United Front coordinator Dinga Sikwebu.

51 Numsa was the biggest Cosatu affiliate, with more than 300 000 members. It was said to generate about R1.8 million in income for Cosatu monthly.

52 The ANCYL proclaimed in 2014 that in five years South Africa will be led by either Dlamini-Zuma or Mbete, national chairperson of the ANC. There were initiatives by Zuma-ists in the ANCYL to get the league to formalise its support for a woman candidate. See Matuma Letsoalo, Andisiwe Makinana and Verashni Pillay, 1–7 August 2014, 'Women's league eyes the presidency', *Mail & Guardian*, p. 15.

2

CONFIGURING ZUMA'S PRESIDENCY

South Africa's and the ANC's presidencies were the heart of state power, fused around the person of an unparalleled, controversial yet commanding head of state and government. The ANC propelled Zuma into power with the twin tasks of rescuing the ANC from subjugation to state power under former president Thabo Mbeki, and ensuring that the many hungry elites beyond the Mbeki circle would get their chance to 'eat' – but the ANC got more than it had bargained for: domination by a powerful and president-centred faction. The party found itself in the hands of a strategic and shrewd president who could operate the organisation and present himself as being in control while bumbling his way past a phalanx of problems.

The state leg of the presidency expanded in the time of Zuma rule. Even so, it was the ANC's Chief Albert Luthuli House and Zuma's hold on ANC power that towered over the president's private office in the West Wing of the Union Buildings. And this is only part of the story of precarious political power in the time of the Zuma presidency. In essence, the ANC under Zuma has more power over the state, but the ANC and the Tripartite Alliance are fractured and under control of Zuma and his associates. Under Mbeki, the ANC had become an increasingly limp attachment to the state. The Zuma-ists reversed this and reinstated the ANC in charge. Few had imagined at the time of Zuma's election the extent to which this reversal would in due course demean the ANC.

The presidency of South Africa has to be considered in conjunction with the presidency of the ANC. Similarly, the power of Jacob Zuma can only be understood with the linked consideration of his potent KwaZulu-Natal ANC power base and his state-wide powers to make appointments and create positions. This chapter explores further the locus of formal and informal power in and around the president, and the trajectory towards the completion of the second Zuma term. It illuminates the tragedy of a powerful, often underestimated president who manipulated his way into and in power, found his way around obstacles in power, and pulled the ANC to a point from where it would be tough to recover.

PRESIDENTIAL IDENTITY

Top-executive state power in the time of Zuma is diffused, with no single and predictable structure definitively representing where all important top-government and strategic decisions are taken. The multiple layers operate concurrently and Zuma commands; he is in many ways the spy puppet master who keeps his operatives sufficiently in the dark to ensure that he and he alone pulls the strings. This act has been challenged, on numerous occasions. The challenges (ranging from the legal contests of opposition parties to the meek opposition of political rivals) failed.

Zuma's power game at the height of his command (a period spanning his re-election at Mangaung in late 2012 to 2015, when repositioning for a post-Zuma period and campaigning for 2017 succession took off in earnest) was undermined, yet he still held a trump card: the possibility of pulling off a succession slate that would bring continuity between the Zuma order and the post-Zuma order.

It is said that Zuma and his presidency lack a galvanising message, that his inner soul is still a matter of conjecture for his compatriots.[1] This chapter argues that it is precisely the absence of definitions that has become Zuma's trademark political identity. He is the Zulu-background president, for a few years up to 1990 the head of the ANC's intelligence department in exile, who slipped into seniority by rising in the ranks of the ANC's top six. Zuma is the common denominator when strategic and important decisions are taken – or not taken, because he either prefers vacillation or uses it deliberately, as much evidence suggests. A series of individuals, groupings and structures nevertheless crams in and out of the presidential power and decision-making sphere. Zuma surrounds himself with multiple concurrent influences. He has the upper hand in the power game because only he knows on whom, and when, he calls. His West Wing and Luthuli House structures compete with a band of kitchen cabinets – a configuration which combines with Zuma's skill to let his loyalists (whom he had often himself appointed to powerful positions) do things for him without involving or implicating him.

To strengthen this 'structure' of power, Zuma personally directs key appointments in the security sector, and accepts Luthuli House directives for many of the other Cabinet appointments. The president has the power to appoint and recall a host of top political figures, including the chief justice and other senior judicial officials, all heads of public institutions, the national director of public prosecutions, auditor general, head of the army, president of the Reserve Bank, members of the independent communications authority, and many others. Some of the appointments are on sole presidential authority, others on advice from the Judicial Services Commission (JSC) for example – even so, the ANC's (and hence Zuma's) wishes largely prevail. The heads of the powerful state-owned enterprises are mostly in their positions at the president's behest – often close associates and confidants – and are better known for presidential connections than for job performance. Zuma holds the key to the fates and fortunes of many of the most powerful names in South African politics. In cases where the president has the sole power to appoint, appointees' durability is as strong as their last defence of or service to the president.

The heart of Zuma's power structure lies in a posse of loyal and trusted figures. They control access, manage the presidential space, facilitate, defend and protect. They enable the president to exercise his personalised power – but this is not always a smooth, coordinated operation. It varies from one occasion to the next, and posse members also compete with one another generally to be the ultimate power pleasing the throne. ANC secretary general Gwede Mantashe pops right into the heart of presidential power. He was the core link between party and state and assumed a *de facto* prime ministerial role. This role was curtailed as succession-related tensions accumulated between him and Zuma, and Jeff Radebe, in his deployment as minister in the Presidency, absorbed much of the 'prime ministerial' function. The SACP's Blade Nzimande is always there to pull thorns from the presidential flesh – from art galleries and newspapers to trade unions (especially Numsa), the EFF and the SACP in the provinces, all because of their 'disrespect of the president'. Former presidential spokesperson Mac Maharaj saw reason in presidential actions that defied all reason. Radebe managed the Presidency and covered when Zuma had legal and personal matters to attend to. The two 'presidential women' of Lakela Kaunda in the Presidency and Jessie Duarte in Luthuli House are pivots in the circle of loyalty.

The subtext in these configurations is the fusion of state and party. At executive level this differentiates the Mbeki and Zuma orders of government. Earlier chapters argued that the fusion is a major ingredient in the ANC's maintaining itself in power in the longer term as its electoral and popular standings decline. The fusion also helps to build Zuma's presidential power. The party prevails over the state in general, while under Mbeki it was more a case of subjugation of *some* institutions to Mbeki's control plans, but not in the name of the ANC. For a long time Luthuli House briefings carried more weight, and had more of a sense of occasion of state than those from the government executive.[2] As Zuma amplified his efforts to build his legacy, and simultaneously avoid the contested forum of Parliament, he escalated presidential briefings from Pretoria.

THE INTELLIGENCE MASTER

The Zuma years were the time in which the seemingly (read 'deliberately self-presented as') naive, victimised,[3] modestly educated president was elected by a masochistic (so it turned out, and then there was no turning back) ANC to enter and play a sophisticated power game. Zuma's power construct went beyond the foundations of his ANC intelligence experience.

Zuma remains the partially defined president, and he thrives on the misunderstandings and underestimations that result. Zuma is intelligence-oriented. Quietly subverting the understanding that he is unambiguously party-centred, he plays both party and state in crafting his power reserve. The state is the arena for Zuma's personalisation of political power. In this process he is not held accountable; instead, he equates himself with democracy in South Africa and dictates that he be protected against onslaughts and conspiracies. As the ANC becomes more challenged, Zuma becomes more assertive and unapologetic about the ANC's majority and his right to be the president. In his words to the NEC, 'the time has come ... to use our majority to assert the right we were given to govern ...'[4]

Zuma is notorious for leading neither from the front nor from 'the surface'. Some of his power lies in working in the style of an intelligence operative. He shares his political directives with Luthuli House and the NEC, Cabinet meetings, and intra-Presidency meetings. It is often not clear precisely what managerial or policy decision is in force. He does not offer hands-on policy leadership and often appears to be out of command. Many of Zuma's policy speeches, even into his make-or-break second-term deliveries, were half-hearted, exaggerating the status of 'new' announcements (which would usually be repackagings of previous efforts). On essential policy issues such as the energy and local government crises, his March and August 2015 verbal answers to parliamentary questions showed a meagre grasp of the issues.

Zuma's absence at the front is part of the *de facto* 'Zuma scheme of governance'. He operates in an opaque, almost secretive way, hardly ever giving away his intentions in meetings.[5] Those who had just been consulted in a meeting might be hopeful, but not aggrieved if Zuma does not exactly follow through on their ideas. Zuma hoists in constituencies and interest groups, including business groupings such as black empowerment business, traditional leaders and cultural organisations. He keeps them in suspense, predisposing them to want to please the president through compliments and appeals. Such audiences often feel satisfied just for the fact of having been engaged by the president.

He is not recognisable through specific, scholarly-intellectual or organically-intellectual writings, or a particular ideological stance beyond that which arises from his inferred roles in Operation Vula (the mandate that brought his ascendancy into ANC and government power in 2007–09), the National Development Plan (NDP) and his 'we are a mixed economy' statements.[6]

'Remember,' an interviewee has said, 'Zuma has seven faces. He will wear the one he wants you to see.'[7] It is only the closest of his associates and defenders who refer to him as an organic intellectual. The only biography to date of Zuma is Jeremy Gordin's,[8] which ended before Zuma assumed state power. As Xolela Mangcu points out, Zuma's eleven predecessor ANC presidents had all written extensively – or were written about extensively.[9] Zuma is yet to publish a single book or treatise of note.

Party and state anchors balance each other in the appointments Zuma makes. He plays gender, provincial and Tripartite Alliance balances in the selections. He retains substantial personal leeway in determining who will be retained and who will be appointed. Appointees are drawn from both state-institutional and ANC bases and he plays these bases against each other. He appoints a Cabinet that limits direct NEC involvement in favour of inputs from full-time Luthuli House functionaries. He retains sole voice in appointment of the security cluster's Cabinet members. He uses a multiplicity of state-institutional friendships and links to build rings of presidential power and protection. He appoints the heads of state-owned enterprises and matches them with ministers who will carry forward his desires, including having a stab at solving his personal and governance problems. His vast network of business and patronage interests makes him a resource kingpin. In many respects Zuma *is* the contemporary ANC – public institutions articulate with his personal pursuits and are presented as extensions of the liberation project. Zuma is also the president who has learned from Mbeki (perhaps he has always known) never to alienate and neglect control over your own organisation and power base. The president is weak in public respect and moral standing, but strong in his understandings of nurturing and exercising control where it matters in the ANC.

The Zuma-ists like to present their president as decisive and clear in his developmental state orientation, emphasising the 'radical' direction, which in this lexicon coheres with 'mixed economy'. Instead, vacillation and faltering stand out. The 2014 post-election State of the Nation address (Sona) was the presumed Zuma flagship as it signalled the start of his second term, or the fifth administration of the ANC since 1994. It repeated the thrust of '*radical* socio-economic transformation' that Zuma inserted into his second-term inauguration speech. The speech showed the mundane reassurance that the NDP offers the long-term vision. The Sona, contradictions and all, became the subject of a fourteen-page newspaper supplement, the Jacob Zuma Legacy Special, sponsored by the Passenger Rail Agency of South Africa (Prasa), whose head Zuma appoints. The 2015 Sona brought mild twists and repackaged existing plans and policies into a nine-point plan.

Instead of showing a consolidated Zuma vision for the rest of his second term, the 2015 Sona was mired in disgrace for the president and his ANC. Zuma-ists so feared embarrassment of the president by the EFF that they oversaw State Security Agency signal jamming and public order security forces entering Parliament to 'restore order'. The public outcry following the night of 12 February 2015 became a signal point, defining South Africa and the Zuma ANC. There was consensus that something broke that night.[10] Zuma was subsequently humiliated by DA leader Mmusi Maimane in his parliamentary speech on Zuma as a broken man, overseeing the broken institutions of South Africa's broken democracy. Zuma then turned this around into a mockery of Maimane, vigorously cheered by the ANC MPs.

Zuma would have been vastly powerful – and never under siege from public opinion and multiple sources of political-party and other opposition – had it not been that he extended his prosperity through the inappropriate use of public funds while public outcries rage; plus that he then denies knowledge of this happening and refuses to be accountable. He takes cover in feigned ignorance, in 'innocent until proven guilty', 'I did not know', 'there are no charges', 'Parliament did not command me' and 'there is no case against me'. The ANC adds, citing the public protector's findings, that Zuma did not use undue influence to get his way. Zuma knows that his aura – rich, successful and affable – will endear him to communities where he makes well-staged entrances. He then demonstrates his common touch, speaking in the vernacular about 'iNkandla, iNkandla, iNkandla. This is because [the opposition parties] have nothing to offer …'[11] and then he charms the crowds with haunting renditions of struggle songs.

Zuma is the president who helped foster anti-intellectualism in dominant ANC circles. 'Clever blacks'[12] were told how to behave and show their gratitude for liberation by the ANC. In contrast, former short-term president Kgalema Motlanthe argued that he was ashamed of ANC members appropriating liberation for the ANC instead of recognising that all South Africans were liberated in 1994.[13] Zuma plays victim, personally and on behalf of the ANC. The ANC, and Zuma himself, pronounced that the voters did not care about Nkandla,[14] the president was the victim. He argued that he and his family needed those upgrades because one of his wives had been raped there in the late 1990s. The ANC in Parliament adds that South Africa owes the president more, rather than the other way around. According to this narrative, only the media and the opposition worry about Nkandla.[15]

Zuma's victim act has been long-lasting. Mzilikazi wa Afrika relates how in 2003 Zuma played journalists and newspapers, planting information to 'expose' Bulelani Ngcuka (former national director of public prosecutions) as 'apartheid spy' (knowing that Ngcuka had not been a spy) at the time that Zuma was at the receiving end of NPA questioning.[16] In 2006, Karima Brown and Vukani Mde wrote that 'the Zuma trials are as much about the tragic downfall of an antihero as they are about reshaping the ANC, the state and the SA of the future'.[17] Close to a decade later we know that the anti-hero has survived against many odds. It was a compromised hero who subsequently pulled state, government and especially the ANC down to the level of a president who was shrewdly clever, and quite possibly greatly gratified with the games he had pulled off with party, citizens and country.

63

EXPANDING AND RESTRUCTURING THE PRESIDENCY AND EXECUTIVE

The elaborate presidency of South Africa was an innovation of Thabo Mbeki's in the days when he was building *his* personalised empire.[18] It was criticised for its ambitious executive orientation in times of dreams about democracy and parliamentarianism. In retrospect, the Mbeki presidency is dwarfed by the elaborate maze that has come about in the days of Zuma.[19] It has grown in size, resources and power. This happened especially in the first few years after Zuma's assumption of power (Table 2.1). Some tapering off in staff numbers, hardly shrinkage, occurred late in Zuma's first term.

Kader Asmal related the essence of the story of the Presidency under Nelson Mandela and Mbeki, the situation that Zuma inherited from Mbeki. He specifically noted the Cabinet-president relationship:

> With Mbeki at the helm, the truly sensitive or difficult topics of state were kept off the agenda even at the level of South Africa's executive branch of government. While power hovered in and around the Mandela cabinet, by the time Mbeki had assumed the presidency, this kind of power resided elsewhere. Cabinet carried on with the day-to-day business of governance and the managing of our individual portfolios. But the difficult, controversial decisions, strategising and policy formulation took place within the rapidly expanding Office of the President.[20]

Table 2.1:   Growth of the Presidency in the time of Zuma

Annual report	Staff numbers	Budget allocation
2006/07	466	R241 019m
2009/10	589	R494 301m
2010/11	636	R807 463m
2011/12	636	R931 000m
2012/13	686	R1 061 940m
2013/14	680	R1 098 934m

Source: Annual reports of the Presidency of South Africa 2006–2014, http://www.thepresidency. gov.za/docs/reports/annual/, accessed July–October 2014.

The Presidency's structure continually changed as departments and special projects moved in and out. Under Mbeki, the unit for women, children and people with disabilities resided in the Presidency. Under Zuma, a separate ministry originated, as Zuma's reward for the ANC Women's League support. It failed, and in the second Zuma term the portfolio was split and 'women' moved back into the Presidency, albeit with a full Cabinet portfolio in tow. Zuma also gave another ANC constituency – the veterans – their own department. By 2015 it was dysfunctional to the extent of its inability to report financial affairs to the parliamentary oversight committee.

The National Planning Commission (NPC), with an associated Cabinet member, and the Department of Performance Monitoring and Evaluation (DPME), with Cabinet member, boosted the image of the Presidency as a centre of direct presidential control over planning, monitoring and execution of core state projects. The second Zuma term saw reorganisation to create the powerful 'minister in the Presidency' (under Jeff Radebe, long-time right-hand man to Zuma; further strengthened by his position as head of policy in the ANC). The ministerial portfolio includes planning, monitoring and evaluation. The formal functions associated with this position have often eclipsed those of the officially designated deputy president of the country. Radebe, trusted to embrace Zuma's interests as his own, hence became the super-minister. Always considered as influential, and consistently in Zuma's Cabinets, Radebe also carries the title of Zuma's firefighter.[21] He defended Zuma in the Guptagate scandal, and against the public protector as part of the pre-2014 election security cluster. Deputy President Ramaphosa had *ad hoc* engagements such as negotiating and sealing the 2014 Cabinet members' performance agreements. Ramaphosa is mostly deployed as the roving peacemaker, moving from South Sudan to Lesotho and then domestically between the Cosatu task team and as leader of government business into negotiations with the opposition parties.

The Presidency was only alluded to broadly when Zuma announced his first second-term Cabinet,[22] but further institutional change loomed. A steering committee on the new 'macro-organisation of the state' would take the organisational lead. So-called super-departments were shaping up – provisionally, and besides the Presidency, the departments of Public Service and Administration, National Treasury, Public Works and Communications. This was a long-standing theme, with a previous heyday in the 2006–2007 Mbeki period. It was shelved then because Cabinet members in the 'ordinary' ministries rebelled. A number of the ministerial kingpins in the Zuma system appeared to be in place in Zuma's first second-term Cabinet – including troubleshooter and fixer Malusi Gigaba; Pravin

Gordhan assuming responsibility for the local government quagmire; Ebrahim Patel pushing infrastructural development; Lindiwe Zulu holding up the image of job creation through small business; Siyabonga Cwele (also the departmental employer of one of Zuma's daughters) albeit now in telecommunications; Thulas Nxesi (public works minister sympathetic to Zuma's Nkandla expenditures); and Maite Nkoana-Mashabane building Zuma's international profile.

The new departments of the second term included Small Business Development (cobbled together out of parts of the departments of Trade and Industry, and Economic Policy) to find a political platform for a long-time Zuma adviser; Telecommunications and Postal Services (incorporating the Government Communication and Information System, taken out of the Presidency); and a new Communications department created for the woman who had forcefully chaired a parliamentary committee to help Zuma out of Nkandla problems.[23] The NPC and the National Youth Development Agency moved into the new Planning ministry in the Presidency. One of the plans was to link all national line departments into the performance management and evaluation (PME) system, their strategic plans to be monitored centrally through the apparatuses in the Presidency. The DPME did not put the 2015 performance plans in the public domain, and one of the few certain things about dismal Cabinet performances was that underperformance would be filtered through individual usefulness to the president.

The president's seamless control over justice, crime prevention and security (commonly known as 'the security cluster') further characterises Zuma's presidency. The first fifth-administration Cabinet restructuring wrought a near-total revamp of the cluster's ministerial members, with most of the fourth administration's security cluster members redeployed into other Cabinet portfolios. In the reshuffles there were new ministers of police, justice and correctional services, and home affairs. Only the minister of defence and military veterans, Nosiviwe Mapisa-Nqakula, remained.[24] The changeovers might have been driven by criticism of the cluster's management of Nkandla and Marikana; it might have been that Zuma had other longer-term plans for previous incumbents; or it might simply have been the power that Zuma centres on himself by not allowing the occupants of senior and strategic positions (on which the sustainability of his Presidency depends) to set down roots and develop power bases of their own.

The president is under no legal obligation to explain and defend his strategic manoeuvres. Because he is not an MP the exact form of accountability due by the president to Parliament is contested. Overall, Zuma has created a personal shield in the justice and security sectors, 'a phalanx of praetorian guards allied to him and to each other, including on-off, suspended or not, crime intelligence boss Richard Mdluli' and with a range of other senior security staff clustered around him.[25] Strategic intelligence deployments have often been sourced from exile days.[26]

CABINETS AND KITCHEN CABINETS

One of the ways to define the presidency of Jacob Zuma is to trace his Cabinets and the executives more generally, and thereby discern how the president positions himself in relation to the centres of executive power. He remains 'under-defined' in terms of how those close to him influence him, determine or co-determine his decisions, and shelter him. In some respects, his presidential story is that of an enigma. He is an intelligence operator whose political survival depends on no one knowing everything about him. We know that when friends and associates of the president become enemies, others will step into the vacancies. The formal Cabinet members are expendable; the composition of its incumbents is an indication of their value to the president at a particular moment in time. Given Zuma's *modus operandi* in governing, his amorphous kitchen cabinets are revealing too, to the extent that they can be pinpointed.

Many crucial issues are handed over to Zuma's Cabinet members, and he often lets them get on with the job without holding them substantively accountable for ensuring that those policies and actions render significant outcomes. On issues close to his power scheme he retains exact monitoring – even more than what was associated with 'big controller Mbeki'.[27] The performance agreements for his Cabinet members (signed off by the president) are often vague, containing broad descriptions that make it difficult to prove that ministers perform poorly.[28] With regard to his own performance, an assessment comes from the president himself:

> I think that people do appreciate what I've managed to achieve. Even those who are generally critical, I don't think they've ever said 'this man is lazy'. The majority appreciates it. They comment about it; many will tell you and even articulate what they think the country has achieved and say 'thank you very much, it is because of you that the country is in this situation'. It's part of life, but South Africans are generally a very critical society, sometime overly critical at times when we need to say actually we have done well. We laugh at that because even when they are critical they are sitting in the RDP house which was given to them by government and they say, 'this government is doing nothing'.[29]

In a statement of May 2009, the Presidency noted that the advisers 'bring a wealth of experience and expertise to the Presidency and will add much value to the president's determination to bring about faster change and improved service delivery'. No matching statement followed in 2014. Zuma prefers his advisers and key Presidency staff to be long-standing friends and professionals who have assisted him over time; for example, in 2005 after Mbeki had fired him as deputy president, Zuma relied substantially on the journalist (then part of his inner circle) Ranjeni Munusamy for public relations, and on Mo Shaik (among others) for political strategic direction. His chief operations officer in the Presidency remains Lakela Kaunda. At some stages, adviser positions went to senior persons who were owed deployment when no other positions were available.[30] Compared with the Mbeki presidency and with Zuma's first term, there was far less profiling of his second-term set of advisers. A few continued, others stepped down, or were promoted, but replacements were not specifically announced. It took a question for written reply, lodged by the DA, to get a full listing of advisers in the president's office. Six were listed in the reply, along with their function and the date of commencement: M Maharaj (communication adviser, from January 2009 [to April 2015]); B Makene (legal adviser, from June 2009); M Hulley (part-time legal adviser, from November 2011); BN Mfeka (economic adviser, from July 2014); VG Mashinini (special projects adviser, from November 2012, appointed as electoral commissioner in May 2015); and VR Shabalala (political adviser, from July 2014).[31] Ebrahim Ebrahim, former Deputy Minister, became the president's parliamentary counsellor in 2014. Zuma announced Silas Mzingeli Zimu as his special energy adviser in 2015.

Some of Zuma's advisers were 'hidden' in departments where they had the status of personal ministerial advisers. In the Department of Energy until September 2015, Senti Thobejane was dismissed by minister Joemat-Pettersson. He is, according to reports, also a close associate and adviser to Zuma. The chief executive of the Nuclear Energy Corporation of South Africa, Phumzile Tshelane, is seen as a linchpin in Zuma's plan for nuclear power stations.[32]

There have been multiple estimations by those close to Zuma (and by occasional participants) about the identity of Zuma's *actual* kitchen cabinet – with reference to who gets consulted and who advises and influences, parallel to the official government structures of Cabinet, NEC top figures and other senior members. Instead of choosing between estimates, this chapter argues that the answer lies in Zuma being advised by multiple trusted sources, often at the same time. This fits the contention that at the broader civil society tier of consultation

Zuma plays all the constituencies, deliberately not choosing publicly or visibly and not accounting to anyone interested in keeping track formally.[33] Links were evident in Zuma's governance style and his intelligence background.[34]

The multiple coexisting kitchen cabinets serving Zuma in his second term of office have constituted different networks of influence and co-optation. There is no central (kitchen) structure that pulls Zuma's multi-network operations together in one, state-centred and concrete institution. The coordination is in the president's head; the overall organisation is opaque. He takes advisers' guidance and insights when needed. In approximate declining order, the groupings and institutions (formal and informal) involved in Zuma's presidential decision-making processes are, depending on the general or specific nature of the issues:

- *Any or all of the top six officials of the ANC NEC, especially Gwede Mantashe in the time when Zuma trusted him.*

   The ANC treasurer general, secretary general and deputy secretary general are the three NEC officials employed by the ANC – by the 2012 ANC election Zweli Mkhize, Gwede Mantashe and Jessie Duarte, respectively. They are closely associated with Zuma, although the evolving succession plans are influencing the relationships. Mantashe is very proximate and a key player, a consistent stalwart by Zuma's side – yet at times considered an adversary. He carries a wide constituency, without being dependent on Zuma to mobilise it. There have been attempts to drive a wedge between them – some see Mantashe as a threat to Zuma and his KwaZulu-Natal backers' succession plans.[35] At the height of Mantashe's influence, Presidency staff members reported that Zuma never took an important decision without informing Mantashe. Mantashe took a central role in senior-level appointments, including Cabinet; he handles important ANC briefings concerning the ANC in government and Parliament and national and government policy. He presents and defends many of the government's policy announcements, and as an SACP politburo member he exercises influence over the SACP. Duarte rose into her position as head of the ANC's monitoring and evaluation unit in 2011, after a time of clashes with Kaunda in the national Presidency. At Luthuli House, Duarte was pivotal to ensuring Zuma's re-election as ANC president at Mangaung.

- *Chief adviser and legal adviser.*

   Michael Hulley, once his personal lawyer, is regarded as Zuma's chief adviser (appointed part-time legal adviser in 2011, and later full-time). Zuma and Hulley are also together in business, sometimes through family members.[36] He has consistently helped Zuma to sidestep the legal traps that come with Zuma territory. Advocate Kemp J Kemp for Zuma in the Bloemfontein High Court made a concession concerning the 'spy tapes' (the recordings of intercepted conversations that were supposed to have proved that Mbeki had conspired to prevent Zuma from becoming president). Hulley indicated his dismay.[37] He is reported also to be present at security cluster meetings.

- *The security cluster.*
  Zuma may have accepted consultation and specific Luthuli House advice in compiling his Cabinets, but for the security cluster appointments he took the bow. The appointments include Zuma loyalist and minister of home affairs, rising in the NEC ranks, Malusi Gigaba. Zuma is secure in the knowledge that the security cluster will take care of his interests.

- *Other Zuma confidant-advisers.*
  With variation over time, they include Mac Maharaj, brought in from retirement in early 2011 to replace Zizi Kodwa and add 'Vula *gravitas*' to a Presidency suffering credibility deficits (Maharaj retired from the position in April 2015); Nathi Mthethwa (despite being moved to a seemingly more junior Cabinet position in 2014);[38] Zweli Mkhize (a former KwaZulu-Natal premier, ANC treasurer general and a likely candidate for the ANC deputy presidency of 2017); and Blade Nzimande (SACP general secretary and minister of higher education).

- *Internal ANC operators and power-mongers.*
  Zuma has managed to keep these operators on his side, for one thing because they could visualise Zuma as key to their rise through ANC ranks. Zuma integrated them into his project to remain in power (Blade Nzimande is in a league of his own in this category). The rest of the list contracts and expands over time, also overlapping with the confidants above. They include Lindiwe Zulu (from her time as international affairs adviser to the president, with special reference to Zimbabwe),[39] Zizi Kodwa, S'dumo Dlamini, Senzo Mchunu and Sihle Zikalala. Stella Ndabeni and Pule Mabe complement the list. Several in this group come from the so-called war council responsible for mobilising support for Zuma among younger citizens. By 2014–15 they were graduating into the heart of power, as ministers or deputy ministers, as part largely of a post-exile generation that was being positioned to take charge in the post-Zuma era.

- *Trusted Cabinet members (a few are also noted in preceding sections).*

Zuma operates with the support of Jeff Radebe, the late Collins Chabane, Nosiviwe Mapisa-Nqakula, Maite Nkoana-Mashabane and Tina Joemat-Pettersson, besides some (like Gigaba) of those mentioned above. Siyabonga Cwele is probably part of this group.

- *A set of KwaZulu-Natal business and professional people.*

They feature consistently as close to Zuma,[40] often backing him in defences against the onslaughts of the new opposition. Participants in the Friends of Jacob Zuma trust, featuring businessman Don Mkhwanazi, are constant. Comfort Ngidi of the Professionals' Association of South Africa and the Concerned Lawyers and Educationists for Equality Before the Law (CleeBlaw) brings in support. CleeBlaw defended Zuma on release of the public protector's Nkandla report. They saw flaws, inaccuracies, inconsistencies and contradictions in the report that they called a 'miscarriage of justice'. Jimmy Manyi, between spells as official and potentially reappointed government spokesperson,[41] founded the Progressive Professionals Forum. KwaZulu-Natal businesspeople such as Vivian Reddy and Philani Mavundla are in business and friendships with the president. The extended Gupta family is frequently mentioned regarding connections and influence with the president. The relationship with the Guptas became marginally more arm's length after public exposures, although connections persisted through their *The New Age* and ANN7 television channel.[42] The 'Zuma Brains Trust' was prominent in Zuma's early days of power (then including Professor Sipho Seepe, Dr Paul Ngobeni and former judge Willem Heath). The structure faded out, but members were still used strategically to help keep tabs on developments around Zuma and to help defend him.

Several senior appointees in government suggest that professional competency does not rank foremost in gaining positions. Several such persons have headed state-owned enterprises, including the contentious South African Airways (SAA) chairperson Dudu Myeni. Former SABC board chairperson Ellen Tshabalala was also among the protected appointees – close to the president but more likely to have been there to help execute wishes than influence decisions. She was also the chairperson of the Jacob Zuma Foundation. There are several signs of Zuma appointing persons to Cabinet because they will execute his wishes. To illustrate, the 2014 minister of public enterprises said, in relation to SAA appointments: 'The president doesn't give me instructions. He doesn't tell me what to do – he gives advice.'[43] The new minister also did not step up on Eskom's R43 million sponsorship of *The New Age*-SABC breakfast shows. Former Eskom interim chief executive Collin Matjila (also seen as a member of the president's inner circle) signed the deal – the sponsorship was a *de facto* transfer of funds to a sympathetic newspaper.[44] A rapid series of Eskom top-level changes in 2015 suggested that 'special presidential appointments' in national crisis situations were exacerbating the crises.

Personalised rules of deployment

One of Zuma's greatest sources of power, even as many started ascribing him second-term lame-duck status, was the right to reshuffle Cabinet. Frequent reshuffles at Cabinet level had the effect of members knowing they constantly have to please the president in order to remain at this political front line. Zuma's first-term reshuffles happened like clockwork: on 31 October 2010, 24 October 2011, 12 June 2012 and 9 July 2013. The first second-term Cabinet reshuffle was minor and followed in September 2015. The new minister of minerals and energy, replacing Ngoako Ramatlhodi, was Mosebenzi Zwane (from the Free State and associated with the Gupta clan). Ramatlhodi (enmeshed in controversies and clashes with powerful figures in the mining industry) was shuffled into the public service and administration portfolio, which had been left vacant with the passing of Collins Chabane. Given the minor status of this reshuffle Zuma retained a core trump-card: senior members must support him in party and government or risk losing portfolios.

There are four cardinal rules of the reshuffle game. First, when things do not go perfectly for the president, such as in the cases of the Guptas' Waterkloof landing and the president's Nkandla homestead security systems, there shall be consequences. Second, a strong alternative senior (including Cabinet) appointment strategy of Zuma's is to appoint known-to-be-flawed persons, possibly like the subsequently suspended and given-the-golden-handshake Mxolisi Nxasana as NDPP[45] and keeping Mapisa-Nqakula as minister of defence (despite Waterkloof) in order to ensure compliance and control.

> Why appoint someone as compromised as Mxolisi Nxasana to head the NPA if not to have some past deeds to use against him should he act independently? Why retain someone as palpably unsuitable as Richard Mdluli as head of police crime intelligence if it were not for the support that his position could lend to those who fear punishment? Why hang on to the likes of Hlaudi Motsoeneng at the SABC if you have nothing to fear from public opinion?[46]

Third, subservience and willingness to take instruction is a common feature. Appointees, generally inexperienced and no power-players in their portfolio fields themselves, are available to be directed by the president and his circle of advisers and associates. Fourth, even if a presidentially led redeployment comes across as a demotion, it may not be that. In some instances it is a Zuma strategy to move that person below radar for a while, tasking the person differently with strategic functions while keeping him or her employed (perhaps in the presidency), or a sideways reshuffle to let a person like Nathi Mthethwa do ANC legacy building and struggle resuscitation from within government.[47]

The power to reshuffle Cabinets

Zuma relies on his Cabinets. He often allows the members to get on with their jobs yet he takes great interest in portfolios that concern him personally – and ensures that some of his senior confidants keep close tabs on his behalf. Zuma has reshuffled with such frequency that incumbents were either settling in or gearing up for handovers for substantial parts of their terms. Accountability has suffered because some ministers are serially settling into new portfolios.

Zuma has used the power to reshuffle Cabinets to great effect for confirmation of his own hand on the levers of power. His Cabinets have retained a few persistent persons, subject to changing portfolio allocations – for example, when loyalists had accumulated criticisms in previous portfolios but were still useful to the president. In his appointment of the first Cabinet of his second term, twelve existing Cabinet members were allocated new portfolios[48] and eleven new persons were added while thirteen retained existing portfolios. The chapter has, so far, mentioned the cases of Cwele and Mthethwa. Joemat-Pettersson (moved from Fisheries to Energy) is a further case in point: Zuma needed a loyalist to secure action on the energy portfolio – his legacy was to be constructed, no questions needed, and he was determined to go the nuclear route. Joemat-Pettersson was also a supporter of the Zumaville presidential project (which entailed looking after the president's flagship rural development initiatives) while she was in her agricultural portfolio.[49]

Regular reshuffles have had the spillover effect of pushing the directors general of the government departments into cycles of high turnover. Gareth van Onselen's analysis of the period from May 2009 to August 2013 found there had been 114 directors general of the thirty-three national government departments.[50] In that same period there had been twenty-four newly appointed ministers, thirty new deputy ministers, and eighty-one new directors general. This destabilised departmental operations and detracted from accountability in policy implementation and financial oversight. The problem extended into the security services that were plagued by suspensions and resignations.[51]

Second-term presidents have reduced powers generally, often becoming lame ducks because appointees are less dependent on this person for their continued positioning. Zuma's reputation for frequent reshuffles and redeployments (and executive members' fear of falling out of favour with the president and becoming victims of the next reshuffle) have, however, helped him retain an upper hand well into his second term.

There is expectedly substantial convergence between NEC and Cabinet membership. Thirty out of the thirty-seven Cabinet members appointed to the signature 2014 Cabinet were also elected NEC members (the NEC is bigger than Cabinet). Inversely, while 73 per cent of the elected NEC members before May 2014 were not in Cabinet, this proportion was reduced in the fifth administration. Other rules come into play on deputy ministerial deployment. Only a small minority of the 2014 deputy ministers (ten out of the thirty-eight of 2014) are also elected members of the ANC NEC. Deputy ministerial status appears as a reward for special service – for example, for loyalty to the president and good service to the ANC, or for standing up for Zuma. Youth League task team members were rewarded, as were those who had blasted opponents of ANC standpoints, the opposition generally, and any attackers of the president. The leader of the National Freedom Party (NFP) was the only non-ANC deputy minister (of science and technology). All 2014 Cabinet members were ANC. The Zuma Cabinet and deputy ministerial ranks boasted many appointments from his KwaZulu-Natal: in Zuma's 2009 Cabinet there were fourteen KwaZulu-Natal politicians, and the figure rose to nineteen in 2014.

Zuma's awkwardness with the government security apparatuses has been evident over most of his two terms in government. There has been continuous evidence of strain,[52] including Zuma's making or inducing resignations and redeployments to keep the apparatuses under control. Observers refer to the paranoia in Zuma's operations.[53] This could be real or feigned fear – in trying to counter a Cosatu split (or trying to show that he was countering it), Zuma argued that 'our enemies are ready to destroy us and if we're not united, we will be easy prey'.[54] The fear is real in that Zuma needs frequent changes around him, especially in the security apparatuses, in order to maintain his own upper hand (although in some cases he avoids changes that ought to be made). Tensions are rife. For example, State Security Agency director general Jeff Maqetuka, head of the agency's domestic arm Gibson Njenje, and head of intelligence's foreign arm Mo Shaik all left amid tensions in 2011. The Special Investigating Unit's (SIU's) Willie Hofmeyr was fired, despite having helped to elevate Zuma into power in 2009. Willem Heath, a Zuma cheerleader and Brains Trust member, was briefly appointed head of the SIU, then removed. In 2015, Hawks head Lieutenant General Anwar Dramat, Robert McBride of the Independent Police Investigative Directorate (Ipid) and Mxolisi Nxasana (NDPP) were suspended or threatened with disciplinary action or other sanction. Dramat and Nxasana followed the lure of the golden handshake, and resigned.

Playing the conspiracy card

Zuma often portrays himself as the victim of political conspiracy. Mbeki was probably the king of conspiracies,[55] but Zuma has offered strong (often subtle) competition, handling the suspected conspiracies differently, probably better. Zuma has played the 'calm statesman' when the rumours started rolling. But he does not forget actions that will wrong him. Retribution follows later. Zuma does not ask too many questions on whether it actually *is a conspiracy*. He sees conspiracy in much of the criticism – for example, according to him the corruption charges against him were inspired by the West.[56]

Zuma's ANC and Tripartite Alliance partners have taken many a cue from him. Mantashe, Nzimande and Duarte are the foremost practitioners. Mantashe accused 'foreign forces' of attempting to use the strike by Amcu to 'destabilise' the South African economy. He accused 'enemies' of Cosatu of taking advantage of its internal battles to try to destroy the labour union – while the battle was in fact over Cosatu's loss of independence to the ANC. Nzimande referred to Nkandla as 'white people's lies', warned of 'an imperialist plot' to divide Cosatu, and accused the country's media of an anti-Zuma 'liberal offensive'. Journalists critical of Zuma were a '[paid] mouthpiece of factionalists' in the ANC. Duarte reckoned that opposition parties in Parliament were 'destabilising' the ANC and South Africa.[57] Nzimande was just one beat away from conspiracy in arguing that the EFF's robust opposition to Zuma's refusing to pay back for Nkandla excesses was 'demagogic' and 'neo-fascist'.[58] Zulu King Goodwill Zwelithini and the ANC reckoned a third force was behind the 2015 xenophobic attacks – compared with Numsa's 2008 argument that the 'third force' lives in the Gauteng hostels among the lumpenproletariat.[59]

The trend has continued in Zuma's second term. The focus remained on Madonsela and alleged links to foreign agencies. Suspect 'intelligence leaks' informed the ANC government, and Julius Malema (EFF), Lindiwe Mazibuko (DA) and Joseph Mathunjwa (Amcu) were added as 'CIA agents'. The state security minister announced that these claims would be investigated, along with an investigation into signal jamming around the parliamentary precinct in Cape Town! The developments converged with the Al Jazeera-leaked 'spy cables' from South African spy agencies which were embarrassing for revealing South Africa's hapless spy operations.[60] The security base of the Zuma government appeared wretched.

MAN OF THE PEOPLE?

Zuma's entrance ticket into his Polokwane 2007 election was 'reconnection with the people'. He was 'the man of the people', close to those who, the Zuma camp argued, Mbeki had alienated.[61] The evidence of this having been achieved is ambiguous. Judged by general citizen sentiment expressed at the grassroots, Zuma failed to bring the ANC closer to the people. Research has shown substantial alienation between the ANC and the communities:

> On general democracy issues citizens felt aggrieved that they frequently only saw their elected representatives at election times, and that ANC leaders care more for themselves than for the people. In election campaigns they are flooded with ANC visitors, leading to another round of 'empty promises' and appeals for support for the 'liberation movement'.
>
> In ANC structures and meetings there are two trends: the insiders that speak glowingly of the great work of the movement; and those who regard themselves as ANC supporters (and often are ANC members), but feel excluded, for example not welcomed into branch meetings.
>
> Research decimates the Zuma camp's argument that the people do not care about Nkandla and similar issues. The people greatly care and deeply begrudge the new political elites and their president for greed and consumption of public resources. This research project showed hardly a word of pardon or praise for the president. Instead, there was a wall of condemnation and ridicule.[62]

The research findings contrasted with ANC staff and workers on the 2014 campaign trail, for example, testifying how Zuma was welcomed with accolades and warmth when he went campaigning. Such images also beamed across South Africa when Zuma's community appearances were televised. Zuma's 'people charm', bolstered by the general pull of power, was his great redeeming factor in his relentless quest to get into and retain presidential power for all of his second term. Prasa's Jacob Zuma Legacy Special proclaimed that he has 'mainly endeared himself to people through his personal charisma and magnetic charm'. In an interview with *Business in Africa* in 2009 on the eve of becoming South Africa's president, Zuma singled out Oliver Tambo as one of his role models in becoming 'a man of the people':

> While Tambo was a great thinker, he was very simple. There is nothing he did not do … When people came to him he attended to them. He would even attend to somebody who comes to raise the issue of the shoe that doesn't have shoelaces, he would ensure that the shoelaces were found … I am not a great man. I am a man of the people. I believe in people and I think that the people are everything. Once there is disconnection with the people you have problems …[63]

Zuma's connection with the people is partial. At least two major events, in Gauteng and in Limpopo (one was Nelson Mandela's memorial service), saw Zuma being booed by large numbers in the audiences. ANC strategists, subsequently, carefully managed Zuma's exposure to avoid public embarrassment. Some 'closeness to the people' was evident in the audiences Zuma has entertained at his residences in Pretoria and Nkandla. Across class, aspirant 'tenderpreneurs' and modest community members with pension and social grant issues rub shoulders while waiting for and then consulting with Zuma.[64] Many of the after-hours visitors are put in touch with relevant government departments. These meetings give insights into the Zuma presidency's creation of personalised patronage networks, the other side of the formal government networks and operations. Aspects of the meetings also resemble traditional leadership community meetings.

These illustrations shed light on the failed initiative of the president's hotline,[65] on which the Presidency breathed hot and cold. While it was obviously a bureaucratic channel to connect with citizens, they had originally believed that the president was taking a personal interest in the service they get from the state. In February 2010, Zuma announced that the hotline was being trans-ferred to the then Department of Performance Monitoring and Evaluation. Early 2012 statistics show that more than half a million out of a total of over one million calls had been dropped – 90 000 were logged for further attention and around 56 000 were resolved.[66] Later, the President's Coordinating Council reported how pleased the Presidency was, with all provinces bar the Eastern Cape having achieved 'complaints resolution above 80 per cent ... since the presidential hotline was established'.[67] Community research findings did not replicate such satisfaction with the hotline.

In refutation of Zuma as the president of the people who understands their culture, research reveals popular ridicule of the president.[68] When focus group participants from across the demographic spectrum received the positive prompt of 'Zuma is a leader, a man who understands our culture', there followed scorn, laughter and comments on polygamy and showering. Further prompts encouraged participants to abandon this tone, to no avail. Both this project and others[69] confirm that voters separate their opinions of the president from their willingness to vote ANC (at least at the time, in 2014).

Zuma has nevertheless carved a safe personal net with many South Africans, especially those also of Zulu origins. Little had the Mandela-Mbeki axis of the 1990s imagined that their deployment of Zuma to get peace in the war fields of KwaZulu-Natal (and bring the province into the national post-liberation ANC) would have the repercussions it did.[70] They helped create the platform on which Zuma would rise into power. The ANC KwaZulu-Natal as electoral giant awoke late, and then sustained the ANC when it started declining in other provinces. Without the KwaZulu-Natal performance in the national elections of 2009 and 2014 (largely facilitated by Zuma) the ANC would have looked pitiful even if still winning.

Quantitative public opinion polls further corroborate the qualitative com-munity studies. The details in Table 2.2 show metropolitan approval ratings for President Zuma that have not been over 50 per cent since early 2012. Except in the aftermath of Election 2014, the president's approval ratings have remained in the thirties, with his lowest approval rating ever in February 2015: 33 per cent of metro South Africans reckoned he did a good job as president. The most impor-tant part of this rating is that the president of the ANC is rated roughly thirty per-centage points lower than the ANC's result in the last national election. Among metropolitan black-African citizens, the president's February 2015 approval rating is 48 per cent (compared with 18, 11 and 11 per cent for Indian-Asian,

Table 2.2: President Jacob Zuma's approval ratings, 2009–2015, in metropolitan areas

Rating (%)	2009				2010				2011				2012			2013			2014			2015
	April	June	September	November	February	May	September	November	February	March	September	Oct/November	February	April	August	February	May	August	February	August	November	February
Approve	52	57	53	58	43	51	42	49	49	48	45	55	55	46	48	41	42	43	34	44	37	33
Disapprove	29	13	19	23	41	33	44	34	35	38	41	38	35	46	44	51	50	47	58	48	53	56
Don't know	19	31	28	12	17	16	15	17	16	14	14	14	10	8	8	9	8	10	8	8	10	11
Net (% point change)	+23	+44	+34	+35	+2	+18	−2	+15	+14	+10	+4	+17	+20	0	+4	−10	−8	−4	−24	−4	−16	−23

Source: TNS-Global, media releases 2009–15: TNS Metro Omnicheck 2014: 'Zuma's approval ratings bounce back post-elections', October 2014; 'President Jacob Zuma's declining popularity in metro areas', 1 June 2015.

coloured and white citizens, respectively). There are multiple highly ranked surveys that confirm these trends in Zuma's popular standing.[71] It is problematic for the ANC that its president actually subtracts from electoral support.

CORRUPTION, SCANDALS, CLOSE SHAVES, PARDONS, DENIALS

Much of President Zuma's variable but generally dismal popular ratings concern his scandals and controversies and the impact these have had on the ANC and South African politics. Negative perceptions of leaders help shape a negative image of the ANC. Nevertheless, voters largely continue differentiating leaders from party, and persist in voting ANC. Even more, Zuma was actively protected by the ANC's parliamentary brigade who, ironically, had been elected to be accountable to the citizens, and not the president.

Zuma could never 'just' be a normal president. He entered office on the wings of the arms deal scandal of the late 1990s and has never shed that association. A series of supplementary scandals has enfolded him. He has suffered continuous condemnation by state institutions such as the public protector and the courts that have the brief to protect democracy. Many ANC-linked office holders within state institutions tread softly for fear of setting off the Zuma-ists in the ANC, the Tripartite Alliance, or the vitriolic Zuma-protective apparatuses of the Presidency.[72]

The ANC by all accounts accepts that its president fulfils his accountability duties in terms of being responsive to issues arising from the 'Zuma scandals'. For example, Zuma (now assisted by a team of accomplished communication advisers) did his utmost in 2015 to persuade opposition parties and the public that he and his government regularly prove their accountability. This is said to be through oral and written answers to parliamentary questions, deliberations of oversight committees, and in debate on departmental budget votes. There is no escaping, however, that the ANC parliamentarians act as ANC operatives in defence of their president in the first instance, and only thereafter as MPs who do valuable work in the parliamentary committees. The ANC in turn actively prevents the opposition parties and the proactive Chapter Nine institutions from enforcing clearer standards of accountability.

One of the ANC parliamentarians' acts has been the appointment of whitewash *ad hoc* committees to exonerate the president. In 2014, for example, Parliament – on whether Zuma was supposed to 'pay back' a portion of the exorbitant sums of public money spent on 'security upgrades' to his private estate at Nkandla[73] – went through the motions and pretended that the issues were dealt with. This was while all of the government reports on Nkandla (and both the original Madonsela report and subsequent ones solicited by government to get 'second opinions' and obfuscate the public protector's findings) converged in some way or another on the point that R246 million worth of 'security upgrades' at the president's private residence is far-fetched, and that public funds are being misspent. There are several such report-based illustrations, besides the Madonsela findings, and Zuma himself admitting to wrongdoing:

- The ministerial task team report: large cost overruns, high consultancy fees, *prima facie* evidence that supply chain management rules were disregarded, all of which point to the 'possibility' of overpricing and collusion;
- Parliament's joint standing committee on intelligence: in response to the task team report it notes the 'high costs' and advises that the auditor general ought to investigate the appointment of contractors and allocation of tenders so as to pinpoint 'abuse' and 'unlawful conduct';
- SIU report: the scale of construction of the Nkandla residence went far beyond security requirements – the report refers to 'indefensible extravagance' and sets public purse damage at more than R155 million;
- Zuma himself: after considering the intelligence committee and SIU reports in his report to Parliament in August 2014, Zuma said 'whilst a legislative framework exists, it was either deficient in certain respects, wholly ignored or misapplied'.

It was only police minister Nathi Nhleko's 2015 report that found that the president had done no wrong – and, instead, that the taxpayer owed the president more security upgrades to the Nkandla bastion. Zuma had designated Nhleko to give effect to the public protector's ruling that part of the excessive Nkandla security upgrades to his private homestead would have to be paid back[74] – a fact of which the protector had reminded Zuma in her letter of 24 August 2014.[75] The determination ought to have been done in consultation with the National Treasury, but Nhleko engineered his own brief.

The Zuma presidency came to be recognised through the debates on whether a person as controversial as this ought to be president (the arms deal, relating to on-off 783 arms-deal-related charges of corruption, fraud, money laundering, and racketeering),[76] should be in power at all (the 2007 spy tapes on preventing Zuma's ascension into power),[77] or should be repaying inappropriate personal benefits from public funds (Nkandla).[78] The arms deal was sold to South Africa on the basis of promised offsets, a part of the project that was 'badly structured'.[79] The charges against Zuma were controversially removed in the nick of time (early April 2009) in order for him to become president of South Africa. It was a 'political solution' to a legal problem. It was only in September 2014 through an extended, tortuous series of legal actions by the DA that there was an order to release the 'spy tapes' – the information on why charges were withdrawn for Zuma to qualify to be president of South Africa. Throughout his first five years in power Zuma and his legal teams toiled (with the help of state funding covering legal representation) to prevent the South African voters from knowing the details.

Zuma used the deferment or suspension of charges – as a result of his own relentless avoidance of the processing of the charges – to his advantage. He could aver in Parliament that 'there are no charges against me'. On 21 August 2014, or EFF Thursday (when the EFF started chanting 'Pay back the money' in defiance of the speaker's order for them to 'leave the house'), the DA parliamentary leader asked the president whether he saw no conflict of interest in personally appointing the national director of public prosecutions who would determine the outcome of his charges. Zuma responded: 'There are no charges against me so the issue of conflict of interest does not arise on this case.'[80] In an approximate replay on 11 March 2015, Zuma retorted while answering, off script, verbal questions in Parliament:

- 'There is no case against me about Nkandla, no pending arrest. Nothing!'
- 'The task team of the government investigated and they did not find that I took even a penny. The SIU also investigated. They didn't find that I took even a penny.'
- 'How can I take a sabbatical leave [suggested by the United Democratic Movement's Bantu Holomisa] when there [are] no allegations against me?'

In mid-2015 President Zuma appointed advocate Shaun Abrahams as the next National Director of Public Prosecutors (NDPP). Abrahams pledged not to use his office to protect anybody – not even the president.[81] Soon thereafter Abrahams dropped cases against Lawrence Mrwebi, head of the Special Commercial Crimes unit and one of Zuma's prime defenders, and Nomgcobo Jiba, deputy NDPP, who denied that she had ever rendered special assistance to Zuma.

The ANC elected Zuma into its Presidency in the full knowledge of his arms deal baggage.[82] It was in the heat of the battle to loosen Mbeki's grip on power. Zuma was the deputy president of the ANC and, until his suspension by Mbeki two years earlier, also of South Africa. He had, by all ANC parameters at the time, a legitimate claim to the presidency of the ANC. In addition, he was openly and defiantly offering a desirable alternative to the Mbeki regime, with promises of more accountable and accessible government and more left-leaning, caring policies. The ANC had netted itself the responsibility to accept the consequences of its elective decision. Zuma's 2012 re-election showed overwhelming support, but the intensity of the campaign was evidence of the internal resistance that the Zuma-ists had to overcome. The Zuma faction knew the importance of establishing and retaining control, not just to let its president sit out his term but also to contain succession pressures.

The ANC thus set itself up for the near-constitutional crisis of August 2014 onwards. It involved the roles that Parliament and the public protector assume when the president of South Africa is the person implicated or accused, instead of one of the final points of authority in the structures of state and governance. One of Zuma's strategies was to remain silent, except when obliged to be in Parliament to answer questions. In an extreme demonstration of not feeling accountable to Parliament, Zuma asked: 'Why must I go to Parliament? I am not an MP.'[83] The ANC in Parliament in effect cheered Zuma's accountability-dodging, working to undermine public protector Thuli Madonsela's Nkandla report.[84] The ANC majority in the parliamentary *ad hoc* committee delivered an attempted 'final absolution' in the wake of the Nhleko report: Zuma no longer had anything to account for. Thereby the ANC MPs had executed the instruction that their president had delivered to the ANC NEC meeting of September 2014 perfectly, as reported:

> We cannot and should not be bulldozed by noisy smaller parties. We should guard our space and our position jealously and lead. The ANC commands more than 60 per cent support in this country … at times we become reluctant to lose our majority, and try to be as accommodating as possible.[85]

Upon execution in Parliament, Mantashe confirmed Zuma's order, arguing:

> What is wrong with that? Why should you give an institution to minority parties? All the time the ANC started by persuading people who

instead kicked it in the teeth. He [Zuma] said you can't tolerate that forever.[86]

The bigger crisis had not dissipated. The Cape High Court gave an ambiguous ruling on another case, concerning the controversy over the appointment of SABC chief operating officer Hlaudi Motsoeneng. It had implications for the status of the public protector's 'recommendations' generally, which also applied to the president in the case of Nkandla. (The minister of communications had appointed Motsoeneng permanently, by all indications with the president's blessing, in defiance of Parliament.) The case went on appeal, to help determine whether state agencies have the right to choose whether they implement public protector rulings. It was deemed likely to end up in the Constitutional Court.

These crises and scandals surrounding the president were compounded by controversies. New ones were added as the old ones hovered, unresolved. The spy tapes, purportedly proving a conspiracy by Mbeki and associates to keep Zuma from rising into power, were the extreme example. A series of polemics marked Zuma's personal and personal-professional lives, in the main covering the period from 2007 to 2015: privileges and fine business deals for family members; having unsafe sex with multiple partners in and out of wedlock; having intercourse with an HIV-positive person, who was also the daughter of a former comrade;[87] later showing that he still practised unsafe sex when he fathered a twentieth child with the daughter of a friend; inappropriately friendly relations with the Gupta family; appointment of his recently graduated daughter in a high-level security sector job; and possible close relationships with board chairpersons of the SABC and SAA, who faced questions about qualifications and professionalism, respectively.

Exceeding all other controversies and scandals was the August 2012 killing of thirty-four miners at Marikana by the South African Police Service (SAPS) at a Lonmin mine near Rustenburg. It was a dual scandal, firstly in the systematic killings themselves and secondly in the reality that the ANC as government, led by President Zuma, refused to assume responsibility. The Farlam Commission of Inquiry also stopped short of explicitly blaming the ANC government.[88] The ANC and Zuma refused to acknowledge that the murders were a mistake for which they were ultimately responsible, and thus failed to apologise to the miners, the affected communities and to South Africa as a whole. South Africa could never be the same after Marikana. Succession politics could also not be the same, given that a lead candidate, Ramaphosa, emerged seriously tainted, although not officially blamed.

CONCLUSION: THE ENDGAME UNFOLDS

By many standards Zuma was the unlikely president, but certainly not if one tracks his relentless rise through ANC ranks before he captured the ANC presidency in 2007, and again in 2012. Zuma spent ten years (1963–1973) on Robben Island. He left the country in 1975 on the instruction of the leadership. In 1977 he was appointed to serve in the ANC's Maputo regional committee. He became a co-opted NEC member in that year. At the 1985 Kabwe conference he was (re-) elected to the NEC. He served on the ANC's politico-military council and in the intelligence department at the ANC head office, Lusaka, from the late 1980s. In November 1990, the ANC's Southern Natal region elected him as chairperson.[89] Then his trajectory entered the ANC top-six positions: 1991 – deputy secretary general; 1994 – national chairperson; 1997 and 2002 – deputy president; and 2007 and 2012– president. In 1999 he also netted the South African deputy presidency when inclusive government power-sharing fell away and Mangosuthu Buthelezi declined the position.

It is, then, almost inconceivable that Zuma would *not* rise into and retain the ultimate position of presidential power. However, when one overlays this power track with his scandals, controversies and lapses in government and policy it becomes almost unthinkable that Zuma could remain in power, probably in a position to see out his second term – if not up to the 2019 national elections, then at least up to the ANC elective conference of 2017. When he showed signs of poor health shortly after the 2014 election, the Zuma-ists made it a prime task to assure South Africans that the president would complete his term as ANC president up to December 2017 and South African president until May 2019.

Zuma knows how to dig himself in. This chapter has sketched the carefully crafted configuration of institutions and power relations that he has shaped. A manipulative-charming-forceful personality, he plays the role of innocent victim persecuted through conspiracy and the president who demands to be seen as the embodiment of deep historical symbolism of struggle against oppression and persecution.

Zuma has been tragic for the ANC. Throughout his notorious tenure he has committed the mistake of not considering the damage he was imparting to the political world in which he operated. He was so much part of the ANC, so strategic and so calculated, that he could pull in otherwise good and wise people around him. Few in the heart of the ANC could imagine an ANC without Zuma as the controller. This movement became frenetic, as evidenced in parliamentary proceedings and the ANC MPs' astounding exoneration of Zuma. Zuma's exceptional hold on the ANC rings out. This was the president, shrewdly intelligent, who knew how to play power games that would bring him the last laugh. Loyal ANC members who did not share the pro-Zuma fervour pleaded that the man should not be equated with the party, but they could not wish away the stark changes in the ANC.

NOTES

1   Barney Mthombothi, 15 June 2014, 'Lessons in courage for a president who has yet to find his voice', *Sunday Times*, p. 21.
2   Ferial Haffajee, 25 May 2014, 'Who really runs the country?' *City Press*, p. 1.
3   Adriaan Basson, 2012, *Zuma Exposed*, Johannesburg and Cape Town: Jonathan Ball, observes that Zuma is master at playing victim.
4   The quotation from Jan-Jan Joubert, Sibongakonke Shoba and Thabo Mokone, 16 November 2014, '"Now you will learn kern:"', *Sunday Times*, pp. 1–2.
5   Charles Molele, Mmanaledi Mataboge and Rapule Tabane, 8 February 2013, 'Zuma's most trusted lieutenants', *Mail & Guardian*, http://mg.co.za/article/2013-02-08-00-zumas-most-trusted-lieutenants, accessed 1 September 2014.
6   This world was light years away from the ideologically defined alternative to the Mbeki-Mandela-ist negotiated world which was imagined by the so-called Vula Boys, the ones that were supposed to be more socialist and radically oriented than the ANC negotiators of the early 1990s. Even then, there were questions as to whether Zuma was really part of this more left-oriented camp.
7   Interview, 27 June 2014, employee in the Presidency, granted on condition of anonymity, Johannesburg.
8   Jeremy Gordin, 2008, *Zuma: A Biography*, Johannesburg and Cape Town: Jonathan Ball.
9   Xolela Mangcu, 20 October 2013, 'Six months to write an opus', *City Press*, p. 21; also André Odendaal, 2012, *The Founders*, Auckland Park: Jacana.
10   Ranjeni Munusamy, 13 February 2015, 'SONA 2015: The day our country broke', *Daily Maverick*; Ferial Haffajee, 15 February 2015, 'Something broke on Thursday night', *City Press*, p. 1; Susan Booysen, 15 February 2015, 'Democracy under siege in its citadel', *The Sunday Independent*, p. 13; Mmusi Maimane, 17 February 2015, 'Zuma: A broken man, presiding over a broken society', Cape Town, State of the Nation debate in Parliament.
11   Babalo Ndenze, 24 April 2014, 'Zuma turns Nkandla into a joke', *The Star*, p. 4.
12   *City Press*, 3 November 2012, 'Zuma scolds "clever" blacks', http://www.citypress.co.za/news/zuma-scolds-clever-blacks-20121103/, accessed 28 November 2013.

13 Mondli Makhanya, 24 May 2015, 'Motlanthe and De Klerk weigh in on the future of SA', *City Press*, http://www.news24.com/SouthAfrica/News/Motlanthe-and-De-Klerk-weigh-in-on-the-future-of-SA-20150524, accessed 4 June 2015.

14 An ANC campaigner in the Western Cape confirmed the opposite: no matter how much the ANC tried to avoid Nkandla, the issue haunted the party on the campaign trail. Anonymous interview, 12 September 2014, Cape Town.

15 See Louise Flanagan, 6 May 2014, 'Zuma justifies Nkandla', *The Star*, p. 1.

16 Mzilikazi wa Afrika, 2014, *Nothing Left to Steal: Jailed for Telling the Truth*, Johannesburg: Penguin.

17 Karima Brown and Vukani Mde, 25–26 February 2006, 'Political fault lines beginning to show', *The Weekender*, p. 8.

18 Susan Booysen, 2006, 'Consolidation of control in the centre: Trends in public policymaking in South Africa', *Journal of Public Administration*, vol. 41 (4), pp. 731–749; Susan Booysen, 2001, 'Transitions and trends in policymaking in democratic South Africa', *Journal of Public Administration*, vol. 36 (2), pp. 125–144.

19 Graphics depicting the institutional landscapes can be found in Susan Booysen, 2011, *The African National Congress and the Regeneration of Political Power*, Johannesburg: Wits University Press, chapter 12.

20 Kader Asmal with Moira Levy, 2011, *Politics in My Blood: A Memoir*, Auckland Park: Jacana.

21 See Makhudu Sefara, 30 May 2014, 'Pushing back lame duck period', *The Star*, p. 14.

22 For the details of the legislatives mandates, see *The Presidency Annual Report 2012–2013*, pp 3–4; 23; 28.

23 Jacob Zuma, 25 May 2014, announcement of the 2014 Cabinet. Statement on SABC-TV3 news.

24 Zuma's control over the security cluster also came a long way. After he assumed power in 2009, Zuma appointed several of the so-called Vula Boys to the security portfolios. See Paul Holden and Hennie Van Vuuren, 2011, *The Devil in the Detail How the Arms Deal Changed Everything*, Cape Town: Jonathan Ball.

25 Sam Sole and Sally Evans, 23–29 March 2012, 'Zuma's praetorian guards', *Mail & Guardian*, p. 4.

26 Interview on condition of anonymity, South African diplomat in Harare, 12 October 2012.

27 Temba Masilela and Sihle Mthiyane, 2014, 'From the RDP to the National Development Plan: The mirage of a super-ministry', in Thenjiwe Meyiwa et al. (eds), *State of the Nation 2014*, Cape Town: HSRC Press. The authors do not differentiate between obviously varying cases, arguing that ministers under Zuma had the space to develop their ministries, more so than under Mbeki.

28 See, for example, http://www.poa.gov.za/pages/overview.aspx, accessed 15 August 2014, 14 March 2015. The new 2014 Cabinet agreements were still not available for public insight well into 2015. A source reported in April 2015 that they had all been signed. It was confirmed that they were aligned to the Medium Term Strategic Framework.

29 Jacob Zuma, 2014, in interview with Kevin Ritchie, 'Zuma – leaner, and confident that SA is on the right track', *Cape Times*, 14 August 2014, p. 10.

30 Zuma's 2009 set of advisers included his second legal adviser, advocate Bonisiwe Makhene, former ambassador to Brazil and at the time deputy chief state law adviser in the Department of Justice and Constitutional Development; political

adviser, Charles Nqakula, former safety and security minister and former defence minister; economic adviser, Mandisi Mpahlwa, former trade and industry minister (until 2012); international relations adviser, Lindiwe Zulu, ANC NEC member; and his parliamentary counsellor, Ayanda Dlodlo, ANC NEC member and MP who became deputy minister in 2012.

31 Question for written reply, number 1682, issued by Parliament, 26 May 2015.

32 Lionel Faull, 27 February 2015, 'Energy minister shields "key Zuma nuclear ally kern:"', http://amabhungane.co.za/article/2015-02-27-energy-minister-shields-key-zuma-nuclear-ally, accessed 22 May 2015.

33 Zuma brings in aides who are not close enough to question his judgement. Surprise prevailed when at one stage he brought in Vusi Mona as deputy director general of communications, and Vincent Magwenya from Standard Bank as spokesperson.

34 See S'thembiso Msomi, Sibusiso Ngalwa, George Matlala and Sibongakonke Shoba, 5 August 2012, 'Who's who in the Zuma web', *Sunday Times*, pp. 1, 14.

35 Qaanitah Hunter, 24 October 2014, 'The rift deepens: Zuma is "sidelining" Mantashe', *Mail & Guardian*, http://mg.co.za/article/2014-10-23-zuma-mantashe-rift-widens, accessed 24 October 2014.

36 Adriaan Basson, 2012, op. cit., analyses Zuma's business interests in detail, based on details from the Company and Intellectual Property Commission, as at 26 September 2012. Also see Jeremy Gordin, 2008, op. cit.; Thulani Gqirana, 8 February 2015, 'Zuma's lawyer faces disbarment over Aurora "perjury" claims', *Mail & Guardian*, http://mg.co.za/article/2015-02-08-zumas-lawyer-faces-disbarment-over-aurora-perjury-claims, accessed 2 March 2015.

37 Zuma's lawyers conceded in the Supreme Court of Appeal that they could not make an argument for refusing to hand over the 'spy tapes' to the DA. The lawyers had been opposing the DA's bid to get the recordings that had been used as a reason to withdraw corruption charges against Zuma in 2009.

38 Mthethwa had saved Zuma at the 2005 NGC meeting by moving that delegates must overturn the decision to suspend Zuma; see Jovial Rantao, 28 October 2011, 'The man who has the president's ear', *The Star*, p. 16.

39 David Moore, May 2014, 'Zimbabwe's democracy in the wake of the 2013 election: Contemporary and historical perspectives', *Strategic Review for Southern Africa*, vol. 36 (1), pp. 47–71, analyses the Zimbabwean incident in which President Robert Mugabe called Zulu a 'street woman'. She swallowed the insults. She became a full Cabinet member on a specially created portfolio in mid-2014.

40 See the 2007 overview by Sipho Khumalo, 5 June 2007, 'Project JZ: The men behind the man', *The Star*, p. 13.

41 Stephen Grootes, 30 October 2014, 'The Communication Cluster: Too late for credibility?' *Daily Maverick*, http://www.dailymaverick.co.za/article/2014-10-30-the-communication-cluster-too-late-for-credibility/#.VFNSLMl6joQ, accessed 31 October 2014.

42 Interview with one-time adviser in the Gupta empire, 23 February 2014, Midrand; 15 March 2015, Cape Town.

43 Interview with Pearlie Joubert, 2 November 2014, '"Iron Lynne" gets tough on failing SAA', *Sunday Times*, p. 2.

44   See Lionel Faull and Sam Sole, 24–30 October 2014, 'Eskom sugars the Gupta breakfasts', *Mail & Guardian*, p. 4. Matjila was also close to the Guptas, dating from his time as chief executive of Kopano ka Matla, Cosatu's investment company.

45   Justice Zac Yacoob called for a judicial commission to investigate the NPA; see 'Yacoob calls for judicial commission into NPA', *City Press*, 2 November 2011, p. 6.

46   Dave Lewis, Corruption Watch, 11 August 2014, 'Pursuit of corruption has its inspiring moments', *Business Day*, p. 9. A March 2015 Supreme Court ruling forced the reintroduction of charges against Mdluli.

47   Interview with former employee in the Presidency, 12 November 2014, Cape Town.

48   The retained Cabinet members included Radebe, Chabane (until March 2015; deceased), Gigaba, Mthethwa, Gordhan, Shabangu, Joemat-Pettersson, Pandor, Cwele, Sisulu, Mashatile and Hanekom.

49   See Yolandi Groenewald, 28 August 2012, 'Minister did budget for Zumaville', *City Press*, p. 11.

50   Gareth van Onselen, 1 September 2013, 'The short life of a DG in the regime of Jacob Zuma', *Sunday Times*, p. 10.

51   For an overview, see *City Press*, 22 March 2015, 'A state of crisis', p. 4.

52   See Mmanaledi Mataboge and Carien du Plessis, 11 December 2011, 'Zuma's cunning paranoia', *City Press*, p. 21, http://www.citypress.co.za/columnists/zumas-cunning-paranoia-20111210/, accessed 12 December 2011.

53   For example, *City Press*, ibid.; Adriaan Basson, 2012, op. cit.

54   Jacob Zuma, 21 March 2015, address at the JB Marks reburial ceremony, Ventersdorp.

55   Susan Booysen, 2011, op. cit., chapters 2, 11.

56   *City Press*, 12 October 2014, 'Zuma: Corruption is a Western thing', http://www.citypress.co.za/politics/corruption-western-thing-2/, accessed 14 October 2014.

57   The list of illustrations is too long to repeat in this chapter.

58   Blade Nzimande, 30 November 2014, SABC-TV3, 18:30 news bulletin (repeated on multiple SABC channels).

59   Numsa, 28 June 2008, 'Xenophobia', *Numsa News*, http://www.numsa.org.za/article/xenophobia/, accessed 2 May 2015.

60   The leaks used by the State Security Agency were from https://africainteli-genceleaks.wordpress.com/2015/02/13/the-cia-has-already-his-instigator-at-home/#more-38; also see Richard Poplak, 6 March 2015, 'The day the State Security Agency started investigating opposition politicians for being CIA agents', http://www.dailymaverick.co.za/article/2015-03-06-the-day-the-state-securi-ty-agency-started-investigating-opposition-politicians-for-being-cia-agents/, accessed 6 March 2015.

61   Much of the Zuma camp's arguments against Mbeki were sophisticated pretence. WikiLeaks cables revealed that Mo Shaik, at the time a trusted Zuma adviser and under Zuma head of the SA Secret Service, told the US embassy Zuma's legal team would subpoena important political figures if he lost a bid to have corruption charges against him reconsidered. See *The Star*, 24 January 2011, p. 1.

62   Susan Booysen, 2013, *Twenty Years of South African Democracy: Citizen Views of Human Rights, Governance and the Political System*, research report, Johannesburg and Washington DC: Freedom House.

63   Jacob Zuma, May 2009, interview with *Business in Africa*, 'Africa has potentials to solve its problems', pp. 31–32.

64   Interview with Nkandla resident and aspirant small business entrepreneur who attended one of the mass queue-ups for personal presidential attention at Zuma's Nkandla estate, Kempton Park, 2 November 2012.

65   The presidential 'hotline' was instituted in 2009 by Zuma, following campaign and other promises, as an initiative to make government more accountable to the people; see Susan Booysen, 2011, op. cit., chapter 5, 'Participation and power through cooperation, complicity and co-optation'.

66   Answer to parliamentary question; see Mandy de Waal, 27 January–2 February 2012, 'Zuma hotline's puzzling statistics', *Mail & Guardian*, p. 8.

67   Presidency, 6 March 2015, statement, http://www.gov.za/speeches/president-jacob-zuma-meeting-presidents-coordinating-council-6-mar-2015-0000, accessed 6 March 2015.

68   Susan Booysen, national focus group study, conducted with participants from all pertinent demographic groupings across the provinces, in the second half of 2013, and drawing on supporters of all political parties. There was only one group (young Zulu men from Richards Bay) that had a handful of positive things to say about the president as a man of culture. Achille Mbembe, 1992, in 'Provisional notes on the postcolony', *Africa*, vol. 62 (1), cites examples of the public ridicule of African leaders – but this in no way indicated that the leader was losing power.

69   TNS survey, reported in February 2010, *City Press*, 11 February 2010, 'Poor services, not sex life affects Zuma popularity: Survey', p. 3.

70   See Prasa, 2014, 'Zuma the peacemaker and seasoned negotiator', *The Jacob Zuma Legacy Special*, p. 4.

71   Susan Booysen, 22 March 2015, 'Zuma isn't exactly Mr Popular', *The Sunday Independent*, http://www.iol.co.za/sundayindependent/zuma-isn-t-exactly-mr-popular-1.1835410#.VWGAgUYQtVM, accessed 23 March 2015.

72   Following the September 2014 ANC NEC, Mantashe intimated that the ANC was facing a threat of persistent humiliation and attacks from a (*de facto*) alliance between the EFF and DA in Parliament. See Lebogang Seale, 23 September 2014, *Cape Times*, p. 5. Scribes in the Presidency using the same template attacked columnists and analysts with faint regard for valid critiques.

73   *Report of the Opposition of Parliament on Powers and Privilege Committee of the National Assembly*, 18 November 2014, https://drive.google.com/file/d/0B_-sl-Gu8-FTxZVNzLWtRdWcyTjg/view?pli=1, accessed 18 November 2014.

74   In a comparable incident *Noseweek*, February 2013, tracked down a former Goldfields CEO who confirmed that in the early 2000s, upon having resolved to build a school at Nkandla, the architect accompanying the Zuma entourage quoted more than double their own architect's estimate. He then asked that architect where the rest of the money goes: 'He looked across the table at Zuma and Zuma just looked at me with this big smile', p. 9.

75 Thuli Madonsela, Office of the Public Protector, 24 August 2014, letter to the president, http://www.politicsweb.co.za/politicsweb/view/politicsweb/en/page71639/page71654?oid=695095&sn=Detail&pid=71654, accessed 2 January 2015.

76 Zuma announced the Seriti Commission in October 2011, after he had failed to meet a Constitutional Court deadline to explain why such a public commission should not be appointed. Zuma now positioned himself to control the commission's processes and terms of reference. There were several reports of a 'second agenda' within the commission, articulating with the president's interests. Staff members resigned and one died, reportedly committing suicide. See Ivor Powell, 'Crawford-Browne rustles up arms deal', 4 August 2013, *The Sunday Independent*, p. 8. Bulk evidence was withheld from the commission. In July–August 2013 a series of witnesses either led mundane ('how much the arms were needed') types of evidence, or a series of whistle-blowers were humiliated for not having their own original information and relying on investigative journalism for their facts.

77 A political solution had to be found for Zuma to get into office. He was the ANC's No. 1 on the 2009 elections list and president-in-waiting. Yet, given the charges against him he would not have been able to assume office. On the eve of Election 2009 the spy tapes surfaced, 'proving', so it has been argued, that the NPA had conspired with Mbeki, in a politically inspired vendetta to charge Zuma for corruption, money laundering and racketeering. The DA filed an application to get the tapes. Protracted legal battles suggested that Zuma and his lawyers had something to hide, perhaps that there is hardly evidence of a 'conspiracy'. In August 2014 court appeals finally succeeded and the tapes had to be handed over after scrutiny and exclusion of portions that were part of Zuma's personal representations.

78 Nkandla summary timeline: 2009: First media reports by Mandy Rossouw for *Mail & Guardian* revealing questionable security upgrades, then priced at R65m; 2010: The security upgrades begin; 2012: *City Press* reveals R200m of upgrades; minister of public works orders interministerial investigation; 2013: Summary of interministerial report released; report is classified (January); Zuma tells Parliament he was not informed about costs of upgrades (March); public protector's provisional report leaked, interministerial task team report is made public; 2014: Public protector releases report; Zuma defends Nkandla in terms of family security issues, delivers cryptic note instead of responding to the Nkandla report; *ad hoc* committee convenes but dismisses investigation; in election campaigning says citizens do not care about Nkandla; letter to Parliament outlining some details of the president's response; president designates minister of police to determine whether he should pay anything; *ad hoc* committee gets blank mandate to consider the reports; opposition parties withdraw when opportunities for interrogating the reports fade; committee finds Zuma has done nothing wrong.

79 Interview comment by director general of the Department of Trade and Industry, Lionel October, in a Swedish investigative programme, *Dokument Inifra°n*, 16 October 2014.

80 Monitoring of parliamentary proceedings, *Times Live* broadcast, 21 August 2014.

81 Shaun Abrahams, 8 July 2015, http://www.timeslive.co.za/politics/2015/07/08/watch-shaun-abrahams-tell-media-he-won-t-protect-zuma, accessed 14 July 2015.

82 The Seriti Commission of Inquiry into the arms deal laboured on in 2015, severely compromised by a chairperson who refused to allow witnesses to testify on any document or information which they had not personally generated, and who presided over an investigative team that had not assessed thousands of available documents.

83 Jacob Zuma, speaking off-script; see 'Verbatim', *Mail & Guardian*, 24–30 October 2014, p. 37.

84 Public protector, 19 March 2014, *Secure in Comfort: Public Protector's Report on Nkandla*, http://www.politicsweb.co.za/politicsweb/view/politicsweb/en/page71656?oid=572814&sn=Detail&pid=71616, accessed 19 March 2014; also see *City Press*, 29 March 2015, 'One year of the Nkandla report', p. 13.

85 Jan-Jan Joubert et al., 16 November 2014, op. cit.

86 Ibid.

87 Over a breakfast meeting in Durban, 2008, struggle stalwart Phyllis Naidoo talked about her revulsion at the fact that the sexual relations were with the woman who as a baby was pictured in Zuma's arms. Naidoo was in the photograph with Zuma and the baby.

88 *Marikana Commission of Inquiry: Report on Matters of Public, National and International Concern Arising out of the Tragic Incidents at the Lonmin Mine in Marikana, North West Province*, publicly released on 25 June 2015.

89 Synopsis from http://www.thepresidency.gov.za/pebble.asp?relid=7, accessed 1 December 2014.

3

CONSTRUCTING THE ANC'S COMPLIANT STATE

The ANC circa 2014–2015 is all but the strident, confident party and movement-in-power of even five years before, and the state in these times matches it. The ANC under Jacob Zuma entrenched itself in state power at exactly the time of persistently ineffectual local government, lack of credibility of policing and public security, and lapses in the legal system. It was overseeing the subjugation of several of the institutions of democracy to the will of a faction of the ruling party.

Earlier in the Zuma period South Africa had lived the hype of the pending reinvigorated, reconnected and more caring ANC state and government under redeemer Jacob Zuma. Instead, South Africa entered a time of unparalleled presidential controversy, which affected the state. There were morbid symptoms of compromised state capacity that merged with 'gross manifestations of corruption at the local level', while 'public discourse is replete with cases of the abuse of state resources' and 'patronage on a grand scale in state-owned enterprises', 'shoddy responses to the injunctions of the public protector', 'strange shenanigans in critical state agencies',[1] and infighting and top-order political agendas in security agencies.[2]

The ANC is not a party to sit back passively watching poor fortune enfolding it. It intervenes, and state action is a useful part of its repertoire. This ANC, strategically shrewd, works to change public perceptions and limit public expressions of dissent and critique. It issues public statements, engages in the media, disseminates history lessons that remind citizens of the ongoing struggle for liberation, and sets out to undermine if not demonise the sources of challenge. The ANC believes it retains the historical mission to fully liberate South Africa from apartheid and its structural legacies – even if it has to recast the struggle and the role of the current leadership ten times over. The ANC does not imagine itself as an ordinary political party: it works to preserve a sense of being special, a party in a distinctive relationship with the people. It equally believes it has the right (if not obligation) to act out its electoral majority in the state.

Many of the ANC's acts of recasting and reinvention rest on compliance, and both the ANC and ANC-as-government use state institutions to manufacture it. Chapter 2 unpacked the major, presidency-centred aspects of this, and showed that the president is in control of a vast construct of state power. The manufacture of compliance extends over two further fronts: intra-state generally (beyond the presidency) and across to the people, the public and civil society in general. This chapter deals with how the state is used to ensure the maximum possible compliance to boost the ANC and, in effect, President Jacob Zuma's dominant portion of the ANC.

The argument demonstrates the extensive control that the ANC and ANC-in-government maintain over the state apparatuses – and over civil society and the media – for the sake of constructing the compliant state. In this time, control over the state is often equated with the protection of the president. Control and manufacture of consent are top-down components of the construction of hegemony – hegemony based on quiescence of the people more than hegemony built on active consent.[3] In the process, the ANC shows how concerned it is about losing the hold it has on the people. The ANC's actions in this period signal that it knows the dangers, but sees the problems as secondary to ensuring that the president is retained in respect and dignity.

This chapter's arguments focus on the ANC's appropriation of institutions of state and government for the battle between, for example, the president, the public protector and Parliament. Overall, compliance emerges internally because of the prevalence of power politics. Externally, it arises through the ANC's labours to manufacture popular acceptance of its governance, optimally through control or influence over the dissemination of information.

SIEGE OF THE INSTITUTIONS OF DEMOCRACY

At the broad national level the South African state is a massive operation and the ship of state sails on, performing and delivering, irrespective of vast stretches of preoccupation with ANC politics, dysfunctional government, hapless policy implementation and corruption. Digging just fractionally deeper, however, reveals a picture of pervasive problems (illustrated in Table 3.1). There are *elements* of a failed state here.[4]

Exploration delivers the picture of the ANC-in-government entangled in cross-cutting political pressures largely caused by the clash between government administration and politics. The protection of political superiors rules supreme and the misbehaving troops (those aligned to a dominant faction and certain that they have licence to make money in the state) are either untouchable or guaranteed to be treated softly. Ostensibly simple government and policy decisions – even at lower levels of the state bureaucracy – frequently come with political baggage and lack of accountability. Damage to the credibility of public institutions is par for the course when it comes to the greater good of the leaders who are gatekeepers to promotions, continuous employment and lucrative business with the state. In this context a *de facto* war on the institutions of constitutional democracy is a small sacrifice for the protection and advancement of the interests of political principals. The institutional playground includes all three spheres of government, in representation and bureaucracy, covering all sectors.

In many instances and at the top level, protection is specifically about protecting *the president* against charges (often legally deferred or quashed) of corruption and related matters. Given that the president appoints his Cabinet and premiers and that these persons intersect with the web of ANC structures, apolitical appointments are rare, and personal and factional political interests are usually advanced. Political loyalty and the politicisation of the state apparatuses would have been less noticeable had it not been that the president is the compelling centrepiece. State operations pause and get paralysed while the presidential act is passing.

'Protecting the president' requires demonstrations of loyalty to him, visible attacks on those who criticise him, or any action (solicited or unsolicited) on his behalf and in his defence. The act includes that practitioners know what the president wants and accept that they will be rewarded. Verbalisation is not required and there will be no paper trail. Such operations have become a far-reaching mission of the ANC in state and government in the time of Zuma. This has

95

Table 3.1: The South African state and the weakened state of governance

Level or location	Illustrations of political and administrative problems				
Top political executive	President avoiding accountability, delegating	Cabinet reshuffles show lack of confidence	Deputy president constrained by political battles	Effective performance evaluations lacking	Turf battles between departments
Legislative, national	Parliament prioritises rules over accountability	Governing party MPs loyal to president above all	Parliamentary process abused to protect the president	Majority in parliamentary committees defer politically	Parliament juniorised due to expansive executive
Civil service	Directors general change frequently	Dubious and compromised political appointments	Provincial administrations' poor resource management	Local government often corrupted, ineffectual, but untouchable	Services delivered but of low quality
Security and judicial system	SAPS struggles to maintain law and order, low credibility	Gangsterism, 'underworlds' rule in many communities	Presidential control over security agencies	SAPS and lower courts often seen to have been corrupted	Wars between security agencies
Government entities	Several SOEs in dire operational and financial straits	Some SOEs suffer dubious presidential appointments	Sars hosted a rogue unit dabbling in intelligence	Pension fund suffers mismanagement	PIC in some questionable transactions
Provincial and local government	Local audits give dismal results; slow improvement	Provinces not coping with load of policy management	Provinces and local suffer poor political deployments	Provinces at odds with national about policy	Local strained to deliver and sustain services

Source: Author's research based on observation, interviews and media monitoring.
Note: Listings in this table are illustrative, not exhaustive.

subjugated politically rational and reasonable behaviour – a demeanour that can nevertheless be deemed 'rational' in the sense of a rapidly emerging political elite gathering around the patrons who can secure their accumulation. Much of what has gone wrong in the South African state at this time requires blind-eye treatment, because the perpetrators are presidential deployees or lower-level appointments with protection networks cascading upwards.

The forms of rent that the deployees pay to master-patron Zuma and other senior politicians in the in-group vary from presidential legacy building to oiling the wheels of presidential trust projects, handling the media and critics, facilitating business opportunities for family members and associates, or simply stepping aside so that the president's advisers can enter. The public protector (a Chapter Nine institution), civil society, opposition parties, and the high courts and Constitutional Court are often lined up against the presidential and other public sector controversies and scandals. Because these are the liberal-style institutions that help form South Africa's constitutional state, they are often put down as 'Western', 'anti-majoritarian' and 'un-African' by those who equalise the president, the party and the state.

The ANC, often arrogant in its abundant power, figures that it can sacrifice the credibility of some of the democratic institutions – Parliament in particular – as long as their actions safeguard the president against new and old charges or accusations. At the height of Zuma power, in the late first and early second Zuma terms, the ANC bargained on government delivery and sturdy campaigning before the 2016 local and 2019 national and provincial elections to counter damages inflicted. The president's handlers excelled at arranging historical domestic or international events to celebrate real experiences but simultaneously divert attention. In typical style, the day in mid-2014 after President Zuma issued an unsuitable non-responsive 'response' to the public protector's Nkandla report (amid raging controversy), he told a specially convened congregation at an anti-apartheid struggle site, the Regina Mundi church in Soweto, that South Africans should not forget their apartheid past, adding: 'We have something to celebrate, our freedom.' On diversionary tactics, Trevor Manuel had cautioned (and Zuma at the time tried to refute the argument):

> Nineteen years into democracy our government has run out of excuses. We cannot continue to blame apartheid for our failings as a state. We cannot plead ignorance and inexperience. For almost two decades the public has been patient in the face of mediocre services.[5]

A TRILOGY OF CONTROVERSIES

The key to understanding how a president who consistently harms the ANC remains so deeply rooted in his hold over state power lies in three issues that all relate to the controversies surrounding him. This trilogy comprises the arms deal (783 on-off charges of corruption, fraud, money laundering and racketeering); the spy tapes (alleging conspiracy and trying to quash the arms deal charges and enable Zuma to become president in 2009); and Nkandla (over-budget and opaque 'security improvements' meaning inflated prices and construction beyond security features to Zuma's private homestead). Details reveal how Zuma evokes notions of victimhood, persecution by enemies, conspiracies by plotting adversaries and 'third force' action, while using the shield of the innocent 'simple' rural man from Nkandla to disarm and demobilise critical citizens, state agencies and departments, and the courts. This section of the chapter distils the essence of the trilogy that distracted the state, with a view to showing Zuma's strategy to get around the charges, all the time pretending to be oblivious to the impact on the state, its government and policy pursuits.

Interrelated, and at the level of the economic definition of Zuma's rule, has been the catastrophe of the South African economy. Up to at least 2014–2015 (and there were no signs of pending improvement) the vast and well-resourced state was defined to a large extent by its inability to reach growth rates that would trigger the required labour absorption ratios, and great (not just reasonable) job-creating infrastructural development. Unemployment persisted and an unattended lumpenproletariat took shape. South Africa suffered serial downgrades at the hand of international rating agencies Moody's, Standard & Poor's, and Fitch, among others, because of growing public debt and energy crises. Yet besides the expenditures on public sector wages (only mildly moderated in the 2015 wage settlement), the World Bank reported in 2014 that South Africa's fiscal policies had helped to reduce poverty and inequality.[6] A batch of redistributive measures such as social spending helped elevate 3.6 million South Africans out of poverty (defined at the level of roughly R750 per month). As one would expect, the report cautions that there is little further scope for redistribution through fiscal policies. It advised that South Africa needs rapidly to address infrastructure constraints and broaden structural reforms (which amounted to further liberalisation) in the form of flexible wages and labour laws. However, borrowing had become more expensive because of the downgrades, and in *this* context economists warned that infrastructural investment had to be scaled down. The much vaunted National Development Plan, offering a broad framework rather than answers to policy dilemmas, did not offer an escape. The contrasting stories of South Africa were those of citizens barely, if at all, climbing out of poverty versus the large new middle class or the elite political and business class.

Events demonstrate the extent of the state's seizure by the Zuma trilogy. By August–September 2014, Zuma's campaign had largely run out of legal procedures to obfuscate and delay further processing of his charges through task teams, interministerial committees and legal appeals. The ANC expected citizens to trust the supremacy of Parliament, acting on the advice of the political executive, to bring the verdict of presidential innocence – despite Parliament's not having held the executive to account since the mini-Prague Spring of the changeover between Mbeki and Zuma, and while legal minds argued that Parliament did not have the authority to play arbiter.[7]

- The spy tapes, origin 2007, refused to go away.[8] The saga epitomises what has become known as the Zuma-ists' Stalingrad strategy,[9] referring to Zuma's use of every legal technicality possible to avoid the reinstatement of the charges against him while unemployment ruled and required consistent attention at the highest level. Zuma fought the DA's bid for the courts to overturn the April 2009 decision by the national director of public prosecutions (NDPP) to withdraw the charges – the DA wanted reinstatement, arguing that it had been a political decision by acting NDPP Mokotedi Mpshe. In the Supreme Court of Appeal in August 2014, Zuma's counsel Kemp J Kemp conceded – to assertive judges – that he had no argument to counter the release of the tapes. Hence followed the 2014 release of the tapes that had let Zuma off the hook in 2009. The DA explained that the tape release was to show 'that the decision to discontinue the prosecution was manifestly irrational and was taken on political grounds. If we can prove *that* the prosecution needs to be reinstated.'[10] After the DA's 2014 spy-tape victory, a serving judge had suggested that a denouement was not in sight (at least not before Zuma has retired):

> Once you have a review application then a whole lot of possible options open to the respondent [Zuma] to make technical points … There's probably still a good year or two ahead before the review would be heard, then the appeals all the way up … It'll be another five-year saga before there is an outcome.[11]

- The arms deal goes hand in hand with the spy tapes. The arms saga continued in 2014–2015, in the form of the Seriti Commission into procurement. This commission had been a long time coming; it was instituted largely because Zuma had run out of options under pressure from the DA. The commission's credibility declined as high-level officials resigned, citing its 'second agenda' as the reason (with reference to predetermination of the verdict), and its partial call for and treatment of witnesses threatened to become as disreputable as the original events.[12] Key witnesses (Andrew Feinstein, Hennie van Vuuren and Paul Holden) withdrew owing to the refusal of the commission to grant them access to large quantities of relevant documents which the commission had not entered into proceedings. Other expert witnesses, including unsuccessful bidder Richard Young, were equally censored by Seriti in the evidence they were allowed to lead. Mbeki's evidence stonewalled investigators and witnesses, giving nothing away and raising race as a driving force in the proceedings: 'At the base of all this lies the racist conviction that Africans, who now govern our country, are naturally prone to corruption, venality and mismanagement.'[13] Government witnesses formed a united front against those who had pegged hope for openness on the commission.
- In the same period, the ANC parliamentary caucus first declared its satisfaction with President Zuma's August 2014 'inclusive response' on the Nkandla matter, in November a parliamentary *ad hoc* committee exonerated Zuma,[14] and in mid-2015 police minister Nathi Nhleko manufactured a 'nothing to pay' whitewash report which was, equally, routed along an *ad hoc* committee. The SIU report, the joint standing committee on intelligence (JSCI) and the interministerial committee on security (IMCS) had by then all been positioned alongside the public protector's Nkandla report. The Public Works report of 2012–2013 (guided by Minister Thulas Nxesi), which had offered ultra-presidential protection and was at first classified as confidential, was a gleam in the background. The president's non-response to the Madonsela report was at the centre of it, until eclipsed by the two *ad hoc* committees.[15] The first four reports noted, in common, that prices were inflated, supply chain regulations flouted and other regulatory frameworks circumvented. The differences lay in whether Zuma should pay, how much he should pay, and whether final responsibility rested with him, his officials, or his privately engaged consultants and architects.[16] The *Mail & Guardian* noted four components to the ANC's master strategy on Nkandla: avoid bringing Nkandla before Parliament,

separate party and state on details but not on the broader picture, embrace and then supplant the public protector's report, and prepare scapegoats.[17]

- A ruling by Judge Ashton Schippers brought a measure of contested clarity for the matter of powers of the public protector: in a case on the SABC's chief executive, Schippers found that the public protector powers are not adjudicative (or binding), but that rational, detailed reasons need to be given for non-compliance.[18] The judgement went on to appeal, which was later granted: Schippers thought there was little chance of success but wanted to allow for the Supreme Court of Appeal to settle the matter of the public protector's power. The public protector had argued that the office of the public protector would be fundamentally and irreparably undermined if the impression is created that the public protector's authority has no material effect.[19] The Nhleko ruling reopened the debate and the public protector pointed out that no reason had been applied in the 'nothing to pay verdict'.[20] A new series of legal challenges followed.

The ANC and its Zuma-ists appeared unperturbed by the damage these Zuma wars inflicted, accepting that when all was said and done the ANC will still be on the path of sufficient self-corrective action. In an alternative sentiment, however, former ANC leader Mathews Phosa had argued in 2013: 'If we want to avoid being consigned to the dustbin of history, we must be demonstrably more decisive, more transparent and totally unforgiving in how we deal with those who steal public money, or abuse positions of trust.'[21]

THE COMPLIANT STATE – CONTROL OF THE BUILDING BLOCKS

The ANC, by design and by default, has been constructing its 'compliant state' for obedience to political leaders generally and adherence to presidential demands and needs in particular. It first took shape under Mbeki, then expanded under Zuma. Cadre deployment remains the most powerful tool at the ANC's disposal to protect its interests within the state structures, to ensure that it occupies the government space that equals access to power and the resources to regenerate that power, and to block opposition parties from gaining formal or informal footholds.

The compliance for which it strives is to let service to the ANC as movement pair with Jacob Zuma's presidency and personhood. The compliant state arrives through appointments and control, which may very well feed elite predatory needs.[22] The ideal (for both the party and the elite within) is appointments that are sympathetic to the ruling elite. Institutions or persons who upset the desired order, *in and beyond the state*, are subverted or subdued, such as in the case of the public protector and much of South Africa's media. Part of the schema is also to deny that this is being done, parade a few accolades and offer seemingly principled assurances of the value that the ANC attaches to the public protector, the courts and the media. Judicial appointments are pivotal in the battle to restrain the executive and get it to comply with the prescripts of constitutionalism and the rule of law. The ANC will act, but will ensure it is not seen to be acting against the judiciary. It will pursue every action possible to maximise influence legitimately and get a sympathetic judicial ear. The Judicial Service Commission (JSC) recommends judicial appointments to the president; it is meticulously constructed,[23] with substantial ANC involvement, to give the ANC the certainty that it is safe to let problems go the legal-institutional route. Yet there can be no guarantees that all appointees will always rule in favour of the ANC; hence with regard to the JSC as well the ANC puts all measures in place to ensure deferment and avoidance. From the early 2000s onwards, Zuma set the example for the use of legal processes to delay, defuse, defer, obfuscate and escape. Overall, however, the high courts and Constitutional Court uphold their role as guarantors of due legal process and the Constitution.

The mass media are a further set of institutions for the state to control, if not by law then more subtly. For example, ANC Secretary General Mantashe argues that 'factions of the media' repeat distorted facts from opposition parties, and those media houses form 'part of the offensive' against the ANC.[24] By 2015 there was even more media heat on the ANC, including *Daily Dispatch* revelations about a toilet tender from which children of politically connected parents were getting rich – the ANC claimed knowledge of a *Daily Dispatch* plot to undermine the ANC.[25] The Zuma government generally threatened control, baulked at implementing it, and instead got improved self-control and facilitated (or pressured for) a far more sympathetic overall media set-up.

Institutional re-engineering

Government during Zuma's time has emphasised institutional re-engineering disproportionately, along with reshuffles and (re)deployment, as evidence that problems of governance and delivery are being addressed. This creates the illusion of government business unfolding relentlessly, whereas widespread paralysis (due to presidential protection and often ineffectual government) prevails.

Such reorganising also creates the space for the elites to play their presidential protection politics. It is easier to redesign an institution, reassign functions and create a sense of movement towards 'the goals of the Freedom Charter' than to get definitive evidence of outcomes and effects in substantive policy action in a public sector that is often paralysed by politics. Institutional rearranging also helps position compliant personnel … who are occasionally also good at their jobs.

One outstanding illustration of institutional reordering substituting for definitive policy action was recorded in President Zuma's June 2014 State of the Nation offerings.[26] There was a task team to reorganise government in the wake of departmental restructuring of May 2014. Additional interministerial committees (IMCs) were the evidence of serious pending top-level attention to the problems of revitalising distressed mining communities and of service delivery. The IMCs were set to report to Cabinet via Cabinet committees which also give oversight and coordination and are headed by senior Cabinet members. IMCs could guarantee government action and they could also sidestep accountability.[27] They have become a standard operating procedure rather than evidence of exceptional attention. They can help create high-level attention to vexed government issues, but are no guarantee. More generally, government departments have been subject to continuous redesign. Both the 2009 and 2014 Zuma Cabinets illustrate the point. New departments and the regrouping of portfolios under existing departments potentially improve functionality and efficiency, but there is little evidence that the policy goals could not equally be achieved if better attention went to the function in its previous setting. The departments of Economic Development, Women, Children and People with Disability (2009) and Small Business Development (2014) were cases in point.

Security apparatuses and presidential protection

South Africa's compliant state commands that there will be *special security protection for the president and those whom he has anointed*. Zuma's personal and professional uncertainty over whether he might be brought to book on corruption, fraud, money laundering and racketeering charges have meant that paranoia is one of the side-effects of his presidency. The president has developed a *de facto* personal intra-state security state, centring on the security cluster (whose appointees he has determined and controlled) and a range of other high-level appointments.

Control over deployments and redeployments in much of the security sector was not negotiable. It was done surreptitiously, by professionals specialising in leaving no traces,[28] but tracking could still reveal smoking guns – such as the

103

links between President Zuma and Lieutenant General Richard Mdluli.[29] The cluster was also the entity that moved in to protect Zuma in the wake of the EFF's humiliation of the president through its 'pay back the money' parliamentary protests of August 2014 and March 2015. The interventions raised questions about the separation of powers (with the executive, in the form of security agencies, operating on parliamentary turf) and the inability of speaker Baleka Mbete to manage Parliament evenhandedly.

The National Prosecuting Authority (NPA) and its range of directors since its inception in 1998, its acting directors and its senior associated staff were in the direct line of fire concerning President Zuma's delayed and quashed charges. NDPPs are appointed by the president for ten-year terms, but in the sixteen years up to 2015 there have been seven permanent and acting appointments, and changes were ongoing (the problems had started when Mbeki tried saving former police commissioner Jackie Selebi from prison while the criminals who had corrupted him were walking free). The line-up of NDPPs included factotums with unconvincing records, but with impeccable loyalties to political masters. Some have been so obviously compromised that the reasons for their appointments could only have been either negligence (by Zuma's advisers) or continuation of an ANC policy to appoint flawed persons in order to ensure that political principals will have a hold over them.[30]

The SIU shared the forefront of compliant state construction. Its leaders were expected to deliver the required investigation results, such as in the case of the supplementary (to that of the public protector's) Nkandla report. The Hawks (Directorate of Special Operations) in 2009 replaced the Scorpions, and is a business unit of the NPA. The change followed the political decision by the ANC at Polokwane to abandon the Scorpions (in reaction to Zuma's prosecution). The Crime Intelligence Unit of the South African Police Service suffered the fate of political interference as well, centring on Richard Mdluli, who had high-level political protection.[31] Businessman Hugh Glenister gained a 2011 Constitutional Court verdict that invalidated legislation to establish the Hawks. The court left it to Parliament to amend relevant legislation. In the process, Constitutional Court judges contemplated how the fact that the Hawks reside under the Ministry of Police (as opposed to the Scorpions, under the NDPP) had hamstrung the unit's independence.

This set of illustrations is but a sample of the manoeuvrings that were unfolding to protect those who are seen to protect the president, or are close to the president, for largely undisclosed reasons. The intrigue deepened when the Independent Police Investigative Directorate (Ipid) fell out with the minister of police and acting leaders of the NPA (with formally appointed leaders con-troversially suspended), and individuals turned to the courts to forestall being suspended themselves after the minister of police blocked attempts to approach the parliamentary portfolio committee on police. The final word still had to be spoken on whether Robert McBride was suspended because of request-ing Nkandla investigation files, or whether McBride had used the request as an attempt to shield his unit against other charges. In the interim, McBride launched a constitutional challenge to the powers of the minister of police to suspend him as the head of Ipid. The saga continued, golden-handshake depar-tures accumulated, and the string of events demonstrated the quagmire that resulted from protection of the president.

Bureaucrats and the war against the great leader

The civil service is a massive operation of close to two million employees[32] working on a huge annual budget, the largest single chunk of which goes towards the state's wage bill of roughly R260 billion in 2014 (Table 3.2). Despite many preceding promises that the size of the civil service would be reduced, the headcount has consistently expanded since 2003. The growth from 2012 to 2013 was the lowest in a decade, but this was no guarantee of future trends. The high levels of growth in the civil service occurred largely before the global recession. From 2009 to 2013, Zuma's first four years in power, the salary bill for civil servants rose from close to R300bn to over R450bn. Government debt by 2014 came to 49.7 per cent of GDP. Total public sector debt – the summation of gross government debt, state-owned companies and local government – was 59.1 per cent of GDP in 2013–2014[33] – and money was being borrowed to pay civil servants rather than doing more on infrastructure.

The maintenance of the expansive state offers insurance to the ANC. It is advantageous to the ANC to have a large and compliant middle class installed, even if some will in due course leave the ANC. While consuming a massive chunk of the national budget, this growth created employment and helped both the ANC's middle-class project and its building of base employment through the Expanded Public Works Programme. The state employees are more likely to tolerate and pardon the president that comes with the party in charge of the state that employs them.

The question arises as to the ways in which the president's shadow affects the work of elected representatives and civil servants.[34] Rather than being seen to be assertive and in pursuit of public sector ethics, bureaucrats often do not

Table 3.2:   Size and salary budget of the South African civil service,
1998–2013

Year	Headcount	Percentage-point difference on preceding year	Total wage bill	Percentage-point difference on preceding year
1998	1 566 896	−1.1	R102.1bn	+10.2
1999	1 523 932	−2.7	R105.6bn	+3.4
2000	1 462 605	−4.0	R110.3bn	+4.5
2001	1 436 272	−1.8	R120.8bn	+9.5
2002	1 441 396	+0.4	R132.6bn	+9.8
2003	1 428 056	-0.9	R139.5bn	+5.2
2004	1 453 547	+1.8	R155.4bn	+11.5
2005	1 495 944	+2.9	R170.9bn	+10.0
2006	1 574 021	+5.2	R190.5bn	+11.5
2007	1 622 622	+3.1	R213.9bn	+12.3
2008	1 700 459	+4.8	R252.8bn	+18.2
2009	1 779 707	+4.7	R298.9bn	+18.2
2010	1 813 564	+1.9	R340.2bn	+13.8
2011	1 897 223	+4.6	R381.3bn	+12.1
2012	1 934 203	+1.9	R419.0bn	+9.9
2013	1 961 963	+1.4	R457.4bn	+9.2

Source: Compiled from data of StatsSA, *SA Statistics 2014*. More recent data was still to be released.

take decisions or initiate actions for fear of antagonising powerful superiors.
The politically inclined and ambitious spend time proclaiming the virtues of
their political principals and ensure they *are seen* to be doing so (this is at least
as important as getting the actual job done). It is common to see civil servants
turn a blind eye to corruption in the procurement chain – rather this than risk
a well-remunerated job with good benefits. These bureaucrats know there is
scope to carve their own careers by choosing moments to praise the president,

and otherwise steer clear of voicing opinions on the president or the behaviour of the presidential warriors in the public sector.

Controlling Parliament and the provinces

It is Parliament that is tasked with holding the bureaucracy to account, but Parliament itself uses blindfolds and holds back for political reasons. The ANC top officials in Parliament, through the ANC chief whip, exercise tight control over the ANC in the parliamentary chambers. The fifth ANC administration practised a different parliamentary game to that before Election 2014. First, the EFF changed parliamentary and opposition politics by discarding parliamentary opprobrium in favour of insisting robustly that Zuma answers questions; and the DA upped its game. Second, Parliament changed because the president was never as weak as in this period of parliamentary politics. Even if in 2015 he became more strident in his responses to the young opposition leaders Maimane and Malema, this failed to veil his avoidance of questions about undue personal benefits from the Nkandla 'security' upgrades. Weakness escalated in the face of more united action between the more assertive opposition parties, and this axis was a threat to the legislative leg of the compliant state. The NEC and Mantashe called the ANC in Parliament to action, 'advising' the ANC MPs to 'restore to the House the necessary dignity and decorum [and] appreciation of its rules ensuring that it becomes once again a House which South Africans can be proud of … The NEC cautions against continuing this trend of negatively exposing the head of state to disrespect and intended humiliation by a fringe group [used with reference to the EFF] committed to undermining democracy.'[35]

The MPs are directly and visibly accountable to party principals because of the chiefs' control over the party's electoral lists.[36] MPs' first priority has been to fend off opposition-party attacks that could cast bad light on the president. Thereafter they have had to defend the executive and ANC appointees in general. Their accountability – for how they advance their party's policy positions and the policy interests of their constituents – has been relegated to third place.

The ANC's local political fiefdoms have had a field day in provincial and local government's political and bureaucratic arms. Political deployment has built power reserves used by leaders to endear themselves to national leadership and enclaves of vocal and powerful citizens. Local government is often in a dismal state. Capacity and political will are chief concerns. In Zuma's time as president, adverse auditor general reports on lapsed or dismal financial management in the bulk of South Africa's 278 municipalities[37] have alternated with national government interventions such as the turnaround strategy or the 'Back to basics' strategy of the Department of Cooperative Governance and Traditional Affairs.

Valiant attempts to redirect local government have had limited effects. ANC local and provincial kingpins have gained their standing through being gate-keepers to principals and in charge of government redistribution, even if delivery does not meet the targets. Top leadership appears loath to act harshly (for example, to stop civil servants from doing business with the state in any decisive way) or to take critical action against underperforming deployees.[38] Tolerance is essential in order to ensure compliance with the movement leadership and sufficient delivery to maintain ANC credibility and electoral support,[39] despite often hapless deployment mismanagement.

ANC STATE STEERING THE PUBLIC AGENDA

As in Guptagate[40] and Nkandla,[41] a mere hint of the wishes or consent of Number One (or reminders that the security of the president is in their hands) has made bureaucrats 'do the right thing'. It is unnecessary to issue a command, perhaps even to order bureaucrats not to leave paper trails. It appears that, for Zuma, operating the South African state is a variation on running the ANC's exile intelligence operations – although the enemy forces now look different and include the media, opposition parties, intellectuals and analysts (irrespective of ideology, when they criticise the president), astute and independent-minded state appointees such as the public protector (and the media are accused of sanctifying her) and, internationally, most commonly, the West (even if the Al Jazeera-*Guardian* cable leaks revealed 'human intelligence' details showing that South African intelligence agencies cooperate extensively with the West).

Besides the omnipresent big stick, the task of 'managing' the mass media into favourable coverage requires steering, manipulation, influence and ownership. The strategies in the time of Zuma have included gaining direct access to the media through ownership deals, suasion in which income or transfers talk, or friendships. The Zuma presidency has used a sophisticated strategy to influence public opinion through the media. Specifically, this has included:

- Persuasion, and appeals to nationalism, patriotism and positivity: Zuma, with the assistance of SABC COO Hlaudi Motsoeneng,[42] propagated sunshine or good-news journalism (Motsoeneng argued for a 70 per cent proportion of good news). The effect of this shrewd move showed not only in the run-up to Election 2014, but far beyond. The ANC's 2014 campaign message was 'the good story'. In the ensuing debates each reference to the need to report good news was an acknowledgement that the media were under-reporting good news about the ANC's achievements. Zuma reiterated: 'We are going to try our level best to engage the media to calculate the spirit of patriotism and the positivity in the country ... because the ANC has overcome many things, I am sure that this is one more thing we will be able to overcome ... I have begun to engage the media where they are falling short. They need to be reporting the success stories ...'[43]

Persuasion extended into the placement of Cabinet-level analyses in the print and electronic media. Some media obliged in the face of assertive ministers, and in particular the Presidency. Personal assistants, advisers and dedicated communication staff do not hesitate to send newspaper editors e-mails, even stating the date on which they expect a contribution to be published.

- Direct or sympathetic ownership: The ANC government has progressed in developing substitutes for a long-standing ANC dream: owning a public newspaper of its own. First, the ANC and Zuma's personal relationships with the Gupta family ensured unhindered access to the pages of *The New Age* (owned by TNA Media [Pty] Ltd) daily newspaper – if indeed the paper was not founded with the exact objective of giving this type of access. Over time, and realising the effect on the president's reputation of a visibly close connection with the Gupta dynasty, the public relationship was toned down. Second, Sekunjalo Investments bought Independent Media from Irish owner Tony O'Reilly. Sekunjalo Independent Media Consortium, with high levels of public sector and union involvement, bought Independent News & Media SA. Sekunjalo Investment Holdings, Cosatu's investment company Kopano Ke Matlaka, SACTWU Investments Group, and the Food and Allied Workers Union and employees held 63 per cent of Sekunjalo's shares, and a number of broad-based, 'value-adding partners' held the other 37 per cent.[44] Sekunjalo did not create outright pro-ANC news coverage but did ensure that ANC events and opinions would get their share of editorial space. In addition, the SABC, the chief executives of which are political appointments, gives access at management level to the ANC, as party and as government. At election times it takes care to balance coverage proportionately between political parties – although coverage of government at this time is excluded from fairness calculations. Directives for political operations and coverage are routinely handed down to station managers. There are, nevertheless, also reasonable opportunities for producers and presenters to report and analyse truthfully.[45] The experience of the (presumably independent) e.tv television broadcaster complying with government coverage wishes in exchange for possible commercial gain in 2014 demonstrated how little guaranteed free-of-government media space is left in South Africa.[46]

- Transfers in kind: Direct calls from senior politicians in state or party often lead to coverage of ANC and government events if they are not already on the news list. The media try to get coverage right, because otherwise censure – and appeals to the SABC management – will result. For private media, advertising revenue through government advertisements (including 'state events', tenders, jobs and special appearances of the political executive) are at stake. Transfers to *The New Age* (TNA) were in a league of their own. In 2014, Eskom transferred R43 million to *The New Age* as sponsorship for breakfast shows. The TNA business breakfasts were the honeypot for ministers and other senior politicians who regularly called in to push for a slot, which would give them extensive prime-time exposure on SABC television[47] and multi-page coverage in the nationally distributed newspaper.
- Advertising revenue and business deals: The ANC needs good circulation destinations for its government advertisements, but will also spread out the advertising. It has on several occasions threatened to starve unsympathetic media of advertising, refusing to 'feed the hand that bites us'.[48] Hence there is a good chance, on the side of the media, that favourable coverage for the ANC and ANC government might bring in advertising revenue, or deals around the set-top boxes for digital conversion. For example, the possibility exists that e.tv had succumbed and offered positive coverage for presidential infrastructure projects, mindful of a set-top box deal. My own research, from June 2014 to February 2015, compared SABC television and e.tv evening open-channel news broadcasts on South African politics: the SABC coverage on several core events was more balanced than that of e.tv until late 2014. Subsequently, e.tv regained more of its earlier reputation for neutrality.

Cumulatively, these strategies contribute to the public image of the ANC and ANC government. It can also be calculated that government is a huge client of most of the commercial banks. Modest switches of government-held accounts between banks will affect bank revenues. This was recognised when First National Bank retracted a public campaign that had an anti-ANC government twist and generated ANC fallout.

BRINGING 'ABERRANT' STATE INSTITUTIONS BACK INTO LINE

For the sake of nurturing hegemony, the ANC feels it has to keep state institutions under control, despite investigations and rulings that regularly fault the political principals and their policy processes. Institutions meting out correctives to the ruling party include the Constitutional Court, Supreme Court of Appeal and high courts generally, the public protector, and, beyond government, the mass media. Trade unions and civil society are other elements of the opposition formation called 'liberal constitutionalists' that also 'require' control. In its 2012 political programme, the SACP defined liberal constitutionalism as one of two opponents of the ANC order that had to be defeated.[49]

Two decades into democracy, South Africans remained proud of their constitutional state, with rule of law as a guaranteed cornerstone. There were no guarantees, however, that the ANC in government would not subtly undermine these values. The ANC often felt hamstrung, but also recognised that for public reputation and trust it was necessary to respect the Constitution and rule of law. It sometimes felt wronged, because as the vanguard dominant party in a multiparty democracy it was supposed to own the right to give effect to its *interpretation* of the will of the majority. The ANC chose to go to war in and with Parliament and the public protector in protection of its president. More subtly, it also took on the judiciary. The ANC conveyed the beliefs that the courts were ganging up against it and were overreaching, and that the judges were second-guessing the ANC as the party that was chosen to lead the country. It argued that the public protector was overestimating her own powers. The ANC further argued that Parliament had become an unruly place where opposition parties embarrass the president. The ANC, in effect, communicated that letting the president be unaccountable was more acceptable than boisterous EFF and DA behaviour aimed at getting accountability. President Zuma's arguments that he was accountable were based, it appears, on counting appearances in Parliament rather than on answering questions meaningfully.

Threats against the Constitutional Court and legal system

The personalisation of state power around the defence of the president reached one of its highs – but subsided in the face of public outcry – when President Zuma argued in 2012 for the review of the powers of the Constitutional Court. The 2012 episode followed a botched attempt by Zuma to reappoint former chief justice Sandile Ngcobo, and the campaign by Zuma-ists to get subsequent chief justice Mogoeng Mogoeng appointed. The ANC continued the thrust in the 2015 aftermath of Sudanese president Omar al-Bashir being allowed to leave South Africa in breach of legislation that domesticated an International Criminal Court agreement. High-ranking ANC voices took exception against a ruling of a full bench of the High Court. In response, Justice Mogoeng, supported by a united legal arm, told the ANC: 'General gratuitous criticism is unacceptable.'[50]

Ngoako Ramatlhodi (former Limpopo premier, in the past subject to suspicions on tender issues, subsequently mineral resources and then public service and administration minister in the Zuma Cabinet) spearheaded the 2012 assault and President Zuma joined in. In the wake of fallout with Mbeki, Ramatlhodi had become part of the coalition of the wounded.[51] He criticised the role of the courts while, in typical ANC style, giving face-value commitment to judicial independence and the rule of law.[52] Ramatlhodi argued that the courts are obstacles to transformation; the Constitution was a compromise that 'emptied the state', and 'forces against change reign supreme in the economy, judiciary, public opinion and civil society'.[53] The Zuma government spin added a procedural trademark of the ANC when it deals with 'aberrant' institutions: unleash debate by threatening action against the Constitutional Court (or, at other times, the public protector and the media), take cover, and deny exactly the motive that constitutionalists, jurists and civic actors attach to the threatening proposals.[54] Then let institutions self-reflect. Hopefully they will become more cautious and less prone to challenging the elite's use of power. Next, the ANC steps back to await a time to follow through with another salvo. Commissions of inquiry also come in useful to win time and then unleash new salvos.

An earlier relevant skirmish was in 2003 when the Constitutional Court rejected Schabir Shaik's application for leave to appeal and declare parts of the NPA Act unconstitutional. It had been ruled that he had to present himself for questioning concerning alleged arms deal corruption. Zuma was a business associate of Shaik's and the debate was about whether Zuma and Shaik ought to be charged separately or jointly. Shaik was then charged separately on two counts of corruption, was convicted, and his appeal was served in the

Constitutional Court two years later.[55] Next, in 2008 Zuma and the arms company Thint Holdings unsuccessfully contested the lawfulness of the Scorpions' search-and-seizure warrants of their premises. Still in 2008, Zuma and Thint challenged the lawfulness of NPA communications to Mauritian authorities in order to access information on their involvement in the arms deal. In 2011, the Constitutional Court found that the Hawks' location within the police insufficiently insulated it from political interference (in the case brought by businessperson Hugh Glenister).[56] In a case brought by the Justice Alliance of SA, Freedom under Law, and the Council for the Advancement of the SA Constitution, Zuma's reappointment of former chief justice Ngcobo was successfully challenged. Soon after the questioning of Constitutional Court powers, Zuma's appointment of Menzi Simelane as NPA boss also reached the court and was rejected. The next of Zuma's encounters unfolded around the powers of the public protector, Thuli Madonsela, and then, potentially, the spy-tapes case.

Public protector in parliamentary and court battles

The ANC worked actively to control the expression of opposition voices in Parliament, even if mainly under the legitimate mantle of exercising the right of the majority to take the final decision. It toiled to counter the impact of the public protector's rulings, especially those against the president, to the point of instigating (attempted) palace coups against her, restraining budget increases, and undermining her report through commissioning supplementary investigations into the upgrades at Nkandla.[57] Most of these endeavours were in a spirit of playing narrowly within the rules – the ANC regards using its force of persuasion, as the dominant party, as entirely compatible with playing within the rules.

It mattered little to the ANC that the public protector herself did not initiate investigations regarding the president, but was doing her work to the point of receiving accolades such as being one of *Time* magazine's 100 most influential people of 2013 and the 2014 winner of Transparency International's Integrity Award. Madonsela strictly adhered to the constitutional responsibilities associated with her office. She demonstrated faith in her office's calls on justice and legality and took judicial rulings on appeal – for example, in 2014–15, to get the Constitutional Court's verdict on the legal standing of her reports. Constitutional experts differ on the public protector's powers. Pierre de Vos argued that Madonsela's position constituted the correct legal position on Nkandla and that neither the president nor the police minister could afford to ignore it or set it aside. Paul Hoffman of the Institute for Accountability in Southern Africa, argued that the president is obliged to respond to the public protector's recommendations and that Cabinet cannot overrule these recommendations.[58] Shadrack Gutto said Zuma had shown that he is disinclined to act in accordance with the Constitution and the rule of law, noting: 'It is clear that the president is trying to dodge the laws of the country.'[59] With reference to sections 181 and 182 of the Constitution of South Africa and section 3 of the National Key Points Act, Gutto noted that the *relevance*, and not the comprehensiveness, of the president's response to the public protector's report matters.[60]

The public protector's investigation of public spending on Zuma's Nkandla homestead was published in March 2014, after numerous delays due to lack of cooperation by the Presidency.[61] The sensitively formulated recommendations were that the president should pay back a reasonable part of R246 million unjustifiably or unaccountably apportioned. After the election, the former parliamentary *ad hoc* committee chair, Faith Muthambi, was elevated into Cabinet and cast into a new, potentially powerful communications portfolio. The EFF, now a vociferous opposition party, demanded answers as to when the president was going to pay. The ANC in Parliament, along with the executive, commissioned several additional reports, some with limited briefs, to ensure it could deflect attention and find other culprits (civil servants who had been sworn to secrecy and could not access documents to defend themselves, the architect, and the former minister and deputy minister of public works). The reports were to come from public works, the security sector and the SIU. All three identified other responsible parties. The public works minister reassured that 'everyone found to have done anything wrong will be dealt with … the SIU is investigating everyone'.[62] The ANC's objective was to reduce and discard the public protector's report, yet be seen to be doing it procedurally and fairly.

South Africa's public protector enjoys standard ombudsperson powers, plus the responsibility to strengthen constitutional democracy. Both the Executive Members Ethics Act 1998 and the Public Protector Act 1994 elaborate on her powers regarding investigations in terms of section 182 of the Constitution.[63] Section 182(1)(c) of the Constitution spells out that the public protector has the power to take appropriate remedial action, while section 181(2) states that Chapter Nine institutions (which include the public protector) are subject only to the Constitution and the law. Even if her powers were merely that of recommendation and not order, Zuma and his forces went to great lengths to avoid them. The ANC entered into a painful and embarrassing chain of defences of the president, on the one hand emphasising its respect for the office of the public protector, and on the other setting off trains of insults and condemnations. The lines of the dispute were complicated given that the ANC, its leagues and tripartite partner the SACP and the SACP's Young Communist League (YCL) often led the attacks on the public protector, on behalf of the institutions of Parliament and the president. Two categories of insults and condemnations of Madonsela reflect the thrusts of the ANC parliamentarians' assault on this Chapter Nine institution:

- Lack of legality and misappropriation of functions: she assumes you are guilty until proven innocent (Bheki Cele, ANC NEC) and commits procedural and substantive mistakes in her investigations (Buti Manamela, YCL); the public protector is usurping the functions of Parliament, rendering it irrelevant (Mathole Motshega, ANC MP, former chief whip); she undermines the constitutional rights of ANC voters, and desperately attempts to dictate to Parliament (Stone Sizani, ANC chief whip).
- *Mala fide* intentions: she plays into an anti-democratic regime-change agenda – the Nkandla report is 'white people's lies' (Blade Nzimande, SACP); she is a CIA spy and she thinks she is God (Kebby Maphatsoe, Umkhonto we Sizwe Military Veterans' Association, deputy minister); Madonsela must stop acting like she is God; people are going on like she is Jesus of Jerusalem (Bheki Cele, ANC NEC). There were also matching insults from beyond Parliament: Madonsela is malevolent, salacious, ordering people around, and uses cheap demagogy (Thami ka Plaatjie, ministerial adviser); the public protector's office leaks reports and blames it on divisions in the ANC (Gwede Mantashe, ANC secretary general); and the leak of a letter she wrote to Zuma was timed and deliberate (Jessie Duarte, ANC deputy secretary general).

When the DA, EFF and other opposition parties combined their voices, these parties accumulated a parliamentary opposition voice that exceeded their joint number of seats in the National Assembly. They could not win the votes, given the ANC majority (with the ANC chief whip ensuring high attendance rates at National Assembly sittings). However, the opposition succeeded in spotlighting President Zuma, his failure to answer questions and his shying away from Parliament because he fears 'embarrassment' in general and on Nkandla specifically.

The Nkandla case clearly showed that the ANC will find ways to use due parliamentary and government process (and, if possible, judicial processes) to derail inconvenient questions. It showed that it would rather focus on 'ill-discipline by opposition MPs' (as it was phrased)[64] who demand accountability than attend to a lack of ANC answerability in the legislative institutions. The EFF and the rest of the opposition united increasingly[65] in the face of the ANC's digging itself into its pro-Zuma trench, demanding general accountability and direct answers from the president.

PUBLIC OPINION AND THE ZUMA STATE

Public opinion surveys, both quantitative and qualitative, show that the ANC had much to be concerned about. The details (Table 2.2) from a research project at the height of controversies about the president and how they reflect on the state demonstrate the negative citizen sentiments. TNS-Global tracks the metro public's satisfaction with the performance of the president. Recognising the differences between survey and electoral data and between metro and rural trends, the results demonstrate for August 2014 (one of his best ratings) that the president was falling far short of the 62 per cent electoral endorsement of the ANC – a total of 48 per cent of respondents said they do not approve of President Zuma's performance as president, compared with 44 per cent who approved (8 per cent were uncertain or chose not to reveal their opinions).

Adverse as this rating was, it constituted a recovery on the same series' measurement of February 2014, which had delivered a mere 34 per cent presidential approval with 58 per cent disapproving The improvement between February and August 2014 probably indicated the relative success of the ANC's election campaign, which had taken pains to shield the president. Ipsos also points out that it is common around the world for political leaders to have improved ratings in post-election periods.[66] TNS monitoring of late 2014 confirmed the lower pre-election trends, while the February 2015 measurement hit rock bottom in the form of a 33 per cent presidential approval rating.

When it comes to the state more generally, South Africans are critical and see the flaws, as well as the institutional abuse by the predominant governing party. Citizen perceptions (Table 3.3) reflect alienation from predominant government institutions. This research preceded the 2014 election and the post-election change in the opposition's style in legislatures which has made the public view Parliament as more robust and engaging. Post-election research shows popular appreciation for the opposition pushing the ANC into better accountability, adding to positive perceptions of opposition parties.[67]

Table 3.3:   Citizen perceptions of South Africa's representative institutions and politicians – focus group findings

OPINIONS IN PARTICIPANTS' OWN WORDS AFTER PROMPTS FOR POSITIVES AND NEGATIVES	
Elected representatives and the president	
Parliament / MPs	Corrupted, lazy, rubber stamp, misuse of power, fighting, dodgy, fashionable, greedy, selfish, party pawns, uninformed, jokers, circus, 'paid for doing nothing', 'just see them on TV' and 'don't know them'
Provincial legislature / MPLs	Corrupt, invisible, cabal, 'caught for fraud and corruption', 'we don't know them', joke, 'they don't have a clue', 'maybe they work behind the scenes'
Local government / councillors	Favouritism, 'we don't know who they are', 'he switches off his phone', corruption, selfish, invisible, poor services
President of South Africa	Once-off mentions: time for communities, cunning, wise, good leader, helps development; Repeated in multiple groups: 'corrupt', 'many wives', 'Nkandla', 'rich', 'cunning', 'uncertain of his own abilities', 'struggles with public speaking'
Civil service and local government	
National civil service, government departments	'No staff shortage, but you wait all day', 'helpless', 'try to deliver, but captain is not driving the ship', 'if it is break time they will not help you', 'do as they please', 'no discipline', inefficient, corrupt
Provincial government departments	'We go for tenders and they just want to know how much we can give them', 'no complaints here', 'you get assistance', 'poor performance', 'empty promises', 'we don't know anything about them', pathetic, corrupt
Local municipal officials	Disorganised, greedy, uncaring, arrogant, 'long lunches', 'ignore us', 'arrive late for work', 'didn't go to school to get their jobs', 'we don't ever see them', 'eating money', lazy, corruption

Source: Booysen, December 2013, *Twenty Years of South African Democracy*, national focus group study. Phrases in this table are verbatim from focus group discussions.

Quantitative survey trends of 2013–2015, based on nationally representative probability samples, corroborate the qualitative indications. Both the World Values Survey (WVS) and the Institute of Justice and Reconciliation (IJR)[68] report declining confidence in institutions that define the South African democratic state. The WVS finds that confidence in the government (at 47 per cent), police (45 per cent), armed forces (58 per cent) and the courts (50 per cent) in 2013 had reached all-time lows since the first post-1994 measurement of 1995. In the decade from 2003 to 2013, the IJR measurement of confidence in the Office of the Presidency and national and provincial government declined from 77 to 55 per cent, 73 to 55 per cent, and 65 to 52 per cent respectively. Although the absolute measurements of IJR are higher than those of the WVS, the overall trend in both cases is one of serial and serious decline. The twenty-two percentage-point decline in confidence in the Presidency illustrates the change that set in as the presidential order changed from Mbeki to Zuma, as the political system was also losing more of its liberation gloss.

The IJR project also measured trust in national leaders and institutions by asking if South Africans agree with the statement (for example): 'Most of the time I can trust the country's national leaders to do what is right.' The IJR results also show that from 2003 to 2013 trust in leaders decreased. In 2003, 55 per cent of South Africans agreed with the statement; ten years later, trust levels for national leaders had decreased by six percentage points, to 48 per cent.

The ANC and government argue that the people are not concerned about corruption and that the media and opposition parties *construct* this concern. In contrast, both focus group and opinion poll research show citizens' wish to have an untainted government, a concern that has also grown over time. Afrobarometer trend analysis (Figure 3.1) on nationally representative data shows that in 2002 just over 10 per cent of South Africans believed there was corruption in the Presidency. By 2011 the figure approached 40 per cent. Beliefs that government officials generally and local government officials specifically are corrupt both reached the 50 per cent mark by 2011. As impressions of corruption grew, the confidence levels in the institutions of the ANC state under Zuma declined further.

CONCLUSION: NEW GOVERNMENT, ENTRENCHED LEGACIES

The ANC government under Jacob Zuma tried repeatedly to present itself as a 'new government' when Zuma entered state office in 2009 and when Zuma's presidency proceeded into a second term. The 'new' was anticipated to be paired with

Figure 3.1: Perceptions of incidence of state corruption

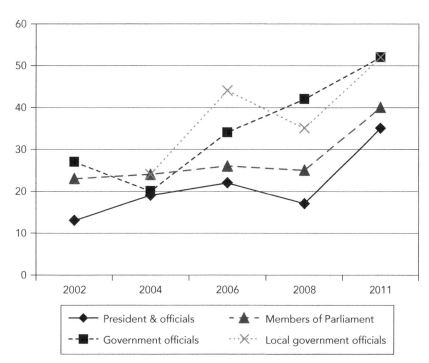

Source: Afrobarometer, 2013, survey of 2 400 randomly sampled South Africans.
Note: Margin of error is 2% at a 95% confidence level. Percentages are based on beliefs that 'all' or 'most' of these persons are involved in corruption.

improved delivery and a reinvigorated local election victory in 2016. However, it interprets the protection of the president as a special case that the people will pardon when it comes to the next poll, for it believes it can use delivery and suasion to retain the old dynamic of the ANC being bigger than any individual leader, and that no leader can break or damage the movement's liberation bond. Research, however, shows that there have been concurrent declines in the levels of support for the president, for core state institutions more generally and for the ANC in election contests. These declines equally co-varied with increases in the perception of corruption in state institutions. The research also showed that Zuma's name was inextricably linked to corruption. Hence, the state and the ANC were taking damage for the protection of the president for his association with corruption – and yet the ANC was moving ahead on the belief that it would be strong and persuasive enough to deliver future electoral victories on *its terms – despite* protecting the president.

119

This goes to the heart of the matter of the ANC and its compliant state. The ANC stands a chance to do well in future elections if it shows it is prioritising government performance along with living out its promises of caring and connection with the people. This competes with the images of the leaders and their political parties. In the case of Zuma and the ANC, the ANC in government in effect informed the electorate that the president is the one sacrifice the ANC is not prepared to make. The ANC trusts that its partial control over delivery and communication media will be sufficient to supplement its state performance and organisational culture, and generate favourable future election results.

However, the state is weakening, with a range of state institutions being mismanaged, malfunctioning, or suffering a war of attrition for daring not to bow before the president and his protectors. This is unfolding while the state does not extract the levels of income necessary to sustain some essential policy projects. The economy is not generating the required growth rates and labour absorption ratios. Neither social spending nor the public sector salary bill is sustainable, yet the ANC's middle-class and patriotic bourgeoisie projects, along with the social security network that is cast in narratives of patronage, need these to sustain the ANC in the longer term.

NOTES

1   All citations from Joel Netshitenzhe, 8 March 2015, 'Is the state losing legitimacy?' *City Press*, Voices, p. 3.

2   Ranjeni Munusamy, 16 March 2015, 'The minister, the watchdog and the hidden hand: Why Nhleko is taking on McBride', *Daily Maverick*, http://www.dailymav erick.co.za/article/2015-03-16-the-minister-the-watchdog-and-the-hidden-hand-why-nhleko-is-taking-on-mcbride, accessed 16 March 2015.

3   See Joseph V. Femia, 1987, *Gramsci's Political Thought: Hegemony, Consciousness, and the Revolutionary Process*, Oxford: Clarendon Press, for a discussion on minimal and maximum hegemony.

4   Alex Boraine, 2014, *What's Gone Wrong? On the Brink of a Failed State*, Cape Town: Jonathan Ball.

5   Trevor Manuel, 3 April 2013, '19 years into democracy, our govt has run out of excuses - Trevor Manuel', Conference of the Senior Management Service, CSIR Conference Centre, http://www.politicsweb.co.za/politicsweb/view/politicsweb/en/page71654?oid=367636&sn=Detail&pid=71654, accessed 4 October 2014. The president did counter Manuel: 'To suggest we cannot blame apartheid for what is happening in our country now, I think is a mistake to say the least ... We don't need to indicate what it is apartheid did. The fact that the country is two in one, you go to any city, there is a beautiful part and squatters on the other side, this is not the making of democracy and we can't stop blaming those who caused it'; http://www.iol.co.za/news/politics/we-can-blame-apartheid-says-zuma-1.1498541#.VFZFeMl6ino, accessed 4 April 2015.

6   The World Bank, 4 November 2014, 'South Africa lifts 3.6 million out of poverty thanks to its fiscal policies', http://www.worldbank.org/en/news/press-release/2014/11/04/south-africa-lifts-36-million-out-of-poverty-thanks-to-its-fiscal-policies, accessed 20 November 2014.

7   Pierre de Vos, 19 November 2014, 'Nkandla and the National Assembly: Little more than a sideshow', *Daily Maverick*, http://www.dailymaverick.co.za/opinionista/2014-11-19-nkandla-and-the-national-assembly-little-more-than-a-sideshow, accessed 20 November 2014.

8   The spy tapes are transcripts of the National Intelligence Agency (NIA) of intercepted telephonic conversations between then NPA boss Bulelani Ngcuka and Scorpions head Leonard McCarthy. Then acting NPA boss Mokotedi Mpshe cited the tapes in his decision to drop charges against Zuma – a step that cleared the way for Zuma to become president of South Africa. The tapes are argued to have identified a politically inspired decision to charge Jacob Zuma for corruption, racketeering and related charges. The charges related to an alleged arms deal bribe and Zuma's relationship with Schabir Shaik. Richard Mdluli, later to become the head of police crime intelligence, obtained some of the recorded conversations, which in turn ended up with Zuma's lawyer, Michael Hulley. It was argued (but contested) that the existence of the tapes tainted the legal process. Mokotedi Mpshe, former acting head of the NPA, on 6 April 2009 hence announced that it would not be possible to continue prosecuting Zuma.

9   The Stalingrad strategy denotes Zuma using technicalities to avoid or delay the possible reinstatement of the 783 charges of fraud, corruption, money laundering and racketeering. Zuma's lawyer, for example, used at least six court applications to stop the release of the spy tapes.

10   James Selfe, interview with Craig Dodds, 16 August 2014, 'Spy-tapes battle nears its climax', *Weekend Argus*, p. 8.

11   Philip de Wet, 29 August 2014, 'Spy tape release may not end with Zuma in the dock', *Mail & Guardian*, http://mg.co.za/article/2014-08-29-release-of-spy-tapes-may-not-end-with-zuma-in-court/, accessed 12 September 2014.

12   See, for example, André Jurgens, 27 July 2014, 'De Lille's arms deal claims "need probing"', *Sunday Times*, p. 2; Louise Flanagan, 20 July 2014, 'Arms critics turn in the firing lines', *The Sunday Independent*, p. 9; André Jurgens and Ernest Mabuza, 20 July 2014, 'Mbeki: No regret over arms deal', *Sunday Times*, p. 14.

13   Thabo Mbeki, 18 July 2014, in response to questions by the Lawyers for Human Rights advocate Anna-Marie de Vos, Seriti Commission of Inquiry.

14   Zizi Kodwa, 14 November 2014, ANC press statement, 'Adoption of ad hoc committee report into Nkandla upgrades', http://www.anc.org.za/show.php?id=11195, accessed 19 November 2014.

15   Jacob Zuma, 2014, *Report to the Speaker of the National Assembly Regarding the Security Upgrades at the Nkandla Private Residence of His Excellency President Jacob G Zuma*. It was the predecessor *ad hoc* committee that in the dying days of the 2014 pre-election Parliament had pulled the plug and disbanded the first *ad hoc* committee. This unravelled while the public protector and Zuma engaged in their duel on the powers of Parliament and public protector, with the Western Cape High Court weighing in. The saga continued through the report by Minister of Police Nathi Nhleko, 28 May 2015, *Report by the Minister of Police to Parliament*

on Security Upgrades at the Nkandla Private Residence of the President, http://www
.gov.za/sites/www.gov.za/files/speech, accessed 6 July 2015.

16   See, for example, Xolani Mbanjwa, 14 September 2014, 'Nkandla blame game', *City
Press*, p. 2.

17   Phillip de Wet, 28 March–13April 2014, 'ANC hones its master plan to save Zuma',
Mail & Guardian, p. 3.

18   Greg Nicolson, 30 October 2014, 'Nkandla, Madonsela and the Schippers ruling',
Daily Maverick, http://www.dailymaverick.co.za/article/2014-10-30-nkandla-mad
onsela-and-the-schippers-ruling/#.VFc0FMl6joQ, accessed 3 November 2014, does
a detailed and expert-driven analysis.

19   Reported in Biénne Huisman, 23 November 2014, 'Madonsela fights for the
authority of her office', *City Press*, p. 6.

20   Thuli Madonsela, 28 May 2015, interview with Xolani Gwala, Radio 702.

21   Mathews Phosa, 2013, 'We need to know the truth', http://mg.co.za/article/2013-
10-09-mathews-phosa-on-nklanda-we-need-to-know-the-truth&views=1&mo-
bi=true&KEY=ac911outpud90pbo79qheii6o4, accessed 10 September 2014.

22   Alexander Beresford, 8 October 2014, 'Power, patronage and gatekeeper politics', University of Johannesburg, Sociology, Anthropology and Development Studies Seminar.

23   Susan Booysen, 2008, 'South Africa', in Vanessa Shields and Nicholas Baldwin
(eds), *Beyond Settlement, Volume I – The Institutional Dimension: Consolidating
Democratic Institutions in Conflict States*, Madison/Teaneck: Fairleigh Dickinson
University Press, pp. 254–275.

24   Mmanaledi Mataboge and Qaanitah Hunter, 19 December 2014, 'Gwede Mantashe
admits ANC could lose power', *Mail & Guardian*, http://mg.co.za/article/2014-12-
18-gwede-mantashe-admits-anc-could-lose-power, accessed 18 December 2014.

25   Stephen Grootes, 19 May 2015, 'ANC vs. the media, again', *Daily Maverick*,
http://www.dailymaverick.co.za/article/2015-05-19-op-ed-anc-vs.-the-media-
again/?utm_source=Daily+Maverick, accessed 19 May 2015.

26   Jacob Zuma, 17 June 2014, State of the Nation address, President of the Republic of
South Africa on the occasion of the joint sitting of Parliament, Cape Town, http://
www.thepresidency.gov.za/pebble.asp?relid=17570, accessed 18 June 2014.

27   There was an IMC task team on Nkandla. It set the scene for a whitewash of security excesses. The IMC on the Gauteng Freeway Improvement Project recommended the implementation of e-tolls. A security cluster IMC visited protest hot
spots before Election 2014 and brought security force deployment to suppress protest and deliver elections.

28   See, for example, Qaanitah Hunter, 5–11 September 2014, 'Paranoid president axes
more top spooks', *Mail & Guardian*, p. 2 – which was followed up with 'SSA defends
Zuma's axing of spooks', *Mail & Guardian*, http://mg.co.za/article/2014-09-06-ssa-
defends-zumas-axing-of-spooks?, accessed 8 September 2014. The officials that
were redeployed circa 2014 were senior (as in a previous instance three years earlier): head of the national intelligence coordinating committee Dennis Dlomo,
director of the domestic branch of the State Security Agency Simon Jabulani
Ntombela and deputy director general of domestic collection Nozuko Bam.

29   Ranjeni Munusamy, 16 March 2015, op. cit.

30   Interview with a former ministerial adviser, 10 July 2009, Johannesburg; Pierre de
Vos, 19 November 2014, op. cit.

31   See, for example, Institute for Security Studies, 8 October 2013, 'A dysfunctional SAPS intelligence division has severe implications for reducing crime', http://www .issafrica.org/iss-today/a-dysfunctional-saps-intelligence-division-has-severe-implications-for-reducing-crime, accessed 20 September 2014; Zelda Venter, 24 September 2013, 'Judge reinstates charges against Richard Mdluli', *The Star*, p. 4; Mondli Makhanya, 2 April 2011, 'Shame on those who sold our integrity to save their skins', *Sunday Times*, p. 4.

32   *Quarterly Labour Force Survey*, October 2014. Mid-2014 there were roughly 15 million formal jobs in South Africa, including the 2 million in state employment.

33   National Treasury, 25 February 2015, *Budget Review 2015*, p. 39.

34   Interviews with nine master's students, deployed mostly mid-level in the public sector, at the University of the Witwatersrand, in the period 2011–2014.

35   Marianne Merten, 22 September 2014, 'Protect the president, NEC tells Parliament', *Daily News*, http://www.iol.co.za/dailynews/news/protect-the-president-nec-tells-parliament-1.1754335#.VFaXdMl6ino, accessed 2 November 2014.

36   Judith February and Gary Pienaar, 2014, 'Twenty years of constitutional democracy' in Thenjiwe Meyiwa et al. (eds), *State of the Nation 2014*, Cape Town: HSRC Press.

37   The reports of the auditor general, over time, show the effects of political deployment. Auditor general South Africa, 2014, *Consolidated General Report on the Audit Outcomes of Local Government: MFMA 2012–13*, http://www.agsa.co.za/ Portals/0/MFMA%202012-13/2012_13_MFMA_Consolidated_general_report .pdf, accessed 27 August 2014; Auditor general of South Africa, 2015, *Consolidated General Report on the Audit Outcomes of Local Government: MFMA 2013–14*, accessed 28 June 2015.

38   In this context, see Ivor Chipkin, Gumani Tshimomola and Ryan Brunette, 1–7 August 2014, 'Decentralised procurement fails the state', *Mail & Guardian*, p. 27; also see NCOP briefing to the select committee on cooperative governance and traditional affairs on the status of financial disclosure and compliance of heads of department, reported in *The Sunday Independent*, 13 March 2013. Then minister of the department Lindiwe Sisulu promised in 2013 that new legislation was being created to stop 1.5 million public servants from doing business with the state; Estelle Setan, Treasury, 9 September 2014, 'Treasury admits to public procurement shortcomings, moves to implement "strategic sourcing"', *Polity*, http://www.polity.org.za/article/ treasury-admits-to-public-procurement-shortcomings-moves-to-implement-strategic-sourcing-2014-09-09, accessed 12 September 2014.

39   See, for example, David Makhura, 2014, 'State of the province address', reported in *Gauteng News*, SOPA special edition 2014, p. 1.

40   Guptagate refers to the landing, on March 2013, of a plane of wedding guests (from India to the Vega Gupta wedding) at a national key point, the Waterkloof Air Force Base. Zuma was implicated in authorising the flight, but insisted he knew nothing about it. SANDF commander Lieutenant General Bruce Koloane was the fall guy. He lost his position but in August 2014 was confirmed as South Africa's ambassador to the Netherlands.

41   See Xolani Mbanjwa, 14 September 2014, 'Nkandla blame game', *City Press*, p. 2.

42   See Andisiwe Makinana and Matuma Letsoale, 11–17 July 2014, 'Motsoeneng's clout reaches the top', *Mail & Guardian*, p. 5.

43 Jacob Zuma, in interview with Malcom Hewitt, *African Business*, 'I am not a great man – I am a man of the people', 1 June 2009, http://www.thefreelibrary.com/I+am+not+a+great+man--I+am+a+man+of+the+people.(Interview)-a0202294929, accessed 7 June 2010.

44 The two Independent News and Media SA group (INMSA) shareholders were Sekunjalo Independent Media Consortium (SIM) (75 per cent) and the Government Employees' Pension Fund acting through the Public Investment Corporation (PIC; 25 per cent). The Food and Allied Workers' Union's role was through a special-purpose vehicle.

45 Interview, SABC station manager, 2 February 2012, Johannesburg.

46 Empowerment group Hosken Consolidated Investments (HCI) owns free-to-air broadcaster e.tv. The South African Clothing and Textile Workers' Union is Hosken's biggest shareholder. Yunis Shaik, a director of the company that controls e.tv, said in a March 2014 e-mail to e.tv Chief Executive Officer Marcel Golding that Economic Development Minister Ebrahim Patel said in an email to him, 'President Zuma this day opened a new dam. He wants us to cover it tonight. As this is a big story, it might be a good lead story.' See http://www.bloomberg.com/news/2014-10-23/hosken-chairman-golding-suspended-over-2-2-million-ellies-deal.html, accessed 23 October 2014.

47 Interview, 2 March 2014, former adviser to *The New Age*, Johannesburg.

48 Mmanaledi Mataboge and Matuma Letsoalo, 12 December 2014, 'State poised to wield advertising axe', *Mail & Guardian*, http://mg.co.za/article/2014-12-11-state-poised-to-wield-advertising-axe, accessed 14 March 2015. The DA in the Western Cape provincial government has been using withdrawal of subscriptions to punish *Independent* for adverse coverage of this government.

49 SACP, political programme, adopted at the SACP congress, July 2012. The second of the tendencies was the 'populist bourgeois nationalist ideological tendency with deeply worrying demagogic, proto-fascist features'.

50 Statement issued by Chief Justice Mogoeng Mogoeng, the heads of court and senior judges of all divisions on 8 July 2015, 'The judiciary's commitment to the rule of law', http://www.politicsweb.co.za/politics/general-gratuitous-criticism-of-judiciary-unaccept, accessed 10 July 2015.

51 Drew Forrest, 17–23 February 2012, 'Comeback kid returns with a vengeance', *Mail & Guardian*, p. 5.

52 Variations on this theme were also used in the case of the media and 'confirmed support' for the freedom of information.

53 Drew Forrest, 17 February 2012, 'Comeback kid Ramatlhodi returns with a vengeance', *Mail & Guardian*, http://mg.co.za/article/2012-02-17-comeback-kid-ramtlhodi-returns-with-a-vengeance, accessed 10 April 2012. Also see Cora Hoexter and Morné Olivier (eds), 2014, *The Judiciary in South Africa*, Johannesburg: Juta.

54 Also see Hugh Corder, 15 February 2012, 'Zuma shocks with pledge to look at powers of judiciary', *Business Day*, p. 9.

55 His argument was that in the context of racial discrimination he had not had equal opportunities and did not have a fair trial.

56 See Pierre de Vos, 2011, The South African Police Service Amendment Bill: Compliance with Glenister v President of the Republic of South Africa, Memorandum, Claude Leon Foundation Chair in Constitutional Governance, Department of

Public Law, University of Cape Town, http://www.nelsonmandela.org/uploads/files/The_South_African_Police_Services_Amendment_Bill.pdf, accessed 20 August 2014.

57   ANC MPs on the justice and correctional services portfolio committee accused Madonsela of being an undemocratic leader running a dysfunctional office, while Parliament and the Treasury were denying her office sufficient funding to run all necessary operations and appoint the staff complement that had been granted to her office; proceedings of this committee, 22 October 2014, Parliament, Cape Town.

58   Oliver Ngwenya, 25 August 2014, 'ANC attacks Madonsela after letter to Zuma', *Public News Hub*, publicnewshub.com/anc-attacks-madonsela-letter-zuma/, accessed 2 September 2014.

59   *Legalbrief Today*, 25 August 2014, 'Madonsela slammed by ANC, backed by experts', Issue No. 3582, http://www.legalbrief.co.za/article.php?story=20140825091841485, accessed 5 September 2014.

60   Shadrack Gutto, 24 August 2014, e.tv 7 pm news bulletin. Gutto is a Marxist scholar who had previously been kicked out of both Kenya and Zimbabwe for being involved in 'anti-state' activities. He is more concerned about civil liberties and constitutionalism than most other analysts.

61   See Public Protector South Africa, March 2014, *Secure in Comfort*, Report No. 25 of 2013/14.

62   Thulas Nxesi, 20 July 2014, quoted in 'Officials to face the Nkandla music', *City Press*, p. 1.

63   Thuli Madonsela, 21 August 2014, letter to President Zuma, entitled *Report to the Speaker of the National Assembly Regarding the Security Upgrades at the Nkandla Private Residence of His Excellency President Jacob G Zuma*', http://www.sabreaking news.co.za/2014/08/25/read-thuli-madonselas-letter-to-the-president/, accessed 4 November 2014, explains nuances of the public protector's powers.

64   See, for example, Thabo Mokone, 2 November 2014, 'Deputy speaker wants "better spin" to counter EFF', *Sunday Times*, p. 10.

65   Annelie Lotriet, L. Filtane and M.A. Mncwango, 18 November 2014, 'ANC did a hatchet job on EFF MPs – DA, UDM and IFP', opposition press statement on the report by the Powers and Privileges Committee, http://www.politicsweb.co.za/politics/anc-did-a-hatchet-job-on-eff-mps--da-udm-and-ifp, accessed 2 September 2015. Cyril Ramaphosa, 18 November 2014, 'Parties commit to restoring dignity, integrity and standing of Parliament – the Presidency', http://www.politicsweb.co.za/news-and-analysis/parties-commit-to-restoring-dignity-integrity, accessed 21 November 2014.

66   Mari Harris, 15 February 2015, quoted in 'Ipsos Poll: Performance of the president and the deputy president', media briefing.

67   Susan Booysen, 2015, *Youth and Political Participation in South Africa's Democracy: Surveying the Voices of the Youth through a Multi-province Focus Group Study*, research report, Johannesburg and Washington DC: Freedom House.

68   World Values Survey, South Africa, principal investigator Hennie Kotzé, 19 March 2015, presentation at the Democracy Development Programme, Durban; Institute of Justice and Reconciliation, 2014, *SA Reconciliation Barometer Survey: 2014 Report*, Cape Town.

4

DESPERATELY SEEKING 'RADICAL' POLICY

The ANC has become adept at straddling the speak-left and walk-right divide.[1] The distinction between the two worlds of policy aspiration and government policy action – and the uneven connecting lines between the two – are a large chunk of the ANC's world of policy in the time of Jacob Zuma. At heart, the ANC is the unflinchingly radical (former) liberation movement with its aspirations anchored in the Freedom Charter. The ANC's quotidian life as South African government is in a different world, one in which progressive enclaves and hard-working individuals battle and often lose against tenderpreneurs and the strident patriotic-nationalist bourgeoisie. This struggle unfolds amid international pressures and the 'global economy' which push leaders to compromise on overall policy positioning. Nationally, the ANC has turned into a middle-of-the-road, perhaps social-welfarist-neoliberal, *post*-liberation policy project.[2]

The government has become skilful at putting on the Janus-faced act in policy practice. It works hard to fit into the liberal-capitalist world order. It prioritises friendships with the BRICS (Brazil, Russia, India and China, besides South Africa), honours the Chinese and obliges the Russians. It has been said that the ANC consistently uses 'left and Marxist rhetoric to justify and mask neoliberal policies'.[3] Numsa cites the implementation of e-tolls, the youth wage subsidy, adoption of the NDP and refusal to ban labour brokers as examples of neoliberalism in the ANC's policy repertoire. Jeremy Cronin of the SACP questions whether BEE has been transformative and developmental. He notes that more public funds were being spent on BEE than on housing and land reform, and links the often disconnected and incapable South African state to tenderisation and agentification (creation of semi-autonomous units within public sector departments). He suggests that BEE has been parasitic and compradorist.[4]

The Freedom Charter of 1955, despite having been overtaken by world ideological developments,[5] remains at the heart of the ANC's frequently restated commitment to the people of South Africa. Official ANC speeches and websites cite the Freedom Charter freely, without reference to discrepancies with prevailing policy practice. Whichever compromise or practical policy deviation is manifested, the ANC is certain to project it as a step towards realising the Charter's ideals – and as revolutionary progress.[6] Its 2012 debate on a 'second transition' versus 'second phase of the transition from apartheid colonialism to a national democratic society' (the latter prevailed) shows deft footwork in matching explanations of the policy mutations over time.[7]

The term 'radical' came to be far removed from the presumed ideological meaning of radical in the sense of extreme left. The assumption in the theory is that if it is left-socialist, the state takes a major role on behalf of citizens and controls the economy – the workers will be central, people will be the beneficiaries and substantive egalitarianism will take shape in society.[8] A crucial part of the ANC's fixation with being seen as radical stems from the realisation that many of its economic transformation objectives remain unfulfilled twenty-years-plus into democracy (this helps deliver the space for the EFF to lock its project into 'economic liberation'). The triple challenge of poverty, unemployment and inequality, combined with continuously recalcitrant economic growth rates and employment creation that simply does not fill the gap, is a daily reminder of the left deficits in ANC policy.

Irrespective of these grand policy-ideological positionings, the ANC's policy making is often bogged down because the public sector has restrained capacity for implementation. Poor accountability in the public sector and in the ranks of its political supervisors (also in the political executive) exacerbates the problem. Deficient accountability, in turn, links to cadre deployment with its flip sides of patronage and corruption. Much of the ANC's *de facto* world of public policy is also characterised by the aphorism of 'formulate but don't necessarily expect implementation'. Rhetorical radicalism becomes the safe option – the

127

ANC knows there will be limited follow-through into implementation. It is thus compatible to speak 'radical' to the people, 'moderation' to investors and 'patriotic bourgeoisie' to the political family.

The rest of this chapter delves into the way the ANC under Zuma's wing positions itself ideologically and on the policy front, and how it straddles the divide between radical and everyday politics and policy. The thread that runs through the chapter is the ANC's compulsion to be seen as ideologically 'radical'. The chapter highlights the two contentious and patriotically centred areas of mining and land, and builds up to assessing the anomalies of the NDP and the task for the ANC at the time to project this plan as South Africa's own, consensual 'end of ideology'. The chapter also reflects on how policy decisions might work in the time of personalised presidential state power.

FAR-REACHING CHANGE, PAPER RADICALISM, IDEOLOGICAL OPPORTUNISM

The ANC as government – in charge of a large state with considerable tax revenue and budgets – has effected far-reaching change, and continues to do so. The ANC leans towards the poor, has put a human face to much of liberal democracy and has established an approximate system of social democracy. Social grants, housing delivery, free basic services and pro-poor taxation have helped to contain the poverty rate. In 2014, Statistics SA noted that close to 60 per cent of government spending in the preceding decade had been allocated to the social wage, and expenditure on these services has 'more than doubled in real terms over the past decade'.[9] Radical (in the sense of far-reaching) change can thus be said to have been achieved if the ANC compares itself with the *status quo ante* of apartheid South Africa.

Yet, even if it is interpreted as substantial cumulative change over more than two decades, it has hardly been a *radical* developmental project. Such radicalism would be reassuring to those who aspire to a more egalitarian and just South Africa in which poverty and unemployment do not remain inescapable burdens. The ANC's actions have not reshaped the economy fundamentally.[10] The Zuma administration has extended policy adjustments away from the Growth, Employment and Redistribution (Gear) strategy initiated in the Mbeki days.[11] On the back of a rising budget deficit the extensions include programmes for industrial revival,[12] continual extension of the social welfare system (including early phases of national health insurance), further development of the social wage, and a public works system. Nevertheless, the pro-poor thrust has mainly been there in the fiscally redistributive sense of the word. In addition, unemployment rates have not budged, despite modest increases in the number of the employed, and much of the social wage has become a stipend for survival.

The ANC government's perspective on its own version of radicalism is clarified in the Presidency's report on the first twenty years of democracy, a document tailored and timed to boost the final phases of the ANC's 2014 election campaign. Systematic delivery and outputs in the twenty years, and the consistent prioritisation of public spending on disadvantaged communities – resulting in undeniable overall transformation – could be termed 'radical', but only by a very extended use of the word.

There is little evidence of Zuma's leading radical innovation and implementation. At the time of Zuma's 2007–2009 rise into power there was some evidence of a left-ANC project taking shape to substitute for more conservative-centrist policy dogma under Mbeki.[13] Zuma's policy style was to let stronger voices in Cabinet and Luthuli House lead – provided it is not in a domain he personally wishes to influence (security comes to mind; possibly also energy and nuclear matters). Mcebisi Ndletyana notes that '[Zuma] is reluctant to lead policy direction … for fear of alienating critical constituencies within the Alliance. This has engendered policy contradictions within Cabinet, projecting the image of a government lacking in clarity over how it seeks to achieve its objectives.'[14] It can be added, however, that Zuma's policy leadership emulates his strategic approach, which is deceptively 'unfocused'.

As the realities of intractable problems of inequality, absolute and relative poverty, and citizens' desperation about no evident escape to the 'better life for all' set in,[15] larger numbers become alienated from the ANC. One of the few instruments at the ANC's disposal to keep its broad church of ideological suasions together is the projection of its policy, superficially, as 'radical'. Thereby it might soften the otherwise incompatible cohabitation of liberals and economic conservatives, those left of the SACP, pan-Africanists and those from black consciousness backgrounds. The renewed societal and ANC focus on unrepentant racism and persistent racial colonialism that were continuously damaging contemporary politics and society also created scope for the ANC to return to the basics of fostering inclusion and cohesion.

The reasons for the compulsion to be seen as radical are thus threefold. First, historically the ANC has been a radical movement, and for the sake of its contemporary credibility it needs to continue at least to be seen as such, to be seen to be in a continuing war against the old regime. Second, it is a way to persuade masses of poor and unemployed, still suffering multiple inequalities and injustices, that there is a better world awaiting them and the ANC is leading them there assiduously. Third, and interrelated, the ANC cannot afford to cede the radicalism tag either to the in-your-face radical rhetoric of the EFF or to a budding workerist party.

This compulsion to express its project as radical thus helps ensure that the discontented constituencies to its left, which include many young South Africans, can find a way to continue seeing the ANC as their home. Vukani Mde unpacks it:

> ... the ANC has neither the stomach nor the inclination for what it calls 'radical change'. It's not in its nature now, nor is it in the interest of its self-interested elites. So the ruling party has taken to repackaging the things that we all acknowledge are needed now – even things they have been doing for two decades, such as delivering water, lights and decent public transport – as radical new ideas that will form part of the 'next phase' of our transition. If the NDP is the central pillar of the next phase of South Arica's transition, then that phase is best characterised as 'doing things better', not 'radical'.[16]

REINVENTING AND RECASTING PUBLIC POLICY

The ANC's duality of almost routinely embracing mainstream policy but pitching it as revolution is a long-standing act that has peaked during Zuma's reign. It can be traced back to the point of preparing the ANC's Election 1994 manifesto, *Ready to Govern*. The document twinned with the Cosatu-drafted Reconstruction and Development Programme (RDP), embraced the aspirations of the pre-1994 popularly anchored policy initiatives, and bonded with the 1955 Freedom Charter. It was a document of hope, and took its place alongside the interim (1993) and final (1996) Constitution.

South Africans celebrated the Constitution as a great founding document, proof that the new political and socioeconomic orders had arrived. The documents, however, also encapsulated the compromises that had accompanied the transitional negotiations. It is widely known that President Nelson Mandela underwent some form of conversion in his economic ideas. Some argue that Mandela decided at a World Economic Forum meeting in Davos in 1993 that the ANC would not go the nationalisation route.[17] Allister Sparks has remarked that Mandela changed a prepared speech to refer to 'a mixed economy in which the private sector would play a central and critical role ...'[18] This event is assumed to have launched the ideological compromises[19] of the constitutional negotiations of the early 1990s.[20] One interpretation of what Robin Renwick wrote[21] suggests that it was a gradual process that had started earlier (in his 2015 publication Renwick credits former British prime minister Margaret Thatcher).[22] Trevor Manuel repackages it with a Chinese twist, arguing that it was a meeting with the Chinese Communist Party that had triggered the change. The Chinese, says Manuel, highlighted the pitfalls of nationalisation:

> [Mandela] had a discussion not with wide-eyed capitalists, but with members of the Communist Party of China about policy. And he spoke about this nationalisation thing, and they asked, 'Why do you want to do that?' Because in China 'socialism with Chinese characteristics' – AKA party-run hyper-capitalism – 'was already developing its own momentum'. He was persuaded that nationalisation can't be the policy of the ANC. However, maybe it was awkwardly handled ...[23]

Manuel does not mention that the Chinese economy remains heavily nationalised: state-controlled companies account for 80 per cent of the market capitalisation of the Chinese stock market and world-class state companies can be found in almost every industry (China Mobile, for example, serves 600 million customers).[24] Irrespective, ANC sentiments expressed after the World Economic Forum event diverged from what had gone before; this was possibly a mere consolidation of preceding ANC inclinations. A few years later the ANC replaced the RDP with Gear. Within Gear, the Accelerated and Shared Growth Initiative in South Africa (AsgiSA) followed, its target to halve unemployment by 2014. These macroeconomics of the Mbeki area – dubbed by the SACP 'the 1996 class project' – handed Zuma-ists ammunition in Mbeki's recall.

The ANC has continually reinvented policy, struggling to accommodate social welfarism, socialism and liberalism. Since 2004, it 'has sought to differentiate its approach from that of a neoliberal capitalist state – by becoming a developmental state that would be more interventionist and more autonomous in relation to capital'.[25] Adam Habib argues that the ANC has a neoliberal base but is 'groping towards' social democracy.[26] The ANC's utterances helped generate the sense of a new policy regime taking shape under Zuma. In substance, there was more continuity than new direction.

In the early days of 2009, when the first Zuma administration carried the new hope and renewal that had originally accompanied the 1993 and 1996 constitutions, it sounded organically radical. A populist, people-first narrative had brought the expectation of a reconnection to the people – but within a year of assuming office it faded. By 2011 it was business as usual, and by 2012 the NDP's contested economic conservatism was ruling supreme. ANC policy documents in mid-2012 became the showcase for compromises that had left behind the populist cloak for Zuma's ascendance into power. Policies and delivery records were presented to sound 'radical'. The NDP metamorphosed from long-term vision to all-term government programme.[27] The NDP is a vast document, covering all policy domains. It offers variable policy frameworks rather than policies, much of it drafted by Presidency and Treasury bureaucrats. It suffers from internal inconsistencies and glossed-over policy problems. The ANC, however, needed a 'policy framework' and the NDP was it.

By 2015, Zuma's State of the Nation address contained only one reference to the NDP: '… we have in the past year introduced some innovative programmes to implement the National Development Plan.' The ANC's October 2015 discussion documents for its National General Council (NGC) more than compensated – the NDP was integrated into the prognoses. The frequent NDP references were in line with departmental budget speeches of mid-2015: multiple references in the rural development and land reform speeches emphasised how the department was giving effect to the NDP. In contrast, the minister of energy's speech proclaimed once-off: 'Energy security is a prerequisite for achieving the 5.5 per cent economic growth target as envisaged by the National Development Plan.'[28] As the term of the first set of national planning commissioners expired, an outgoing commissioner enthused that the president 'truly sees the NDP as important, and personally endorses it'.[29] President Zuma announced the new NPC commissioners in September 2015 and tasked them with advancing NDP implementation.

The ANC conceived the New Growth Path (NGP),[30] which divided the Tripartite Alliance but was welcomed at the NGC meeting of 2010. The ANC cites the NDP, its industrial policy action plans (IPAPs) and the NGP as evidence that it is progressing towards realisation of the 2007 ANC Polokwane resolutions.[31] The ruling party draws the link between the policy documents by stating that 'central to meeting the vision enshrined in the NDP is the implementation of the NGP, the IPAP and the National Infrastructure Plan'.[32]

The NGP centrepiece was the proposed massive investment in infrastructure, along with investment in people through skills development. It was presented as the answer to unemployment and inequality. Yet the problems worsened, even if infrastructure gained more focused attention. The trade and fiscal deficits widened; the promise of five million decent jobs turned into six million 'job opportunities' – not 'real' jobs but offering reprieve and some improved prospects for millions.[33] The IPAP[34] (with several sequential iterations) followed. Infrastructural advancement became one of the Zuma administration mainstays and showed improvements, articulated with the NDP, but was also overshadowed by the NDP, labelled by some in Cosatu the 'recycled Gear'. The SACP cites NGP- and IPAP-related actions as 'radical' realisations of SACP influences on the ANC. After Polokwane the SACP also interpreted the 'developmental state' rhetoric as evidence of the ANC's 'turn to the left'.[35]

The SACP became thoroughly embedded in the ANC's pro-Zuma project – while rooting itself in government and in less-than-radical policy making. It gained more prominence through its attacks in defence of the ANC president than for being at the coalface of ideological contestation. For example, it gained Zuma-era exposure through assaults on artist Brett Murray's depiction of Zuma in Stalinist pose with exposed genitals, later on the 'liberal constitutionalists', and later still on the EFF as 'proto-fascist', 'neo-fascist', 'demagogic' and 'bourgeois-nationalist'. The president of Numsa described the SACP as no longer the voice of the working class, but rather the 'megaphones of ANC neoliberal policies'.[36] Indications of some reconsideration of support for Zuma followed in a 2015 SACP discussion document that questioned the party's wisdom in putting all its eggs in the Zuma basket.[37]

Cosatu had endorsed the post-Polokwane order conditionally at the time of conception, and subsequently fractured over Zuma's leadership.[38] Many Cosatu members sided with Numsa and backed a left-labour split from Cosatu, strategising towards a left political party in the absence of capturing Cosatu. At stake were policy and ideological issues, plus (and especially) the Zuma project to nullify voices that oppose the president. It was, however, not going to be a clean break; several affiliate unions were divided. Cosatu's former secretary general, Zwelinzima Vavi, Numsa and the budding United Front became prime targets, through their outspokenness against Zuma and his policy-ideology

133

compromises, for marginalisation from the pro-Zuma sanitised Cosatu. The battle for ownership of Cosatu continued but swayed towards Cosatu's Zuma-ists.

The 'second (radical) phase of the transition'

The Tripartite Alliance divisions and the Zuma faction's ideological obfuscation led to the ANC's 'second transition' turned 'second phase of the transition' documents of 2012.[39] These documents, entangled in arguments for Zuma's second term, sealed the ANC's economic policy of the period and set the foundations for projecting all that is happening in the Zuma regime's policy world as radical and unquestioningly part of the evolving, phased revolution.[40] The ANC's December 2012 confirmation of the resolutions revealed much about the character of the ANC at the time of the Mangaung conference and the expulsion of Julius Malema and his ANCYL group.[41] The ANC's ideas to guarantee a better life for more *in the foreseeable future* were concretised through this document. The 2012 planners argued that a second term for Zuma was necessary for realisation of the first term's promises. The 'Lula moment' was the 2012 pre-Mangaung Zuma-ist vessel to carry the factional belief that Zuma was the 'good president' who had just been too busy during his first term to make good on his Polokwane promises.[42] The policy conference's formulations first promised turnarounds to the national democratic society in the thirty- to fifty-year term. Later, the compromise posed twenty years as realistic. The final announcement of the resolutions was silent on the delivery date.

The fact that this debate hinged on whether transformation was to be carried out in a 'transition' or a 'phase' within a transition illustrates the often farcical nature of the National Democratic Revolution (NDR) discourse and its stages.[43] At the policy conference the great debate was about proclaiming the second phase of the transition to a national democratic society, instead of the NDR's second transition (the latter in line with Marxist proclamations of two sequential transitions, the political and the economic). By then the die was cast for new moderation. The NDP was already a *de facto* presence. The defeat of the 'two Marxist revolutions' was an admission that the ANC's revolutionary rhetoric was aspirational rather than real-world.

Subsequently, ANC KwaZulu-Natal chairperson Senzo Mchunu used revolution-speak to mobilise for Election 2014, claiming that 'we are facing the challenge of defending our national revolution'. This 'threat and defend' narrative became one of the trademarks of the Zuma regime. More sedately, the SACP's 2014 post-election statement hoped that the 'radical second phase of our democratic revolution [will be] pursued with greater rigour'.[44] It contained more emphasis on explicit radical rhetoric. Ingredients of this radical quest were listed as state intervention in the economy to ensure job creation, re-industrialisation, greater beneficiation of natural resources, a sustained public sector-led infrastructure programme, salary and wage policies that ensure greater equality, land reform that focuses on sustainable livelihoods, and corruption to be tackled in line with commitments in the shared ANC election manifesto.

Workmanlike definitions of 'radical' appear in the NDP document and the ANC government's 2014 Medium Term Strategic Framework (MTSF). In the NDP's executive summary, 'radical' emerges as 'radically improved government performance'. The MTSF notes that the 'NDP provides the framework for achieving the radical socioeconomic agenda set out in the governing party's election manifesto' and then posits a series of points that would fit in positions all over the ideological spectrum:

> Government's programme of radical economic transformation is about placing the economy on a qualitatively different path that ensures more rapid, sustainable growth, higher investment, increased employment, reduced inequality and deracialisation of the economy. The NDP sets an annual growth target of above 5 per cent by 2030 and emphasises measures to ensure that the benefits of growth are equitably shared.[45]

In this style, Mondli Makhanya suggests, there will be emphasis on a more activist and interventionist state.[46] Ministers in the economic cluster are likely to be vocal about business issues, black empowerment, employment equity and land redistribution – not directly interventionist but putting pressure and seen to be doing so. An illustration in the field of equity was in the enactment of regulations to support implementation and enforcement of the Employment Equity Act: the regulations were stricter, fines higher, policing tighter and escape clauses substantially reduced.[47]

Amid public debate on exactly where and how much of the 'radical' in the ANC's policy regime is to be found, the SACP increasingly tried to step in and show that it bequeaths the radical in the ANC policy repertoire. By 2014, the SACP took the liberty to insert 'radical' into the assumed blank spaces in the 2012 resolutions of the ANC's 53rd national conference. The SACP's 'Going to the root' discussion document[48] aspires to inform the move to the second radical phase [not 'stage'] of the National Democratic Revolution. In order to help get its government project in shape it needs to support the NDP.

Speaking in radical tongue

Zuma's use of the term 'radical' in a series of ANC and government engagements illustrates the added use (but watering down of) 'radical' in his ANC, and 2014 was a good year for clarifications. In the ANC's January 2014 anniversary statement 'radical' was linked to 'the economic emancipation of our people', which might still allude to radical ideology. When Zuma moves into government events the tune alters. In explanation of his February 2014 State of the Nation address Zuma argued that South Africa would enter 'a new radical phase in which we shall implement the second transition policies and programmes that will meaningfully address poverty, unemployment and inequality'. This may or may not have left ideological connotations.

At the start of the second Zuma administration the ANC revived the 2012 national policy conference wording on the second phase of the transition. In his inaugural speech Zuma announced that South Africa was entering that second phase – as had been announced two years before as well. In his 2014 mid-year State of the Nation address Zuma used 'radical' only to characterise the far-reaching scope of change envisioned – equally possible in radical and reactionary systems: 'The journey towards prosperity and job-creation generally involves radical change in the manner in which we undertake planning, implementation and monitoring ...' He also used it in relation to the second phase of the transition: 'As we enter the second phase of our transition from apartheid to a national democratic society, we have to embark on radical socioeconomic transformation to push back the triple challenges [of poverty, unemployment and inequality]. Change will not come without some far-reaching interventions.'

The ministers in the same debate demonstrated how to use 'radical' repeatedly and thoroughly removed from ideology. In delivering their departmental budget statements many assured the president of how they are following his inspirational lead by articulating the 'radical' in their policies. When Edna Molewa used 'radical' in relation to environmental affairs, it was about dramatically transforming towards managerialism. Basic Education's Angie Motshega proclaimed that '(t)he time for radical transformation has come' and 'as we embark on this radical transformation, both the NDP and the ANC manifesto will guide our programmes' (there was nothing ideologically radical to her educational plans). When Economic Development's Ebrahim Patel ventured into the radicalism minefield he was explicit, albeit 'radical' only in the sense of government's getting together a particular economic development act, prioritising an 'economic transformation' agenda that it calls radical, comprising infrastructure, industrialisation, investment and innovation, inclusion and integration. Patel was driving the Presidential Infrastructure Coordinating Commission (PICC). Similarly, in his 19 February 2015 response to the debate over the State of the Nation address Zuma made two non-radical references to 'radical': 'We have called for radical economic transformation' (in racially transforming the Johannesburg Stock Exchange) and 'radical transition from colonialism of a special type to a national democratic society'. There was not even an allusion to 'radical' when President Zuma delivered his mid-year State of the Nation address implementation update in Pretoria in August 2015.

CONSENSUS WITHOUT NDP POLICE

The NDP is a remarkable story of the emergence of ANC grand policy – a long-term policy framework – in the time of Zuma. As South Africa moves well into the third decade of ANC rule the heights of NDP contestation might have been eclipsed. The NDP story nevertheless remains instructive in how the ANC handles issues of macropolicy and 'policy certainty'. There were appointments and consultative processes[49] that unfolded along with an ideological contest – and shift – in the heart of the Zuma-ANC. The plan originated with the Zuma group; after the 2009 election they aspired to show that they could do policy planning (in effect, consolidate previous policy planning), and do it with better transformation results than the Mbeki-ists. The expectation was the leftward shift that Zuma had promised upon becoming ANC president. In the period that followed, Manuel was legitimated as the National Planning Commission (NPC) chairperson – against the odds, given that he was the Zuma-ists' detested Mbeki-Gear man. Relative NDP consensus emerged. Yet argument over the plan's economy section continued, in both the ANC and Cosatu.

The ANC's doublespeak on the NDP matches the radical-speak, neoliberal-do in its general world of policy. On the one hand it broadcasts the NDP as its policy vision and guiding document. On the other hand, it keeps opponents of the NDP on board – for example, via a task team to 'resolve differences'.

Three levels of NDP dialogue dominated the ensuing period. One was that the plan is work in progress and merely the broad vision. This was gradually matched and then surpassed by the narrative of 'this *is* the policy framework' and 'there is policy certainty in South Africa'. There was little evidence of 'left' in the NDP – the radical narrative became the cotton wool in which it had to be packaged. Next, around 2015 there appeared increasing suppression of the NDP chronicles, a time in which explicit NDP debate was effectively replaced with 'all that is happening in the policy and governance world is implementation of the NDP'.[50]

The ANC wanted to get its acceptance of the NDP on record, and in August 2012 Cabinet endorsed the NDP well before the Mangaung national conference could do the policy-making honours. There was a rush to show rating agencies and investors that there is policy certainty in South Africa. The Zuma-ists campaigned for a second term for Zuma on the platform that it would be the 'Lula moment'. In contrast, the ANC's 2012 national conference and Zuma's Cabinet, in their acceptance of the NDP, showed that the second term was *not to be* a Lula moment. Mangaung delegates, uninterested in policy matters after having cast their ballots for the leadership election, endorsed rather than revolted against a policy framework that was contentious, before and after Mangaung.

The ANC in Mangaung was ambiguous in endorsing the NDP. The conference declaration stated 'we embraced the NDP as a platform for united action by all South Africans … an important basis for the development of a long-term plan'.[51] Yet a contrasting economic transformation resolution had it that the 'NDP is a living and dynamic document and articulates a vision broadly in line with our objective … [the] ANC will continue to engage with the plan'.[52] Cosatu's Neil Coleman argued that the economic section of the NDP needed redrafting. The pre-conference ANC policy discussion documents had been vetted for approximate convergence with the NDP. Aspects of the documents were also tweaked in relation to controversial Reserve Bank and Constitution statements after more contentious versions had been leaked prior to the conference.[53] Three years later, in the aftermath of its 2015 special national congress, Cosatu, through its president S'bu Dlamini, *still* argued that the economic chapter needs revision!

Several 2013 clampdowns on contests around and criticisms of the NDP suggested a potential collision track. However, the ANC was quick to deny that NDP policing was happening.[54] The SACP's Cronin[55] was critical, and encouraged further engagement on the document, in line with a September 2013 Tripartite Alliance statement. Trevor Manuel, having led the development of the NDP, took a cautious approach to the ANC's endorsement and remembered to insert the word 'radical':[56] the NDP 'commits the ANC to a radical programme of economic transformation aimed at growing the economy faster and in a more inclusive manner. It commits the ANC to seek collaboration with other social partners in pursuit of the ANC's long-term objectives.'

A glossed-over NDP consensus followed, in line with the Mangaung decisions. It appeared, largely through the pressure on government, to be seen as investor-friendly, stable and predictable on policy. 'Regulatory certainty' had to be asserted. The National Development Plan was preferred over the New Growth Path,[57] but the policy compromise seekers stressed that the NGP was part of the realisation of the NDP goals.

From 2013 onwards, the ANC took the NDP as basic point of departure for all policy action. In the medium-term budget statement of October 2013 the minister of finance stated that this budget statement and all future budget statements would be 'the accounts' of the NDP. Multiple subsequent statements, including the State of the Nation addresses of 2014 and 2015 and the ANC's 2014 election manifesto, declared that the NDP was *it*. The 2014 Medium Term Strategic Framework stated that the 'electoral mandate of the fifth democratic government is to deepen transformation and implement the National Development Plan'.[58] ANC Secretary General Mantashe reminded Cosatu at one stage that it was failing to defend the ANC against 'the liberal offensive' against the NDP. NDP enforcement also followed with Cosatu's effort to punish general secretary Zwelinzima Vavi for his criticism of it – Vavi had suggested, for example, that the workers are expected to be the self-sacrificial 'bacon' in the NDP breakfast.[59]

The ANC commitments were renewed in the wake of serial ratings agency downgrades.[60] The pressures emanating from the ANC for everyone to endorse the NDP as Zuma's signature policy statement overwhelmed critical reflection. The strategy paid off largely, despite the contradictions. In November 2014, for example, Moody's did a further downgrade (due to poor medium-term growth prospects and prospects of further rises in the government debt-to-GDP ratio) but with a stable instead of negative outlook (to reward policy makers' 'commitment to reining in government debt growth over the medium term and the broad political support for the NDP, tighter monetary policy and fiscal restraint').[61]

There were phases of critical reflection, followed by the advocacy of (relatively) radical (and sometimes more workerist and/or working-class) options. A cyclical pattern shows. The conservative resolution of the complex debate is followed by a phase of nationalist mobilisation to legitimise the compromise, probably in the name of radicalism, which all then tapers off as the unresolved issues (of the previous solution) push to the surface again.

POLICY CENTRALISM AND PRESIDENTIAL RULE

With radical-speak from leaders who talk revolution but come across as narrowly capitalist experts in self-advancing business, the Zuma epoch is the time of an ANC with leaders who affirm and follow their president – and these are obviously acts that have policy implications. Those who refuse to do so get purged, as happened in the case of rebels within Cosatu. The ANC of 2014–2015 is structured around personalised presidential rule, a system that includes Luthuli House monitoring members and putting a premium on conformity and deference to ambiguous leadership – and, to some extent, also on policy conformity. Zuma is obviously affluent, well-remunerated and with ample official presidential benefits (his presidential salary also rates among the highest in international stakes), along with extensive business interests,[62] and does not see (or acknowledge seeing) anything wrong in accumulating additional wealth. Little is known about the president's directly benefiting from leveraging his own position, but ample 'beneficiation' has enfolded many of his family members. The wealth has come his way substantially through using his top political status for business opportunities to family members (and indirectly also to him).

The ANC implements pro-elite, nationalist pro-black business enhancement policies and programmes and has put substantial effort into such transformative policy work. The legislative framework for broad-based BEE (BBBEE) nests in the Broad-Based Black Economic Empowerment Act No. 46 of 2013, the Department of Trade and Industry's BBBEE strategy document ('South Africa's Economic Transformation: A Strategy for Broad-Based Black Economic Empowerment'), and the BBBEE Codes of Good Practice of 2007, along with the Amended BBBEE Codes of Good Practice of 2013 (effective from 1 May 2015). The revised BEE points-earning formula for tenders was announced in mid-2015, yet was rapidly withdrawn when the 'broad-based' component was judged to have been scrapped and the industry revolted.[63] In addition there is the Employment Equity Act, Skills Development Act, Skills Development Levies Act, Preferential Procurement Policy Framework Act, National Small Business Act and National Small Business Amendment Act.

While the ANC does deft footwork to project itself as revolutionary, middle class growth is a centrepiece of the evolving and normalising society. The ANC also includes these middle classes as part of its motive forces for change. The black business lobby is successful and has the ear of government. At election time many in the recently empowered classes rise politically, bask in the glory of being rich alongside the ANC leaders, contribute to campaigns and flaunt their partnerships with the ANC government.[64] The ANC relies on business practitioners' longer-term contribution through enterprise and industrial development to bring higher economic growth and job creation to South Africa, to the extent that it is materialising. In the words of Gauteng ANC leader Paul Mashatile,[65] a particular Gauteng ANC congress resolution makes it clear that 'we want the benefit to accrue to all … (T)he elite … must create employment, must bring change in life as the economy grows. The middle class has grown from two million in 1994 to six million in 2014. This is our achievement.' Large proportions of the new middle classes, however, are state employees and, by definition, are rent-seekers rather than value-producers. Others are both: ANC and government leaders by now also own farms, mines and multiple businesses of note.[66] These corrections of the racial character of the middle classes[67] have arisen through honourable work (even if it is over and above their work as public representatives), and through connections into tenders and other state contracts. The ANC and its supporters are not unique in undergoing this change – it is the ANC's attachment of the radical label to the process that provokes censure.

The Zuma faction has learned that public sector corruption undermines its credibility and thus speaks anti-corruption – for example, in the ANC's Mangaung conference. However, it then soft-pedals on implementation and sidesteps the question in the debates on whether both future and current leaders will be subjected to discipline.[68] Mangaung undertook strict anti-corruption action, *inter alia* by means of integrity commissions at all levels of the movement, with powers to dismiss members or public servants linked to the ANC.[69]

Overall, the ANC creates unconvincing impressions of determination to stamp out corruption.[70] Up to 2014–2015 there had been only a modest number of disciplinary interventions. Loopholes abound. For instance, in the appointment of the government executive, elected politicians and deployed civil service functionaries go through the rituals of declaring financial interests. Declaration does not mean that the cadre will be prevented from entering into deals; it may simply mean that those who consider the bid will take note and probably condone the transaction, sometimes happy to please the comrade by awarding the bid to him or her.[71] Directors general and a mass of other civil servants often do not declare.[72] Local government is rife with blatant 'insider trading'.[73] Level of compliance in the civil service does improve, however, even if it is often not a meaningful action *per se* to have declared. The ANC's May 2015 NEC meeting recognised corruption as an issue that turns voters against the ANC.[74]

The Public Service Commission (PSC)[75] reported that in mid-May 2014, 97 per cent of the 4043 senior managers at provincial level and 77 per cent of the 5777 at national level had submitted declaration forms. The 2014–2019 Medium Term Strategic Framework records that government 'will focus on limiting the scope for conflicts of interest by prohibiting public servants and public representatives from doing business with the state as well as ensuring transparency in public expenditure and contractual relations with the business sector', adding that the 'capacity to investigate and prosecute corruption cases will also be improved, from both a disciplinary and criminal perspective'.[76] Undertakings of this nature have circulated since the early days of the Mbeki administration, without much effect. Political principals are either afraid that action will alienate their followers or are thoroughly enjoying the fruits of inaction themselves.

Parliament, policy and presidentialism

The ANC in Parliament has wanted to guard the level and type of exposure to interrogation that the president may undergo. 'Radical and revolutionary' are in the distant background when it comes to this process – as in much of ANC deliberations in Parliament generally. Instead, ANC parliamentarians' driving force is their president's right to accumulate non-security, publicly funded upgrades to his Nkandla residence. This became taxing on the ANC during the EFF's presence in Parliament, conducting its campaign for President Zuma to 'pay back the money' (in line with what the public protector had recommended in 'Secure in Comfort'). The ANC blamed parliamentary questioning of the president on the 'hooliganism and insult' that had become rife in Parliament. In reaction to the EFF's insistence that Zuma answer their questions, the ANC promised to turn to Izimbizo processes to engage with the people, sidelining Parliament to safeguard its president. The NEC connected this protection to 'the revolution':

> Any revolution is about people and people need ongoing attention so that the revolution is not derailed. Political consciousness is a function of the ongoing work being done among the people. This will include organising and mobilising all strata of society. The emergence of a right-wing coalition among political parties is one of convenience and is brought together only by their common animosity towards the ANC. Their only intention is to derail the revolution, and therefore qualifies to be called a counter-revolutionary coalition …

It is this reality that informed the decision that in order to account to our people, the ANC should continue to rely more on direct contact with them in Izimbizo. The ANC has a revolutionary duty to defend itself, the revolution and democracy. Similarly, Parliament has a duty to protect its dignity and integrity and thus be less tolerant of deviant behaviour. Parliament cannot be a battleground. Its members have been elected by voters and thus carry their hopes and aspirations for progressive and constructive engagement.[77]

This was a mark of historical note for the ANC. Opposition parties in Parliament asking uncomfortable questions which embarrass the ANC do not get answers but will be designated as enemies of the revolution. The ANC statement neglected the fact that the ANC's 2014 election strategists had a massive task to ensure public appearances for President Zuma in places where he could be assured he would not be booed. The 'protected president' could not be safeguarded in Parliament or in the communities, but this changed partially in 2015 when the ANC used force in the form of 'white shirt' special forces to 'restore order' in Parliament and the President started doing policy reports from the bunkers of the Union Buildings.

Kingpin of nuclear policy-making

Parliamentary committee events in October 2014 illustrated another dimension of presidential rule over Parliament. ANC parliamentarians set substantive policy direction in pursuance of apparent wishes of the president, did so without asking questions, and handed over responsibility to the state bureaucracy. It demonstrated that for ANC MPs the president's word is often policy, and that the executive makes policy – nuclear in this instance – allowing Parliament to enter and add elements to the policy. While considering the Department of Energy's 2014–2015 budget, the ANC committee majority wanted to add to the committee report that the committee 'reconfirms nuclear as its supply-side solution to meet environmental and macroeconomic development objectives'.[78] The DA pointed out that the government's energy master plan, the Integrated Resource Plan (IRP) 2011, updated in 2013, had downgraded projected reliance on nuclear, coal and wind technologies while increasing solar photovoltaic and gas. This meant that the nuclear programme should have been delayed until a proper financial framework and economic controls had been in place. Government promotes its 'Nuclear New Build Programme' as premised on the

143

Nuclear Energy Policy of 2008, the Nuclear Energy Act 46 of 1999 and the IRP adopted in 2011.

The IRP contrasts with the 2014–2015 'intergovernmental framework agreements' that government entered into with Russia, France, China and others, with suspicions that the Russian 'framework' was in fact a done deal.[79] The *Mail & Guardian* remarked: 'Zuma is now firmly directing what is expected to be the largest, most complex tender process in South African history. At stake is the development of new nuclear power plants, potentially worth up to a trillion rands.'[80] Zuma signed the Russian version of nuclear cooperation agreements with state-owned nuclear company Rosatom, in a meeting in Russia that only Zuma attended. None of the usual accompanying officials was present. The Russians implied that a deal had been reached for the procurement of eight nuclear reactors.[81] South Africa's nuclear authorities subsequently did a full vendor parade of potential nuclear partners.

There had been semi-clandestine sequences of creating decision-making structures on nuclear policy. It appeared as an ever-tightening circle with growing centralisation around Zuma. Shreds of evidence of the processes involved arose after media exposés, which were then followed by, for example, statements from the Presidency or brief references in presidential speeches. To illustrate the shifts in locus of decision making by stealth, in November 2011 Cabinet approved the establishment of the National Nuclear Energy Executive Coordination Committee (NNEECC) to implement a phased decision-making approach to the nuclear programme. It was a Cabinet committee, and the minutes of Cabinet and substructure meetings are not available to the public. Cabinet further approved the establishment of the nuclear energy technical committee to support the NNEECC. No details of its composition were announced. In his July 2014 budget vote speech the president announced the Cabinet Energy Security Subcommittee, created out of the NNEECC. This was a smaller committee than the NNEECC to 'strengthen its efficiency' in decision making, and oversee and achieve the development of an energy mix that includes nuclear, coal, gas, solar, wind and hydro. Zuma assumed the position of committee chair.[82] Glimpses into the committee's operations and decisions were few and far between.

Besides the fact that huge amounts of nuclear were not part of the agreed understanding regarding the unfolding energy mix, no funding mechanisms or frameworks were specified – apart from departmental claims that such planning exists. A few months before the May 2015 announcement that government would start procuring nuclear power by July 2015, and have a successful bidder by year end, the Treasury still maintained that it had not calculated the cost of the Department of Energy's politically driven new nuclear plants,[83] and did not know whether they were affordable. In a July 2015 briefing the Department of Energy's deputy director general, Zizamele Mbambo, claimed that the department had completed the financing model and the technical studies 'strengthened our case to proceed'. He admitted that government still had to negotiate the price tag, something that would happen in the course of the procurement process. Zuma confirmed in August 2015 that the procurement process was to be concluded within the financial year.

It emerged that government was aiming at spending an estimated US$85 billion on a nuclear energy programme that would add 9 600 megawatts to South Africa's embattled energy grid by 2030. There are comparative analyses of cases of dismal international nuclear funding, cost-setting and timely delivery issues which lead to the conclusion that South Africa might be on a wild nuclear goose-chase.[84] In addition, the announcement on pending procurement came notwithstanding the dated IRP and lack of clarity on whether South Africa would require the mooted 9 600MW of nuclear power, given the other anticipated expansions.

As in many other cases of policy making, the ANC MPs did not interrogate these announcements and actions because their president and a set of Cabinet members (largely NEC members and also their political superiors) were in charge.

VARIATIONS ON NON-RADICALISM – MINING, LAND AND JOBS

The ANC in government readily produces evidence (and presents the statistics) that it is working for the people.[85] Much of the state is at work, and projects get implemented, although often with substantial delays, with trickle-down instead of bursts of delivery, and with few guarantees that the outcomes will match the original plans. The president's State of the Nation addresses excel at using dipstick cases as evidence of national progress on policy issues. The ANC is good at ensuring a sense of motion on core issues, even if it is through well-profiled consultations or breakfast briefings, task teams or interministerial committees. The ANC's late 2014 consultations on stopping farmworker evictions and a minimum wage for workers were cases in point.[86]

ANC tongues when it comes to 'radical' policy and government plans are illustrated in the nationalisation of land and mineral resources. In the ANC, at best and as this chapter has been illustrating, 'radical' is used to designate far-reaching change. Hence 'radical' was in the title of the Gauteng ANC policy documents for its September 2014 conference, but the content was short on radical substance.[87] The Gauteng ANC tried to take the lead and push for higher levels of mine ownership to formerly disadvantaged South Africans, arguing that the mining charter's 26 per cent black ownership should go up to 49 per cent.[88] State ownership should be established on the basis of the state buying in; the state bank should assist, and the Public Investment Corporation (PIC) would hold shares, along with private investors. Accentuated BEE has emerged as the bottom line. It entails far-reaching racial restructuring of business, but contains little radicalism unless changing the racial face of the business class is denoted as radical.

On the transformative, gradualist path, mining companies had been making some progress in implementation of the mining charter.[89] Empowerment schemes were being put in place; others were progressing slowly towards converted and humane housing conditions. In his June 2014 State of the Nation address President Zuma availed a committee under his guidance to drive the implementation of the charter – some low-lying fruits were in sight.

Land reform, redistribution and the mirage of 'radical'

The story of land and radical transformation in South Africa illustrates the contradictions between the NDP and radical. The land reform-redistribution process evolved in the time of the Zuma administration through the Green Paper on Land Reform of 2011,[90] and a series of policy and programmatic interventions.[91] It was a slow and frustrating process, with some progress and good intentions,[92] although again definitively not radical.

In 2014, land affairs minister Gugile Nkwinti evoked radical expectations (fears, for some) when he proposed that existing white farmers split their farms and farming assets in half and let their workers have half (the 50/50 proposal). Richard Calland at the time reported that the NPC informed the minister in the Presidency (Radebe, by then also NPC chairperson) about the land affairs minister diverging from the NDP.[93] This had cast doubt on the NDP as a united vision and programme of action.[94] The unfolding story is illuminating: Radebe contacted Mantashe; Nkwinti was summoned to Luthuli House, told to get in line; Radebe issued 'clarificatory statements'; and 'Nkwinti met with the big farmers to assuage their fears'. Nkwinti subsequently appeared at an AgriSA summit, appeasing farmers:

> When we published the 50/50 proposal, the very first call I got on a
> Sunday morning was from the secretary general of the ANC Gwede
> Mantashe. He said 'I have bought myself a farm for R2m and now you
> want to nationalise R1m' … In South Africa it's not going to work. Even
> as we say the 50/50 [proposal], farmers say 'we don't agree'. They say 'no,
> it's wrong' … They say it's unconstitutional, and they are right. That is the
> beauty of our country. Our country is a constitutional democracy …[95]

As a compromise measure the proposal went ahead tentatively with pilot studies and voluntary participation by farm owners. President Zuma announced
that by 2019 government would conduct fifty pilots on the policy, now called
'Strengthening the relative rights of people working the land', or the 50/50
Policy Framework.[96] Beyond the 50/50 intervention various discussions, briefings and debates on the proposal continued, yet had the status of consultations.
This showed that the ANC government was using an extended public engagement space to play for time on how radical (or not) its land policies would be.

The policy formulations of 2012 on the redistribution of land and nationalisation of mines were rhetorically promising even if substantively showing much of the BEE *status quo* (BEE was promising to many in the national
bourgeoisie even if not to a broader segment of the population, except in an
aspirational sense). Nationalisation of the mines – in addition to the more conventional meanings – in South African policy phraseology could well entail that
empowerment-operations-gone-wrong in the minerals industry could be res-
cued, or that the state should own 51 per cent that would be farmed out for management by an expanded class of patriotic capital. Right-wing and neoliberal
lobbies, such as the Solidarity Research Institute (SRI) and the South African
Institute of Race Relations (SAIRR), nevertheless managed to see and scorn
what they saw as the highly radical nature of the NDP.[97]

ANC policy formulations show distinct restitutive and nationalist (as
opposed to nationalisation) orientations, which impeded business autonomy,
and again were hardly 'radical'. The SAIRR refers to existing and proposed
legislation to make foreign-owned security companies transfer 52 per cent of
ownership to South Africans, and the proposals that the state will be entitled
to acquire up to 100 per cent of new oil exploration and production operations
(20 per cent free and a potential further 80 per cent at a price that government will concede). Distinct possibilities for elite beneficiation arise from these
proposals. Resource nationalism and beneficiation of the middle classes are

supreme. This was in line with Malusi Gigaba's announcement that the 2014 election had given the ANC the mandate to 'radically' boost black business as a way to eliminate perceptions of continued social and economic injustice.[98]

Policy on land reform and redistribution wavers, and touches on radical suggestions, yet with limited follow-through. Much attention goes into rural development plans and strategies (of which land is but one dimension). Yet land reform is allowed to continue on a chequered path. Ruth Hall argues that this has amounted to policy not being effected. The Proactive Land Acquisition Strategy of 2011 entailed government buying land, retaining ownership and leasing it rather than transferring it to beneficiaries. This is a recipe for the elite to take over, despite framing of the initiative as radicalisation:[99]

> Smallholder farmers and the rural poor are often named as key beneficiaries. This populist discourse masks the reality that under the Zuma administration the rural poor and small-scale farmers have not been the main beneficiaries of land redistribution; rather those who are able to comply with the government's requirement of 'production discipline' are an elite, often urban, who have incomes to invest in commercial farming – rather than farmworkers or the 2.5 million households farming in the communal areas of the former Bantustans.[100]

The objective of the 2014 Restitution of Land Rights Amendment Bill is to reopen the period for lodging claims.[101] Parliament heard that an estimated 397 000 valid claims might be lodged upon enactment (in 2014 there were still close to 30 000 outstanding claims, lodged up to 1998, with 77 610 settled at a total cost of R29.3bn).[102] There would still be substantial settlement costs for the remainder (up to R20bn estimated), the new window carrying an estimated cost of R180bn.[103] By April 2015, according to Nkwinti, about 56 000 new claims had been lodged. In a 2015 EFF written parliamentary question as to where government would find the budget to fund the proposals, the minister of land affairs responded abruptly: 'From the fiscus'. Aninka Claassens[104] argues that government has neither the funds nor the capacity to implement the promise. She stresses the extent to which traditional leaders will be advantaged in the process, recalling that in February 2014 Zuma opened the House of Traditional Leaders and advised them to 'put together their resources' to file restitution claims:

> Restitution was intended to undo the boundaries of the former bantustans, but the government seems to have changed tack since 2004. New laws

re-entrench those boundaries and this bill will be used to bolster the power of traditional leaders at the expense of those who were actually removed. This is exactly the opposite of what was envisaged when the Restitution of Land Rights Act was passed to a standing ovation in Parliament in 1994.

In Zuma's corresponding 2015 speech he urged traditional leaders to hire lawyers jointly to handle their land claims. The Centre for Law and Society (CLS) observed that the president's remarks framed the failure of land restitution as a consequence of communities being unable to afford lawyers to help them claim land, and traditional leaders not claiming land on behalf of communities. Zuma had told the traditional leaders in off-text remarks: 'You should be charging people that are not farming … the land should be taken from people that are not using it productively and be given to those that are diligent.'[105] The CLS pointed out that the remarks accentuate the president's doublespeak: amid the closed dialogue (excluding communities) on land reform between government and traditional leaders there is the exclusion of interests of the communities.[106] It also notes the president's failure to acknowledge the experiences of communities (and in particular women) in living under autocratic traditional leader rule. In addition, President Zuma and ANC ministers concerned with land affairs disregarded the fact that the national budgetary allocation for the land reform programme had been slowly decreasing, while the costs of the land restitution programme were due to rise exponentially.[107]

Research shows that it is black descendants of the groups that bought the land prior to the 1913 Land Act who are now being dispossessed by the traditional leaders converting indigenous land rights into leasehold. Some of these leaders were working with mining companies to claim and explore mineral resources in former bantustan areas. In 2013 the Constitutional Court struck down interdicts preventing one such traditional leader from being called to order.[108]

Jobs and elusive liberation

The greatest policy and transformation failure in democratic South Africa has been government's incapacity to create sufficient jobs – or to generate a level of economic growth that will trigger the necessary jobs – to absorb new entrants into the labour market. Authors such as JP Landman,[109] along with the ANC, point out that more South Africans than ever before are in employment. However, the proportion that was unemployed is stubbornly dismal – for 2014 generally above 25 per cent (although 24.3 in the seasonally good fourth quarter). The rate again rose to 26.4 per cent annualised in the first quarter of 2015. These figures represent the narrow unemployment rate (excluding those who have not been actively looking for work). At this time the economically active working-age population is 21 million, of which 5.5 million are unemployed. With inclusion of the discouraged work seekers (2.4 million) the expanded unemployment rate reached 36.1 per cent (up by 1.5 percentage points). These unemployment rates were South Africa's highest in eleven years. President Zuma, for his first administration and in the context of global economic crisis, had promised to create 4 million jobs – only 1.4 million materialised. (Between 2003 and 2008 the Mbeki administration had created 1.9 million jobs, albeit before the global recession set in.) By 2014 the one million jobs lost during the recession had been recovered, and were exceeded by 300 000, but the unemployment rate did not budge. Zuma's words at the official twenty years of democracy celebration demonstrated the struggle for the ANC to keep alive hope for higher levels of employment – and hinted at the odds against the ANC adding new working-class support: 'Over the past twenty years employment, both formal and informal, has grown by around 5.6 million people, which is far faster than it was the case previously. More work however still needs to be done to expand the capacity of our economy to absorb more people, especially the youth.'[110]

Slow economic grow means that not enough jobs are being created to employ the annual increased numbers of labour market entrants. The South African population had grown to an estimated 51 million in 2012 and was in excess of 53 million in 2014. The Presidency's figures on South Africa's economically active population show that the number of employed grew by 5.7 million from 1994 to 2013. In the same period, the number of unemployed, discouraged and economically inactive grew by 5.4 million. This reflects a virtual stalemate, also evident in the quarterly labour force survey statistics: unemployment rates remain consistently high and promises of job creation that exceeds population growth and labour market entrance have come to nil. For many millions of South Africans the 'revolution' and the 'radical' policy tags mean little.

THE 'GOOD STORY' IS NOT THE END OF THE STORY

A government five-year self-assessment stated that the ANC government had been failing against the five-year objectives it had set for itself in 2009. The 'Close-out Report on the Implementation of Government Priorities for 2009–2014'[111] was tabled before a Cabinet lekgotla. It assesses ANC performance over the five years of Zuma's first term, in contrast to the Presidency's twenty-year report. The government's five-year view pointed out failures in fighting corruption, creating decent work and rural development. This report articulated with the details in comparable reports.

The ANC's successes over the first twenty years of democracy are recorded extensively, especially in the Presidency's 'Twenty Year Review: South Africa, 1994–2014'. The realisations show why South Africans can unambiguously concur that the ANC government has changed the face of the country. The failures that are recognised in the five-year period, the twenty-year Presidency report and the Goldman Sachs report[112] shed light on the extent of transformation *not achieved*, and whether the label of 'radical' could even be assigned in the sense of far-reaching contemporary ANC policy:

- Government corruption: The government five-year report observes that only a small number of the people with assets gained from corruption had been prosecuted. Inadequately skilled investigators contributed to the low success rate. It also notes that suspects tend to remain in office after having been charged. Goldman Sachs, in a general opinion on the public sector, asserts that performance leaves much to be desired – in the internal management performance and assessment tool (of the Department of Performance Monitoring and Evaluation in the Presidency) assessment, 60 per cent of government departments fail on accountability and 73 per cent on human resource management.

- Inequality: Goldman Sachs reports that in 1994 altogether 40 per cent (15.8m) of the population lived on less than US$2 per day compared with 31.3 per cent (16.6m) in 2013. The World Bank stresses that fiscal policies have elevated 3.6 million South Africans out of poverty (in this instance defined as a paltry R750 per month). South Africa's Gini coefficient, however, remains high – and higher than that of 'rival' Brazil. It was at a peak of 0.72 in 2006 and went marginally down to 0.69 in 2011 according to Goldman Sachs, or in 2005 according to the Presidency. The Presidency cites 0.65 as the Gini coefficient for 2010–2011 (compared with Brazil's 0.55, according to Sachs for 2011; the 2012 NDP gave it as 0.69). Further 2010 statistical manipulations showed that starting with a general Gini of 0.70 it goes down to 0.65 if social grants to the poorest of society are fed into the equation (this is probably how the Presidency derived its figure). If free services, water, electricity and sanitation are added, the Gini goes down to 0.61. Finally, if progressive income tax is added, the Gini emerges as 0.59. The 2013 Gini without manipulations was 0.70.[113]

As Statistics SA notes, albeit with setbacks only seen as globally caused:[114]

> Poverty levels in the country have dropped since 2006, reaching a low of 45.5 per cent in 2011 when applying the upper-bound poverty line ... this translates into roughly 23 million people living below the upper-bound poverty line. When one looks at extreme poverty, defined as those living below the food poverty line, we can see the dramatic impact the global financial crisis of 2008–2009 has had on the livelihoods of South Africa's poorest. The number of people living below the food line increased to 15.8 million in 2009 from 12.6 million in 2006, before dropping to 10.2 million people in 2011. Despite this adverse impact of the financial crisis, poverty levels did noticeably improve according to 2011 estimates. This was driven by a combination of factors ranging from a growing social safety net, income growth, above inflation wage increases, decelerating inflationary pressure and an expansion of credit.

- Poverty versus middle class: Poverty remained at haunting levels (see Table 4.1), even if general indicators show notable growth in the middle classes. The number of people dependent on social grants increased. In the decade 2002–2012 the percentage grew from 12.7 to 29.6. The Eastern Cape at 40.3 per cent in 2012 was the province with the highest household dependence on social grants, followed by Limpopo at 37.7 and KwaZulu-Natal at 36.1 per cent.[115] In the nine years from 2004 to 2013 the size of the black middle class grew from 1.7 to 4.2 million. These figures are anchored in a University of Cape Town study[116] that takes middle class as households earning between R15 000 and R50 000 per month, with their own transport, a tertiary education, employment in a white-collar job, and owning their home or spending more than R4 000 a month on rent. On a total figure of 4.2 million for 2012, the Centre for Development and Enterprise concludes that black South Africans at that point constituted more than half of South Africa's middle class.
- Unemployment: The ANC's employment targets were not achieved serially. This was due to the rising number of job seekers entering the labour market and a low-growth economy unable to absorb the new entrants fast enough. The Goldman Sachs report shows that by the narrow definition

Table 4.1:   Poverty rate and poverty gap, comparison of 1993 and 2013

Year	Level	Poverty line (nominal rand)	Poverty rate without social grants	Poverty rate with social grants	Poverty gap reduction as % GNI
1993	Subsistence	88.71	0.41	0.33	0.95%
	Lower	131.27	0.50	0.45	1.29%
	Upper	193.61	0.60	0.57	1.59%
2013	Subsistence	336.18	0.43	0.25	1.48%
	Lower	497.45	0.50	0.38	1.99%
	Upper	733.69	0.58	0.52	2.44%

Source: Economic Policy Research Institute, 2013, from Presidency of South Africa, *Presidency's 2014 Review*, p. 44.
Note: GNI per capita refers to dollar value of the country's final income in a year, divided by its population.

20 per cent of the working-age population was unemployed in 1994 (or 24.1m) compared with 31.5 per cent (34m) in 2013. Owing to the slow rate of national economic growth, inadequate progress with smallholder farm development and lack of growth in employment in the commercial farming sector, unemployment in rural areas was also not addressed. The government five-year report specifically notes the failure to create rural employment.

The successes across the five- and twenty-year report perspectives include (albeit with ominous reverse sides):
- Food security: It is regarded as a relative success, although the South African National Health and Nutrition Examination[117] found that only 46 per cent of the population is food secure, contrasting with 28 per cent at risk of hunger, and 26 per cent who experience hunger (the latter mostly in urban informal and rural formal areas). About 11 million South Africans, or about one-fifth of the population, do not know where their next meal will come from, and are thus 'food insecure'.
- Education: There is progress in terms of matriculants passing, and at the foundation stage of education, *amid lowering of standards and adjustment*

of marks. Problems remain in school infrastructure and curriculum coverage. Learner-support materials are also short of the initial objectives. Goldman Sachs confirms that the bulk of education and health expenditure goes to employee remuneration and that 77 per cent of 11.4 million learners will receive poor to medium quality of education.

- Health care: Progress is evident in maternal and child health, as well as life expectancy, reduction of HIV-AIDS and tuberculosis infection levels. The provision of quality health care, however, remains a significant problem.

The blend of successes and failures in this selection of procedural and substantive policy areas cuts to the bone of the tragedy of policy making and implementation in South Africa. There have been big successes, but the lives of many millions have barely changed. They might have arrived at a level of subsistence through social services and the social wage, but their own lives have not changed to the level of well-being that was part of any version of the dream of 1994. The high-flyer lives of the political class and the middle classes, however, remind them what should have been possible for them as well.

CONCLUSION: FORWARD TO THE FREEDOM CHARTER

The ANC in power has been good news for South Africa's hard-working and growing black middle classes, the middle class generally and certainly white South Africans, large numbers of South Africans who suffered less poverty because of expansive social spending, and for the predatory elite who were delighted to be affirming and emulating President Zuma and his cohort of political elites. Policy action (and inaction) in the time of Jacob Zuma in ANC and government power affirmed the far-reaching ways in which the face of South African politics and society is changing. Most of the changes that were outlined in this chapter emanated before Zuma's confirmation in the highest office in the land, but were sealed by the Zuma stamp.

The level of delivery boils down to the half-full, half-empty criterion. If the point of departure is that South Africa needs to be better than it was in the days of apartheid, the ANC government wins hands down. This is the criterion that the ANC uses widely to assert that it has performed remarkably. If the test is set against the ANC's Freedom Charter, an aspirational document of great historical significance, which the ANC proclaims as its leading star, then verdicts of insufficient progress and outright deviations are inevitable. If it is set against the promises and undertakings of the ANC in earlier Zuma-regime days, there are mostly also vast shortfalls. The ANC has devised and revised the old Soviet Union-style phrase 'phases of transition' because it tries to explain the shortfalls in relation to the reasonably radical vision of the Freedom Charter. The ANC needs to have a message for the deprived (or relatively deprived) citizens – to show that the current deficits are 'just a phase'. Hence the ANC implies that the currently deficient levels of transformation have actually been foreseen, and that the governing party knows how to get out of the problems of ongoing and extreme poverty, unemployment and inequality.

The ANC hardly figures the 'doctrine of the divine right of the leaders to accumulate courtesy of public position' into its transformation delivery equations. Research tells us that there are repercussions for the party's lapses. People wonder if the state of delivery and transformation would have been better had the leaders been more focused on dedicated and selfless service to the people. We know that policy inconsistencies and leadership excesses do not, yet, substantially detract from ANC electoral support. However, the ANC dropped a total of eight percentage points at the national level in the two elections spearheaded by President Jacob Zuma. The policy message is in the gap.

NOTES

1   The discourse of 'talk left, walk right' was first triggered in South Africa by Patrick Bond, 2004, *Talk Left, Walk Right: South Africa's Frustrated Global Reforms*, Pietermaritzburg: UKZN Press. Some earlier uses of the term appear in the *Financial Express*, Mumbai, India.

2   James Ferguson, September 2007, 'Formalities of poverty: Thinking about social assistance in neoliberal South Africa', *African Studies Review*, vol. 50 (2), pp. 71–86; and 2010, 'The uses of neoliberalism', *Antipode*, vol. 41, supplement 1, pp. 166–184; and 2013, 'How to do things with land: A distributive perspective on rural livelihoods in southern Africa', *Journal of Agrarian Change*, vol. 13 (1), pp. 166–174, explains how neo-liberalism and South African-style social welfare merge well.

3   Mazibuko Jara, 2014, 'Marxisms', in Michelle Williams and Vishwas Satgar (eds), *Marxisms in the 21st Century: Crisis, Critiques and Struggles* (Democratic Marxism series), Johannesburg: Wits University Press.

4   Jeremy Cronin, 24 May 2013, 'Let's not monumentalise the NDP', presentation, Chris Hani Institute, http://www.chi.org.za/Public%20Engagement/CHI%20NDP%20Cronin%2024%20May.pdf, accessed 14 October 2013.

5   Scandinavia offers possible exceptions.

6   Stephen Ellis, 24–30 January 2014, 'Ideologists with cast-iron theories don't like unpleasant facts', *Mail & Guardian*, p. 30, details the ANC's manipulation of

155

historical facts to help place the ANC as central to the 'liberation' (rather than compromise) of 1994, as predominant force in the attainment of democracy (marginalising the UDF, Black Consciousness Movement), and attaining a military victory (rather than withdrawal of the SANDF from Angola). Also see Stephen Ellis, 2012, *External Mission: The ANC in Exile, 1960–1990*, Cape Town: Jonathan Ball.

7   ANC, January 2013, 53rd national conference resolutions, Mangaung, http://www.anc.org.za/docs/res/2013/resolutions53r.pdf, accessed 30 January 2013.

8   Leon Baradat, 2011, *Political Ideologies*, New York: Pearson.

9   StatsSA, 2014, 'Poverty trends in South Africa: An examination of absolute poverty between 2006 and 2011', http://beta2.statssa.gov.za/publications/Report-03-10-06/Report-03-10-06March2014.pdf, accessed 12 March 2015.

10   Colin Bundy, 2014, *Short-changed? South Africa since Apartheid*, Pocket Guide, Auckland Park: Jacana.

11   Susan Booysen, 2011, 'Policy, pursuit of the "turn to the left" and the paradox of continuity', in *The African National Congress and the Regeneration of Political Power*, Johannesburg: Wits University Press.

12   In April 2014 the Trade and Industry Ministry launched the sixth three-year iteration of the IPAP, for 2014/15 and 2016/17. The plan aims to raise competition in the production and services sector. It had already spurred around R143bn in private sector investments and created 144 000 jobs.

13   ANC, December 2007, 52nd national conference resolutions, Polokwane, http://www.anc.org.za/show.php?id=2536, accessed 3 January 2008.

14   Mcebisi Ndletyana, 2013, 'Policy incoherence – a function of ideological contestations?' in Umesh Pillay, G. Hagg and F. Nyamnjoy (eds), *State of the Nation: South Africa 2012–2013*, Cape Town: HSRC Press.

15   The quotation refers to the ANC's 1994 campaign slogan.

16   Vukani Mde, 25 May 2014, 'ANC gives "radical" a new meaning', *The Sunday Independent*, p. 8.

17   See Anthony Sampson, 1999, *Mandela: The Authorised Biography*, London: Harper Collins Publishers, p. 496.

18   Allister Sparks, 2003, *Beyond the Miracle: Inside the New South Africa*, Johannesburg: Jonathan Ball, p. 175.

19   See Anthony Sampson, 1999, op. cit., p. 496.

20   See Susan Booysen, 2011, op. cit.; also see Willie Esterhuyse, 2012, *Endgame: Secret Talks and the End of Apartheid*, Cape Town: Tafelberg; Richard Spitz with Matthew Chaskalson, 2000, *The Politics of Transition: A Hidden History of South Africa's Negotiated Settlement*, Oxford: Hart Publishing.

21   Robin Renwick, 1997, *Unconventional Diplomacy in Southern Africa*, London: Palgrave Macmillan.

22   Robin Renwick, 2015, *Mission to South Africa*, Cape Town: Jonathan Ball, was British ambassador to South Africa during the period leading up to the release of Nelson Mandela.

23   Richard Poplak, 21 April 2014, 'Exit stage right – the final days of Trevor Manuel', *Daily Maverick*, http://www.dailymaverick.co.za/article/2014-04-21-hannibal-elector-exit-stage-rightthe-final-days-of-trevor-manuel/#.VF3d_sl6joQ, accessed 26 April 2014.

24   David Moore, November 2014, 'Notes on nationalisation', Toronto, Working paper.

25 Colin Bundy, 25 April–1 May 2014, 'What happened to transformation?' *Mail & Guardian*, p. 36. Also see Tom Lodge, 2009, 'The South African developmental state?' *Journal of Southern African Studies*, vol. 35 (1), pp. 253–261.

26 Adam Habib, 2013, *South Africa's Suspended Revolution: Hopes and Prospects*, Johannesburg: Wits University Press.

27 Cosatu, 2013, 'Summary of critique of the National Development Plan, March 2013', http://www.cosatu.org.za/docs/discussion/2013/NDPcritiquesummary.pdf, accessed 26 February 2015.

28 Gugile Nkwinti, 8 May 2015, Department of Rural Development and Land Reform, Budget policy speech, Parliament, Cape Town; Tina Joemat-Pettersson, 19 May 2015, 2015/16 policy and budget speech, Parliament, Cape Town.

29 Outgoing NDP commissioner, 14 May 2015, interview, Centurion.

30 Details of the NGP were first presented to the Cosatu central executive committee in November 2010. Aspects were endorsed but concern also expressed that it remains rooted in the belief that strong economic growth will lead to the redistribution of benefits and income. See Terry Bell, 26 November 2010, 'New Growth Path: Different acronym, same old direction', *Business Report*, p. 2. The SACP endorsed the NGP; see Sibongakonke Shoba, 29 November 2011, 'Patel plan divides SACP, Cosatu', *Business Day*, p. 1.

31 ANC, January 2013, op. cit.

32 The Presidency, Republic of South Africa, Department of Planning, Monitoring and Evaluation, 2014, *Medium Term Strategic Framework (MTSF) 2014–2019*, Tshwane, p. 20.

33 Two phases of the Expanded Public Works Programme's job opportunities rolled out: first the 1 million for 2004–2009, next the 4.5 million from 2009 to March 2014. A further 6 million opportunities of varying duration are projected for the 2014–19 cycle. See Jeremy Cronin, 5 February 2014, 'Jobs claims is not bogus, posturing is', *The Star*, p. 12.

34 Industrial Policy Action Plan: Economic sectors and employment cluster IPAP 2013/14, fifth iteration, http://www.thedti.gov.za/news2013/ipap_2013-2016.pdf, accessed 20 August 2014.

35 Jeremy Cronin, 2007, 'ANC delegates support major left policy switch: The climax of a festival of ideas', *Umsebenzi*, Congress Special, July 2007.

36 Andrew Chirwa, 12–18 September 2014, 'SACP is leading the Nkandla cover-up', *Mail & Guardian*, p. 31.

37 SACP discussion document, 'Meeting the challenges facing the trade union movement'.

38 Cosatu's moderated policy influence in due course would also emerge from two sets of legislation, enacted in late 2013. First was the Transport Laws and Related Matters Amendment Act. It enabled implementation of e-tolling on Gauteng highways, opposed by Cosatu, some political parties and civil society. Second, the Employment Tax Incentive Bill, or the 'youth wage subsidy', was promulgated.

39 ANC, January 2013, op. cit.

40 The 'phases' discourse first came up in the 1920s, when the Marxists realised that 'communism' was not unfolding in the exact anticipated ways, and a different explanation had to be established.

41 Also see Susan Booysen, 2012, *The ANC's Battle of Mangaung*, Cape Town: Tafelberg Shorts e-Book series.

42 Cosatu has referred to the economic success of former Brazilian president Luiz Lula da Silva, and the Zuma-ist lobby embraced this as promise of what Zuma would achieve should he be granted a second term. See Leon Schreiber, 8 October 2012, 'Why a "Lula moment" is not possible in SA', *Politicsweb*, http://www.politicsweb.co.za/politicsweb/view/politicsweb/en/page71619?oid=331216&sn=Detail&pid=71619, accessed 5 November 2014.

43 On the interpretation of the NDR in the South African context, see David Moore, 2010, 'A decade of disquieting diplomacy: South Africa, Zimbabwe and the ideology of the National Democratic Revolution, 1999–2009', *History Compass*, vol. 8 (8), pp. 752–767. The analysis highlights Mbeki's interpretations. Zuma has not yet offered any updates or personalised reinterpretations.

44 SACP, 9 May 2014, 'ANC victory: A decisive mandate to press ahead with the radical second phase of our transition', statement.

45 *MTSF*, 2014, op. cit., p. 6.

46 Mondli Makhanya, 25 May 2014, 'New term, new slate', *City Press*, p. 13.

47 See Marleen Potgieter, 23 September 2014, 'New employment equity rules leave errant employers no place to hide', *Cape Times*, p. 9.

48 SACP, October 2014, 'Going to the root: Discussion document on the second, more radical phase of our transition', *Bua Komanisi!*, vol. 8 (2).

49 NDP, 2012, 'A conversation with South Africans', Addendum, pp. 479–484, http://www.npconline.co.za/MediaLib/Downloads/Home/Tabs/NDP%20 2030-Addendum-A%20conversation%20with%20South%20Africans.pdf, accessed 2 December 2014.

50 As illustration, see Presidency of South Africa, 10 March 2015, 'Call for nominations to serve on the National Planning Commission', press briefing, http://www.thepresidency.gov.za/pebble.asp?relid=19195, accessed 12 March 2015.

51 ANC, December 2012, Conference declaration, Mangaung.

52 ANC, December 2012, Resolution on economic transformation.

53 See Sharda Naidoo, 9–15 March 2012, 'Draft policies are "not the final word"', *Mail & Guardian*, p. 8.

54 See Joel Netshitenzhe, 31 May 2013, 'NDP an attainable vision', http://www.iol.co.za/the-star/ndp-an-attainable-vision-1.1525327#.VF39_cl6ino, accessed 2 May 2014.

55 Jeremy Cronin, 24 May 2013, op. cit.

56 Trevor Manuel, 2013, 'Why did the ANC endorse the National Development Plan?' *Umrabulo*, First Quarter, pp. 16–21.

57 See Attard Montalto, 7 September 2013, 'NDP getting heavy competition', *Saturday Star*, p. 14.

58 *MTSF*, 2014, op. cit., p. 4.

59 Susan Booysen, 28 April 2013, 'Plan's thought police undermine ANC's character', http://www.iol.co.za/news/politics/plan-s-thought-police-undermine-anc-s-character-1.1507367#.VFyYoMl6ino, accessed 17 September 2013.

60 Standard & Poor's downgraded South Africa's sovereign credit rating in June 2014, and Fitch ratings put South Africa's outlook on negative watch. The main reasons were labour unrest, South Africa's slow growth path, the fiscal and current account deficits, and external vulnerability. See *Business Times*, 15 June 2014, 'Downgraded', p. 1; *Business Day*, 17 June 2014, p. 8. In March 2015 it downgraded Eskom to 'junk' status.

61   *Politicsweb*, 6 November 2014, http://www.politicsweb.co.za/politicsweb/view/politics web/en/page72308?oid=787722&sn=Marketingweb+detail&pid=90389&utm, accessed 7 November 2014.

62   See, for example, Adriaan Basson, 2012, *Zuma Exposed*, Johannesburg: Jonathan Ball, insert between pp. 140 and 141; pp. 302–307. Gareth van Onselen, 20 August 2012, 'The billion rand president: How much Jacob Zuma costs the taxpayer', http://inside-politics.org/2012/08/20/the-billion-rand-president-how-much-jacob-zu-ma-costs-the-taxpayer/, accessed 12 July 2014, calculated details (on conservative basis in 2012, with some amounts not adjusted since 2009) and surmised that President Zuma would cost the taxpayer around half a billion rand, just for his first term. Also see https://ca.finance.yahoo.com/news/salaries-13-major-world-leaders-103900861.html, accessed 7 January 2015.

63   Clarification by the minister of trade and industry, 12 May 2015, *Government Gazette*. The Black Business Council had supported the clampdown on broad-based ownership and employee schemes. The minister would also appoint a task team to reconsider code content.

64   Richard Poplak, 2014, 'Fantasia', in *Until Julius Comes*, Cape Town: Tafelberg.

65   Paul Mashatile, 8 October 2014, interview, SABC-SAFM.

66   Gugile Nkwinti, 2014, quoted in Media24, 16 October 2014, 'No Zim-style land reforms for SA, says Nkwinti', http://www.fin24.com/Economy/No-Zim-style-land-reforms-for-SA-say-Nkwinti-20141016, accessed 21 October 2014.

67   A substantially larger proportion of the upper tiers in South Africa's living standard measure (LSM) classifications have become black; see data presented in *City Press*, Voices, 8 April 2015, p. 1.

68   Personal observation of media briefings and select deliberations at the ANC's 53rd national conference, Mangaung, December 2012.

69   ANC, January 2013, op. cit.

70   See Susan Booysen, 2013, *Twenty Years of South African Democracy: Citizen Views of Human Rights, Governance and the Political System*, research report, Johannesburg and Washington DC: Freedom House; Mcebisi Ndletyana, 1 March 2015, 'No way is Zuma seriously fighting corruption', *The Sunday Independent*, p. 16.

71   Personal communications and observations of cases where the author is acquainted with the persons involved.

72   Public Service Commission (PSC), commissioner, presentation to parliamentary committee. Repeat offenders were the departments of Correctional Services, Agriculture, Forestry and Fisheries, Communications, Defence, Military Veterans and the State Security Agency. In 2013 eleven national departments, including their directors general, did not submit any financial disclosure forms. It is within the powers of the ministers to hold their official to account; it is not done.

73   Term is used to refer to government employees, their family members or other associates doing business with government. Evidence is found in Auditor General South Africa, 2014, *Consolidated General Report on the Audit Outcomes of Local Government: MFMA 2012–13*, http://www.agsa.co.za/Portals/0/MFMA%202012-13/2012_13_MFMA_Consolidated_general_report.pdf, accessed 27 August 2014.

74   ANC internal report on a survey concerning the 2014 election trends, discussed at the NEC meeting of 16 May 2015, Tshwane.

75   See multiple links accessed from http://www.pmg.org.za/briefings.

76   *MTSF*, 2014, op. cit.

77   ANC, 22 September 2014, Statement of the ANC National Executive Committee following meeting held 19–21 September 2014.

78   Paul Vecchiatto, 29 October 2014, 'MPs accused of rewriting nuclear policy', *Business Day*, p. 2.

79   Also see Sibongakonke Shoba, 7 December 2014, 'Outwit. Outlast. Outfawn. The bizarre survival of Teflon Tina', *Sunday Times*, p. 21.

80   Lynley Donnelly and Lionel Faull, 26 July 2013, 'Zuma slips into nuclear driver's seat', *Mail & Guardian*, http://mg.co.za/article/2013-07-26-00-zuma-slips-into-nuclear-drivers-seat, accessed 20 March 2015.

81   On the latter point, Jeff Radebe, quoted in Paul Vecchiatto, 7 November 2014, 'Cabinet still not briefed over nuclear agreements – Radebe', *Business Day*, p. 2. There were denials of the conclusiveness of the agreement with Russia, but no documents were released.

82   Department of Energy, http://www.energy.gov.za/files/media/pr/2014/MediaStatement-South-Africas-nuclear-new-build-programme-01-October-2014.pdf; http://www.the presidency.gov.za/pebble.asp?relid=181, accessed 20 March 2015. Also see Department of Energy, July 2015, *Sawubona*, advertorial.

83   Carol Paton, 20 January 2015, 'Nuclear budget? What budget, asks Treasury', *Rand Daily Mail*, http://www.rdm.co.za/politics/2014/12/02/nuclear-budget-what-budget-asks-treasury, accessed 25 May 2015.

84   Steve Thomas, 25 May 2015, 'Pursuit of nuclear energy likely to be more wasted time', *Business Day Live*, http://www.bdlive.co.za/opinion/2015/05/25/pursuit-of-nuclear-energy likely-to-be-more-wasted-time, accessed 25 May 2015.

85   The Presidency, 2014, *Twenty Year Review: South Africa, 1994–2014*.

86   See, for example, Shanti Aboobaker, 5 November 2014, '"Game-changing" minimum wage to be mandatory', *Cape Times*, 5 November 2014, p. 4. As one follow-up the ANC announced a rise in the minimum wage for domestic workers; it was dismissed as meaningless because it was so marginal.

87   ANC Gauteng, September 2014, Base document II: Framework document towards the ANC Gauteng 12th provincial conference; theme: 'United in action to advance radical social and economic transformation', Johannesburg.

88   Paul Mashatile, Gauteng ANC chairperson, 8 October 2014, interview, SABC-SAFM.

89   Department of Mineral Resources, October 2009, Mining charter impact assessment report, http://www.dmr.gov.za/publications/summary/108-mining-charter-downloads/126-miningcharterimpact-oct-2009.html, accessed 2 July 2014.

90   Department of Rural Development and Land Reform, Green Paper on land reform, 2011. The paper proposed a four-tier land system – state or public land (leasehold), private-owned land (freehold with limited extent), foreign-owned land (freehold but precarious tenure) and community-owned land – with institutions to support the system, in the form of the land valuer general, land management commission and land management board.

91   Michael Lyne, 2014, 'Two decades of land reform in South Africa: Insights from an agricultural economics perspective', http://c.ymcdn.com/sites/www.aeasa.org.za/resource/collection/900D509D-5F84-43AB-8875-A2220BAAB38D/Tomlinson_Lecture.pdf, accessed 21 October 2014.

92 *MTSF*, 2014, op. cit., p. 25.
93 Richard Calland, 29 August 2014, 'First 100 days: The good, bad and dire', *Mail & Guardian*, http://mg.co.za/article/2014-08-30-first-100-days-the-good-bad-and-dire, accessed 4 September 2014.
94 See Jan-Jan Joubert, 2 July 2014, 'Nkwinti sticks to land proposal', *Sowetan*, p. 5. His proposal had been that farmers give up half the value of their farms to labourers that had proved disciplined, who will then co-own the farm with them. Nkwinti argues that his proposals were in line with ANC policy conference decisions of 2012.
95 Gugile Nkwinti, 2014, op. cit.
96 Gugile Nkwinti, 8 May 2015, op. cit.
97 Solidarity Research Institute, 18 July 2013, 'The dark side of the NDP – SRI, Solidarity Research Institute' (Piet le Roux), http://www.politicsweb.co.za/politicsweb/view/politicsweb/en/page71619?oid=392692&sn=Detail, accessed 12 September 2014; South African Institute of Race Relations, Frans Cronjé, 'Confidence in NDP misplaced', letter to *Business Day*, 12 May 2014, p. 8.
98 Malusi Gigaba, 12 May 2014, quoted in 'The danger of policy paralysis', *Business Day*, p. 8.
99 Ruth Hall, 2014, 'Land redistribution: The politics of not making policy', in Thenjiwe Meyiwa et al. (eds), *State of the Nation 2014*, Cape Town: HSRC Press, pp. 171–182.
100 Ben Cousins and Ruth Hall, 24–30 January 2014, 'ANC land policies: Talk left, walk right?' *Mail & Guardian*, p. 27.
101 This Bill followed in the footsteps of the 2004 Communal Land Rights Act, which was struck down in its entirety by the Constitutional Court in 2010. In 2014 Zuma noted that this act is again in the process of development. Also see Department of Rural Development and Land Reform, 7 September 2010, Briefing, Communal Land Rights Act: Constitutional Court judgment, http://www.pmg.org.za/print/report/20100908-department-constitutional-court-judgement-communal-lands-right-act, accessed 2 April 2011.
102 Commission on Restitution of Land Rights, 2014, Annual report 2013–2014, 'Reversing the legacy of the 1913 Natives' Land Act'.
103 Ruth Hall and Michael Aliber, 25 February 2015, 'Big talk, but there's less money for land reform (again)', http://www.plaas.org.za/blog/big-talk-there%E2%80%99s-less-money-land-reform-again, accessed 2 March 2015.
104 Aninka Claassens, 10 April 2014, 'Haste over land rights bill not just in aid of buying votes', *Business Day*, p. 11.
105 For the rest of the speech, see address by President Jacob Zuma on the occasion of the annual official opening of the National House of Traditional Leaders, 27 February 2015, Parliament, Cape Town, http://www.thepresidency.gov.za/pebble.asp?relid=16947, accessed 28 February 2015.
106 Centre for Law and Society, 9 March 2015, http://www.customcontested.co.za/cls-comment-on-president-zumas-address-to-nhotl/, accessed 9 March 2015.
107 Ruth Hall and Michael Aliber, 25 February 2015, op. cit.
108 Nomboniso Gasa, 14 October 2014, 'Laws for traditional leaders emulate the logic of apartheid', *Business Day*, p. 4; Aninka Claassens, 16 November 2014, 'Double dispossession for rural poor', *City Press*, p. 8.
109 J.P. Landman, 2013, *The Long View: Getting Beyond the Drama of South Africa's Headlines*, Auckland Park: Jacana/Stonebridge.

110 Jacob Zuma, 2014, Address on the occasion of the 2014 Freedom Day celebrations, 27 April 2014, https://www.dac.gov.za/content/address-president-jacob-zuma-oc cassion-2014-freedom-day-celebrations, accessed 13 May 2014.

111 ANC, 2014, 'Close-out report on the implementation of government', Johannesburg. See Lebogang Seale and Piet Rampedi, 27 January 2014, 'ANC report admits party has "failed dismally" in delivering on goals for 2009–2014', *The Star*, http://www.iol. co.za/news/politics/anc-report-admits-party-has-failed-1.1637176#.VF0b3cl6inol, accessed 28 January 2014.

112 Goldman Sachs, *Two Decades of Freedom: A 20-Year Review of South Africa*, 2013, http://www.goldmansachs.com/our-thinking/outlook/colin-coleman-south-africa/ 20-yrs-of-freedom.pdf, accessed 2 December 2013.

113 See Adél Bosch, Jannie Rossouw, Tian Claassens and Bertie du Plessis, September 2010, 'A second look at measuring inequality in South Africa: A modified Gini coefficient', Working Paper No. 58, School of Development Studies, University of KwaZulu-Natal, http://www.sds.ukzn.ac.za/files/WP%2058%20web.pdf, accessed 30 September 2014.

114 StatsSA, 2014, op. cit.

115 StatsSA, 2012, *General Household Survey*, reported in *City Press*, 25 August 2013, p. 15.

116 *News24*, 4 June 2014, 'Rise of the black middle class', http://www.news24.com/ MyNews24/Rise-of-the-black-middle-class-20140604, accessed 5 June 2014.

117 Human Sciences Research Council (HSRC), *South African National Health and Nutrition Examination Survey*, August 2013, Tshwane; also see Tanya Farber, 27 May 2014, 'Now it's a case of cry the hungry country', *The Star*, p. 5.

5

THE WAKE-UP CALLS OF ELECTION 2014

Election 2014 offered a microcosm of insights into how the ANC maintains power in South Africa. It concerns more than endorsement by the people. The ANC's victory showed how skilled strategists in a well-resourced campaign of long duration, well supported by the state, and shrewd in the use of media and information can help build a victory of note in circumstances of attitudinal discontent and budding voter realignment. Before the election the ANC's vulnerable underbelly had become all too visible. Then the ANC used the election campaign to refurbish its liberation credentials and mobilise the national consciousness.

The ANC built its campaign on the fertile soil of deep voter loyalty. Even if ANC supporters were critical, they found it difficult to take the step of switching to other parties. This orientation assisted the 'chosen party' to produce a victory above 60 per cent. Nevertheless, the ANC remained on shifting ground. Neither its iconic liberation status nor the delivery potential that might have assured seamless electoral allegiance was working as well as desired. The ANC received wake-up calls. The result showed that substantial segments of the middle and working classes who had benefited from ANC rule were now willing to either vote against the ANC or to abstain. The ANC's own analyses of its 2014 result told the story of how it felt betrayed by those who had switched their votes to the EFF or the DA. The ANC was seemingly unable to contemplate how 200 000 fewer voters, despite an electorate that had grown by 2.5 million from five years before, refused to accept its campaign's 'good story' as sufficient reason to endorse it.

The electoral verdicts in the metropolitan areas pointed to the crux of the matter: the ANC's decline despite its dominance, especially in the Gauteng metro trio of Ekurhuleni, Tshwane and Johannesburg. Nelson Mandela Metropolitan Municipality voters confirmed the slippery slope. Evidence of slippage had already emerged in the 2011 local elections, and the 2014 national and provincial elections continued the trend. The ANC prevailed in Gauteng, but it received a chilling message. Work had to be done to stop the bleeding. Could the ANC change in the post-election period to show its willingness to listen to voters on issues of poor governance and representation, compromised leadership and policy issues touching the people's pockets and stomachs? Would such improved government appease voters in the face of the ANC *not yielding* on issues such as Nkandla, President Zuma himself, unemployment and e-tolls?

This chapter dissects the story of the ANC in Election 2014, with emphasis on the lessons that the ANC may derive from it.[1] It first assesses the campaign. Then it analyses the apparatuses that carried the campaign. The chapter then unpacks the election results, identifying the main trends and assessing the explanations. Finally, it considers the implications for the ANC – foremost that the ANC had fragile outright majorities in several metropolitan centres; that South Africa is urbanising and the ANC's predominant support bases are rural; that the KwaZulu-Natal vote bonuses of recent elections were becoming lacklustre; and that ANC majorities in protest communities were increasingly eroded.

THE LONG-HAUL CAMPAIGN

In no election since 1994 did the ANC have to work so hard, against such odds, to keep the party-movement elevated as a political family bound by an enduring thread of struggle. The ANC's result was boosted by South Africa celebrating twenty years of democracy, the ANC's association with iconic Nelson Mandela, the generous use of state patronage, and the circular and self-perpetuating project of knowing that the ANC is likely to remain in power. Of course, the ANC was also rewarded for its 'good story' of twenty years in power and its liberation credentials. Had it not been for the deep-seated loyalty to the former liberation movement, and the ANC being considered as the big political family, much more could have gone wrong than the loss of four percentage points of national support.[2]

It was a long-haul election campaign. It came together with the ANC centenary celebrations that had been rolling out since January 2012 and 2014's nationwide celebrations of twenty years of democracy. Mobilisation included events around ANC President Jacob Zuma's re-election at the national ANC conference at Mangaung in December 2012 and the illness and passing of Nelson Mandela in December 2013. The four months of dedicated campaigning from early 2014 until election day of 7 May 2014 were merely the final stretch.

The ANC's main message was the 'good story' of twenty years of government delivery and transformation, combined with the 'vote for Mandela' mantra and promises that the time of policy implementation (or realisation of hope for more substantive change) had now truly arrived. The ANC presented its past and present policies as generating hope, especially for employment and relief from extreme poverty. It worked hard to present itself as the responsible governing party, true to the National Development Plan but 'radical' in order to withhold oxygen from the EFF. The campaign issued reassurances that the ANC and its leadership were attending to corruption and that a page had been turned towards a better ANC. This extended into the 'hands off Zuma' campaign by the ANC in KwaZulu-Natal,[3] unapologetic in its belief in Zuma, its own son. This narrative ensured at the time that the ANC remained the hope, the continuous liberator and a party bigger than any contemporary stain on its name.

In spite of all these reassuring strains, Campaign 2014 was no plain sailing for the ANC. The party had to counter multiple obstacles to its reputation as a 'caring and competent' (former) liberation movement and contemporary governing party. The main controversies centred on policy and governance issues, leader and government scandals, and rising community protest and labour disputes, including the state of play in Cosatu. The major policy issues featuring in the campaign were the government's failure to address unemployment: labour absorption had not improved, so neither had unemployment rates. How did a scandal such as the Marikana police shooting of striking miners square with a caring and accountable governing party? Zuma featured personally in contentious arenas, all of which cast doubt on his suitability as president. The Waterkloof landing debacle of the Gupta family featured too, displaying special privileges for special citizens and thus inequality before the law. The arms deal and other suppressed charges against Zuma were never far from public eyes and ears. The DA persisted in interrogating Zuma's role in the scandals. Zuma's first term ended with his narrowly escaping an impeachment debate in Parliament concerning the Nkandla scandal and presidential accountability for undue use of public funds for private benefit. The campaign question for the ANC was how to relate and explain these issues to the electorate.

The conceptualisation of the electorate as 'political family' seen through eyes of loyal ANC voters helps to explain much of voter allegiance in South Africa. Even when the parent's behaviour disappoints, substantial numbers of the voter 'children' believe they have more bargaining power with this political party than with any opposition party.[4] A modern-day deviation from the family theme is that of transactional voting. Among the young voters there is evidence that the ANC gets support because it has the power, including the say over who gets jobs – they know their best chance of coming into favour and becoming eligible for jobs is by voting ANC, and making it as clear as possible that this is how they had voted, in case someone in power is watching.

The people and the face of public discontent

In defensive rather than expansive mode, the ANC worked hard to persuade supporters to bear with it. The main questions with which its strategists battled were whom to target and what issues to prioritise. ANC leaders across the provinces proclaimed they would increase their support. Spreading a pre-election message of the ANC as an unchallenged top party was an important part of its campaign positioning.

ANC campaigners on the ground were confronted with citizens who were critical of campaign promises, absentee representation and the political elite taking care of itself instead of the people. They confronted ANC leaders, interrogated them and insisted on explanations for government's insufficient or uneven delivery – yet most would nevertheless close ranks later to vote ANC. Large numbers of voters continued to *want to* believe in their ANC. David Moore points to a feeling of ritual at these elections, which 'is almost religious'; communal yet private, reminiscent of confessional behaviour.[5] Ben Turok[6] elaborates on the contemporary variations on the continuous bond: '… the African people of South Africa love the ANC. They don't love Zuma. The ANC is your family. The ANC is your neighbour, the ANC is your mother and father.' Campaigners did not take chances, reminding voters of *who* it is who had been looking after them. A member of the KwaZulu-Natal ANC provincial government told voters: 'Nxamalala [Zuma] has increased grants, but there are people who are stealing them by voting for opposition parties.'[7]

Minorities were often inconsequential additions to the campaign. The ANC nevertheless targeted coloured voters, asserting that the DA was racist. Early in the campaign the ANC had stated that it would be a 'waste of time' to canvass whites – deals with whites were rather in backrooms and meetings with special interest groups.[8] In the final weeks of the campaign the tone became more inclusive.

The entrance of the EFF to the left of the ANC meant that the ANC had to refocus to counter both the DA and the EFF. The ANC said it was unperturbed, as it was accustomed to a new opposition party per election. It had seen the heydays of the United Democratic Movement (UDM) and the Congress of the People (Cope), and thus far all these opposition parties had been modest pop-up parties, one-election wonders before fading into microparties. The EFF, however, was speaking to a growing audience, mostly of young and disaffected voters, a demographic grouping that concerned the ANC. The pro-EFF voter rebellion entailed that the EFF was intercepting first-time voters from both the ANC and the DA.

ANC campaigners and leaders used sly and other-worldly tricks when the going on the ground got tough.[9] Malusi Gigaba said the DA is a 'party of demons'. Fikile Mbalula averred that the Western Cape is 'run by witches' and that 'tokoloshes' are needed to run the DA's provincial government out of power. Baleka Mbete suggested that the struggle spirits would deal with those who become disloyal. Jacob Zuma and Cyril Ramaphosa warned voters that the ancestors would turn on them if they did not vote ANC. Nomvula Mokhonyane was down to earth: she told Bekkersdal that the ANC did not need their 'dirty votes'.

ANC supporters did not automatically blame the ANC as a whole for the shortcomings of its leaders. The masses streamed to the rallies, but the party's campaign strategists had to protect the president from booing at rallies and from audiences that wanted to talk Nkandla rather than the approved campaign narrative of the 'good story'. Zuma suffered several booing experiences, most strikingly at the December 2013 memorial service for Nelson Mandela. Strategists changed campaign schedules suddenly to shelter the president. Rallies with Zuma as the key speaker were minimised.[10] Organisers moved him to safer forms of campaigning and cancelled some appearances at short notice.[11] The huge ANC Siyanqoba national and provincial rallies became controlled events – seating was arranged in provincial blocks and records were kept of everyone attending and from which regions they came. 'The extraordinary measures taken to screen and control the crowd when the ANC released its election manifesto in January in Nelspruit may be a measure of how uneasy the leadership feels in the face of public discontent.'[12]

Anchors of the ANC campaign

The ANC's centenary celebrations of January 2012 set the foundation for its rolling election campaign. The base message was that the ANC had brought liberation and far-reaching transformation. Failures in the first two decades of ANC governance were merely small diversions in a great historical project. It is the story of progress, hope and trust, said the ANC.

Jacob Zuma as incumbent president of the ANC and South Africa took centre stage at the year-long twenty years of democracy festivities that simultaneously reminded South Africans of the link between liberation, democracy and the ANC. These were controlled state events and Zuma was free to appear without humiliation such as booing. The celebrations of the ANC's centenary also doubled for much of Zuma's ANC presidential campaign at Mangaung in December 2012. By 2014, Zuma could hardly be separated from the contemporary ANC, even if he was pulling it down by as much as six to eight percentage points.[13] ANC Secretary General Gwede Mantashe chose to interpret attacks on Zuma as efforts to destroy the party, and defended Zuma as the symbol of the ANC, going as far as suggesting that Zuma was the head of the ANC snake: 'If you want to kill a snake you crush its head ... The party is not something to play around with.'[14]

The ANC's campaign thus benefited from convergence with the government's all-encompassing democracy celebrations. The messages from multiple government departments on the feat of twenty years articulated with the ANC's 'good story'. Perhaps the best part of this story for the ANC was that large amounts of state funds could be channelled legitimately into events that assisted the party's campaign.

The tragedy of the passing of an iconic leader of the ANC's struggle against apartheid, who became the symbol of the democratisation and reconciliation process of 1994, was manna from heaven for the ANC's campaign. The focus on Mandela frequently highlighted all that came to be seen as virtuous about the ANC – indeed, the ANC promoted itself as the embodiment of Nelson Mandela.[15] Several reports[16] confirm that medical assistance sustained Nelson Mandela's life from July to December 2013. The eventual time of his passing fitted snugly with the ANC's campaign process – the ANC used the relatively quiet spell in December 2013, prior to the main campaign period, for memorial services and respectful mourning. The focus on Mandela helped elevate the ANC campaign above the reaffirmation of Zuma as the face of the ANC election. Mandela's passing and the renewed focus on the ANC's honour was not, however, an unambiguous gift. The attention to Mandela's merits and contributions to South Africa's democracy highlighted contrasts with the prevailing ANC leadership. While the ANC campaign implored voters to remember Mandela with their ballots, there were no campaign appeals to choose the ANC for Zuma's sake.

Even the kowtowing South African Communist Party (SACP) ran poster campaigns urging citizens to vote ANC for the sake of Mandela and Chris Hani (two ANC leaders who diverged in their ideological inclinations). Zuma's face featured as a modest inclusion on the ANC election posters, contrasting with that of 2009 on which a beaming Zuma face was the whole of the ANC's anchor poster.

The ANC devised the core campaign message of 'a good story to tell'[17] with a palpable 'us and them' theme between the lines. 'Us', those experiencing the good changes, were contrasted with 'them', those who are not telling the truth, for various suspect motives, about South Africa today. The tale ended with 'together we move South Africa forward'. Despite criticism about the 'good story' as a half-truth, the narrative worked politically. No South African, even if hostile towards the ANC, could disagree that South Africa in 2014, warts and all, was a better place than it had been in apartheid days. This message helped draw attention from critical pre-election debates on the ANC, its leadership, corruption and many ineffectual policies. Malusi Gigaba, the ANC's head of elections, remarked: 'We knew we were not going to outcompete negative public debate and discourse about the ANC. We didn't even try to contest all the negative views that were being peddled at the media level. Our focus was getting down to the voters ...'[18]

To narrate this story, the ANC cast the twenty-year period of ANC power and would not be drawn out on what proportion of the 'good story' had been accomplished in Zuma's time (as extenuating circumstances, the ANC reminded voters that Zuma had assumed power in the aftermath of the 2008 global economic meltdown). The 'good story' and its accompanying realities created a complicated election task for opposition parties. The DA had hoped to extend its support into the black-African voter bloc to capture disaffected ANC support and could not risk alienating potential converts by being hostile to the early days of democracy. Instead, it focused on the woes that had befallen

169

South Africa and the ANC under Zuma's rule. ANC campaigners countered that the DA had previously also been critical of the ANC in pre-Zuma days.

The ANC conducted its powerful campaign in the face of the recognised weakness of its Number One, its president and repeat presidential candidate, Jacob Zuma. In the end, the Nkandla-Zuma factor did not lethally detract from ANC support, but much strategy and campaign labour went into minimising its impact, and the party could count on an electorate that for the most part still regarded the ANC as a bigger entity than its individual leaders.

ANC elections head Gigaba shed light on how the ANC 'made Nkandla go away'.[19] The ANC maintained that voters on the ground were preoccupied with issues of basic service delivery, not taking much note of Nkandla – although this is contrary to 2013 research demonstrating that citizens *were* troubled by Nkandla, not to the extent of generally changing their vote away from the ANC, but detracting from the ANC's legitimacy and credibility. Media coverage featured a host of reports of ANC leaders on the campaign trail confronted by angry voters about corruption in government.[20] Gigaba explained[21] that the ANC began fashioning its Nkandla message in late 2013, before the public protector's Nkandla report had been leaked to the media. Further into the campaign, the ANC emphasised an interministerial report (strategically produced by the ANC in government) that had exonerated Zuma. Once the public protector's report was released in March 2014, the ANC used the interministerial report to counterbalance the public protector's findings.

A moment on the campaign trail in Mpumalanga illustrated this approach. Zuma asserted that the opposition parties focused on Nkandla because they did not have policies to match the ANC's: '[A]ll they say is iNkandla, iNkandla, iNkandla. This is because they have nothing to offer …' For Zuma, all that opposition parties knew about was how to run to the court. 'How can we respect such people?' As for Madonsela's report, it 'didn't say the president misused money … it did say there was something unclear with those who built and bought material … Government asked the Special Investigating Unit to investigate …'[22]

DENTED CAMPAIGN APPARATUSES

The ANC's structures for the battle of 2014 were weaker than in previous elections. The most important changes were in the Tripartite Alliance and in the ANCYL – the veterans and women's leagues had both already suffered capacity and credibility issues over time. Two replacement apparatuses came into play, which helped the ANC produce a powerful campaign and deliver a certain victory: the ANC's volunteer formations operated as a formal and mass structure and the state institutions brought in significant resources. The ANC campaign gained from staff, projects and programmes, and advertising associated with both the celebration of twenty years of democracy and the delivery records of specific government departments.[23]

Cosatu had been a pinnacle of past ANC campaigning, providing foot soldiers and resources through its organised formations in all the elections since 1994. At its December 2013 congress, Numsa resolved that the metalworkers would not campaign for the ANC if the National Development Plan featured in the ANC election manifesto – and the NDP did feature centrally. At election time Cosatu was divided. The ANC silenced its general secretary Zwelinzima Vavi, and Numsa withheld campaign support. Yet although Numsa was not campaigning for the ANC, it also did not actively oppose it. An ANC-led pre-election task team's intervention delivered an accord that forestalled further fallout, at least up to election time. ANC elections head Gigaba conceded that Cosatu infighting and Numsa's decision not to campaign for the ANC had affected the campaign.[24] Later that year, Numsa was expelled from Cosatu, accused of resisting Cosatu resolutions – for example, by not supporting the ANC in the May elections.[25] With Cosatu's subsequent disintegration and the emergence of a counter-union from 2015 onwards, it became evident that the ANC's heyday of tripartite election campaigning had come to an end.

In addition to the ANC's Tripartite Alliance losses, the statures of its leagues at the time of the 2014 campaign had become substantially reduced and they could not emulate the roles they had had in most previous elections. The ANC Women's League (ANCWL) stayed subdued and the ANCYL was non-existent except for a marginal role played by the appointed task team that prepared the ground for a youth league to replace the disbanded 'Malema League'.

At election time, the ANCYL was the appointed youth task team, on the unaccomplished mission to construct a compliant league in the place of its predecessor. In the past, and particularly in Election 2009, the ANCYL had been an election stalwart, driving grassroots campaigns and doing footwork – it was the kingmaker then. The 2014 results would show that the task team failed to activate the four million born-free voters in favour of the ANC. The Veterans' League, formed in 2009, remained ineffectual, besides, in part, also becoming critical of Zuma.[26] The Umkhonto we Sizwe Military Veterans' Association had split roughly a year prior to the election, and one part, the Umkhonto we Sizwe War Veterans' Union, alleged and offered evidence of corruption in the Association.[27] It then contested the election through the vehicle of a new political party, South Africa First, but had scant resources and was poorly organised. In the end it forfeited its election deposit.

Beyond the faltering leagues, luminaries such as Nobel Peace laureate Archbishop Desmond Tutu withdrew his support for the ANC very publicly, because of its loss of moral authority: 'I will not vote for them … I say it with a very sore, very heavy heart because on the whole they have tended to be close to the kind of things we dreamt about.'[28] Veteran and member of a prominent 'ANC family' Mavuso Msimang[29] referred to the ANC's handling of the Nkandla affair as embarrassing and asked the ANC to 'put a stop to the cancer that causes power to be abused'. ANC stalwarts such as Ronnie Kasrils and Noziziwe Madlala-Routledge led the 'Sidikiwe!' campaign for a non-ANC vote: it meant vote but don't vote for the ANC – and in most cases also don't vote for the DA.

The volunteers were organised by province, with huge launches and toolkits of typical queries, and with suggestions of the most appropriate answers. Zuma described the campaign volunteers as an 'important additional structure in the ANC'. The 2013 launch statements referred to them as disciplined, no-stipend, campaign-implementation forces activated at voting district level and subject to ANC branch executives. The brigades were named after struggle icons. Gauteng's 6000-strong Moses Kotane brigade was launched in Johannesburg mid-2013. The Western Cape had the 5000-strong Chris Hani detachment. KwaZulu-Natal followed with the Volunteer Corps Movement called 'a re-launch of the 1952 Volunteers of Inkosi Albert Luthuli'.[30]

Gigaba noted that 'the biggest strength in the ANC lies in its ground capacity … the existence of the sheer force of troopers of the ANC, who can get into every household and mobilise everyone. We relied on our volunteers to carry our message across … That was the heartbeat of our campaign.'[31] Zuma's address at the final Johannesburg election rally echoed: 'ANC leaders and volunteers have visited every corner of the country, humbly engaging our people.'[32] The 2013–2014 version of the ANC volunteers was a reinvented formation, mobilised for campaign purposes from mid-2013 onward. Volunteers had played a substantial role in previous elections, specifically in 2009, but their 2013–2014 profiling was that of a major campaigning formation. This worked, because citizens wanted to be in favour with the powerful party, the ANC. Reporting for duty in a volunteer corps could very well leverage the visibility to the ANC that would in due course bring access to jobs and state contracts. Potential voters were said to have been reached at least three times in the course of the campaign.

Part of the outreach formula was to let Zuma himself go only to carefully selected houses, as was the case in his door-to-door outreach in Mpumalanga and the East Rand.[33] However, the volunteers were not always good news. In the Western Cape they were seen as faction-aligned and insufficiently informed.[34]

RESOURCES AND STATE RESOURCES

The ANC ran a high-profile and expensive campaign. It gained from public resources, but also had ample organisational funding.[35] An ANC report referred to the party's campaign having cost R450 million[36] and the figure might be even higher – in excess of R17 million was spent by the ANC on television advertisements alone. The cost of its campaign could be estimated at around R500 million,[37] based, for example, on the cost of hosting mass rallies with associated transport, food and T-shirt costs, across the provinces (the final Johannesburg rally required 2 000 buses and twenty-nine trains). Musicians were hired to provide entertainment. More than three million ANC election T-shirts were procured, and millions of election leaflets and pamphlets. A dedicated social network team went on the election trail with top leaders and ANC officials. Taxi services were procured to transport voters to the polls.

Volunteer action extended into the ranks of municipal functionaries with control over local resources. ANC strategy included obstructing opposition party campaigns. A Community Agency for Social Enquiry (Case) report showed that typical ANC campaign tactics include large doses of such sabotage.[38] For example, there was the attempt to prevent the EFF from holding a final closing rally at the Atteridgeville stadium in Tshwane. The local authority feigned stadium maintenance work after the EFF had booked and paid its deposit. The EFF only regained access upon taking urgent legal action.

ANC election manuals covered the final year of the extended ANC campaign cycle and indicated the type of activities that had to be financed. Activities were organised in phases, aiming at identifying potential ANC voters, ensuring that eligible citizens acquire identity documents, getting them registered in cooperation with mobile Electoral Commission (IEC) units, and then ensuring they got to the polls on election day.[39] The phases up to mid-2013 centred on laying the foundations, organising nominations and researching the communities that would be canvassed. Then it was 'back to the people' until the end of 2013, doing the first round of outreach, listening and dealing with

173

questions. The *mayihlome* (prepare for battle) phase prevailed until mid-April 2014, ensuring that voter registration continued right up to cut-off dates, in cooperation with the Department of Home Affairs and the mobile units. The Siyanqoba (we are winning) phase rolled out from mid-April up to election week. It required mobilisation, with meetings in parks and community precincts, handing out pamphlets and putting up posters at workplaces. Finally, election week reminded voters to go out and vote, and transported them to the voting stations. Taxi transport was put in place and T-shirts and refreshments were often available for voters as they finished.

The ANC might have become weakened on some fronts, but the state came to its rescue. Multiple national and provincial government departments delivered services, handing out food parcels and other gifts as close as possible to election time and high-profile campaign visits. The celebrations for twenty years of democracy created high levels of awareness of ANC government achievements. Government advertising of its achievements in the twenty years of democracy articulated perfectly with the ANC campaign message, as in the case of a Department of Water Affairs advertisement with the slogan 'Government can't do it alone'.[40] It uncannily resembled the ANC's slogan of 'Together we move South Africa forward'. There was a deluge of such celebratory advertisements in print and electronic media. Billboards, advertorials and building wraps amplified the message,[41] often in ANC colours. No opposition party could compete.

More advertisements – including some run by the South African National Defence Force – reinforced leadership images. The SANDF variety depicted the faces of commanders-in-chief over the last twenty years, ending with the face of Zuma and the slogan 'Twenty years of freedom and democracy'. This form of security sector contribution to the ANC's campaign was supplemented in the final two campaign weeks with security cluster visits to protest hot spots. The cluster issued statements 'reassuring' South Africa that the elections would be peaceful. In essence they were deploying state resources to safeguard the ANC in campaigning.

State agencies were *de facto* election agents. Super-delivery was the phenomenon of timing and suspension of routine and legitimate deliveries, so that there could be a visible deluge in the final run-up to election day. Government departments and the Presidency specialise in stacking the completion, announcement and launches of public sector work in the weeks prior to the election. This ensures that voters are conscious of governing party achievements when they cast their ballots. Media coverage is guaranteed and is not recorded as campaigning by the media monitors – prime-time radio and television coverage thereby accentuates the ANC in full performance flood. The rapid succession of official openings in the last three campaign months showcased the ANC's delivery record. For example, there was the April 2014 launch by President Zuma of the Umzimvubu water project in the Eastern Cape, and the De Hoop dam in Limpopo.[42] Many schools, houses, bridges and power stations had official openings – and generous community celebrations.

The South African Social Security Agency (SASSA) and provincial departments delivered truckloads of campaign gifts, including food parcels and blankets, to communities, in particular in the run-up to campaign visits by ANC luminaries.[43] Other departments and their provincial counterparts heightened delivery, including bicycles for schoolgoers. At many of these events people dressed in ANC gear were bussed in to lend an ANC aura to the event.[44] 'We are the real election agents,' remarked a senior SASSA official in a pre-election interview.[45] The government budget for food relief had grown by an additional R200m (for a total of R419m) in the election year.[46] The DA took the ANC to court for one such activity, but lost the case. Lines between party and state were blurred; hence it was impossible to prove legally that senior ANC leaders were not also legitimately involved in departmental events.[47]

Tenderpreneurs ploughed back financial goodwill after having benefited from state contracts. The SABC also banished borderline campaign advertisements of the DA and EFF which assisted the ANC in filtering out some in-your-face anti-ANC campaigning through the public media.

SERIAL DECLINE AND 'TREASON' IN THE METROS

Given the frequently adverse political and social context to Election 2014, the ANC's result of above 60 per cent was a feat. It contrasted with pre-election debates about the ANC, in particular its leadership and organisational ethics, but this was understandable given the South African people's deep historical and current-day state-patron links with the ANC. The good result also needs to be interpreted with caution. The 62 per cent level of support confirmed the ANC's serial decline and revealed the extent to which the party required massive resources and powerful campaigning to sustain itself. The winning percentage was unevenly constituted. The ANC barely sustained its majority status in four of the eight metros, three of which are in Gauteng. The ANC was losing its hold in these condensed urbanised centres and political-economic heartland. It felt cheated by the emerging middle classes in the province – and intense post-election resurrection work would follow.

Two of the ANC's biggest electoral assets are its continuing popular trust and voters' ongoing separation of the ANC and its leaders, affording higher value to the party – although opposition parties made inroads (Table 5.1) into the ANC base, testifying to some shifting trust. Zuma's words in response to the result rang true, but also had the ring of an ominous misinterpretation: '[t]his election victory has re-confirmed just how deeply rooted the ANC is in the hearts and minds of the overwhelming majority of South Africans' and '[t]hose parties who spoke so violently in Parliament … spent more than a year discussing my homestead Nkandla, instead of telling us what they'll do for the country. They remind me of Shakespeare … "It is a tale / told by an idiot, full of sound and fury, signifying nothing".'[48]

The details show that the ANC's 2014 result was roughly on the same level as the 2011 local election result, albeit on the basis of a different dynamic. In two consecutive national elections the ANC declined by four percentage points at a time. Table 5.1 demonstrates that the ANC does about two to three percentage points worse in the local election that follows on the national. If this trend holds, the ANC can be expected to touch 60 per cent at best in the 2016 local elections, all other factors being equal. The DA generally gets better results in local than in national elections. The EFF in the 2016 local election could detract from the ANC vote, but will also keep some disaffected voters away from the DA. The ANC's overall result in the 2009, 2011 and 2014 elections has depended on the growth of support in KwaZulu-Natal to bolster its sagging national averages. However, from 2011 onwards this effect had become less robust. Three post-election 2014–2015 tracking polls by Ipsos confirm that the ANC's surge in KwaZulu-Natal has run its course. May 2015 data show that ANC support in this province is notably declining.

Six trends tell the ANC's 2014 results story:

- The ANC is recording a serial decline in results – in 2014 for the second national election in a row (and the fourth consecutive election if one includes local elections).
- Lowered national and provincial levels of turnout register a form of alternative non-ANC voting, to the extent that it can be differentiated from apathy or total rejection of the system.
- Voting trends across the provinces vary and the two most populous provinces, KwaZulu-Natal and Gauteng, salvaged ANC in Election 2014 but with fewer votes.

176

Table 5.1: National election results: Proportional party support in nine national and local elections, 1994–2014

Parties with national representation	1994 National	1995/6 Local	1999 National	2000 Local **	2004 National	2006 Local ***	2009 National	2011 Local ****	2014 National
ANC	62.6	58.0	66.4	59.4	69.9	67.7	65.9	62.9	62.2
DA (DP+NP*)	22.1	21.5	17.0	22.1	12.4	13.9	16.7	24.1	22.2
EFF	–	–	–	–	–	–	–	–	6.4
IFP	10.5	8.7	8.6	9.1	7.0	8.4	4.6	3.6	2.4
NFP	–	–	–	–	–	–	–	2.4	1.6
UDM	–	–	3.4	2.6	2.3	1.98	0.9	0.6	1.0
FF+ (FF+CP)	2.2	2.7	0.8	0.1	1.0	1.0	0.8	0.4	0.9
Cope	–	–	–	–	–	–	7.4	2.2	0.7
ACDP	1.2	1.4	0.8	0.4	1.6	1.2	0.8	0.6	0.6
AIC	–	–	–	–	–	–	–		0.5
ID	–	–	–	–	1.7	1.4	0.9	–	–
Agang SA	–	–	–	–	–	–	–	–	0.3
PAC	1.3	0.7	1.2	1.2	0.7	1.2	0.3	0.4	0.2
MF	–	0.4	0.3	0.3	0.4	0.3	0.3	0.4	0.1
Azapo	–	–	0.2	0.3	0.3	0.3	0.2	0.2	0.1
UCDP	–	–	0.8	1.0	0.8	0.8	0.4	0.2	0.1

Source: Electoral Commission, www.elections.org.za, multiple windows, accessed 1994–2014.
Notes: * In some instances the IEC website combines the support for the DP and NP/NNP; the current table does not dissect it.
** Stated by the IEC website to be the percentage for the 'proportional representation' component of the local vote.
*** Stated by the IEC website to be the percentage for the 'party overall'.
**** Percentages on the proportional representation ballot.

- Voting tendencies of the middle classes affect the outcome, especially in metro areas of Gauteng, and they affect the ANC's future prospects.
- In the context of South Africa becoming a highly urbanised country, the metros delivered hair-raising results for the ANC, which either lost its outright majority or came close to losing it in the metros that do not have rural tracts within their boundaries.
- There was reduced support for the ANC in trouble spots, which ranged from substantial concentrations of EFF support in Gauteng townships to a handful of ANC ward losses to the EFF in North West informal set-tlements and mineworker communities. Despite securing a 6 per cent national proportional result, the EFF attained wins in three wards only, among them Madibeng Ward 26, which included Wonderkop, where the Marikana massacre had unfolded. The other two wards were in the Rustenburg municipality.

Serial decline, while dominance persists

Election 2014 confirmed the ANC as dominant party, gaining 62.15 per cent of the national vote, the support of around 11.5 million out of 18 million voters, and 249 out of 400 National Assembly seats. Impressive by most standards, this performance nonetheless raises questions about the ANC's liberation-movement invincibility, the amount of effort and resources required to leverage this continued dominance, and the qualitative changes that opposition parties have undergone. The result of Election 2014 is the story of a gradually declining behemoth, rather than another ringing endorsement.

The ANC garnered 213 827 votes fewer nationally in 2014 than it had in 2009. This represents a 1.84 per cent decline if calculated in relation to the 11.7 million votes the ANC had won in the national election of 2009. However, more than two million new voters had been added to the voters' roll between the 2009 and 2014 elections. With this taken into account, the ANC's real national loss becomes a 10.4 per cent decline.[49]

The difference (based on the national result) between the ANC and the larg-est of the opposition parties, the DA, consequently slipped below 40 percent-age points marginally for the first time in the five national elections from 1994 onwards – stopping at 39.9. At the 2004 peak of ANC national electoral power, the gap between it and the closest opposition party (the DA) came to 57.3 percentage points. This gap has narrowed by roughly 20 percentage points in a decade.

Cope's distintegration from 2009 to 2014 probably helped to moderate the ANC's national decline. In 2014, Cope released the bulk of 7 per cent of the national vote of 2009 back into the electoral marketplace, losing 1.19 million votes in this election compared with its 2009 result. It is likely that at least three of the seven percentage points had reverted to the ANC (four of the seven had its origins in ANC support).[50] Without this 'correction' the ANC might have been below the 60 per cent mark. Collected evidence from public radio interviews suggested that much of the rest of the previous Cope support moved on to the DA, which helped give the DA its increased chunk of black-African voter support.

Turnout, the hidden story

Turnout has been called the 'hidden story' of the 2014 election.[51] The turnout rate in the four national elections since 1999 has been 89.3 per cent, 76.7 per cent, 77.3 per cent and 73.5 per cent. Out of 25 million registered voters (with an estimated 10 million eligible voters not bothering to register, mainly the born-frees) 18.7 million voted, yet just over one-quarter of those registered did not go to the polls in 2014. The total voting age population is 32.7 million. These figures mean that the ANC governs with the proactive consent of 35 per cent of voting-age South Africans (Table 5.2).

Table 5.2:   ANC result relative to voting population, 1994–2014

Voting populations	Election				
	1994	**1999**	**2004**	**2009**	**2014**
Voting-age population (VAP)	22.7m	22.6m	27.4m	30m	32.7m*
Number of registered voters	No registration	18.2m	20.7m	23.2m	25.4m
VAP registered percentage		80.4%	75.4%	77.4%	77.7%
Turnout percentage	-	89.3%	76.7%	77.3%	73.5%
Number of valid votes cast	19.5m	16.0m	15.6m	17.7m	18.4m
Turnout percentage of VAP	86.0%	71.8%	57.8%	59.8%	57.1%
VAP percentage for ANC	53.8%	46.9%	39.6%	38.8%	35.0%

Source: www.elections.org.za; various windows.
Note: *Census 2011 gives this figure as 31.4m, which gave a 36% VAP percentage for the ANC in Election 2014.

Turnout had several effects on the ANC result. ANC voters consider abstention as a moderate form of opposition, and angry or disaffected voters are more likely to abstain than to switch their vote to an opposition party. Lower turnout is thus likely to have contributed to the ANC's four percentage-point decline. Lower voter turnout also moderated the ANC's slippage in that disaffected voters did not add their votes to opposition party tallies. My detailed analysis of ward results shows that the ANC's top performances (in terms of numbers of votes it won) came from wards with high turnout levels, many of them in the metropolitan areas of KwaZulu-Natal. In contrast, the wards in which the EFF gained its highest vote proportions tended to be those in which there had been a below-national-average turnout.

The exact impact of the 'Sidikiwe!' campaign, in protest against the current ANC and its leadership, was limited. Opposition party gains were probably only marginally linked to that campaign. The proportion of national spoilt votes remained consistent – 251 960 in number (and thus a smaller proportion, given the increased number of registered voters). The percentage of spoilt ballots in 2014 was 1.4 per cent, compared with 1.6 per cent in 1999. Ronnie Kasrils remarked that 'Sidikiwe!' succeeded in that 'we have created a national debate about blind loyalty to the ANC'.[52]

Differential provincial turnout affected the ANC result tangibly. In both Limpopo and the Eastern Cape the 2014 turnout was six percentage points down from 2009, and five percentage points each in the Free State and Mpumalanga. These four provinces' declines thus exceeded the 3.8 percentage points of national decline in turnout. The changes are nevertheless dwarfed in comparison with the 'big two' provinces, Gauteng and KwaZulu-Natal. Gauteng's turnout was 76.5 per cent (four percentage points lower than 2009), a drop that was well in excess of the national figure. KwaZulu-Natal's turnout was 76.9 per cent (four percentage points lower than in 2009), but also still above the national rate. On the variable turnout rates in these two provinces, therefore, the ANC continued to increase its KwaZulu-Natal share, but in Gauteng its vote share declined dramatically.

KwaZulu-Natal as ANC saviour

The ANC's provincial proportions of the vote were up in four and down in five provinces. This constituted a nominal improvement on 2009, when KwaZulu-Natal was the only province in which the ANC increased its share. The 2014 provincial increases, however, were minor and only KwaZulu-Natal added significant numbers. The ANC's KwaZulu-Natal vote went up by 274 579 votes from 2009 to 2014. This is modest, considering that the number of registered voters had increased by 2.2 million. Still, it dwarfed the increases that the ANC realised in some other provinces. The other three provinces with proportional rises were the Eastern, Northern and Western Cape, besides KwaZulu-Natal. KwaZulu-Natal and Northern Cape were the only two provinces in which the ANC did much better in 2014 than in 1994 – in contrast, the Western Cape ANC did marginally better and in all other provinces the ANC declined (Table 5.3).

The ANC won 22 per cent of its national ballot total in each of Gauteng and KwaZulu-Natal, leading into the total of 44.2 per cent of all ANC national ballots coming from these two provinces. It demonstrates the extent to which the politics of these two provinces has come to symbolise the erosion and perseverance of the ANC's share in Election 2014: Gauteng contributed much of the decline, and for the third election in a row KwaZulu-Natal went counter-trend to bring in substantial numbers of additional votes for the ANC.

The breakup of the Inkatha Freedom Party (IFP) benefited the ANC. The ANC bloomed late in KwaZulu-Natal (after a few elections), because the IFP had been well entrenched in bantustan politics and continued its hold when liberation came. At first, voters did not trust the ANC so it started off from a lower base than in most of the other provinces (comparable only to its 1994 base in the Western Cape). The ANC's KwaZulu-Natal surge in the 2009 election (related to Zuma's ascendance) continued in 2014. By the time of local election 2011, however, it had been clear that this provincial source of gains, although still on the rise, was losing momentum. The rise of the National Freedom Party (NFP), splitting from the IFP, also usurped a proportion of the votes that became available through the latter's decline. The inevitable tapering off of this KwaZulu-Natal pro-ANC trend, which compensated for ANC losses in other provinces, holds adverse implications for the ANC, unless it can engineer turnarounds in other provinces in times to come.

The ANC had to come to terms with the fact that 2014 did not win back the Western Cape from the DA (ANC pre-election research had shown that it would not win the province). The ANC emerged in the Western Cape with a growth of one percentage point on its 2009 result, off a small base – a result nowhere near the potential that it might have had, given in-migration from the Eastern Cape. Voter registration figures revealed that the ANC had not done its work to ensure that potential voters would be registered.[53] The ANC in the province was also wracked by factionalism, which affected its operations.

Table 5.3: ANC provincial election results over five elections, 1994–2014

ELECTION	1994	1999	2004	2009	2014	Change 2009–2014	Change 1994–2014
NATIONAL	62.65	66.35	69.69	65.90	62.15	-3.75	-0.5
PROVINCES							
Eastern Cape	84.4 (2.5m)	73.8 (1.6m)	79.3 (1.8m)	68.8 (1.6m)	70.8 (1.6m)	+2	-13.6
Free State	76.6 (1.0m)	80.8 (881k)	81.8 (827k)	71.1 (735k)	69.7 (721k)	-1.4	-6.9
Gauteng	57.6 (2.4m)	67.9 (2.5m)	68.4 (2.3m)	64.0 (2.7m)	54.9 (2.6m)	-9.1	-2.7
KwaZulu-Natal	32.2 (1.2m)	39.4 (1.2m)	47.0 (1.3m)	63.0 (2.2m)	65.3 (2.5m)	+2.3	+33.3
Limpopo	91.6 (1.8m)	88.3 (1.5m)	89.2 (1.4m)	84.9 (1.3m)	79.0 (1.2m)	-5.9	-12.6
Mpumalanga	80.7 (1.1m)	84.9 (959k)	86.3 (959k)	85.6 (1.1m)	78.8 (1.4m)	-6.8	-1.9
Northern Cape	49.7 (201k)	64.3 (211k)	68.8 (219k)	60.8 (246k)	63.9 (279k)	+3.1	+14.2
North West	83.3 (1.3m)	80.0 (1.0m)	80.7 (1.1m)	72.8 (784k)	67.8 (764k)	-5	-15.5
Western Cape	33.0 (706k)	42.1 (668k)	45.3 (709k)	31.6 (621k)	34.0 (737k)	+2.4	+1

Source: Figures from www.elections.org.za, various windows, accessed January and August 2014.
Note: All first-row figures in columns 2–6 are percentages (%); remaining rows are vote totals; figures in columns 7–8 are percentage points.

C05.indd   182

14-10-2015   09:23:37

The ANC in the Western Cape was assisted by the Ses'Khona movement. Its main operation up to the time of Election 2014 had been the so-called poo protests, which embarrassed the DA-governed Cape Town and highlighted poor living conditions in the city's vast informal residential areas. The ANC first expelled and then reinstated the Ses'Khona leaders. In both the poo protests and many of the 'standard' community protests there were hints of creating ungovernability against the DA metro and provincial governments. Ses'Khona was a vehicle to capture angry anti-ANC sentiment and then route it back into the ANC (also preventing these voices from siding with the EFF). The ANCYL in the province had a big role in the anti-DA 'service delivery' protests and the Western Cape war that the ANC failed to win at the polls continued on the streets of Cape Town and other towns in the post-election months.[54] The ANC was gearing up for a major assault on the DA in the Western Cape in 2016.

Middle-class ambiguity, working-class indecision

The 2014 results confirmed that the ANC was increasingly subject to the fracturing of its black middle- and working-class voting blocs. New class solidarities were reflected in a percentage of socially upwardly mobile black South Africans voting for the DA. ANC's Mantashe felt a sense of betrayal:

> We describe the forces of the revolution as those who stand to benefit from change and those who are prepared to defend change … If they vote for anybody else, it should not be because they are revolting because of an incident … I find it strange for someone in the black middle class to neglect a party that promotes BEE and employment equity.[55]

It raised the question 'about what disincentives social mobility represents for the ANC's continued political hegemony'.[56] In the words of the Gauteng ANC, the middle classes '… in this phase, are part of the motive forces of fundamental change. They are a by-product of the ANC's transformation agenda.'[57] Yet the ANC noticed that the middle classes, including those who had benefited from ANC policies, did not *all* feel obliged to continue voting ANC. While the ANC continued to receive high-profile electoral endorsements from many of the newly enriched beneficiaries of its twenty years of rule, the 2014 results (especially in Gauteng) were a wake-up call about rising middle-class readiness to vote against it. The ANC noted problem areas as the hostile reception of e-tolling on Gauteng's freeways, the high cost of living, corruption and the slow pace of economic transformation. The Gauteng ANC acknowledged the importance of the black middle classes when it assessed its own 2014 performance, noted signs of multi-class snubbing, and held forth on the need to reverse these threats to ANC hegemony:

> The ANC needs a comprehensive strategy to deal with [the middle-class] constituency, especially in the province where the black middle strata ha[ve] significant social, economic and political weight in determining the balance of power.[58]

The document further observes that while the working class generally sustains its electoral support for the ANC, large numbers did vote against it in 2014, enabling the EFF to win 'an average of 10 per cent of the vote in working-class townships, including the suburbs'.

These signals of change in the traditional pro-ANC alliance of class forces nevertheless did not cancel out the availability of large numbers from both the 'ordinary' middle classes and the high-flyer independently rich, BEE or tender-preneurial beneficiary rich to endorse the ANC. These middle-class groupings have diverse attachments to the ANC. Many continue to see it as struggle icon and/or governing party that has earned their ongoing loyalty. Others view it as vehicle to opportunity for employment or enrichment. An event hosted by the Progressive Professionals Forum (PPF, brainchild of the ANC itself) sketched the contours of the ANC's ideal version of the new middle-class dynamic – it was about political glamour and public flaunting of membership of the ruling class.[59] In short, power and political connectedness are beautiful. The PPF, along with the ANC's Progressive Business Forum, showed off professionals and aspirant BEEs in a parade of ANC electoral endorsements. The message was that the ANC brings prosperity to its associates, while these indulged middle classes, in turn, 'pay back' to their ANC.[60]

The trap of urbanisation

ANC support is adversely affected by urbanisation. The differential levels of support typically associated with urban-rural status, as well as differential urban and rural turnout, compound the problem. While the population has been urbanising, the ANC's urban vote has been declining in comparison with its more stable rural vote. Census 2011 reported that 62 per cent of South Africa's population of 51.8 million was urban. In contrast, 56 per cent of registered voters were urban while 44 per cent were rural; this proportion could increase in the future and come closer to the census statistic. The urban election turnout rate rose from 76 per cent in 2004 to 80 per cent in 2009, but returned to 76 per cent in 2014. Rural turnout started higher than urban in 2004 (at 78 per cent), declined to 75 per cent in 2009, and declined further to 70 per cent in 2014.[61] This places the ANC at a disadvantage for the future.

The ANC's greatest 2014 metropolitan vulnerability was in Gauteng (Table 5.4), a province in which more than 90 per cent of the population live

Table 5.4: ANC decline in four metropolitan municipalities, 2009–2014

PARTIES	METRO FIGURES FROM PROVINCIAL BALLOTS		
	2009 (%)	2014 (%)	Percentage-point gain/loss
Tshwane			
ANC	60	50.96	−10.6
DA	25.1	31.32	+8.7
EFF	–	11.41	+10.1
Johannesburg			
ANC	62.4	53.63	−10.1
DA	21.8	29.76	+10.6
EFF	–	10.15	+11.5
Ekurhuleni			
ANC	66.8 / 67.53	56.41	−11.7
DA	20	26.88	+6
EFF	–	10.65	+10
Nelson Mandela Bay			
ANC	49.6	49.17	−0.8
DA	28.1	40.16	+12.7
EFF	–	4.3	+4.2

Source: Figures from www.elections.org.za, accessed 1 June 2014.
Note: ANC decline in eThekwini, Buffalo City and Mangaung was more moderate. Cape Town was confirmed as increasingly DA-controlled.

in the metros. Metropolitan results in other provinces – apart from the Eastern Cape's Nelson Mandela Bay – showed only small declines. These other ANC metropole results were, for 2009 and 2014 respectively:

- Cape Town: 31.3 and 31.1 per cent;
- eThekwini: 66.3 and 64.6 per cent;
- Mangaung: 64.6 and 64.4 per cent; and
- Buffalo City: 67 and 66.9 per cent.

These last three metros, where the ANC continued to stand strong, all incorporate a substantial portion of rural-traditional areas within their municipal boundaries and are therefore not typically metropolitan. In the run-up to local election 2011 the ANC had already extended the borders of the Pretoria metro to include the district municipality of Metsweding in the Tshwane borders and help the party to retain this metro.

The ANC in Election 2014 received 47.3 per cent of its vote from rural South Africa, compared with 46.5 in 2009 and 48.7 in 2004; with 52.7, 53.6 and 51.3 per cent as the matching urban percentages. These internal rural-urban proportions have been relatively stable, but when compared with the proportions of the ANC's national vote the ANC's urban decline stands out. The ANC's proportion of the overall South African rural vote has remained relatively stable, only declining from 73 per cent in 2004 to 71.3 in 2014. However, serial urban slippage occurred. In 2004 the ANC had 67.8 per cent of the urban vote, declining to 61.3 per cent in 2009 and 55.8 in 2014.[62] The DA's support is overwhelmingly urban, and the EFF made some of its main inroads in Gauteng's urban areas.

Community protest as harbinger of vulnerabilities

It was tough going for the ANC in a range of protest-prone trouble spots. A widespread result in these areas was that although the ANC won the voting districts, they did so by reduced margins.[63] In some instances turnout was low; in others opposition parties fared better than they did nationally. The ANC followed a dual strategy in trying to minimise damage. On the one hand, ministers in the justice, crime prevention and security cluster made a series of high-profile visits across provinces and claimed responsibility for stabilising the areas ahead of the elections, but many voters felt intimidated by the high security force presence, which included soldiers.[64] It promoted the image that the ANC government was in control, yet also contributed to lower turnout.

On the other hand, and low-key, the ANC went into the protest areas after initial hostile receptions, campaigning strategically and thereby minimising damage. Gigaba explained the approach:

> We were strategic when we went to those areas … We went there [after the initial clashes with ANC representatives] when we had done our home-work, even in Bekkersdal. After all the hype in Bekkersdal, we quietly cam-paigned. We quietly campaigned in Rustenburg among the miners. We engaged people away from the glare of the media ... We engaged people directly and talked to influential individuals and turned them around, and used those individuals to continue engaging the masses of our people.[65]

ANC support in protest communities declined, but did not collapse. In pro-test communities generally the ANC lost more support than in communities that had not experienced protest in the six months prior to Election 2014.[66] The ANC still won the voting districts, yet by margins that declined more than the descent suffered in non-protest voting districts.[67] Several of the protest hot spots experienced violent pre-election resistance against IEC voter registra-tion and other electoral preparations, along with public embarrassments of the ANC on campaign visits.

CONCLUSION: CAN CORROSION BE ARRESTED?

The ANC's 2014 election result was a duet of dominance and decline – dominance nationally and in seven of the nine provinces, yet with substantial segments of decline. Decline showed in serial slippages in the national vote proportion, a lower turnout that contributed to the ANC decrease, provincial decay that turned Gauteng into an Achilles heel, and KwaZulu-Natal as the redeemer running out of steam. Middle-class ambiguity and damages to work-ing-class support blended with increasing ANC dependence on the shrinking base of rural votes, in addition to fragility in protest communities. Election 2014 showed concrete evidence of ANC losses in metropolitan areas, especially (but not only) in Gauteng.

The ANC in Election 2014 was far from being voted out, but it was captured in a pattern of serial electoral decline that was unlikely to get reversed. The DA was on a modest forward march, with each election accumulating bigger proportions and mildly pushing back the racial ceiling, yet with a vast support gap remaining between it and the ANC. The EFF added injury through its feats in ANC catchment areas and its ability to reach out to young and disaffected voters (in fact, the voters on whom the ANC will depend should it hope to reverse its 2014 declines). The EFF also damaged the DA's anticipated performance, offering an alternative to young voters who vote in anger or disappointment rather than great ideological belief (although the EFF support base includes fervent ideological believers).

The ANC's downward slope appears gradual but relentless. Post-election polling by Ipsos, however, shows that the ANC's support is holding up – across the provinces there are both declines and increases, including a modest recovery in Gauteng. The party is known for reinventing itself – and, on occasion, for self-correcting as well. The question is whether the ANC can dig deep and get to the point of sincerely and consistently engaging with communities through elected representatives. Can incumbent leaders show that they have the ability to rise above self-interest? Do they have the ability to rescue the ANC from an organisational cave-in that could wreak far more damage than any opposition party could possibly inflict?

NOTES

1   The chapter builds on Susan Booysen, 2015, 'The ANC's duet of dominance and decline', *Journal of African Elections*, vol. 14 (1), pp. 7–34.

2   Susan Booysen, 2013, *Twenty Years of South African Democracy: Citizen Views of Human Rights, Governance and the Political System*, research report, Johannesburg and Washington DC: Freedom House. This orientation was also evident in the DA's research. The DA leader noted the party's research shows that South Africans will continue voting ANC even when they believe it is corrupt (Helen Zille in interview with SABC-SAFM, 30 October 2010). My research showed that there is a deep popular cynicism of political parties; voters believe that any political party in power will be corrupt.

3   Sibusiso Ngalwa, 6 April 2014, 'ANC calls in pros to sing Zuma's praises', *Sunday Times*, p. 10.

4   This orientation compares with Michael Schatzberg, 2001, *Political Legitimacy in Middle Africa: Father, Family, Food*, Bloomington, IN: Indiana University Press.

5   David Moore, December 2014, comment on first draft of the manuscript.

6   Babalo Ndenze, 15 May 2014, interview with Ben Turok, 'Bumpy road ahead for ANC MP', *The Star*, p. 4.

7   As related in Bongani Hans, Leanne Jansen and Kamini Padayachee, 9 April 2014, 'Those voting for opposition parties "stealing grants"', *The Star*, p. 4.

8   Carien du Plessis and Sabelo Ndlangisa, 1 September 2013, 'ANC won't waste its time on white votes', *City Press*, p. 4.

9   See *The Sunday Independent*, 13 April 2014, p. 4; *City Press*, 13 April 2014, p. 3; *The Star*, 20 April 2014, p. 4.

10   Sibusiso Ngalwa, 4 May 2014, 'Zuma sticks to the poor and avoids the haters', *Sunday Times*, p. 4.

11   Sibusiso Ngalwa, 20 April 2014, 'Zuma booed by own party in Limpopo', *Sunday Times*, p. 2.

12   Ben Turok, 2014, *With My Head Above the Parapet*, Auckland Park: Jacana.

13   Pollster (anonymous), 2014, interview, major polling company, Johannesburg.

14   Babalo Ndenze, 12 April 2014, 'Zuma is head of the ANC and must be defended', *Saturday Star*, p. 4.

15   Rushil Ranchod, 2013, *A Kind of Magic: The Political Marketing of the ANC*, Auckland Park: Jacana.

16   Mandela family member, 10 November 2013, interview on condition of anonymity, Johannesburg; Zelda le Grange, 19 June 2014, 'My boss, my friend', *Times Live*, http://www.timeslive.co.za/lifestyle/2014/06/19/my-boss-my-friend-zelda-la-grange-talks-about-her-love-for-madiba, accessed 14 October 2014, notes that she last saw Madiba on 11 July 2013. On that occasion he recognised her.

17   Brendan Seery, 15 March 2014, 'ANC does deliver when it comes to poll advertising', *Saturday Star*, p. 17.

18   Sibongakonke Shoba, 11 April 2014, '"Direct contact" strategy and avoidance of negative debate won it for the ANC', *Sunday Times*, p. 5.

19   Natasha Marrian, 25 April 2014, 'Cosatu infighting has affected ANC election campaign', *Business Day*, p. 3.

20   Lebogang Seale, 13 April 2014, 'ANC "good story" gets jeered', *The Sunday Independent*, p. 4.

21   See Natasha Marrian, 25 April 2014, op. cit.

22   Babalo Ndenze, 24 April 2014, 'Zuma turns Nkandla into a joke', *The Star*, p. 4.

23   The author compiled a database of instances that evidenced the ANC drawing on, or benefiting from, state resources and campaigns throughout the period of January to May 2014.

24   Natasha Marrian, 25 April 2014, op. cit.

25   Amy Musgrave, 13 August 2014, 'ANC wants more time to fix Cosatu strife', *IOL News*, http://www.iol.co.za/news/politics/anc-wants-more-time-to-fix-cosatu-strife-1.1734611#.U_unrGN6ino, accessed 25 August 2014.

26   Setumo Stone, 3 December 2014, 'ANC leagues run out of good ideas', *Business Day Live*, http://www.bdlive.co.za/national/politics/2014/12/03/anc-leagues-run-out-of-good-ideas, accessed 4 December 2014.

27   Setumo Stone and Karl Gernetzky, 26 April 2013, 'MK veterans body rejects plan for new political party', *Business Day*, http://www.bdlive.co.za/national/politics/2013/04/26/mk-veterans-body-rejects-plan-for-new-political-party, accessed 26 July 2014.

28   David Smith, 25 April 2014, '"Desmond Tutu: Why I won't vote ANC"', *The Guardian*, http://www.theguardian.com/world/2014/apr/25/desmond-tutu-mandela-wont-vote-anc, accessed 17 July 2014.

29   Mavuso Msimang, 3 April 2014, 'ANC owes it to itself and SA to halt its abuse of power', *Business Day*, p. 8.

30 Sihle Zikalala, 2013, 'Brief outline on Volunteer Corps Movement', www.anckzn.org.
za/sites/.../briefoutlineonvolunteercorpsmovement.pdf, accessed 2 August 2013.

31 Sibongakonke Shoba, 11 April 2014, op. cit.

32 Jacob Zuma, 4 May 2014, address to the ANC national Siyanqoba rally, FNB
stadium, Johannesburg.

33 Sabelo Ndalangisa and Paddy Harper, 4 May 2014, 'How ANC made Nkandla
disappear', *City Press*, p. 4.

34 Interview, ANC Western Cape organiser, 10 November 2014, Cape Town.

35 There were reports that the ANC was broke; see Qaanitah Hunter and Matuma
Letsoalo, 31 October 2014, 'The ANC is broke', http://mg.co.za/article/2014-10-
30-broke-anc-may-have-to-cut-jobs-for-comrades, accessed 1 November 2014;
and several denials that the ANC is broke, including Sapa, 31 October 2014, 'ANC
denies it is broke', http://mg.co.za/article/2014-10-31-anc-denies-it-is-broke,
accessed 1 November 2014.

36 Qaanitah Hunter, 28 November–4 December 2014, 'Elections cost battling ANC
R450-million', *Mail & Guardian*, pp. 2–3.

37 This is a personal calculation. *Mail & Guardian* (Qaanitah Hunter), 28 November–4
December 2014, 'Elections cost battling ANC R450-million', pp. 2–3, based its
account on a leaked ANC report, which may have excluded some of the typical
campaign expenses.

38 Community Agency for Social Enquiry (Case), 2014, *Just Singing and Dancing*,
research report, Johannesburg.

39 ANC Gauteng, 5 May 2013, provincial election manual, Johannesburg.

40 Department of Water Affairs, 21 March 2014, '20 years of water delivery for social
and economic development', *The New Age*, p. 9.

41 Verashni Pillay, 11–23 January 2014, 'Gauteng ads show ANC's true colours',
Mail & Guardian, p. 6.

42 Sithandiwe Velaphi, 14 April 2014, 'Zuma's water vow', *The New Age*, p. 4.

43 Shanti Aboobaker, 6 April 2014, 'State agency gives blankets at ANC rally', *The
Sunday Independent*, p. 1; Nathi Olifant, Mervyn Naidoo and Agiza Hlongwane,
6 April 2014, 'DA, ANC big guns out to woo voters', *The Sunday Independent*, p. 4.

44 Carien du Plessis and Sabelo Ndlangisa, 1 September 2013, op. cit.

45 SASSA official, 23 April 2014, interview on condition of anonymity, Johannesburg.

46 Sabelo Ndlangisa, 4 May 2014, 'How the ANC won the elections', *City Press*, p. 2.

47 Philani Nombembe, 4 May 2014, 'DA faces hefty legal bill after food-for-votes
court bid fails', *Sunday Times*, p. 4.

48 Jacob Zuma, 10 May 2014, acceptance speech at the announcement of the 2014
election results, IEC National Results Centre, Pretoria, http://www.anc.org.za/
show.php?id=10898, accessed 13 May 2014.

49 Jonathan Faull, 2014, 'Analysing South Africa's 2014 election results', Institute for
Security Studies (ISS), *Policy Brief* 54, June; Judith February and Jonathan Faull,
2014, 'Slicing and dicing the 2014 election data: What are the implications for the
ANC, DA and EFF?' https://www.issafrica.org/uploads/2014-Election-Data-Ju
dith-Februrary.pdf, accessed 13 June 2014. These authors first highlighted these
actual decline figures to my attention.

50 Zaid Kimmie, Jan Greben and Susan Booysen, 2010, 'A review of the 2009 South
African election', *Politeia*, Special edition: Elections in Africa, vol. 29 (1), pp. 98–120.

51   Henning Melber, 9–11 May 2014, 'South Africa's elections 2014: And the winner is?' Essay. Pretoria and Uppsala.

52   Fiona Forde, 11 May 2014, 'Today's ANC had no moral cause, says Kasrils', *The Star*, p. 9.

53   For a detailed analysis, see Troye Lund, 27 February 2014, 'ANC misses Western Cape boat', *Financial Mail*, http://www.financialmail.co.za/features/2014/02/27/anc-misses-western-cape-boat, accessed 6 May 2014.

54   See Kieran Legg, 2 September 2014, 'Nyanga buses to get armed escorts', *Cape Argus*, p. 1. Ses'Khona leader Loyiso Nkohla denied involvement, while Mayor Patricia de Lille linked the bus and taxi violence to Nkohla's threat to destroy the N2 freeway express service in anger about the inequality of public transport services in the city.

55   Janet Heard, 16 June 2014, 'Mantashe's rules for clever blacks', *City Press*, p. 4.

56   Ebrahim Fakir and Waseem Holland, 2011, 'Changing voting patterns?' *Journal of Public Administration*, Special Issue 1, p. 46.

57   ANC Gauteng, September 2014, Base document II: Framework document towards the ANC Gauteng 12th provincial conference; theme: 'United action to advance radical social and economic transformation', Johannesburg.

58   ANC Gauteng, September 2014, op. cit., p. 6; Sibongakonke Shoba, 24 August 2014, 'ANC concedes it lost middle class in Gauteng vote', *Sunday Times*, p. 6. Also see Robert Mattes, 2015, 'South Africa's emerging black middle class: A harbinger of political change?' *Journal of International Development*, 27, pp. 665–692.

59   Richard Poplak, 30 April 2014, 'Welcome to Fantasia: The ANC manifesto endorsement and the reality left behind', *Daily Maverick*, http://www.dailymaverick.co.za/article/2014-04-29-hannibal-elector-welcome-to-fantasia-the-anc-manifesto-endorsement-and-the-reality-left-behind/#.U_uVyGN6joQ, accessed 25 August 2014.

60   Nondumiso Mbuyazi, 3 May 2014, 'Mpisanes throw big beach party for ANC', *Independent,* www.iol.co.za/ios/news/mpisanes-throw-big-beach-party-for-anc-1.1683018#.U_xnFWN6ino, accessed 2 June 2014; Kwanele Sosibo, 2–8 May 2014, 'EFF, Nkandla unite ANC in KZN', *Mail & Guardian*, p. 14.

61   Judith February and Jonathan Faull, 2014, op. cit.

62   Ibid.

63   Michael O'Donovan, 16 July 2014, interview, Johannesburg.

64   Siyabonga Mkhwanazi, 3 June 2014, 'Army stabilised "hot spots"', *The New Age*, p. 3.

65   Sibongakonke Shoba, 11 April 2014, op. cit.

66   Susan Booysen, Alta de Waal, Hans Ittmann and Peter Schmitz, August 2014, 'Testing persistence of the dual repertoire hypothesis on Election 2014 data: Community protest still co-existing with ANC support?' Workshop deliberations, Pretoria.

67   Michael O'Donovan, 16 July 2014, op. cit.

6

THE DA'S ENCROACHING MARCH

Opposition political parties in South Africa are on a long march to dent ANC majorities. Although the parties take part in the uphill slog to close the gap, the succession of new parties falling in battle against the ANC hangs over their heads. And even 'great opposition performances' are only modestly reducing the ANC's lead.

The Democratic Alliance (DA) has grown more steadfastly than any other opposition party in democratic South Africa. It grew by six percentage points from 2009 to 2014, while the ANC shrank by four percentage points. In the decade from 2004 to 2014 it grew incrementally and systematically from one national election to the next without setbacks, and this was despite new opposition parties detracting from its potential performance. Despite such achievements, however, the DA's growth has been modest and it has no guarantee that a new party may not still rise and eclipse it. The EFF made a notable 6 per cent entrance onto the electoral landscape in 2014, yet its performance was only marginally better than the six percentage-point *growth* that the DA registered.

Three futures need to be considered for the DA: on its own, incrementally growing as a predominantly liberal party (with or without added momentum that could allow catch-up with the ANC); becoming more like the ANC in policy and ideology (offering a cleaner, less corruption-prone party while extending rapidly into the black-African voter bloc); and largely suspending prior ideology to become a vote-catching party machine that would also align with other parties in governing coalitions.

The thread of these alternative futures runs through this argument. The DA as predominant opposition party anchors the chapter, counterbalanced with the rest of the opposition right of the ANC. The analysis places DA growth, identity changes and leadership dilemmas and change in the context of a weakened but always dominant ANC. The chapter dissects the DA's gradual accumulation of support, its strategies for reinventing itself, and its barriers to becoming the next government – and compares the DA's fortunes with the hopes of new opposition parties, which rise and fall at an approximate rate of one per major electoral event.

POSITIONING OPPOSITION AMID ANC DOMINANCE

The DA – along with other centrist opposition parties – has encroached on ANC territory. In the process the DA cracked, but did not crush, the ceilings that racial and liberation identity impose on South African voter allegiances. The DA has been making modest inroads into new voter constituencies and, in the process, has become in some respects a smaller version of the ANC's broad church. It increasingly looks like an ideological hybrid, with its quest to attract black politicians and voters watering down its classic liberalism. It is now a political home to an incongruous collection of cultural, political and ideological identities,[1] tied together with a thin and sometimes frayed string of a liberal, open society vision, and/or simply criticism of the ANC. Its Vision 2029 document is intended to synthesise a new DA identity.

The DA has also recognised that leadership image – and that includes racial image – has played a role in new voters' ability to identify with it, and this has informed many of its leadership decisions. The DA has reinvented its image and replaced leaders to try to fit the bill. It tried twice to recruit and parachute a black celebrity leader, Mamphela Ramphele, into a high-leadership position. Then it turned to the fast-track-home-grown leadership option and in May 2015 it elected Mmusi Maimane as national leader in place of Helen Zille. In the course of this transformation process the DA shed (for the time being) former parliamentary leader Lindiwe Mazibuko, for reasons of policy mistakes, divisive leadership and generally for not being the 'designer leader' that the DA reckoned it required for its vote-catching quest.[2]

These dynamics demonstrate the curse of opposition politics in the age of ANC dominance. To challenge the ANC effectively, opposition parties need to grow. To grow, they need to conquer chunks of the ANC support base; in turn, they need to speak in the liberation-style, 'great power working on delivery' voice that the ANC has mastered – and the DA has had to do this while remaining the essentially liberal party. To acquire such a voice it needs to expand its identity and incorporate new policy-ideological ideas – but new policy-ideology orientations are bound to bring contradictions and discord, and even become self-defeating. For example, to what extent can the DA's liberal and veering-towards-social-democrat ideas make room for patron-client relations? How can its open society and equal opportunity ideas take off in a society that expects the democratically elected government to bring restitution and correct the wrongs of the past? To help reposition itself, the DA in 2015 adopted its Values Charter,[3] promising social security to protect citizens against 'extreme poverty' combined with high-quality education, health and basic services. For government, the DA strives for honesty, transparency and accountability.

While these identity-public appeal struggles unfolded, the ANC was on a relentless trail of onslaughts. The ANC strives to minimise the opposition parties' influence, preferably preventing them from gaining representation in the national and provincial legislatures. If they achieve sound levels of representation nevertheless, the name of the ANC's follow-up game is to dishearten and undermine, or mock and try to reinvent opposition attacks on the ANC and its president as opposition weaknesses, as Zuma did in Parliament in May 2015. In the post-2014 time generally, the DA has been more certain than ever of its reinvented identity. It had captured noteworthy numbers of black-African supporters, even if not at the level of definitively breaking through into ANC territory. It also managed to further consolidate opposition to the ANC's right. Such progress came despite the emergence of the EFF and its scooping-up of much of the available youth and born-free vote.[4]

The repositioning of the DA was also in the context of a 'revolutionised' 2014–2015 Parliament where opposition matured, and, bolstered with larger numbers, it no longer appears as a pushover that submits to ANC majoritarianism. Hence, Parliament is no longer a secure rubber-stamping zone for the ANC but has become more of a forum where opposition voices are asserted. The occasionally united opposition is vocal and robust. The two-front DA-EFF parliamentary opposition, joined by the United Democratic Movement (UDM), Freedom Front Plus (FF+) and others, has been evident where it hurts the ethically compromised ANC the most – on the issues of presidential corruption, the separation of powers and the autonomy of Parliament. The ANC has tried to present this new parliamentary opposition as busy destabilising South Africa and disrespectful of Parliament.

The DA's influence on politics in South Africa has also become bigger than its electoral performances. Its between-election opposition is often powerful and has detracted from the esteem and legitimacy of the ANC. There are high seasons of contest with and victories over the ANC. The DA has excelled at using legal recourse and due process, supported by constitutionalism and rule of law, to help hold the ANC to account. But these feats do not necessarily convert to electoral gains.

OPPOSITION POLITICS VERSUS PROTECTING THE PRESIDENT

The ANC's version of protecting the president in Parliament exposed the governing party's dilemma at the time – the president had become difficult to defend, but there was no turning away. The parliamentarians were also essentially weak and had to be guided and coached by Luthuli House on how to protect the leader. Gradually in 2015 the president himself, by now coached by a new communications team, acted more strongly and counter-attacked the opposition. With media and civil society watching every move in the parliamentary drama of how to act legally and constitutionally yet not 'deliver' the president, the ANC was compelled to use its parliamentary majority to force through the protection of the president. ANC Secretary General Gwede Mantashe, and the president himself, had decreed such protection at the ANC's September 2014 NEC meeting[5] (although many ANC MPs were so closely aligned to the president and his wishes that this protection would have been automatic in any case).

Instead of recanting, the ANC answered by attacking and accusing opposition parties of undermining democracy and destabilising South Africa. The subsequent 2015 leg of the 'protection of the president in Parliament' spectacle elicited a set of legal actions – mainly pertaining to the argued violation of Parliament through the entrance of SAPS public order forces and the jamming of cellphone signals in the parliamentary precinct in order to limit the dissemination of potentially embarrassing scenes of the opposition challenging the president.

This ANC presidential protection dogma has been prevalent throughout 2014–2015 parliamentary sessions. The EFF's direct challenges and 'pay back the money' parliamentary assault on the president opened the way, but the DA quickly grew into the new 'robust' style of opposition and started using it to good effect. Parliament had never before been the host to opposition that was in-your-face and honest to the point of insult. The DA became a new parliamentary presence, ranging from opposition big brother, to matching EFF outspokenness, to considered presence. Micro-opposition parties, such as the UDM, Cope and the FF+, added to the concerted opposition voice. Collectively, the opposition parties demonstrated that minorities in party politics can forge joint opposition.

The ANC's protection of the president brought previously unimagined windfalls to the DA and rest of the parliamentary opposition: they found a rallying point with easy common ground.[6] Mutual issues were mostly corruption and the president, or inaction and delayed processes as these apply to required actions by the president. The small steps of cooperation between opposition parties[7] did not, however, suggest the emergence of a new, united opposition party. It was pragmatic cooperation, and without the numbers contributed by the DA the new parliamentary opposition presence would not have taken shape.

Presidential protectionism thus saw two modest opposition parties, to the right and the left of the ANC, along with a host of micro-parties, placing the majority party and its leadership problems under the magnifying glass. The opposition revealed an ANC that was weaker than suggested by its 62 per cent.

DA and opposition by legal process

The use of the courts to challenge appointments, legislation and, in general, defence of the Constitution has become standard in the DA's opposition repertoire. The DA anchored its actions by focusing on the rule of law, due legal and political process and the constitutional state. ANC structures have also used recourse to the courts, one example being between the rival Free State factions in the run-up to the Mangaung conference, but Luthuli House was very critical both of these internal tactics and the DA's strategy of legal challenge.[8] Cope, too, had resorted to the courts to resolve the issues between leaders Mosiuoa Lekota and Mbhazima Shilowa. President Zuma himself is the foremost practitioner.[9] Several of his battles have entailed challenges to controversial appointments that the president makes, or attempts to make.

Menzi Simelane's appointment as national director of public prosecutions (NDPP), and the attempted term extension of former chief justice Sandile Ngcobo, illustrate the point.[10] The biggest cost, by far, has been the president's defence of his own presidential appointment despite 'charges' against him.

The DA's persistence in legal challenges resulted in the release of the spy tapes in 2014 – after five years of legal counteraction from Zuma to avoid it. The DA went to court to contest the NPA's withdrawal of charges against Zuma in 2009. The spy tapes contain details of a so-called political conspiracy against Zuma – details which, it is said, prompted then acting NDPP, Mokotedi Mpshe, to announce the withdrawal of the charges.[11] (It was subsequently said that threats to shut down the NPA, rather than the validity of any conspiracy claim, had persuaded Mpshe to make this call.[12]) The DA kept on pursuing the reopening of the trial, and it started rolling by mid-2015. The DA pursued a series of other cases as well, notably also in the Cape High Court, where it won a battle against the appointment of the SABC chief operating officer, Hlaudi Motsoeneng (the judgement was appealed). The DA is part of the Opposition to Urban Tolling Alliance (Outa) collective that has been opposing e-tolling in Gauteng and the Western Cape. A further illustration was the DA's 2015 exploration of legal action to stop armed police from entering Parliament unless there is a clear and present danger.

THE DA'S ELECTORAL GROWTH PATH

The DA's growth nevertheless has been insufficient to catch up with the ANC, which is also unlikely to happen in the foreseeable future. Ever optimistic, the DA has never failed to anticipate some turning point of mass conversion that would make it the national government and its leader the president. Notwithstanding its propensity for inflated claims, the DA is the only opposition party in democratic South Africa that has not relapsed – its growth has been continuous since it merged with the support base of the former New National Party (even if the last of the NNP leaders standing had merged with the ANC).[13] Far more black voters – and in particular also black-African voters – than before voted DA in Election 2014. Its white-to-black leadership change from Helen Zille to Mmusi Maimane was inspired by prospects of gaining additional windfalls of black support. An internal DA poll at the time of Maimane's election indicated that the percentage of blacks supporting the party would rise from 6 to 8 per cent, at that time.[14] In the minds of the voters, however, the DA was not gaining traction as an alternative *governing party*,[15] except in the Western Cape, where it consolidated its previously modest outright majority.

South African elections are still played in the mode of large numbers of voters forgiving and forgetting ANC misdemeanours and embarrassments when elections arrive. They then celebrate liberation once again, reward progress since the start of democracy, and align with the ANC as the party of power. Opposition parties are up against the ANC's quadruple winning ticket – liberation icon, political family, party that has brought change in delivery, and party of power in charge of patronage. The DA in the Western Cape, and in municipalities like Cape Town, had of course become a party of provincial patronage, polishing its own networks.

Whatever it takes within a liberal-democratic context to grow its party, the DA was attending to it, staying as true as possible to its vision and ideology. The two main thrusts of its strategy were to grow its membership and electoral support, with special effort in black-African constituencies, and to usurp smaller opposition parties. To this effect it recruited black leadership, imported well-profiled leaders, pursued nonracial membership, projected itself as the inclusive, diverse home for all South Africans, developed policies, and became 'Watchdog No. 1' over the ANC's excesses in power. The DA's electoral growth often came on the basis of opposition party supporters abandoning their smaller parties to join the more visible opposition party. Political parties also follow their voters' verdicts. The Independent Democrats (ID) started aligning with the DA after most ID voters had abandoned it in favour of the DA. Elections 2009 and 2014 saw several of the opposition parties shrink as their followers changed parties. Opposition parties that had previously ceded support to the DA included the Freedom Front Plus and the UDM.[16]

The DA's 2014 campaign rendered several achievements, although not to the extent of catching up with the ANC:

- It grew its national support from 16.7 per cent in 2009 to 22.2 per cent in 2014 – a gain on the national ballot of 1 145 755 votes and a six percentage-point growth, just marginally lower than the total percentage that the EFF gained. On the national interpretation of the local vote it had received 24.1 per cent in 2011 compared with 22.2 per cent in 2014. The DA, however, is known to perform better in local than in national elections. It is therefore possible that it will continue its upward trend in the 2016 local elections.

- The DA was the only party to grow in all provinces (apart from the EFF, which grew off a zero base). The gains were sometimes marginal, but in fact the DA grew across all provinces in each election since 1999, with the single exception of Limpopo, where it declined by a fractional 0.2 percentage points between 2004 and 2009. The DA increased its Western Cape majority from the slim 51.4 per cent of 2009 to 59.3 per cent in 2014.
- The DA made substantial further progress in metropolitan areas, particularly in Johannesburg (up by nine percentage points), Nelson Mandela Bay (up by twelve percentage points), Tshwane (up by seven percentage points) and Ekurhuleni (up by six percentage points). This suggests that in the 2016 local government elections there is a good chance that the DA could advance sufficiently to lead coalition governments (if the ANC does not find a minority party to help it continue governing). The DA itself foresees that it will be the lead coalition party in many more municipalities across the country. In Cape Town, where it is already in power, it gained a further eight percentage points.

The rapid phase of DA growth was first apparent in the 2009 national-provincial elections. It continued in the 2011 local and 2014 national-provincial elections. The 2014 growth achievements stand out when viewed in the context of DA performance in three elections in the decade from 2004 to 2014:

- Election 2004: 1 931 201 votes for the DA (12.93 per cent of votes cast), growth of 4.29 per cent;
- Election 2009: 2 945 829 votes for the DA (16.66 per cent of votes cast), growth of 2.81 per cent; and
- Election 2014: 4 091 584 votes for the DA (22.23 per cent of votes cast), growth of 7.83 per cent.

These feats would have been accepted as more remarkable had the DA not *hoped for much better* and *advertised its hopes* early in the campaign. The DA's progress in 2014 was thus less than its widely broadcast targets of 30 per cent nationally,[17] and the capturing of Gauteng by pushing the ANC below 50 per cent. From 2012 onwards the DA had claimed that it would take Gauteng and the Northern Cape in 2014 and from there move toward a national election victory in 2019.[18] Its logic was that it had moved from close to 13 per cent in the 2004 national elections to approximately 24 per cent in the 2011 local elections, thus roughly doubling its base in seven years. If there had been a linear trend taking local and national into account, and if other opposition parties had not started fishing in DA waters, the party might have been closer to its 2014 target. The DA's positioning for taking over power has continued: its Vision 2029, launched in June 2015, suggested that 2019 might be *the date*.

The mirage of capturing Gauteng

The DA had predicted that it would crack the ANC's outright provincial electoral majority in Gauteng in 2014. It assumed that it would be able to pull together alliance majorities there and in other provinces, pushing the ANC below 50 per cent. Lindiwe Mazibuko[19] argued: '… we can push the ANC below the 50 plus 1 per cent and that will give us the opportunity to form a coalition government with other opposition parties.'[20] On the eve of Election 2014, the DA's Gauteng percentage share of opinion survey votes was reported to be in the low 40s,[21] and it was not giving up hope for a provincial coalition government. In contrast the party's national tracking showed it was nowhere near the originally estimated 30 per cent national level of support.[22] It was only shortly before Election 2014, and when the impact of the EFF among young and angry voters was starting to solidify, that the DA realised it would *not* win its anticipated chunk of the Gauteng vote.[23]

The DA had been targeting the disaffected ANC vote, citizens who were saying *ayisafani* ('the ANC is not the same anymore').[24] It had, however, failed earlier on to enter the EFF into its equation. And the EFF – from within the ANC kraal – would be an easier protest vote destination than the DA, which had anticipated that it would win a bigger portion of the new, young voters from the born-free ranks.

Although the DA did not win Gauteng, its performance in the province pushed the ANC close to ceding an outright provincial majority to the joint opposition. This was the most pronounced of the wake-up calls to the ANC in Election 2014. The ANC lost ten percentage points off its 2009 Gauteng vote, only managing to convince 54 per cent of the Gauteng voters that it was fit to govern (Table 6.1). The DA's failure to win the province veils its gain of an additional 450 000 new votes that were added to its 2009 provincial total. Its Gauteng vote proportion rose from 22 per cent in 2009 to 31 per cent in 2014.

The DA did well in the Gauteng metros of Tshwane, Johannesburg and Ekurhuleni (Table 5.4), to the extent of flagging them as potential future ANC losses. In Ekurhuleni the DA grew from 227 000 (rounded figures) votes in 2009 to 328 000 in 2014 (a 44 per cent increase), in Tshwane from 245 000 in

Table 6.1: Biggest parties in three elections, 2004–2014: National and provincial

Election %	National	Eastern Cape	Free State	Gauteng	KwaZulu-Natal	Limpopo	Mpumalanga	North West	Northern Cape	Western Cape
2004	ANC 67 DA 13 IFP 7	ANC 79 UDM 9 DA 7	ANC 82 DA 9	ANC 68 DA 21 IFP 3	ANC 47 IFP 37 DA 8	ANC 89 DA 4	ANC 86 DA 7	ANC 81 DA 5	ANC 59 DA 11	ANC 53 DA 27 NNP 11
2009	ANC 66 DA 17 Cope 7	ANC 69 Cope 14 DA 10 UDM 4	ANC 71 Cope 12 DA 12	ANC 64 DA 22 Cope 8	ANC 63 IFP 22 DA 9	ANC 85 Cope 8 DA 6	ANC 86 DA 7	ANC 73 Cope 17 DA 8	ANC 61 Cope 17 DA 13	DA 51 ANC 32
2014	ANC 62 DA 22 EFF 6	ANC 70 DA 16 UDM 6 EFF 4	ANC 70 DA 16 EFF 8	ANC 54 DA 31 EFF 10	ANC 65 DA 13 IFP 11 NFP 7	ANC 79 EFF 11 DA 6	ANC 78 DA 10 EFF 6	ANC 67 EFF 13 DA 13	ANC 64 DA 24 EFF 5	ANC 33 DA 59 EFF 2

Source: IEC, www.elections.org.za, various windows accessed over time, 2014–2015.
Note: All figures indicate percentage of the vote gained.

2009 to 354 000 in 2014 (another 44 per cent increase), and in Johannesburg from 323 000 votes in 2009 to 508 000 in 2014 (a 57 per cent increase). In other Gauteng municipalities DA growth ranged between 21 and 65 per cent,[25] the latter in Westonaria, which included areas where there had been acrimonious protests in the months prior to the election. There was no substantiation of the DA's Northern Cape pre-election claim that it could beat the ANC. In addition, the DA had stagnated in comparison with the 2011 local election result.

DA and the black-African vote

Through the period of Election 2014 the DA continued its incremental growth, but without the exponential surge that it had anticipated, the kind of growth required to catch up with – and overtake – the ANC. Black-African voters remained overwhelmingly loyal to the ANC, despite the multiple problems they acknowledge regarding ANC government and leadership. The DA's 2014 result nevertheless testifies to the fact that it had captured black-African votes to a greater extent than before. The DA itself claimed that it had grown by 760 000 votes in this voting bloc.[26] My analysis of the ward results shows that the DA's black-African vote gains came from a spread of votes across the country's wards, often centred on middle-class and mostly urban and metropolitan communities. These findings are corroborated by Zwelethu Jolobe.[27] He delves into a series of voting station results in typical township areas in Gauteng and the Western Cape, for example, and finds but a few cases that can be described as DA breakthroughs.

A comparison of the demographic profiles of the DA's support base with those of the ANC and EFF shows (and this corresponds to the profile of the votes it earned):

> Employment: Half of DA supporters are employed either full-time or part-time, whereas those who are unemployed and looking for work are more prevalent among ANC and EFF supporters.
>
> Population group: 20 per cent of DA supporters are black-African, whereas the vast majority of ANC (96 per cent) and EFF (99 per cent) supporters are black-African. The DA draws support from all main population groups (unlike the ANC and EFF).
>
> Education: The majority of supporters of the DA, ANC and EFF have either completed their school education or have some high school education, and 25 per cent of DA supporters, compared with 9 per cent of ANC supporters and 10 per cent of EFF supporters, have post-matric education.

Urban-rural: DA supporters are the most 'urbanised', with about three-quarters living in metropolitan areas, cities or large towns. About a third of ANC and EFF supporters live in metropolitan areas, while more than half of the supporters of both these parties live in rural areas.

Income: DA supporters tend to be more affluent than those of the ANC and EFF (but large proportions of survey respondents do not share income information easily).[28]

The DA had become the party of choice in minority communities: coloured, Indian and white. The DA displaced the Minority Front, which lost close to 80 per cent of its previous support (linked to the passing of its leader Amichand Rajbansi and subsequent turmoil in the party). The Minority Front decline continued in municipal by-elections later in 2014. Leader Shameen Thakur-Rajbansi complained that its supporters of many years 'hardly know the DA and yet they want to vote for it'.[29]

THE DA REINVENTING ITSELF

The DA has constantly attempted to reinvent itself. Its 2014 campaign was an integral part of this process; its 2015 election of a black-African national leader followed through. First, ideologically and policy-wise, it moved somewhat closer to the ANC but had to stay mindful of its liberal roots and of the conservative white and coloured-working-class constituencies that remained an essential base. The change happened manifestly yet haltingly: some true believers in the DA were concerned. In its 2014 campaign, for example, the DA nested itself in the ANC's 'good story', up to the point of saying that Thabo Mbeki had done good work.[30] There was sense in this approach, given that the DA was targeting ANC supporters who still believed in the ANC but were resenting its leadership malfunction in the form of Jacob Zuma. However, such moves led to charges that the DA was inconsistent, given its harsh criticisms of the Mbeki regime not so long beforehand. Second, at election time the DA tried to show its new, reinvented, close-to-Mandela and more-ANC-than-the-original-ANC character. In the words of then national leader Helen Zille, campaigning in Bellville, 'the DA is living up to Madiba's vision … The DA unites, the ANC divides.'[31] Third, an ANC-ish character was infused via a new generation of black leaders slotted into prominent positions, either elected by conference or selected and groomed for leadership by Zille. At the time of the 2015 leadership elections the party focused strongly on repositioning and was strained to remain the DA while becoming the ANC.

Between *ayisafani* and Stan Greenberg

The DA's expensive,[32] well-tuned and glitzy campaigns (with some help from turncoat pollster Stanley Greenberg)[33] helped notch up its DA achievements. An outstanding feature was the way parliamentary leader Mmusi Maimane (also the DA's Gauteng premiership candidate at the time) was pitched. He was recreated in a Barack Obama image, with his head tilted and an optimistic facial expression, eyes lifted towards the hope on the horizon, and immaculate speech delivery. The phrases of 'change', 'hope' and 'believe' drenched the voters, delivered in a messiah-is-arriving style, in blue (DA colour) suede shoes[34] at party jamborees. It was a consummate approximation of campaigning through imagery. However, this political style did not fundamentally change South Africa's party dynamics.

Many of the issues that Greenberg relates as problematic of the 1999 ANC (derived from research when he still worked with the ANC)[35] remained evident and were often exacerbated by 2014.[36] Examples were the distance between ANC leaders and their communities, and the business transactions with their obvious ethical lapses. Despite the *ayisafani* description of the ANC, and notwithstanding agreeing that the ANC is frequently corrupt, the bulk of voters did not believe that the DA or another opposition political party could be better trusted to govern and look after them.[37] Voters' relationship with their ANC was rocky and more tempestuous than before, but the space was not available for opposition parties to claim. Many voters chose to abstain rather than switch their vote to an opposition party (Table 5.2).

The DA tried consistently to demonstrate the distance between the ANC and communities that the ANC purports to represent. A controversial election advertisement showed images of police firing rubber bullets at two unarmed citizens.[38] The offending line was: 'We have seen the police killing our people.' The South African Police Service (SAPS) appealed to the Independent Communications Authority of South Africa (Icasa), arguing that the advert might incite violence against the police, and the SABC banned the advert.[39] The SABC later reinstated it; the Icasa ruling, however, instructed the advert to be changed. The DA gained campaign mileage by crusading into ANC strongholds such as Soshanguve, a Gauteng township north of Pretoria. In some instances at least, this strategy was carried out with imported, paid 'crowds', a common party practice in South Africa.[40]

Building blocks to reinvention

The DA's 2014 election campaign depicted the party as more ANC than the ANC originally. To grow substantially it had to penetrate the ANC support base – and the ANC's great strength was that it was the liberation movement party that makes things happen for the people. More modest reinvention continued through the party's 2015 conference that spawned the slogan 'Freedom, fairness, opportunity'. Its Values Charter was designed to build trust between party and voters, informing voters about some fundamentals of the DA. It placed family values at the centre.

The DA believed its following would increase if only the voters could understand it better. For its 2014 campaign positioning, the DA used a multipronged approach:[41] emphasise the liberal and progressive roots of the DA rather than the nationalist and reactionary ones (the 'Know your DA' campaign); showcase the DA's delivery record as governing party in the Western Cape since 2009; implement assertive social media and television campaigns (centring on *ayisafani*). The Values Charter saw the DA go back to basics, trying to find common ground between new voter constituencies (especially black-African) and conservative white constituencies. Former DA leader Tony Leon said Zille was the person to have brought family values into the DA as part of her negotiation deal to bring the old National Party into its alliance with the Democratic Party, later to become the DA.[42]

The DA circa 2014 tried to appropriate the criticisms of the ANC, as articulated in *ayisafani*, but it could not give a sufficient mass of black-African voters enough reason to trust the DA more than they trust the ANC when it comes to voting. The DA inserted 'experience of solid government in the Western Cape' as explanation for why voters should trust it better, but that was not enough. The DA also attempted recasting itself as liberal *and* progressive, and in the struggle, but damaged its own effort by showing how flimsy its link with Nelson Mandela really was. Specifically, the main components of the DA's 2014 campaign were that the DA is the party of continued resistance against apartheid and the party of struggle with a special Madiba connection – but few voters could forget that the DA had also become home for the majority of former

National Party supporters or their political descendants. Reminiscent of the ANC's limited memory mode, the new DA paired – and then exorcised – that phase of its existence with former leader Tony Leon, and his DP's 'Fight back' (interpreted as 'Fight black') in the 1999 election campaign. The DA was only formed later, but this campaign and its conservative-nationalist followers fit snugly into the box under the reinvented DA bed.

The campaign positioned the DA as a party that is more moral than the ANC: Jacob Zuma was the arch-enemy of good government and he had to be impeached. Gareth van Onselen opines that the DA has become a moral edition of the ANC:

> The party has certainly positioned itself relentlessly as the sole vestige of political moral virtue – the one incorruptible force for good left stand-ing. With that and a relatively impressive track record, it has come to embody more and more moral authority in the public mind … What it really seems to be saying is that 'we are the ANC – we remember the ANC of old, we supported Thabo Mbeki, we love the NDP, we do BEE better than the ANC … only, we don't suffer the same moral shortcom-ings; we are the ANC without corruption and maladministration'.[43]

The DA also emphasised that it has a sound record in Western Cape gov-ernment and voters would earn clean-audit government with a DA vote in Gauteng.[44] It used the public protector's Nkandla findings against President Zuma. In one move it bulk-disseminated the SMS: 'The Nkandla report shows how Zuma stole your money to build his R246m home. Vote DA on 7 May to beat corruption. Together for change.' The ANC's urgent application in the Johannesburg High Court to stop this dissemination saw the first ruling going in favour of the DA. The ANC then appealed to the Electoral Court sitting at the Supreme Court of Appeal in Bloemfontein. Just prior to the election the advert was banned (post-election, the Constitutional Court found the message expressed to be an opinion and this did not contravene the Electoral Act). In a comparable election time move on DA advertising, the SABC banned a DA campaign advert on corruption and Nkandla, arguing that the Nkandla matter remained untested by a court of law.

The DA also portrayed itself as the one party that can create jobs, even if much of its policies and claims were contentious. It contrasted itself with the ANC in an area where the ANC had graphically failed during Zuma's tenure, but instead of accolades the DA ran into trouble. When it undertook a jobs march on Luthuli House, the ANC felt provoked and counter-mobilised to defend its headquarters.[45] The event turned out to be a precarious and tension-ridden showdown in downtown Johannesburg. There were no winners.

The DA's policy conflicts were part of its desire to be 'the real ANC' and capture support from it, but at the same time the DA was hard-pressed to show how it is different from the ANC. Its policies suggested that it differs often only marginally from the ANC – as it reassured voters with regard to social grants, and the general role of the state in delivering services. Predominant among them was its battle over the 2013 Bill on Equal Employment, first endorsed and then opposed. A close second was legislation on reopening land claims in February 2014: it was supported by the DA's parliamentary spokesperson on land but withdrawn after Zille intervened.[46]

The DA's proposed jobs strategy itself entered troubled waters. The perception ruled that 'the DA just wants to fine-tune what the ANC is doing'.[47] The proposals – a melange of free-market policies with a tinge of interventionism – pertained to quality education, increased funding for students, creation of internships and Expanded Public Works Programme work opportunities, the cutting of red tape, black economic empowerment (BEE) and infrastructure development. The DA promised to create six million 'real' jobs through a plan that included cutting corruption and improving education, guaranteeing free higher education, creating one million internships for those leaving higher education, boosting support for small businesses, and investing 10 per cent of GDP in infrastructure. The finance ministry accused the DA of manipulating statistics and misleading the public about the credibility of its economic policies – for example, by claiming support from the Reserve Bank and Treasury.[48]

The DA took these messages to the voters without explaining the contradictions in its own ranks, or why there were different opinions on issues such as BEE, long criticised by 'true liberals'. Vision 2029 focused on clarifying more of the party's values, and how these differentiate it from other parties. Thus, the DA's 'founding philosophy' of an open opportunity society for all was being explained in a 'few basic value-laden concepts'. It presented a picture of South Africa after ten years of DA rule, starting in 2019.[49] Translated into a vision, the DA wishes to 'create a South Africa that is free and fair, with access to opportunities for all; that is more equal and where the barriers of the past have once and for all been removed; where citizens are safe from crime; and that is dynamic and vibrant with a growing economy creating millions of jobs'.[50]

Designer leadership change – 'Godzille' style

The most imperious of all DA self-reinventions was leadership replacement and renewal. One of Helen Zille's post-Tony Leon projects, it came in several phases. The party's fixation evolved into one of wanting palpably to take power, and thus, clearly, to take out the ANC in the process. In response, the ANC frequently employed the image of the DA as a party for whites, looking out for minority interests.[51] The DA was indeed changing away from being 'the white party', even if there were more whites (and often more conservative whites) in this party than in any of the other big parties. As black caucuses became more powerful and assertive, the initiative for who the new leaders should be started moving away from direct Zille control. At the DA's 2012 national congress a broad wave of leadership change was effected, with numbers of black and youth leaders moving into positions of importance. At the time of the May 2015 elective federal congress the new recruits were ready to step up.[52] Mmusi Maimane became the first black DA national leader, but also the first black-African official opposition leader in South Africa.

In the evolving battle to succeed Zille, aspiring leaders knew that their political lives would be more secure with Zille's endorsement. In an early phase of transforming the DA through the positioning of black leaders, Lindiwe Mazibuko went from young graduate to DA national spokesperson to DA parliamentary leader, on Zille's design. Her mistakes led to clashes when Zille stepped in to correct them. The DA had also become factionalised in Parliament as Mazibuko used her power to build her profile. Mazibuko resigned from Parliament when it became clear that Maimane was the new anointed one to carry the DA's black profile.

Zille's Mamphela Ramphele project was a failed initiative to get the DA a transformed profile. Zille conceded that offering Ramphele the DA's presidency candidacy in the run-up to Election 2014 had been one of her biggest mistakes.[53] The specifics of the error tell the story of the DA's desperation to expedite political realignment in South Africa: in 2012–2013, Zille offered to take Ramphele into the DA as successor-leader, which would bring the DA the trophy of a credible, high-profile black national leader.[54] Ramphele chose to go it alone. In February 2013 she launched Agang as a 'platform' on which consultation would take place and then lead to her new party. Early optimism faltered. Opinion polls showed that Agang SA, by then a political party, was a pipe dream. Zille and Ramphele attempted a merger in early 2014. It was poorly considered and badly planned, and mutual embarrassment ensued. It exposed the DA to ANC charges of 'rent a leader'.[55] Agang SA also made no headway in Election 2014. It barely made it into Parliament – and it failed to bring in a notable black-voter constituency that would have made it attractive merger stock to the DA. Ramphele refused to lead a two-seat party in Parliament, and left Agang SA.

The next phase of front-line leadership Africanisation came with the rise of Mmusi Maimane – from Johannesburg metro council, to national spokes-person, to Gauteng premier candidate, to DA parliamentary leader in less than three years. The task was Maimane's to lead the DA to its promised land. Maimane's main opponent was Wilmot James, outgoing DA federal chairper-son. Maimane won overwhelmingly. In Parliament, Maimane had to forge a new opposition identity for the DA, in the context of the EFF-ANC war. As the opposition parties found ways to keep ANC malfeasance and associated gov-ernment malfunction on the front burner, the focus often moved to the ANC scandals and away from the DA's own internal contradictions.

THE FATE OF OPPOSITION PARTIES THAT FISH IN ANC WATERS

The DA, problems and all, is by far the pre-eminent opposition party, and it appears set to remain that way. Only a few opposition parties survive their early years if they fish in ANC support-base waters.[56] The ANC does not take prisoners when it comes to split-off opposition parties, the EFF, Cope and the UDM being cases in point. Equally, the DA had been consolidating support from under the feet of smaller opposition parties. The ANC has a reputation of containing opposition party tendencies and preventing early presences from becoming electoral threats or embarrassments in the legis-lative institutions (much earlier, the Pan Africanist Congress had also been a target). Several elections showed that challenges to the ANC come from both left and right, but up to 2014 the only ones of note have been margin-ally to the right. The EFF was to be the exception, to the extent that it can be regarded as definitively left of the ANC.

New opposition parties regularly pop up, especially in the run-up to elec-tions and when they have the prospects of post-election reimbursement from IEC funds for the representation gained. Only a few of these parties will gain substantial representation in Parliament and the provincial legislatures, and if they do there is a good chance that they will be one-election wonders, soon slipping into the zone of micro-parties that get one to two per cent support in subsequent elections. The cases of the UDM in 1999, ID in 2003 through floor-crossing, and Cope in 2009 all illustrate how opposition parties find initial footholds and then become shadows of their original expectations. The 2014 new entrant, the EFF, still needs to prove itself and Agang failed even to make a credible entrance. These new parties generally fade under ANC-initiated and self-inflicted destruction, the latter often due to feuding leaders and failures of internal processes (but it should be remembered that such battles are often fomented by the ANC).

Smaller opposition parties regularly attempt degrees of cooperation and coalition to help them assert some form of political power while suffering the status of minimally resourced micro-parties.[57] For example, when Cope was still a going concern, soon after the 2009 election, the main opposition parties agreed to cooperate on issues of mutual interest. The agreement was largely ineffectual. As Cope disintegrated[58] and the FF+ enjoyed a deputy ministerial position, the DA (itself in the process of some internal conversion) was left to lead the opposition attacks on the ANC.

Whether by design or instinct of self-preservation, the ruling party – directly or induced, but unremittingly – sabotages competing parties, especially those that have emerged 'from the loin of the ANC'.[59] Most debilitating to the split-off parties is the ANC counter-attack veiled in the discourse of the aberrant child who will again see the light and return to the lap of the forgiving parent. There are also ways of containment, besides using the perks of incumbency. The Community Agency for Social Enquiry (Case) report on intimidation in party politics details how the ANC, being the guardian of state power, disarms opposition parties.[60] Withholding access to meeting and rally venues is a mild example; opposition parties reserve venues and pay deposits but 'keys go missing' on the day of the meeting, supervisors go AWOL or 'double bookings' are discovered. Employment and business opportunities evaporate (the ANC has boasted to other political parties that this is standard practice).[61] The ANC keeps a watch over businesses that might make contributions to opposition campaigns, and does not hesitate to censure.[62] The emergence of the EFF had some similarities with previous splits off the ANC. The EFF, however, had no illusions of life post-ANC. It had been subjected to the ANCYL travails at the hand of Luthuli House (when the Malema-Shivambu group was expelled), and had been the perpetrator of much ANC action on Cope. This did not diminish its susceptibility to ANC attack, given that it operates in crucial ANC territories – youth and the space to the ANC's left – and that its leaders come with vulnerabilities.

The cases of Cope, Agang SA, and the Inkatha Freedom Party–National Freedom Party (IFP-NFP) – opposition parties that at some time, in some way, posed a challenge to the ANC and suffered severe consequences – illustrate the fate of parties that played, failed and stayed.

Congress of the People (Cope) – shooting star, fatal crash

Cope regressed consistently from its pre-launch consultative meeting of 2008. In its early days there were high hopes of gaining around 40 per cent of the national vote, in line with Mbeki's Polokwane proportion. This was naive. Cope came to constitute one of the quickest party political implosions of South Africa's democratic era, retaining only 1 per cent in 2014 after its 7 per cent of 2009. Cope's destruction was mostly self-imposed, even if there were suspicions of an ANC hand behind the protracted leadership war between Mosiuoa Lekota and Mbhazima Shilowa.[63]

The ANC's dark hand was illustrated by its action during the earliest phase of Cope's existence. In September 2008, when aspiring Cope supporters exuberantly sang Mbeki's praises at the pre-launch consultation in Sandton (Mbeki had just been recalled as South Africa's president), ANC cadres were flooding the delegates' home villages to check who was absent. They identified their latest enemies.[64] Armed with that knowledge, countering Cope was a seamless operation. Cope's 2009 election campaign was fraught with obstruction. Donations dried up, business people reconsidered financial support, and suspicions of infiltration and involvement of intelligence agencies haunted those who had dreamed of dashing ANC power only a few months earlier.[65]

ANC spokesperson Zizi Kodwa reassured the nation of his party's innocence, claiming 'there was no internal *structure* to destroy Cope' (author's emphasis; notably, no denial of *activity*). The legal battles to assert leadership of the party came to a close shortly before Election 2014, when Lekota finally 'won'. Avoiding political sudden death, nineteen candidates on Cope's list turned to support the ANC days before Election 2014, noting 'we have to accept that Cope as a credible alternative has run its course'.[66] They were ready for their 'homecoming'. As Cope split into multiple fractions, the party declined to 0.6 per cent national support in 2014.

Cope in effect committed assisted suicide. Internecine internal leadership wars played out in the courts instead of conference rooms.[67] Throughout its brief period of credible existence figures of note were returning to the ANC, all forgiven, especially as it became clear that Cope would be a 2014 casualty. In the North West the ANC declared its operation *Khumbule ekhaya* a success. The only price for the returnee to pay was a public statement to mark the event.

These return journeys were the best possible warnings of how cold it is outside the ANC. (In the years to come EFF leaders would be subjected to the same torments suffered by Cope in its early days in the legislatures, where corridor whispers of 'don't worry, you will be back' approximated psychological intimidation.)

There were several illustrations of the 'cold outside'. By election time in 2014 Shilowa sided with the UDM[68] while former Cope spokesperson Smuts Ngonyama and several other Eastern Cape Cope MPs returned to the ANC.[69] Mluleke George, the main Mbeki apostle in the run-up to Polokwane 2007, left Cope and started the United Congress (Unico). It contested but did not survive the 2014 race. Provincial electoral confirmation of the 2009–2014 Cope implosion came through its fall from 13 to 1 per cent in the Eastern Cape provincial election; 12 per cent to 2 per cent in the Free State; 8 per cent to 1 per cent in Limpopo; and also 8 to 1 per cent in the North West. Cope fell from being the official opposition in five provinces in 2009 to official provincial opposition in none of the provinces five years later (Table 6.1). All this was in the fog of allegations of financial irregularities, including the appearance in court of treasurer Hilda Ndude for fraud relating to party funds.

Agang SA – fleeting opposition hope

Agang SA was synonymous with its leader, Mamphela Ramphele, whose afflictions became those of the party. Ramphele had hoped to position Agang as a fresh political voice to battle for accountability and bring the politically estranged back into the system. The ANC was its obvious target. Instead, Agang SA limped between disasters. There were not nearly as many 'politically estranged' as she had thought (at least not to the point of abandoning the ANC for Agang), and her motivational 'lecturing' style did not win over voters. In early 2014 it was reported that a broke Agang was failing to pay its staff; at around the same time national opinion polls[70] revealed that Agang was faring dismally at around one per cent national support. The abortive merger with the DA followed rather than precipitated the collapse in Agang's poll support.

Like Cope, Agang SA self-destructed – and largely without ANC help, although ANC pressures might have been behind Agang's inability to get sufficient financial backing. Donor funding dried up in the wake of business not wanting to side publicly for fear of angering the ANC. Early on, the ANC was vocal about the fundraising that Agang had undertaken in the United States, falling back on the argument of 'foreign interference' in South African politics.

212

Those still prepared to help made funding conditional on opposition unity.[71] Ramphele attempted fusion with the DA – in which she would have stood as presidential candidate – without consulting her party. She was called to task. Her erstwhile followers attempted to remove her and the executive she had selected.

Its 0.28 per cent national electoral support was the nail in the Agang SA coffin, even if two MPs went to Parliament. Fellow leaders interdicted Ramphele after she refused to step down, refused to go to Parliament to lead a two-MP delegation, tried to impose a youth leader in her vacant slot instead of adhering to the party list, and then stepped out of party politics. Upon her departure, two little-known deputies welcomed her leaving, saying she had become 'a poison to her own child'.[72]

IFP and NFP – fishing or being fished?

The ANC was pivotal to the decline of the IFP and the rise of the NFP. The ANC had already been on a track of relentlessly gaining KwaZulu-Natal electoral ground to the detriment of the IFP. The process gathered momentum towards the 2009 national and provincial elections. At this election the ANC support levels in the province started resembling the earlier peaks in other provinces, and it happened on the back of IFP decline. The IFP became subject to further pressure in the run-up to the 2011 local elections, when the NFP split from the IFP. This happened either spontaneously or with strategic ANC encouragement. The NFP, however, captured support that might otherwise have gone to the ANC. At this time the momentum of the ANC's provincial gains started to decline, although its growth continued. The ANC and NFP cooperated after the local election, constituting a series of joint municipal governments in cases where hung councils unfolded. In the process, both the ANC and NFP gained footholds in previous IFP strongholds. The NFP was aware that being in office (even shared office with the ANC in local government) would be a springboard to resources and better performances in the next election.[73]

In 2014, the IFP ceded substantial support to the NFP, but still exceeded it in both the national and provincial stakes (the NFP won 6.4 per cent of the provincial and 1.6 per cent of the national vote). In the run-up the NFP had anticipated greater growth than was realised. The IFP declined from eighteen to ten seats in Parliament from 2009 to 2014, but remained the fourth-largest (though still very small) party. NFP leader Zanele kaMagwaza-Msibi's 2014 campaign went through the rituals of attacking the ANC for corruption and looting. Zuma rewarded her with a deputy ministership in the national executive, which she accepted amid divided opinion in her party. Her ill health, soon thereafter, stifled the party's further rise. By the time Msibi returned to public life in 2015 the NFP had lost momentum and there were returns to the IFP. IFP politicians[74] harboured suspicions that Msibi might have been planted by the ANC to undermine the IFP, hence consolidating the ANC's relatively new dominance of KwaZulu-Natal.

CONCLUSION – OPENINGS IN THE OPPOSITION'S LONG MARCH

Will the DA overcome its internal contradictions – or begin to appear as a political party with a heart and a heartfelt belief system instead of a machine to take votes from the ANC – and manufacture a majority? Can it do this well enough to take power from the ANC one day? In Election 2014 the DA faltered in its ambitious plans seriously to damage ANC majorities and proceeded more modestly, on a path of incremental growth ... but then hoped that the insertion of black-African leader Maimane (who indeed has leadership qualities) would be the fuel for the magical forward surge. In the process the DA enlarged its edge over other opposition parties, even as the EFF established a striking first performance. The new challenge for the DA was to persevere on this growth path, although the EFF often stole some of its thunder, using its irreverence and in-your-face opposition style to attack the most obvious of ANC weaknesses.

The test will be which – if *either* has the capacity – of the DA or the EFF has the ammunition that best combines anti-Zuma-ism with substantive policy and government alternatives, and whether that party will swing the increasingly young, somewhat alienated and often angry new electorate. In Election 2014 the EFF was probably better believed than the DA to have an economic alternative. The DA, however, has the advantage of an established party organisation that is also relatively immune to sabotage and psychological warfare by the ANC. The EFF is still approaching and negotiating these hurdles.

The DA saw all the ANC's flaws. Yet however much it tried, irrespective of all the right noises reflecting a more inclusive ideological repositioning, new black supporters trickled rather than cascaded in. Was 2014 the time when the

DA could and should have made better progress, before being countered by the high-profile EFF? If anything, the DA's 2014 campaign taught it the lesson that it cannot rush changes in voter allegiance. The period 2014–2015 showed that the DA, short on potential to lift the ANC from power, nevertheless retains a marked edge over the rest of the opposition. Maimane's election will make a difference to the DA's profiling and positioning, but the party would need a racial repositioning and a 'political street-fighter for the underdog' reputation for it to make further headway.

The biggest deterrent to far-reaching DA or EFF expansion is the South African political and voting culture. Voters might agree with the criticisms of the ANC, but they are (admittedly in gradually decreasing numbers) still likely to continue voting for it. In the 2014–2019 parliamentary term the DA and other opposition parties often closed ranks, forcing the ANC to use its majority at a price. The next stage of this evolution appeared to reside in pragmatic alliances rather than in outright defeats of the ANC. Maimane said 'something broke tonight' in the aftermath of the November 2014 parliamentary breakdown when the ANC *ad hoc* committee report exonerated Zuma of Nkandla wrongdoing.[75] Maimane reiterated in 2015 that Zuma is a broken man, presiding over a broken system. Did this break affect voters' perceptions of their ANC? If it did, what pieces can the DA pick up? Or, could the EFF or another party walk away with the prize?

NOTES

1   Christi van der Westhuizen, 9 May 2014, 'Race: The DA's elephant in the policy room', *Mail & Guardian*, http://mg.co.za/article/2014-05-08-race-the-das-elephant-in-the-policy-room, accessed 4 December 2014, unpacks the phenomenon further.

2   Two prominent young female black leaders were sidelined – former parliamentary leader Lindiwe Mazibuko and DA Youth leader Mbali Ntuli (who resigned from her position but remained a DA MP). Both resignations linked to leadership errors or clashes.

3   DA, 2015, Values Charter, http://www.da.org.za/wp-content/uploads/2015/05/DA-Value-Charter.pdf, accessed 17 May 2015.

4   Also see Julius Malema, 2014, in interview with Rian van Heerden, Radio Jacaranda, 20 September 2014, www.jacarandafm.com/.../julius-malema-vs-rian-van-heerden-the-video/, accessed 2 October 2014.

5   *Sunday Times,* 21 September 2014, quotes Gwede Mantashe that the ANC's NEC cautioned against 'continuing this trend of negatively exposing the head of state to disrespect and intended humiliation by a fringe group committed to undermining

democracy', p. 1. In November 2014 Deputy President Ramaphosa told the NCOP, 'I want to call on members of opposition parties to be respectful to the president of the Republic …', 5 November 2014, NCOP.

6   Minor opposition parties rejoiced in the opportunity to become an effective part of a working opposition alliance in Parliament, united against ANC corruption and lack of accountability. This was evidenced in the UDM, IFP and FF+ participation in the *Forum at 8*, SABC-SAFM, 3 December 2014.

7   DA and four opposition parties worked to bring a motion of no confidence in Baleka Mbete after August 2014 events. They were the EFF, Cope, FF+ and UDM. In the parliamentary fallout of November 2014 all opposition parties in statements in Parliament converged against the speaker.

8   See Greg Nicolson, 18 December 2012, 'ConCourt slams ANC Free State, but clears delegates for participation in Mangaung', *Daily Maverick*, http://www.dailymaverick.co.za/article/2012-12-18-concourt-slams-anc-free-state-but-clears-delegates-for-participation-in-mangaung/#.VE4O_xZ6joQ, accessed 18 January 2013.

9   The details of the cost of the president's court battles are never released – there are mere glimpses when reports on unauthorised expenditure reach, for example, Parliament's standing committee on public accounts (Scopa).

10 Dikgang Moseneke (deputy chief justice), 12 November 2014, 'Reflections on South African constitutional democracy – transition and transformation', Keynote address at the Mistra-Tmali-Unisa conference, 20 Years of South African Democracy: So Where to Now?, Pretoria, Unisa, comments on the overconcentration of powers in the president.

11 In March 2012 the Supreme Court ruled that the NPA should hand over the recordings to the DA. By mid-2013 this was still not done. The DA returned to court in an attempt to force compliance with the ruling. In July 2013 the DA in the South Gauteng High Court again sought to access the spy tapes.

12 Drew Forrest, 21–27 November 2014, 'New spy tape salvo spells trouble for Zuma', *Mail & Guardian*, pp. 12–13.

13 See Susan Booysen, 2011, *The African National Congress and the Regeneration of Political Power*, Johannesburg: Wits University Press, chapter 8.

14 Charl du Plessis, 10 May 2015, 'Polls shows Maimane will win by a landslide', *City Press*, p. 4.

15 Susan Booysen, 2013, *Twenty Years of South African Democracy: Citizen Views of Human Rights, Governance and the Political System*, research report, Johannesburg and Washington DC: Freedom House.

16 Zaid Kimmie, Jan Greben and Susan Booysen, 2010, 'A review of the 2009 South African election', *Politeia*, Special edition: Elections in Africa, vol. 29 (1), pp. 98–120.

17 Proclaimed by then DA parliamentary leader Lindiwe Mazibuko in Glynnis Underhill, 28 October–3 November 2011, 'Historic moment for the DA: The rise of Lindiwe Mazibuko', *Mail & Guardian*, p. 8. Also see Richard Calland, 2013, *The Zuma Years: South Africa's Changing Face of Power*, Cape Town: Zebra Press, p. 238, where the DA's Wilmot James also articulates the 30 per cent target for 2014. Youth leader Mbali Ntuli also referred to this target; see Moloko Moloto, 26 August 2012, 'Toppling ANC at 2019 polls not seen as mission impossible', *The Star*, p. 4.

216

18   Marianne Merten, 29 January 2012, '"Much work ahead to seize control in 2014"', *The Star*, p. 4.

19   Mazibuko, parliamentary leader of the DA up to Election 2014, rose into the position as a protégé of party leader Helen Zille. In the process she won a bruising and divisive caucus election. A range of further details are captured in Donwald Pressly, 2014, *Owning the Future: Lindiwe Mazibuko and the Changing Face of the DA*, Cape Town: Kwela.

20   As quoted in Bezekela Phakathi, 21 October 2011, 'ANC infighting "will give DA gap to rule"', *Business Day*, p. 3.

21   Mmusi Maimane, 30 April 2014, 'Battle for Gauteng', *The Sunday Independent*, p. 8.

22   Carien du Plessis, 27 April 2014, 'Zille warns against complacency', *City Press*, p. 6.

23   Interview, DA Gauteng politician, 9 May 2014, Pretoria.

24   This phrase, adopted by the DA for one of its conversion campaigns, was in use in the research fieldwork for Susan Booysen, 2013, op. cit. In a DA campaign advertisement (for example, in *Sowetan*, 6 May 2014, p. 9) the DA says: 'The ANC has changed. Under Jacob Zuma they have become arrogant and corrupt. They have forgotten about us because they believe they will rule …'

25   See Helen Zille, 23 November 2014, 'The DA is growing and the ANC disintegrating in Gauteng – Helen Zille', http://www.politicsweb.co.za/politicsweb/view/politicsweb/en/page72308?oi=818854&sn=Marketingweb+detail&pid=90389&utm_source=Politicsweb+Daily+Headlines&utm_campaign=1be88e91b3-, accessed 24 November 2014.

26   Zwelethu Jolobe, 2014, 'The Democratic Alliance election campaign: "Ayisafani"?' in Collette Schulz-Herzenberg and Roger Southall (eds), *Election 2014 South Africa: The Campaigns, Results and Future Prospects*, Auckland Park: Jacana, p. 69. See Helen Zille, quoted in Govan Whittles, 'Zille: DA gets 760,000 black votes', http://ewn.co.za/2014/05/09/DA-receives-760000-black-votes, accessed 17 May 2014.

27   Zwelethu Jolobe, 2014, op. cit.

28   Ipsos, analysis of parties' demographic support bases, gained from pre-election opinion polls, 2014, http://www.ipsos.co.za/SitePages/Profiles%20of%20the%20supporters%20of%20the%20three%20biggest%20political%20parties%20in%20South%20Africa.aspx, accessed 12 February 2015.

29   See Clive Ndou, 7 July 2014, 'Minority Front: End of the road?' *The Citizen*, p. 6.

30   See Helen Zille, 2014, *DA Election Manifesto 2014*, 'Letter from Helen Zille', p. 1; also see Gareth van Onselen, 16 March 2014, 'DA split over Zille's take on the Mbeki era', *Sunday Times*, p. 8.

31   Report by Shanti Aboobaker, 27 April 2014, 'SA "bluenami" set to hit SA', *The Sunday Independent*, p. 2.

32   Around R100 million, about half the DA's national election budget, was pumped just into the DA's Gauteng campaign. See, for example, Jan-Jan Joubert and Thabo Mokone, 11 May 2014, 'Doubts over DA strategy despite healthy gains', *Sunday Times*, p. 4.

33   US pollster Stanley Greenberg, campaign adviser to the ANC, crossed lines to the DA. Mmusi Maimane, 28 July 2013, Statement, http://www.politicsweb.co.za/politicsweb/view/politicsweb/en/page71654?oid=394474&sn=Detail&pid=71616, accessed 29 July 2013. Also see Melissa Levin, 5 August 2013, 'Little Stan Greenberg

is dead', http://africasacountry.com/little-stan-greenberg-is-dead/, accessed 12 October 2013. Greenberg's exact amount of influence on the DA campaign remained unspecified.

34   Observed at the DA's final pre-election rally, 3 May 2014, Northgate Dome, Johannesburg.

35   Stanley B. Greenberg, 2009, *Dispatches from the War Room: In the Trenches with Five Extraordinary Leaders*, New York: Macmillan.

36   Susan Booysen, 2013, op. cit.

37   Ibid.

38   The image was captured by *The Citizen* photographer Alaister Russell, March 2014, in Bekkersdal.

39   See Emilia Motsai and Sapa, 25 April 2014, 'DA sends "wrong" message', *The Citizen*, p. 3.

40   Interviews on the ground on campaign trail; two different locations in Western Cape and Gauteng townships.

41   Several of these points are also highlighted by Zwelethu Jolobe, 2014, op. cit., which also differentiates these three legs of the DA's campaign.

42   Tony Leon, quoted in 'Family values first, DA decides', *City Press*, 10 May 2015, p. 4; Susan Booysen, 2011, op. cit., chapter 8.

43   Gareth van Onselen, 13 July 2014, 'High-handed DA needs political rehab to cure its "must" addiction', *Sunday Times*, p. 16.

44   See Mmusi Maimane, 6 April 2014, 'Eliminate corruption and create jobs', *City Press*, p. 5.

45   See Jackson Mthembu, interview with Chris Barron, 16 February 2014, 'So many questions', *Sunday Times Review*, p. 2.

46   See the detailed analysis by Philda Essop, 25 February 2014, 'Briesende Zille kap lei-ers oor grondeise', *Volksblad*, p. 2. Mazibuko had reverted to the more conservative backbone of DA support, highlighting the uncertainties of employment, the rural economy and food security that would be created by the proposed legislation.

47   Thami Mazwai, 5 March 2014, 'DA's jobs strategy merely borrows ANC ideas', *Business Day*, p. 11.

48   Pravin Gordhan, 2 May 2014, 'DA's economic claims fail to pass scrutiny', *The Star*, p. 15.

49   Paul Boughey, DA chief executive officer, 22 March 2015, interview with *City Press's* Carien du Plessis, 'All systems go as DA readies for 2016', p. 4.

50   Democratic Alliance, 10 May 2015, 'Our vision', advertorial, *City Press*, p. 6.

51   Zuma continued this approach, also after Maimane had been elected national leader; see Jacob Zuma, 27 May 2015, debate on the Presidency's budget vote, Parliament, Cape Town.

52   See, for example, Jan-Jan Joubert, 29 March 2015, 'Youth versus experience in DA poll battle', *Sunday Times*, p. 4.

53   Helen Zille, 25 May 2014, 'Should I remain premier or go to Parliament? Personal reflections on political advice', *SA Today*.

54   Jan-Jan Joubert, 19 May 2013, 'No deal: How Mamphela Ramphele dumped Helen Zille', *City Press*, http://www.citypress.co.za/politics/no-deal/, accessed 24 September 2014.

55 For example, the ANC's Ebrahim Patel argued that the ANC looks for leaders that are caring and connected, and did not have to resort to 'renting a leader'; Wits Great Debate, University of the Witwatersrand, Johannesburg, 4 May 2014.

56 Parts of this section are based on Susan Booysen, 13 July 2014, 'Split-off parties in survival race', *The Sunday Independent*, p. 13.

57 Susan Booysen, 2014, 'Causes and impact of party alliances and coalitions on the party system and national cohesion in South Africa', *Journal of African Elections*, vol. 13 (1), pp. 66–92.

58 Cope regressed all the time. The legal battles to assert leadership of the party came to a close shortly before Election 2014, when Mosiuoa Lekota finally won (although by then there was not much of a party left for him to lead).

59 Expression used by Pallo Jordan, 2008, 'A letter to Comrade Mtungwa, an old comrade and dear friend', address to the Platform for Public Deliberation, University of Johannesburg, 14 November 2008: 'In many respects, Election 2009 will be remembered for the participation of an opposition formation sprung from the very loins of the ANC and led by former ANC leaders …'

60 Case, 2014, *Just Singing and Dancing*, research report, Johannesburg.

61 Sidebar discussion in a parliamentary committee meeting, 2014, where ANC MPs told EFF counterparts that one of its senior members would not get a senior job she had been offered. Interview, 24 November 2014.

62 ANC Secretary General Gwede Mantashe slammed Nedbank chairperson Reuel Khoza in 2012 for writing in the Nedbank annual report that the country's leadership could not lead because of their 'sheer incapacity to deal with the complexity of 21st-century governance and leadership'. The ANC also criticised First National Bank's 'You can help' (2013) campaign. It featured young people expressing concerns on the state of the country. In 2007 FNB withdrew an anti-crime campaign to escape from ANC interpretation that it was anti-government.

63 Interview, Cope official, 3 May 2014, Randburg; also Susan Booysen, 2011, op. cit., chapter 9.

64 Telephonic interview, ANC MP deployed to the Eastern Cape, 28 September 2008.

65 Interviews as cited in Susan Booysen, 2009, 'Congress of the People: Between foothold of hope and slippery slope', in Roger Southall and John Daniel (eds), *Zunami: The 2009 South African Elections*, Johannesburg: Jacana, pp. 85–113.

66 Statement by nineteen former Cope members and MPs upon siding with the ANC, 28 April 2014.

67 Susan Booysen, 2011, op. cit., chapter 8.

68 Hlengiwe Nhlabathi, 7 February 2014, 'Shilowa loyalists "join" UDM', *Sowetan*, p. 4.

69 See Sithandiwe Velaphi, 1 May 2014, 'ANC accepts ex-members', *The New Age*, p. 20.

70 Mogomotsi Magome, Shanti Aboobaker and Candice Bailey, 5 January 2014, 'Funds dry up for Agang', *The Sunday Independent*, p. 1; information from Ipsos, from a national client poll.

71 Verashni Pillay, 13–19 February 2014, '"All donors" behind the Agang-DA deal', *Mail & Guardian*, p. 6; Helen Zille, interview, Radio 702, February 2014.

72 Babalo Ndenze and Sapa, 9 July 2014, 'Ramphele was a "burden" to Agang', *The Star*, p. 7.

73 Interview, NFP official, September 2014, Cape Town.

74 See Nokuthula Ntuli, 6 June 2014, 'Anger as NFP leader is made deputy minister', *The Star*, p. 4; IFP parliamentarian, interview (on condition of anonymity), 24 March 2014, Randburg.

75 Rebecca Davis, 14 November 2014, 'Parliament diary: Scenes of shame', *Daily Maverick*, http://www.dailymaverick.co.za/article/2014-11-14-parliament-diary-scenes-of-shame, accessed 14 November 2014.

7

EFF AND THE LEFT CLAIMING ANC TURF

The Economic Freedom Fighters have inflicted multiple damages on their one-time parent body and present nemesis the ANC, changes realised precisely in the time of the tortuous and staggered disintegration of the Tripartite Alliance and its constituent member Cosatu. Cosatu's mutation is still unfolding but it is clear that South African politics has entered a new phase. The emerging period stands out for the weakening of the ANC internally (pivoting around the faction that spins for Zuma), and Alliance-wise for the emasculation of the SACP and Cosatu. Two sets of developments were crucial: the remaining part of Cosatu trying to sustain a compliant federation, on the terms of the S'dumo Dlamini faction; and the Numsa-based Irwin Jim grouping, expelled but still claiming the Cosatu tradition, while advancing the formation of a workers' party.

Had it not been for the fallout around Zuma a different ANC, Cosatu and Alliance would have prevailed. Highly significant as it is, the EFF is but one streak on the left political landscape, although admittedly one with strategic and electoral advantage – for the time being – over the rest of the left. It has solid populist-nationalist support, high-profile leadership, and enjoys sound media coverage – besides having established a credible electoral footing in 2014.

This chapter focuses on the EFF and the labour-aligned left, both important for longer-term left politics and the weakening of the ANC. It assesses the
'moment' of Cosatu fragmentation and the associated failure of the Tripartite
Alliance. It takes stock of the political conjuncture, considering whether a left
party is rising. It then focuses on the EFF and its ideological-policy positioning, also asking whether the EFF is in fact a left project with sustainability in
terms of organisational, electoral and grassroots appeals. Can it fend off the
'Cope curse'? The chapter explores both the enigmatic EFF leadership and the
nemesis it finds in President Jacob Zuma, and then returns to the fallout from
the Cosatu war, issues around the formation of a rival union organisation, and
the emerging workers' party. It reflects on the hurdles a workers' party would
have to overcome in order to become an alternative to the ANC, the EFF and
the DA.

THE REBELLION OF THE LAMBS

The EFF rapidly grew out of its ANC Youth League shoes to become a
6 per cent opposition party. The performance gets more credit given that the
chunk largely comprises votes that would otherwise have been on the ANC
tally. The EFF's presence in Parliament changed opposition politics from polite
silences and opposition party submission to the ANC majority. Parliament is
the ANC's comfort zone no more. The EFF (bolstered by the rest of the parties
in Parliament, which also gained new impetus) has held the ANC to ransom.
The ANC's most corporeal current weakness, President Jacob Zuma, has been
on public display and the EFF has ensured that the scandals and embarrassments caused by the ANC leader have remained at the top of the public agenda.

The EFF also gradually developed its policy and popular positioning,
becoming more than an anti-Zuma voice in Parliament to be a party growing
through engagement on the ground. The EFF programme of land occupation
started taking shape in 2015, although haltingly and amid member complaints
of insufficient grassroots action. It played out in the arena of rapid urbanisation, faltering local government and the ANC government's unconvincing land
reform, along with police arrests of EFF leaders of illegal land settlement and
shack construction. In one such instance, EFF MP Fana Mokoena and EFF supporters were arrested by Umtata police in 'a protest to stop the King Dalinyebo
Municipality from illegally demolishing people's homes. The municipality was

in contravention of a standing court order which barred them from demolishing these homes.'[1]

This new space for a left opposition is vulnerable in many respects. The EFF operates in borderline spaces between the legal and illegal, especially concerning grassroots campaigns. In Parliament it gained a more secure footing when the Western Cape High Court ruled that it is within parliamentary rules and the Constitution to pronounce, as the EFF had, that 'the ANC government massacred workers in Marikana'.[2] In another judgement, the Western Cape High Court found, on Parliament's Powers and Privileges Act, that it is problematic for the police to enter Parliament upon a 'disturbance' to arrest MPs – it could impinge on MPs' freedom of expression. The ANC and most of the opposition nevertheless subdued the EFF by tightening the rules and bolstering the parliamentary protection services. EFF and left opposition also remained vulnerable through the matter of legal charges against Malema. Legal charges against Malema for tax matters and tender-related improbity had, however, not dissipated. The Polokwane High Court struck the charges off the roll in August 2015 but the National Prosecuting Authority threatened to reinstate. ANC and intelligence service infiltration was in full flood, although the EFF itself also contributed handsomely to the party's problems.[3] The top leadership did not cultivate unity among founding groupings, and lost some along the way, manufactured a congress leadership slate, did not treat all office workers fairly, and occasionally slipped on leadership ethics.

Internal strife in the EFF is a drawback. In 2015 there was fallout as grievances about electoral authoritarianism at its December 2014 national people's assembly reached the courts. Groupings within the EFF became disillusioned with the leaders, in particular with commander-in-chief Julius Malema and his close associates. A common complaint was about their ways of handling internal finance and party funding, and for not being more visible in grassroots campaigns. There was dissidence – four rebel (and suspended from the EFF) MPs, Andile Mngxitama, Mpho Ramakatsa, Khanyisile Litchfield-Tshabalala and Lucky Twala, wanting to 'save the soul' of the EFF.[4] Twala was disciplined and the others expelled. The EFF then removed them as MPs. They refused to accept the decision, arguing the *sub judice* rule due to their having approached the High Court to nullify the national people's assembly elective outcomes. They also sought an urgent interdict in April 2015 to prevent the EFF's action against them, but the case was struck off the roll. Others rebels, including from the Gauteng EFF leadership, decided there was no soul in the EFF to save.[5] They

223

resigned, along with some in the leadership of the Free State, Mpumalanga and Northern Cape. Later in 2015, Mpumalanga members and representatives followed. Some considered forming their own mini- or *real* EFFs. The strongest guarantee that the EFF would remain standing despite dissidence and leadership drawbacks was its powerful resonance with youth and people on the ground.

Enter expelled-from-Cosatu Numsa and former Cosatu general secretary of sixteen years Zwelinzima Vavi, and opposition to the left of the ANC becomes even more tangible. By late 2015 the Cosatu break-up was in full swing, but with the exact form of the split still contested. There was vacillation around expulsions after Numsa refused to campaign for the ANC in the 2014 election, and Vavi was foremost among the Zuma critics. This was followed by attempted intervention by a senior ANC task team and a truce at election time. Next was the actual expulsion of Numsa, withdrawal of seven other sympathetic unions from some Cosatu activities, including their boycotts of the Cosatu Central Executive Committee (CEC) and Vavi's defiance of March 2015 followed by expulsion. President Zuma – much of the cause of the discord! – promoted the mid-2015 Alliance peace summit. This unfolded as Cosatu's CEC was forced to legally commit to the Cosatu Special National Congress (SNC) of July 2015. The ANC NEC task team reported to the NEC that the Cosatu factions had been ignoring the team's advice.[6] The SNC finally arrived, and collapsed. Nevertheless, the event showed that Numsa-Vavi could not count on majority support within Cosatu, that several of the unions on both sides of the split were divided over whom to support, that the support for an alternative union federation was uncertain, and that the labour organisation overall was in disarray. Here, too, there were losers and no immediate winners – Cosatu was withered, and the Numsa faction was facing an uncertain future.

The part of Cosatu that was controlled by its pro-Zuma CEC argued that there was so much discord that a smaller Cosatu without the Numsa disruptions would be preferable – less paralysed. This group failed to acknowledge that Cosatu had become dependent on Numsa, its strongest affiliate union, which contributed around R1 million per month to Cosatu finances. In the words of Cosatu's Patrick Craven (later associated with the Numsa rebels), when Cosatu expelled Vavi and failed to bring Numsa back in, the federation was 'shooting itself in both feet'.[7] The ANC had been trying to some extent to keep Cosatu together, for the sake of Tripartite Alliance survival, but the CEC refused to abandon contrived charges against Numsa, denying that the charges boiled down to an attempt to silence Numsa's independent political voice. Simultaneously it maintained the pressures on Vavi, until Vavi publicly revealed Cosatu's financial matters – a step the ANC described as 'bordering on delinquency'. Numsa and Vavi had still held out the hope that it could capture the whole of Cosatu – the first prize in the 2014–2015 contest. By late 2015 it appeared that the worker-party offspring may very well complete the process of the ANC being stung by the dissidents. Whatever their eventual fates, the EFF and Numsa-Vavi developments signal a tumultuous third decade in power for the ANC.

Thus, the question has arisen whether at long last a viable left opposition[8] was finding traction – on the one hand the EFF; on the other hand Numsa, Vavi, the United Front (that struggled to get off the ground) and a possible socialist or workers' party. Summary prognoses for the EFF and a Numsa party are:

- The EFF had a credible though highly complicated start and then a contested time in the legislatures. In just a few months as the third-biggest political party it changed legislative politics: it destroyed some barriers between the system and the socioeconomic world outside of the polity. It laid claim to a 'radical' ideology and space, with emphasis on what was possible then and now. Its concept of a 'led revolution' suggests a degree of realism on the pragmatic side of instantaneous utopia. But EFF flaws, if not carefully considered, could induce party suicide. The worst of the EFF's immediate problems are potential factioning and fractioning through internal contests, battles as to how radical and revolutionary the EFF actually is, members succumbing to the ANC's luring them back, less than immaculate management of party finances, being consumed by office and parliamentary politics instead of grassroots action, losing the spark that comes when new parties are born, and running aground in local elections. Furthermore, the evolving workers' party would fish in exactly the same political waters as the EFF – many workers voted EFF in 2014.

- Numsa has been a long-standing left critic of Cosatu's stances in relation to the Tripartite Alliance and ANC government as vultures and tenderpreneurs. By 2014–2015 Cosatu was further weakened through its determination to embrace the ANC and thus to play in ANC palace politics. Tripartite Alliance partners were required to show their loyalty to Zuma. The SACP showed the way to the extent that it was void of critical engagement (apart from a few regions that have become more critical as the Zuma era draws to a close). Cosatu was expected to play its full role in protecting the president and desist from asserting that Zuma is 'predatory', as accused by Vavi.[9] The Numsa-related party could help build a left movement, but a contest between the EFF and a workers' party would also distract from and divide an emerging left challenge to the ANC (if the EFF remains as a going party political concern). One of the dangers is that election hopes will be deflated and voters might get entangled in a competitive left contest, splitting a left vote and helping the ANC to maintain power. Malema has issued appeals for a new labour union that would find the EFF as a party political base. Numsa and the United Front were not committing themselves.

The ANC's mostly unchallenged party political status at this time resulted from its work to ensure that opposition parties remain contained and, when they arise, to minimise their progress: one of its solutions is to ensure, as far as it can, that opposition parties will be pinned down through sustained hostile narratives, operational obstacles and infiltration attacks. Both the EFF and the United Front were subjected to the ANC's maximising obstacles. Public narratives were just one of the ANC strategies: 'Demonise, stigmatise and sabotage' was its battle cry in relation to the EFF. It attacked Numsa for wanting 'regime change', citing a document purportedly authored by 'concerned members within Numsa'.[10] (Numsa responded by highlighting the legal methods through which it is working for change.) The ANC pretended to ignore the EFF during the 2014 election campaign and beyond, despite campaigning tooth and nail in EFF geographical catchment areas such as Ekurhuleni. The ANC was forced to formally acknowledge the EFF only when the upstart party used its power in Parliament, and even then the EFF was noted in dismissive and patronising terms.

The policy void to be filled by a left party

There is no certainty that the EFF-style left, or a new worker-left party (with the United Front as a possible social movement precursor to the Socialist Movement), will practise the belief systems and practical politics that can capture the ideological and policy delivery voids in and around the ANC. But the twin EFF-Numsa challenge was the first of a series of options that emerged at the time of Election 2014 and its 2015 aftermath. This period was characterised by the new political bloodhounds going after Zuma and the Zuma faction – the faction that had become the *de facto* ANC.

Political activists have argued over time that the ANC can only be challenged effectively from the left and through a split in the ANC. The ANC has moved to the centre, and South Africa is a place of vast inequality and waves of disappointments; hence, this argument goes, there is fertile soil for a left-wing party. Continuous deprivation and poverty tell the story of a large proportion of South Africans, often youth, who fear there may be no escape from the socioeconomic conditions that is life in the poor parts of the townships and informal settlements.[11] Many recipients of social services also ask if there is life beyond substandard free education, better than a social wage that substitutes for public works jobs and real jobs, superior to service delivery that spews sewerage on the streets and health services dispensing drugs of a better quality than light painkillers as the mandatory treatment. Are there job queues with places for more than the political in-group? Politicians have presented the NDP as the placebo that masks the ills – but it does not cure. Then the government appears to let the NDP fade; or alternatively suggests that it is mainstreamed and now simply in the phase of implementation. Few officially acknowledge that the required growth rates are nowhere near what the NDP requires, and they are not catching up either. Thus jobs do not catch up with the labour market, the National Health Insurance (NHI) building blocks are not materialising, and fixing the education system is simply a block too far. There is neither a convincing turnaround plan nor matching human resources to control crime. The policing and judicial systems seem unable to cope with community-level justice. Corruption is rife – among politicians and politician-bureaucrats alike.

The only riddle in this reality is that a significant left-wing party, with liberation credibility, has not yet evolved to challenge the ANC. This testifies to the ANC's resilience, along with continuous voter beliefs that the party is bigger than the individuals leading it, that the ANC policies are more likely to deliver results than could the opposition, and that there is still hope that the ANC can do better. Either way, the ANC has become a narrowed-down, factional party that nevertheless still manages to spread inspirational election campaigns and draw in many millions of votes. The splits that still appear realistic in the time of Zuma are intra-factional ones rather than grand centre-left ones.

THE EFF BEARING THE LEFT FLAG

In many respects the time is ripe for an organised and system-directed left-opposition party in South Africa – a party that contests elections and engages in Parliament. During South Africa's first two decades of democracy, formal opposition politics routinely unfolded to the right of the ANC. For a long time the ANC remained regarded as a left party, without sufficient recognition of its actual positioning at the centre, and with small deviations either to the right or left of the centre. The ANC deeply desired to be regarded as left, because much of its credibility hinged on whether citizens accepted that its current policies held a longer-term possibility of improved delivery and deeper transformation. Whether or not South Africa's citizens interpreted the concept of the 'second phase of the transition' in this way, the ANC's intellectuals tried. The ANC laid claim to epithets of 'radical' and 'revolution' in the sense of the multiple (and ever receding) phases towards the left goal of the National Democratic Revolution.

EFF claiming socialism, radicalism and revolution

The EFF is as much defined by its criticism of the ANC as through its proclamation of ideological difference. In the EFF's own estimation it holds the radical solutions to South Africa's political and policy problems. The EFF uses the ideological tag of 'sell-outs' to describe the ANC, which in this discourse suffers from 'cognitive dissonance around neoliberal policies that have kept the country trapped in a neocolonial enclave for the enrichment of white monopoly capitalism'.[12]

The EFF's ideological and policy critiques follow from its ANCYL days. Its challenges on nationalisation and redistribution entered ANC policy deliberations, only to exit with the departure of Julius Malema's unruly ANCYL.[13] The EFF brought in its own definition of radical, and it differed from the radical associated with clear working-class control.[14] The EFF's radical is not 'revolutionary' in the sense of an overthrow of the prevailing political system. It reflects, in many respects, the ANC main body's style of 'speak left, do right'. The EFF speaks revolution and proposes policy actions that appear to be radical nationalist,[15] but in the end are populist and only mildly left of the ANC (examples can be found in its positions on nationalisation and black-nationalist empowerment). Its style and its appeal to people, however, are very different from the ANC's. It may very well be that the people to whom the EFF relates will pull the EFF into radical grassroots action and keep it on that track.

In February 2010, the ANCYL produced a discussion document on nationalisation while the senior body watched from the sidelines. The 2010 ANC National General Council meeting in Durban, with the ANCYL in full challenge mode, was one of the notable moments of the ANCYL's policy contests. It tried to force its positions through the economic transformation policy commission,

228

but was thwarted.[16] The debates about more radical policy followed the ANCYL metamorphosis into the EFF. The EFF argues that the ANC had formed an elite pact and is now part of a system that has abandoned the poor.[17] It emphasises that the lack of economic liberation is evident in the high levels of poverty, inequality, inadequate land reform, unemployment and underemployment, starvation, and lack of direction in political and economic policies. It stresses seven pillars through which it will attain economic liberation.[18] Some of the pillars appear highly radical, but have been accompanied by reassurances of moderation to business, and nationalism rather than outright radicalism:

- expropriation of South Africa's land, without compensation, for equal redistribution;
- nationalisation of mines, banks and other strategic sectors of the economy, without compensation;
- building state and government capacity, which will lead to the abolition of tenders;
- free quality education, health care, houses and sanitation;
- massive protected industrial development to create millions of sustainable jobs, including the introduction of minimum wages to close the wage gap between the rich and the poor;
- massive development of the African economy and advocating for a move from reconciliation to justice in the entire continent; and
- open, accountable, corruption-free government and society without fear of victimisation by state agencies.

The EFF takes aim at a multitude of deficits in ANC policy practice; its election campaign appeals encapsulated twenty-seven realities of deficits and suffering, also listed in its election manifesto. The EFF positions itself as the party to fill the delivery gaps. Its list of deliverables is aspirational. Among the promises it made in its election manifesto were a R7 000 monthly minimum wage for builders, and R6 500 for manufacturing workers. It pledged to introduce a monthly R2 500 grant for the terminally ill. In the EFF future there will be better houses and running water in the households, not just public taps down the lane.[19] 'Do not celebrate mediocrity when black people are undermined,' said Malema in Daveyton, Ekurhuleni.[20]

Ideological aspiration and compromise

Andile Mngxitama, one-time foremost EFF intellectual (before he was expelled for his allegations of corruption against the leadership), land rights campaigner by background, and always an outspoken advocate of black consciousness ideology, was critical of the EFF's populist language, then joined the EFF but soon became part of an internal black consciousness minority lobby. In 2011, Mngxitama had described Malema as 'an opportunist who raised these issues [nationalisation, land expropriation, etc.] not to solve them, but to trick the poor who have been waiting for a better life for all for almost twenty years …'[21] Three years later, and ensconced in Parliament, Mngxitama wrote that the EFF was the embodiment of Frantz Fanon's dream.[22] Next, he fell out with the Malema-ists, for this group's undue influence over the national people's assembly elections.[23]

The EFF's criticism of the socioeconomic and political order focuses in the first place on the blights of South Africa's socioeconomy, which include rampant poverty and racial inequality: continuously critical unemployment, wage inequities, failed delivery on sustainable jobs and livelihoods, and decline in labour-absorptive sectors. Second is land and its associated wrongs: skewed land ownership; farm evictions and forcible evictions from mineral-rich land; race and class bias in deriving benefits from mineral extraction; high proportion of citizens in shacks and informal settlements who also have low service delivery; rural areas remaining underdeveloped; violence and substance abuse in residential areas. Third, the EFF implores that essential social services need correction: apartheid trends are still reflected in education; adult literacy is not addressed; post-secondary education is neglected; the low success rate of African students in higher education with students excluded from higher learning for financial reasons; many going without access to clinics and basic health care amid low provision of health-care practitioners; food insecurity is high in both urban and rural areas; exorbitantly expensive imports of consumer goods; and social grant increases lower than inflation. Fourth, the EFF wants to see the problem of corruption corrected.

Malema emphasises that the EFF preaches 'Marxism in a practical form'. He sees socialist success stories and models for the EFF in Venezuela, Cuba, China and Zimbabwe, stressing that socialism has been developing differently in each of these countries.[24] The EFF emphasises the role of a highly capacitated and skilled state, which will manage state companies in housing, road construction, cement, pharmaceuticals, mining, food stocking and banks. Key components to realising the EFF goals are the expropriation of land without compensation; the nationalisation of mines, private banks and strategic sectors of the economy; the creation of a fully state-owned bank; refocusing strategically controlled state-owned enterprises on development; the advancement of the

African economy; and building progressive political, ideological and economic partnerships in the world.[25] The EFF often adds a racial dimension to the sharing proposed through nationalisation, with frequent references to white people who must learn to share, and to white monopoly capital being a root cause of socioeconomic problems. Black capitalists like the billionaire Patrice Motsepe are also targeted.

The EFF policy positions are thus basically radical, but they are also moderated on occasion, showing some ideological incoherence. The party does not talk full-scale nationalisation: only 60 per cent of resources, and only in select sectors. In the 2014 election campaign, Malema reassured JP Morgan, Coronation Asset Management and Investec of the moderation of the EFF's proposals for economic liberation.[26] Mngxitama added that Malema had been compromising on the EFF principle of expropriation of land without compensation: first in Mangaung Malema referred to expropriation of unoccupied land, and subsequently in Stellenbosch to unproductive land, both in the context of 'without compensation'.[27]

Malema's radicalism is not averse to bling and high-end labels.[28] EFF leaders target billionaires but acquire expensive material possessions. Malema argues this away, saying that in the EFF-envisaged South Africa everybody should have access to such prized goods. As in most left-wing political parties the EFF leaders are not required to live as paupers to demonstrate commitment to the poor, even if its legislative representatives often wear workerist red uniforms. Questions remain as to how Malema affords his lifestyle, and how he can get away with arguing 'luxury items for all'.

When the EFF and the Workers and Socialist Party (Wasp)[29] failed to reach an agreement to cooperate in 2013, the ideological critiques followed. Wasp identified some of the differences:

> The EFF appears to look towards this radical capitalist variety of nationalisation [in which the state is used to accelerate the development of a black capitalist class]. Wasp, on the other hand, fights for nationalisation on the basis of democratic control and management by the workers and working class communities … [30]

Agreements with either Wasp or the Democratic Left Front (DLF) would have burdened the EFF ideologically and practically. Notwithstanding its ideological incoherence, the EFF has emerged with an electoral presence far outperforming

Wasp's minuscule polling achievement (a national total of 8 331 votes or a national-level performance of 0.05 per cent).[31]

EFF RESULTS IN ELECTION 2014

In Election 2014 the EFF established a considerable national and provincial footprint. At less than one year old and with just over six months of formal registration as a party, it gained just over 6 per cent of the national vote and over one million votes nationally. Comparatively, its performance was marginally better than the improvement registered by the DA over its 2009 national election performance, and its mark was one percentage point lower than Cope's 2009 score.

The EFF emerged from the election with a confirmed youth and worker following. It became a new political home to more than a million of the 18 million who voted. It had twenty-five seats in the National Assembly and six in the National Council of Provinces. It became the official opposition in the Limpopo and North West provincial legislatures, and earned representation in all of the provinces. That it had not fared better (as it had anticipated) was due to a large bloc of its supporters being either too young to vote or not registered. The EFF had neither the time nor resources to roll out an EFF-centred voter registration plan and in the end it accused the ANC of rigging, especially in places such as Alexandra in Gauteng. It nevertheless accepted the 2014 election result.[32]

As it turns out, the EFF gained a head start over a possible workers' party by moving into the field when the time was ripe to start capturing an angry and rebellious youth and worker vote. The EFF continued to grow after the 2014 election, with specific breakthroughs in student communities – in October 2014 the EFF won the student representative council (SRC) elections at the University of Limpopo, convincingly beating the Progressive Youth Alliance comprising the ANCYL, the Young Communist League and the South African Students' Congress (Sasco). The EFF again won these elections in 2015, along with a landslide in the Vaal University of Technology SRC elections of March 2015.[33]

The party became the home for large numbers of the unemployed or informally employed. An Ipsos opinion poll conducted just before the 2014 election sheds light on the demographic profile of EFF supporters. It found that 40 per cent of EFF supporters are unemployed, while close to 25 per cent are employed full-time – mostly blue-collar and generally dissatisfied with their lot.

On income, 20 per cent of those who said they would vote EFF earn between R2 500 and R5 000 per month, 13 per cent between R5 000 and R7 000, and the rest are scattered across the remaining income categories. A total of 44 per cent are born-frees aged eighteen to twenty-four and a further 49 per cent are between twenty-five and fifty.[34] Poverty and blackness are the common denominators of EFF supporters.

The EFF is an uncomfortable presence for the ANC, given that many of the ANC's hitherto loyal followers felt free to support it. The EFF is a struggle-compatible 'loyal opposition'. But the EFF also represents Marikana's children, metaphorically speaking. Many saw the massacre of August 2012 as a symbol of how the ANC leadership had come to elevate itself above ordinary citizens' conditions and concerns.[35]

THE EFF IN THE PORTALS OF PARLIAMENT

There is no doubt that the EFF threats of an extra-parliamentary revolt have traction. Besides challenging ANC insincerity on the ground, the EFF also channels anger into Parliament, institutionalising it and helping to ensure that those with grievances feel represented. It is not unique in this respect though – and it is known that citizens who protest in their communities often are not politically alienated and may still vote ANC.

The EFF is on ambiguous ground when it vows to take power through elections and the Constitution via a 'led revolution'. Malema notes widespread discontent, but asserts that the EFF's leadership can guide this discontent carefully to impose order on the upcoming chaos:[36]

> There is going to be an uprising in South Africa if we are not careful, and that's why we founded the Economic Freedom Fighters – to give guidance and direction on how the struggle should be conducted so that it doesn't become anarchic, or doesn't become violent and directionless …

Ultimately, the EFF is not about overthrowing the system; it is about intent to overthrow the ANC and to steer the system towards more caring for its citizens. In the meantime, embarrassing the ANC, exposing corrupt leadership and taking away chunks of its support will suffice. When talking about the hope that the EFF brings, Malema speaks in surprisingly optimistic tones about components of the South Africa political system. 'There is hope,' he says. 'We have multiparty democracy … Our Constitution and electoral system give us hope.' Malema stresses that the EFF's revolution is intended to occur within the ambit of the law and that South Africans appreciate their constitutional and electoral opportunities to change their lives.[37] He explains the 'led revolution' – a vanguard will lead the revolution, but it is to be a soft vanguard that works through the institutions of Parliament.[38]

Malema has integrated 'radical' and 'revolution' into the legislature's work. 'It is not a different game … it's a different terrain. It remains the same struggle.'[39] Andile Mngxitama wrote cautiously but critically about this approach: 'We would do well to remember that warning of Lenin about the dangers of "parliamentary cretinism": the excessive belief that Parliament can change society towards a revolution without mass struggle outside the corridors of Parliament.'[40] At the same time, the EFF also makes the ANC carry responsibility for whether the EFF adheres to the law; it would depend on the force the ANC brings to bear on it. Resistance rhetoric flows easily off EFF lips – and the ANC retaliates with propaganda of treasonous, destabilising EFF behaviour. The ANC argues that the EFF is counter-democratic, as articulated by Zizi Kodwa, ANC spokesperson: 'We warn them not to take us back to the past where we will have no option but to defend our hard-won democracy.'[41] In the wake of the Gauteng legislature's banning of EFF red overall uniforms (later reversed), Malema argued: 'The continuation to remove EFF from the legislature using wrong rulings will cause instability in this province of Gauteng. We are not relying only on the courts, we will fight. We have got the ability to mobilise our people and fight these people, physically.'[42] The state's Joint Centre on Intelligence signalled that it would closely monitor the EFF.

The question was whether the EFF could sustain the balance between parliamentary work and ongoing engagement in communities to build the base that could propel the party into improved standings in future elections. Observation of the EFF 2014 campaign and subsequent community engagements suggests that under Malema's leadership the EFF has enough credible community standing to alternate and swing parliamentary channelling back to community rebellion. Mngxitama, on popular energy around EFF rallies and protests, had said: 'We have to harness this energy [after the May 2014 election]. We're not a political party. We're a revolutionary movement. Expect some disruptions … Expect trouble … Julius is our best gift.'[43] In this context Malema's words, addressed to the ANC, ring out: 'A different baby is born … a child that walks immediately … You must be afraid of that child.'[44] In the final analysis, the ANC would be afraid of spectacle and embarrassment at the hands of the EFF – and most of all, embarrassment of its president. The ANC also loathed being upstaged by the EFF in terms of urban land invasions (predominantly municipal land) and other forms of populist activism. As governing party, the ANC had far less leeway than an opposition party even if it negotiated with protesters behind the scenes.

The EFF's constituency of disillusioned, angry and rebellious citizens, largely youth, was thus brought into party politics, multiparty democracy and the established institutions of democracy.[45] It is important that as long as the EFF operates in terms of party politics and the constitutional order it is a conservative influence on South African politics. It is ironic in this context that the ANC has tried to project the EFF's intra-Parliament protest – all about getting accountability and fair treatment – as disrespecting and disregarding Parliament and democracy. In the words of the ANC:

> The actions of some opposition parties undermine democracy and the Constitution. The ANC therefore understands the responsibility it has to defend democracy. It is for this reason we welcome and wholly support the intervention by the deputy president in his capacity as leader of government business in Parliament.[46]

The ANC adopted the mantra that it was the champion of the dignity of Parliament, arguing that the EFF had made it seem like a circus – whereas, on the contrary, prior to the arrival of the EFF it was Parliament's sleeping MPs and irrelevant speeches that inspired many citizens to label it a circus.[47] It is clear that the EFF employs well-intended populist sentiment but simultaneously it double-speaks, veering between vowing to use the Constitution and its institutions to bring peaceful revolutionary change and stating that it will take its pro-poor campaign to the streets.

The EFF is the only party in Parliament that plays both these worlds seamlessly. Yet, as Richard Calland asks: '… will Parliament be a springboard or will it, over time, slowly swallow the EFF?'[48] If the EFF maintains the extra-parliamentary leg, and its leaders uphold their challenges to parliamentary conventions, it will not become just another struggling small to medium-sized establishment party. When faced with the disputed deal that Deputy President

235

Ramaphosa brokered with opposition parties in Parliament, the EFF appeared willing to submit to ANC authority.[49] Social media were abuzz, asking whether the EFF parliamentarians had sold out in order to keep their salaries. The deal collapsed and the EFF returned to its anti-ANC, insurrection mode. In the process the EFF lost some esteem and the ANC surged into its propaganda about how the EFF was anarchistic, disruptive and disorderly, even alleging that through its parliamentary actions the EFF had prevented accountability functions from running.[50] Further down the line, rebel officials breaking away from the EFF in Gauteng, and later in Mpumalanga, cited as one of their grievances the fact that the EFF had become 95 per cent 'parliamentary show' and 5 per cent community.[51]

Demanding accountability, accused of disrespect

The ANC claimed the EFF to be dangerous – demagogic, even fascist; later it changed to simply disrespectful. It feared that the EFF was dismantling the carefully constructed type of dignified silence among established parliamentarians through the convenient system of undisputed ANC majoritarianism. Yet the EFF was not easily silenced. With its public defiance of Zuma, its history of contrariness, the exorcism of the Malema ANCYL, Malema's ability to coin sound-bite truths about ANC mistakes, and the resonance EFF rhetoric (and even demagoguery) finds on the ground, it would always capture media attention, probably irrespective of scandals. After all, scandals were on display in the governing party as well.

Seven events in the first year of the EFF's life in Parliament illuminate the ANC's accusations that opposition parties were belittling Parliament, whereas opposition parties were demanding accountability from the ANC:

- 20 June 2014: The EFF walks out of the State of the Nation debate in the National Assembly when Malema is requested to leave the House after refusing to withdraw his remark that the ANC committed a massacre at Marikana (in April 2015 the Western Cape High Court finds that it was a reasonable and permissible statement).
- 21 August 2014: Riot police are summonsed when the EFF MPs refuse to leave the House after having insisted during presidential question time that Zuma say when he would 'pay back the money', as the EFF chanted. The unruly challenge is preceded by Zuma's sweeping aside DA parliamentary leader Maimane's question of whether the president's corruption charges created a conflict of interest in his appointing the NPA boss.

Vintage Zuma, his answer is, giggling-style: 'Your question is really not a question, a serious question. I have no charges against me so the issue of conflict of interest does not arise.' Then the president avoids the EFF question about when he intends paying back the money determined by the public protector's Nkandla report: 'As I said in answering the questions I have responded to reports about Nkandla, it's not only the public protector. I've responded to all the reports as I am supposed to.'

- 13 November 2014: Opposition parties jointly take over the National Assembly, filibustering through motions to debate issues of Nkandla, the president, policy and ANC governance, to delay and possibly thwart the ANC-dominated *ad hoc* committee report on Nkandla, which had exonerated Zuma. EFF MP Reneilwe Mashabela repeatedly states, 'The president is the greatest liar in the world' and refuses to leave the House.[52] Riot police are ordered to remove her, and DA MPs, trying to stop police from entering Parliament, are injured. The report is adopted.

- 26–27 November 2014: Opposition parties boycott the reconvening of Parliament for a twenty-five minute session to pass the adoption of the report of the Powers and Privileges Committee, which recommended disciplining twenty EFF members for the 21 August events. On 27 November, despite objections (also from other opposition parties), these EFF MPs are suspended. They vow to get Zuma to answer questions, if need to be in his 2015 State of the Nation address. The suspensions are then suspended through an EFF application to the Constitutional Court.

- 12 February 2015: The president's State of the Nation address is interrupted when the EFF insists on his response to the question of when he will 'pay back the [Nkandla] money'. There is a sense that 'something had broken' that night: a jamming device scrambled cellular network signals and blocked communications. Journalists and opposition parties protest as the president enters the chamber. The DA, EFF and FF+ raise points of order, demanding that the device be switched off. It is done. (A senior Cabinet member was in charge but the event would be explained in terms of a technical glitch.) When the president's speech starts the EFF rise on a point of order: 'We are asking the president when he is going to pay back the money.' Men dressed in white shirts (at least some of them public order police) remove the EFF MPs, punching and hitting them. The EFF MPs resist and are dragged outside while ANC MPs cheer. The DA protests the presence of the white shirts in the National Assembly and walks

237

out, followed by the UDM, Cope and Agang SA. President Zuma giggles and returns to reading his speech to the half-full chamber.[53]

- 11 March 2015: It is presidential question time in the National Assembly and Zuma mocks the public interest in Nkandla, accusing the EFF (and opposition generally) of wanting the answers they want on Nkandla and not accepting the answers he gives, ignores the speaker's efforts to halt him to allow a point of order, and denies that he had ever dodged getting to Parliament to answer questions. Questions arise as to whether the speaker and the Presidency had been sheltering the president from accountability to Parliament.

- 27 May 2015: In response to the debate on the Presidency's budget statement, Zuma takes aim at the opposition parties, repeatedly mocking and mimicking both the EFF and the DA, and accusing them of being disrespectful. The president already knows that the minister of police would the following day pronounce that his boss (the president) would not only not have to pay back a cent for Nkandla but was also deemed to be entitled to additional publicly funded security measures.

When Kodwa had earlier tried to turn the tables on the EFF's insistence on Zuma's accountability to Parliament, he declared that the EFF's disruption had deprived South Africans of the opportunity to get the president's answers, or the MPs from representing their constituencies, and had undermined the exercise of accountability overall. According to Kodwa, the EFF behaviour 'undermines the integrity, the aura and the decorum of the House …[54]. In contrast, the ANC caucus's mission had deferred to the executive and president, protecting them from scrutiny and questioning by the opposition parties.

The EFF started forming strategic alliances with other opposition parties to make it inconvenient for Zuma and the ANC in Parliament. Cooperation followed on the motion of no confidence in the speaker, on the *ad hoc* committees on Nkandla, to some extent on the disciplinary action against the EFF members, and in their rejection of the speaker after the 13 November session.[55] The EFF, DA, UDM and FF+ parties all cooperated by leaving the first Nkandla *ad hoc* committee; only the EFF boycotted the second. The most remarkable aspect was the extent to which the parliamentary game was played on territory defined by the opposition parties. ANC veteran Mavuso Msimang summed up this new terrain of embarrassing battle for the ANC: 'You don't allow your opponents to choose the battleground. Once the battleground has been chosen by somebody else, their rules dictate [action].'[56]

The EFF and opposition parties' relationship with the speaker (also ANC national chairperson) Baleka Mbete was central to the parliamentary fallout. Her emotive and irrational defences of the president helped foster a bond between opposition parties. She argued, for example, '… in the African tradition, you don't interfere with a man's kraal … the issue of a man's kraal or the kraal of a family is a holy space'.[57] Mbete, ambitious, had one eye on becoming South Africa's first woman president. She was not going to miss a beat in protecting the president. The plot thickened later in 2015, against the backdrop of questions to the president that proceeded relatively smoothly. The 'pay back the money' theme featured last in the string of August questions, while tightened rules (the product of ANC-DA parliamentary cooperation) came into in force. The president had the chance to answer questions – but embarrassed himself through hapless responses to the unprepared follow-ups. The EFF next turned to the Constitutional Court to rule on President Zuma's compliance with constitutional prescripts pertaining to, amongst others, giving effect to the public protector's findings and the Constitution's requirement of high standards of presidential conduct.

MALEMA'S TRAIL OF ACCUMULATING AND FORFEITING RICHES

Malema's clashes with the tax and 'business with the state' laws is useful, up to a point, in helping to assess prospects of eventual subjugation to, and even reabsorption into, the ANC. Malema has a chequered history when it comes to building up riches but then seeing the light and converting to condemnations of the ANC under Jacob Zuma.[58] In many respects he is at the mercy of the ANC and this vulnerability has raised suspicion among some adversaries in the EFF.

The public protector's reports tell an important part of the story of Malema in business and politics.[59] The reports speak to lapses in state procurement, accounting for projects and funding, and the Malema-centred elite benefiting from projects in Malema's Limpopo province. The quality of the delivery of infrastructural services ranged from fine to dismal. The public protector's findings read much like auditor general reports on government practice of periods before and subsequent to Malema's tender travails. What Malema did – entering into preferential public sector contracts in association with partners and contractors who execute the work – was similar to many transactions that unfolded across multiple municipal and provincial sites. In this respect Malema was no more involved in unsavoury deals with government than were large numbers of ANC members.[60] However, he was targeted. Malema learnt through his own rise and demise in the ANC that as long as a cadre serves Zuma's contemporary ANC with deference to the leadership, the sky is the limit. If that line is crossed, sanction and expulsion may very well follow.

Malema faced two sets of legal encounters. One concerned the specific transactions for state projects, where there was alleged corruption, fraud, money laundering and racketeering (the exact categories of arms deal charges that Zuma faced and used state resources in legal fees to avoid). The other was with Sars for non-declaration of income, non-payment of taxes and interest, and, subsequently, challenges of how he had afforded to pay.

Malema's tax encounters had started in 2009, when Sars launched checks on his tax affairs, as they also check on many other citizens (there was a good possibility nevertheless that Malema's case received special attention).[61] Malema started filing tax returns in late 2010. He became more visible when, in 2011, he invested in Sandton real estate. From 2011 to 2012, Sars tightened its investigation and issued statements for the payment of taxes. Shivambu relates that during the Marikana moment of 2012, when Malema intervened on the side of the workers, senior government officials met in Cape Town to consider charging Malema for inciting violence.[62] In the meeting, a Sars representative was reportedly asked how the investigation into Malema was progressing. In 2013 Sars notified Malema of its refusal to compromise on payments, and court proceedings began. In 2014, deals of the payments were agreed and Malema started paying, including interest.

Former Limpopo premier Sello Moloto observed that Malema had used Zuma's campaign for the presidencies of the ANC and South Africa 'to intimidate everybody to give him tenders'.[63] When the reports of Malema's tenderpreneurship started emerging, Zuma stressed the right of all citizens to engage in legitimate business, including with the state, given that Malema was not a state employee.[64] When the bubble of Malema's insubordination burst, Nzimande countered on behalf of the ANC that Malema was not breaking away from the ANC for deeper policy or ideological reasons: 'Julius was expelled from the ANC because he wanted the ANC to protect him from his corrupt activities. When that did not happen he started throwing his toys out of the cot.'[65] In contrast, Malema notes the 'special attention' that came his way: 'I am the victim of a political onslaught … All of them are doing business [with the state] … The only crime I did was to stop supporting Jacob Zuma.'[66]

Subsequently the EFF adopted a strong anti-corruption stance. At its July 2013 launch, Malema had said the EFF was founded on the principle of anti-corruption. Also, given that the public protector did not find against Malema, the EFF felt free to condemn the ANC, and Zuma in particular, for their corruption, especially in the large personal benefits that Zuma accrued courtesy of the state-sponsored improvements to Nkandla, security related and not, or whitewash by the minister of police.[67] Malema's problems with Sars did not dissipate either. He documented details of Sars reneging on deals with him to repay, and adding queries about the sources of the funds which had enabled him to settle debts.

Malema started playing one of his trump cards – knowledge of how Zuma had sustained his own lifestyle through donations by secret donors into trust funds. While ANC and presidential spokespersons denied anything untoward in Zuma's finances, Malema explained that he followed the formula he had used when fundraising for Zuma:

> More or less formal trust structures were formed into which donations were made – some large, some small – for the benefit of the leaders. I have first-hand knowledge of this: I dealt with donations to President Zuma. I, myself, was maintained in the same manner. Sometimes money was simply paid into my bank account by anonymous donors, sometimes known supporters paid my expenses or made gifts of money, clothes and other necessities of life and sometimes also luxuries.[68]

VICISSITUDES IN THE EFF'S LIFE AS A POLITICAL PARTY

On the more mundane side of party politics in Parliament, the EFF's early impact was significant. It pushed the rules of procedure and opprobrium, calling a spade a spade, especially when it came to President Zuma and his government. In terms of both institutional politics and grassroots action, the EFF was improving on Cope's track record. In several other ways, however, the EFF was dangling close to the Cope trail. In particular, there was no certainty that the EFF would not still become victim to ANC (and its own internal) pressures.

The EFF continues to face the challenge of whether it can sufficiently differentiate itself from the ANC, and further develop a counterposing identity. That will be essential when the time arrives for Zuma to go.[69] Zuma is much of the EFF's focal point, and compulsion for rapprochement might be strong. This would depend on whether other EFF arch-enemies (like ANC Secretary General Mantashe) remain in top-ANC positions of power. In concrete and campaigning terms, the EFF would have to stand strong against the ANC's infiltration, the EFF top-leadership's legal battles with the ANC state, and sabotage of election campaigning including violence and intimidation.[70] The EFF seemed to handle ANC insults better than Cope had done – including the ANC regularly calling the EFF fascists led by Hitler, loud-mouth demagogues, tenderpreneurs in red berets, people who 'have never done an honest day's work in their life' (Jeremy Cronin), who 'hijack real grievances' and are 'provocative hooligans' (Blade Nzimande).[71]

EFF holding off the Cope curse

Cope, the EFF's predecessor as split-off from the ANC, had suffered the results of poor policy differentiation from the parent body. It had incessant leadership struggles. It focused its energies almost solely on legislative survival, neglecting grassroots organisation. Most of its experienced people were sent to Parliament, and did little else. It suffered suspicions of inappropriate dealings with party finances and was insufficiently transparent. Most of all, when the going got tough Cope members succumbed to the pressures of ANC insults in Parliament and business pressures. Many returned to the ANC; many had never stopped regarding the ANC as their political home.

The EFF still has to prove its ability to survive in the war zone of new opposition parties in conflict with the ANC. It is more streetwise and fighting-fit than was Cope. The EFF has been at the front line of intra-party wars and harbours no illusions about being an ANC target. It draws much attention (some in the EFF say too much), especially through challenges in Parliament. It has somewhat better (although still ambiguous) policy differentiation from the ANC than Cope had had. It applies the legal recourse strategy on the theme of South Africa as a constitutional state. The EFF associated itself with the victims of the August 2012 Marikana killings. It helped care for the workers and their relatives, extended legal representation to the victims, campaigned for the release of the Marikana report, and for due punishment for the Marikana crimes. One of the Marikana widows, Primrose Sonti, became an EFF MP.[72]

This illustrated the presence that the EFF maintains outside Parliament, although unevenly. The party's community roots were neglected when the party was preparing for its provincial and December 2014 elective people's assemblies. The EFF had to show that it was an internally democratic, formally elected and constituted party, yet getting there was tough. Vulnerability showed in its leadership elections, and then escalated around party finance issues. In the run-up to the internal elections much of the EFF's energy was diverted into branch quorums and nominations. Most positions, in both the elections of the national command (December 2014) and provincial command structures (mostly November 2014), were heavily contested. The provincial results went occasionally against the emerging national leadership's wishes, but they were accepted, for then. Disgruntled excluded members approached the courts.[73] Discontent surfaced about Floyd Shivambu being the *de facto* kingpin with Malema depending on him excessively. The Gauteng grouping (comprising the ones who were elected against national leadership's wishes) was on a collision path and in effect left the EFF. Some were expelled after going public without substantiation at the time with allegations of corruption at top-leadership level.

The Malema centre of the EFF held, despite the challenge. An EFF advantage over Cope was that Malema's position as top leader was clear. His authority over the party was undisputed – yet, he was vulnerable to ANC goodwill on his outstanding legal issues.[74]

EFF's eggs in the anti-Zuma basket

The EFF's alter ego is nemesis Jacob Zuma – to such an extent that the EFF is in large part defined by its contrary relationship to Zuma and the Zuma-controlled ANC. When Zuma is replaced or steps down, much of the EFF's character and edge over the ANC will recede. The EFF would then rely more on policy differences to distinguish it from the ANC – provided it posits and retains such differentiation. There may be a compulsion to move back into the ANC but the evolving policy differences, if sustained, could be an effective barrier. As the EFF engages more with community initiatives to occupy land, especially in urban areas, the communities might also function to pull the EFF more strongly into differentiation – especially in the face of the police's readiness to block the EFF from strengthening and sustaining popular roots.

The main differentiators from the ANC nevertheless remain matters of degree, emphasis, labels and rhetoric, and the modest number of substantive policy and ideological differences raises the question of whether the EFF could reconcile with the parent body after Zuma's departure.[75] When this possibility was broached Malema said he will be buried with a red beret. He tweeted: 'I will never do that to my people [defect back to the ANC], the EFF remains my only political home now and for the rest of my life. I will be buried with the red flag'[76] (in a previous era Malema had proclaimed that his blood would forever be the ANC colours of black, green and gold).[77] The EFF released a statement calling the story about Malema reconciling with the ANC ridiculous and hinted that the EFF dissidents might have been manipulating information:

> We believe there is no disciplined member of our organisation who would go to the media with such a story without clearing it with the organisation first, or they would at least go to the media with facts. We have no proof that our member and former national coordinator fighter Mpho Ramakatsa went to the media with such a ridiculous story. We are also not inclined to believe that such a decorated former liberation stalwart would stoop to that level. We note that the ruling party's spokesperson Zizi Kodwa has also refuted these preposterous claims. We urge our disciplined members not to feed the papers with unfounded statements about our president, leadership and our organisation in general.[78]

The EFF's existence is distinguished by progress amid intrigue and suspicion. The lines of tension are internal around the oversupply of potential leaders and community activists versus a leadership around Julius Malema who exercises ownership of the party. To some extent this has followed logically, given that Malema was the pivot around which the EFF revolved. His standing both at grassroots and in the media bolstered the Julius phenomenon. The second line of tension, external, pivoted around the EFF's relationship with the ANC. It was never quite certain what pressures the ANC was putting on whom to abandon the EFF and 'return home'.

NUMSA, VAVI AND LEFT ALIGNMENT

Will the EFF together with Numsa's slowly emerging United Front be the forerunner of a great and united (or at least mutually cooperative) left-opposition party?[79] When the Numsa-linked party finally arises, possibly called the Socialist Movement, could it be the nail in the coffin of ANC hegemony and party political dominance? Such developments are but two advances in a whole new and continuously unfolding battlefield. The ANC is fighting back. It is trying to cut back the EFF's parliamentary presence and restrain its party political development. Until July 2015 it had also tried to roll back Numsa's expulsion from Cosatu (to keep Numsa subjected within Cosatu), while keeping Vavi in the equivalent of internal Cosatu detention. Numsa and Vavi equally did not capture the whole of Cosatu (their first prize): first they were expelled and then sidelined through the Special National Congress (SNC) of July 2015. In the course of 2015 onwards a 'peace' process ensued, through the tripartite summit instructed by Zuma.[80] The summit itself was ineffectual with regard to the Cosatu wars. The SNC mobilised an anti-Numsa-Vavi majority and further forced the rebels out. The Numsa-associated unions issued their statement in the name of the Progressive Block of Cosatu Unions,[81] refusing to let go of their Cosatu association.

The ANC and Tripartite Alliance (to the extent that the latter existed in more than name by 2015) ceded its left position to the EFF and Numsa as the ANC's wars of presidential protection meant that the Alliance partners no longer helped to reserve that space for the ANC. Cosatu's once-powerful role as the internal ANC opposition that could capture issues and debate and deflect the externalised party political opposition had been written out.[82] As Cosatu ousted Numsa from its ranks, despite support for Numsa from seven additional unions, the consent in the internal tripartite-ANC alliance was now very much manufactured (Table 7.1).[83] Cosatu realised, however, the mortal blow it would suffer if these seven left alongside Numsa – 40 per cent of its membership (and as much of its budget) would disappear.

The ANC was no longer the hegemonic juggernaut.[84] The decline of the SACP as a presence on the left of the South African political spectrum is an integral factor within what may be a new and rising left space. This opening had been ceded at the time around the 2014 elections to the EFF, trade unions, a selection of civic movements, and a handful of other small left parties. Cosatu had been assumed to be left of the ANC, and some of its member unions continued to be, especially the 'worker unions' as opposed to the 'professional unions'. However, Cosatu fractured amid the fervour to ensure compliance and loyalty to Zuma and 'the president's ANC'.

Whether Numsa's unfolding United Front and the EFF could cohere to help constitute a wider-ranging socialist-left formation is the first of the many factors determining the sustainability of a left opposition. Achille Mbembe argues that the EFF 'singularly complicates the institutional left's political equation. For the left to emerge as a genuine counter-hegemonic force, it will have to forge a *modus vivendi* with the EFF…' A range of left formations and the potential growth of the left project on the labour front contributed a large part of the optimism for such an alliance to become the site for development of an alternative to the ANC and its government. Regarding a broader left movement, Mbembe continues:

> In its attempt to radicalise the current crisis it faces a real choice: insurrection or the electoral path. To keep straddling both sides as it is currently doing might well lead to its early demise. Instead it must actively create the ideological conditions for an eventual alliance of the forces of labour with the youth and other segments of the subaltern classes. Only such an alliance is likely to open the way for the emergence of a new post-ANC historic bloc.[85]

Irrespective of many questions as to how authentically left and socialist the EFF really is, it has positioned itself as the most viable party left of the ANC. Numsa is a more 'authentic' left, given that it is a workers' organisation, but it lags behind the EFF in organisation and experience at electoral contests. In addition, the EFF demonstrated in elections that a large number of workers were supporting it electorally, and at the same time many Cosatu workers indicated that they were not ready to support an anti-ANC workers' party.[86] Numsa and its associated unions also realised that if it forms a political party to oppose the ANC it would not gain a clean sweep of union-member loyalty. This reality, in all likelihood, helped inform Vavi's tactic to provoke and have himself expelled from Cosatu rather than take the initiative and break away.

Both the EFF and Numsa with its United Front are cautious in seeking cooperation with other left or socialist-oriented political parties and organisations, in and out of Parliament. As is common among similar organisations everywhere, the South African socialist-left organisations exhibit much discord and distrust regarding one another's political and ideological credentials. Agreement on African-nationalist convergence appears easier than the secular theologies of socialist theory. The Pan Africanist Congress (PAC), although approximating extinction, comes relatively close to sharing EFF policies. Before the 2014 election it was announced that the two parties would merge.[87] They cooperated in the campaign but the PAC in effect self-destructed when it only won one parliamentary seat – thanks to the residual vote.[88]

In the run-up to Election 2014 the EFF cooperated variously with other (mostly small, with minor effect on the overall political landscape) political organisations, absorbing remnants of the black consciousness and pan-Africanist traditions, as these remained in micro-party form. The Socialist Party of Azania (Sopa) and the Black Consciousness Party (BCP) merged into the EFF, and their leaders were incorporated in the EFF candidate list. The EFF also cooperated with the PAC and the Azanian People's Organisation (but Azapo lost its single remaining seat in May 2014). Less successful talks with Wasp took place. The Democratic Left Front (DLF),[89] with its eco-Marxism, participated in neither the 2011 nor 2014 elections, despite its founding ambition to grow into a political force of note. The shack-dwellers movement of Durban, Abahlali baseMjondolo, which abstained in previous elections, brought out a technical vote for the DA – in search of protection from ANC attacks[90] – rather than playing out a conventional left alignment. In the ranks of these left organisations the EFF was the only one operating at a mass political level.

In earlier 2013 days Wasp agreed to cooperate with the EFF in organising young people and workers. Wasp then stressed the major difference between itself and the EFF as being the EFF's intent to go into Parliament, whereas Wasp saw its own mission as extra-parliamentary, raising worker consciousness.[91] Wasp formally proposed to the EFF, days after the EFF's formal registration as political party, that they should constitute a Wasp-EFF electoral bloc for the purposes of contesting the 2014 elections. The EFF response was anti-coalitionist, insisting instead that Wasp endorses the EFF. Wasp's microscopic election result of 2014 (0.05 per cent compared with Azapo's and the PAC's 0.11 and 0.21 respectively) probably sealed its fate.

Numsa, the EFF and the quagmire of competing socialisms

The EFF, along with all members of the Tripartite Alliance, uses socialist rhetoric with variations on the theme of the two phases of the revolution or, as rendered recently, the phases to a 'national democratic society'. The ANC claims it is 'not a socialist government but … pursuing many policies that are benefiting the workers and the working class'.[92] For the EFF this may be projected in terms of Malema's declaring that each country creates its own version of socialism. The EFF focuses on leaders such as Hugo Chávez; Numsa, on the other hand, focuses on worker control. The EFF considers interracial redistribution positively. In contrast, Numsa has a primary class focus.

The EFF-Numsa differences led to the EFF not attending Numsa's consultative learning forum, the Symposium of Left Parties and Movements, to learn about the meaning of left politics in the world today and inform its political decision making about a strategic way forward.[93] Numsa, rooted in a form of Marxist-Leninist thinking, distrusts the EFF's ideological positioning, especially questioning its commitment to worker control. The EFF gave two reasons for non-attendance (and these remained relevant at subsequent consultative meetings). First, it disliked Numsa's media-based rebuffs of its efforts to set up a meeting with the Numsa leadership, thus recognising the EFF insufficiently 'as a leading left force on the continent'. Second, the EFF noted that Numsa was still part of Cosatu at the time and subject to the ANC's peacemaking project. Devan Pillay questions EFF ideology by musing on whether it is only a brand of militarist economic nationalism, or a heady cocktail of 'Marxist-Leninist-Fanonian' (an EFF phrase) symbolism and racialised populism.[94] Numsa's general secretary, Irvin Jim, argues that his union's is a clear class position, but the EFF is explicitly anti-capitalist (not socialist) and vague about the type of society to which it aspires. Numsa took its ideological positioning seriously, with its political school 'fleshing out theories to give effect to [conference] resolutions'. Shivambu stresses the EFF position as 'democratic and community control' rather than 'worker control'. Vishwas Satgar casts Numsa as a broader front, 'thinking about a new future for South Africa, in which workers play a central role, democracy is strengthened and transformation happens.'[95] Numsa and the EFF both see white monopoly capital as hugely problematic, and identify with the Freedom Charter and the national democratic revolution.[96] However, Numsa sees the EFF as more nationalist than proletarian. After its 2014 election performance the EFF felt confident about its ability to attract worker support – and thus less reliant on cooperation with a United Front and a Numsa party. As the 2016 local elections drew closer and it became more certain that the United Front would not be a formal participant, Malema repeated appeals for Numsa to form an alternative *labour union* and for workers to support the EFF.

The EFF's postmodern socialist ideological base gets additional texture by Malema's fashioning himself as a revolutionary-insurrectionary leader. He sees himself as a Hugo Chávez (Venezuela), Thomas Sankara (Burkina Faso) and/or Fidel Castro (Cuba). In the final analysis, however, there are only a few aspects of EFF policy that have not at some stage or another been expressed by the ANC. Yet the coordinated and concerted package is projected as radical and as the fix for an ANC-gone-wrong. It could nevertheless also project the ANC onto a more radical policy path. The EFF mix of militancy and institutional moderation is developed as the new party finds its feet in the portals of the provincial and parliamentary legislatures. Assuredly, pressures are on in the EFF to let serious debate on policy issues overtake attention-grabbing antics.

The EFF also maintained a working relationship with Amcu. Amcu, led by Joseph Mathunjwa,[97] arose in the wake of a dysfunctional Cosatu-aligned National Union of Mineworkers (NUM). NUM's lapses made the ANC vulnerable – without working representation by Cosatu in the troubled mining sector it had no effective agent to enter protest and strike areas for peacekeeping (a role Malema assumed with ease). Lines of division became somewhat muddled when NUM changed leadership from Frans Baleni to David Sipunzi, a new general secretary who was more sympathetic toward the Vavi and Numsa rebels. Amcu remained a potential participant in a future counter-Cosatu union congress.

The 'Numsa moment' – gone or going on?

The broad Cosatu base, and especially the Numsa component within, remained the anticipated launch pad for a great break in party politics, for a mass base that would concretise hopes for realignment to the left of the ANC. However, a Cosatu break-up was not going to be clear-cut or incontrovertible and immediate. It would also be contested, especially by the Zuma-aligned ANC. Potential movement will also be affected by the ANC order that will follow after Zuma.

Hopes for the unleashing of left realignment blossomed in the heyday of Vavi as Cosatu general secretary, when he operated at political level there, did not mince words in criticising corruption in the ranks of Tripartite Alliance leader, the ANC and enjoyed the moral high ground.[98] Cosatu grew as a base for a future anti-ANC opposition as Vavi spoke out against the vulture elite in government. He harnessed Cosatu's opposition to e-tolls. He warned that Cosatu could no longer stand up to protect the president or condone the draconian Protection of State Information Bill.[99]

A turning point came when a virtually untouchable Vavi was tripped up for his workplace affair and sale of the Cosatu building – on the first he apologised in different ways; on the second he denied wrongdoing. The ANC had been working on Cosatu to contain the growth of an intra-Cosatu opposition base. Vavi then faced expulsion and submitted to the pro-Zuma line of Cosatu president S'dumo Dlamini. The ANC used the opening to move in and strengthen the non-Vavi, pro-Zuma Cosatu faction. Vavi, effectively silenced with his eight-month suspension, had been reinstated through court action just before Election 2014.[100] He regained his position at the behest of the ANC, which he

249

Table 7.1: Cosatu's 'Numsa moment' – unions lining up pro- and anti-Numsa

ANTI-NUMSA			PRO-NUMSA		
Union		Membership	Union		Membership
1	NUM (National Union of Mineworkers)	310 382	1	Numsa (National Union of Metalworkers of South Africa)*	291 025 (350 000 in 2015)
2	Nehawu (National Education, Health and Allied Workers' Union)	**260 738**	2	Fawu (Food and Allied Workers' Union)*	126 930
3	Sadtu (South African Democratic Teachers' Union)	**251 276**	3	Saccawu (South African Commercial, Catering and Allied Workers' Union)*	120 352
4	Satawu (South African Transport and Allied Workers' Union)	159 626	4	Denosa (Democratic Nursing Organisation of South Africa)*	**74 883**
5	Samwu (South African Municipal Workers' Union)	153 487	5	CWU (Communication Workers' Union)*	18 666
6	Popcru (Police and Prisons Civil Rights Union)	**149 339**	6	Pawusa (Public and Allied Workers' Union of South Africa)	**17 146**
7	Sactwu (South African Clothing and Textile Workers' Union)	85 025	7	Sasawu (South African State and Allied Workers' Union)*	7 074
8	Ceppwawu (Chemical, Energy, Paper, Printing, Wood and Allied Workers' Union)	80 658	8	Safpu (South African Football Players' Union)*	693

9	Sasbo (South African Society of Bank Officials)	67 402
10	Sadnu (South African Democratic Nursing Union)	**8655**
11	Sama (South African Medical Association)	**7759**
12	Cwusa (Creative Workers' Union of South Africa)	Official numbers not available
COLUMN TOTAL WITHOUT SAMWU		1 380 860

COLUMN TOTAL WITHOUT SAMWU
656 076

Source: Cosatu, November 2014; range of media reports.

Note on percentages in the divide: Without Samwu added to the pro-Numsa side, this side has 32 per cent of the membership; when Samwu is added to the pro-Numsa side, it amounts to 40 per cent of Cosatu membership willing to back Numsa, November 2014. Unions marked with an asterisk (*) were by Vavi's side, April 2015, when he conducted his first post-expulsion briefing. Public sector unions are indicated in bold.

Notes on dates of the details: This was the line-up of November 2014; Samwu (in italics) was meant to have joined the pro-Numsa unions but did not join at this stage. The union is struggling with its own leadership problems. By mid-2015 several of the pro-Numsa unions were either divided (like Samwu) or wavering.

C07.indd   251

14-10-2015   09:30:23

could then no longer openly criticise. Beholden to the ANC, he was effectively trapped[101] until the break of March 2015. Vavi did an exposé of Cosatu's financial affairs, and was expelled.

ANC negotiators Cyril Ramaphosa and Jessie Duarte had earlier created a task team to intervene for unity in Cosatu, especially with a view to preventing Numsa from campaigning against the ANC. Days before Election 2014 Duarte reminded the delegates that the decisions that were to be taken on continuing Cosatu unity would exceed the importance of the vote to be cast on election day.[102] The ANC continued to do water-treading mediation for well over a year to keep Cosatu going and in the ANC fold throughout the rest of 2014, yet Dlamini and his union line-up pushed first for Numsa's expulsion and second for its return on the Dlamini-and-Zuma faction's conditions. Towards the end of 2014, just on the verge of going with Numsa, Vavi pulled back again, but would follow through three months later.[103] In 2015, the task team lamented to the NEC that the Cosatu parties had disregarded the team's advice for peace.

The Cosatu war thus continued,[104] through the SNC and towards the November 2015 national congress. Cosatu had become feeble, no longer constituting an effective internal tripartite opposition. The ANC became the negotiator that was simultaneously working to ensure that Cosatu would not split and overseeing the formation of a Numsa substitute union, Liberated Metalworkers' Union of South African (Limusa – around 1 700 members were claimed, compared with the roughly 340 000 of Numsa by the time of Vavi's exodus), with the objective of having a substitute ready to step into Numsa's shoes.[105] Several other new or replacement unions were also being cultivated to be launched if the existing pro-Numsa-Vavi unions could not be swayed or split. Cosatu and the emerging left political-labour force went into operation to regroup and consolidate. There was no end in sight for the prolonged 'Numsa moment'.[106]

CONCLUSION: THE LEFT BEYOND THE EFF, IN FOR THE LONG HAUL

The left in South African politics is haltingly finding its feet. Politics is maturing in that the ANC and the Tripartite Alliance's claim to occupy the left corner of the 'political market' is being shown as fragile while left initiatives are accumulating and solidifying. The process of solidifying the left is gradual and piecemeal. A workers' party will take time to come into place. By 2015 plans were taking shape, slowly and haltingly nevertheless, to let Numsa's United Front build a base on which to anchor a future workers' party. For this project to gain traction workers would have to be ready *en masse* to break with the ANC. At the point of the 2014 election a survey showed that only 8 per cent of Cosatu members (40 per cent of them from Numsa) believed there should be a workers' party.[107] An earlier survey of Cosatu shop stewards showed that 40 per cent would support a workers' party, provided Cosatu endorses it.[108] Despite initial expectations that a new workers' party might be ready to contest 2016 local elections, it now appeared to be a longer-term project. The vacillation about whether to break from Cosatu indicated that the great break was not yet happening, Movement towards it, however, was stronger than ever before. As in the case of the EFF, it had been the ANC's determination to protect its president and the Zuma-ists in government that had been a great stimulus.

While these processes were evolving the EFF was the 'left' available. Its 'left' is quite possibly only marginally left of the ANC's 'left' and ideologically rather compromised, but it combines its 'partial left' with powerful identification of the dishonesty and corruption of today's ANC. It was by force of the ANCYL's expulsion from the ANC that the EFF had its immediate start in organising as a left political party. It had a rehearsed left position, shaped while it was trying to influence the ANC from within and further evolved subsequently. The party proclaims socialist positioning and supports workers without being specifically workerist. The embryonic, authentically left parties might have legitimate doubts about the genuineness of the EFF's particular brand of socialism, but 2014 showed an uptake of well over a million voters for the EFF. This segment of the electorate consciously subscribed to the EFF's brand of 'left'.

The EFF has so far outplayed other left parties through its electoral performance and in positioning and citizen appeals. The war to be the 'left of the ANC' is the EFF's to lose, should it succumb to ANC and internal pressures (the latter sometimes due to ANC interventions and infiltration). In the years to come this party needs to survive its own internal politics battles and it needs to keep up the momentum, excitement and public hype that characterised its early days. It has to keep on showing rapid electoral growth, retain both the enthusiasm of the youth and some left-socialist positioning, counter all compulsion for reverse-defection to the ANC once Zuma goes, convince voters that it has a separate right to existence, have clear minds when it comes to alignment

253

with a likely new worker party, and have answers, when the time comes, to the resurgence of ANC support that might reward the ANC for moving beyond President Jacob Zuma.

NOTES

1   EFF statement, 29 May 2015, by email.
2   Mbuyiseni Ndlozi, 15 April 2015, 'The EFF welcomes the Western Cape High Court judgment that it is parliamentary to say "ANC government massacred workers in Marikana"', EFF statement. The ANC appealed the judgement.
3   Interview, senior EFF politician, 18 February 2015, Cape Town, based on communication between the politician and an ANC parliamentarian involved in intelligence matters.
4   They did not want to leave the EFF and went on a mission to go up against Malema and Floyd Shivambu. The EFF locked them out of their parliamentary offices. S'thembiso Cele, 22 March 2015, 'Defiant MPs return to Parliament', City Press, p. 2.
5   Tweet, 18 March 2015, 'Why would EFF leaders resign? Zorro Boshielo, spills the beans'. S'thembile Cele @City Press.
6   Matuma Letsoalo, 22 May 2015, 'Cosatu "ignored" ANC advice on healing rift', Mail & Guardian, http://mg.co.za/article/2015-05-21-cosatu-ignored-anc-advice-on-healing-rift, accessed 28 May 2015.
7   Patrick Craven, 31 March 2015, interview SABC-SAFM.
8   Left-wing politics denote political positions that advocate for social egalitarianism and elimination of injustice and inequality. It assumes collective responsibility, and gives much of this role to an interventionist state. Left politics de-emphasise nationalism. Workers and the working class take a leading role, and workers, not the bourgeoisie or fractions of the middle class, are to own the means of production.
9   Ranjeni Munusamy, 23 November 2014, 'Vavi's impossible dream: Numsa genie goes back in the bottle', Daily Maverick, http://www.dailymaverick.co.za/article/2014-11-23-vavis-impossible-dream-numsa-genie-goes-back-in-the-bottle/?utm_source=Daily+Maverick+Mailer&utm, accessed 24 November 2014, summarises Vavi's dilemmas.
10 Numsa, 3 December 2014, 'On the plot claims against us – Numsa's response to the "Exposed: Secret regime change plot to destabilise South Africa" document', http://www.politicsweb.co.za/politicsweb/view/politicsweb/en/page72308?oid=847450&sn=Marketingweb+detail&pid=90389&utm_source=Politicsweb+Daily+Headlines&utm_campaign=f363303162-DHN_Dec_4_2014&utm_medium=email&utm_term=0_a86f25db99-f363303162-140175425, accessed 4 December 2014.
11 Susan Booysen, 2015, Youth and Political Participation in South Africa's Democracy, research report, Johannesburg and Washington DC: Freedom House.
12 EFF, 27 November 2014, 'Zuma and his ANC gangsters must admit writing is on the wall – EFF', media statement.
13 Fiona Forde, 2011, An Inconvenient Youth: Julius Malema and the 'New' ANC, Johannesburg: Picador Africa, relates the details of the ANCYL-ANC split.

14 See Floyd Shivambu, 2014, 'Where do we come from? Political and ideological reflections on the struggle for economic freedom', in Floyd Shivambu (ed.), *The Coming Revolution*, Auckland Park: Jacana, pp. 1–32.

15 Roger Southall, 2014, 'The South African elections of 2014: Retrospect and prospect', *Strategic Review for Southern Africa*, vol. 36 (2), pp. 80–95.

16 Observation of NGC deliberations, interviews with delegates who had participated in the closed sessions, Durban, July 2010.

17 Julius Malema, 2 October 2014, interview with Ashraf Garda, *Afternoon Talk*, SABC-SAFM.

18 *Economic Freedom Fighters 2014 General Election Manifesto: Now Is the Time for Economic Freedom!* Also see Floyd Shivambu, 21 July 2013, 'Who are the real freedom fighters'? *The Sunday Independent*, p. 17. Memorising these pillars is part of EFF public representatives' political education.

19 Floyd Shivambu (ed.), 2014, *The Coming Revolution,* op. cit., pp. 170–172.

20 Phindile Chauke, 3 February 2014, 'ANC "values cattle's lives over yours"', *The Citizen*, p. 2.

21 Andile Mngxitama, 26 July 2011, 'Comrade Malema, you are just another ruthless politician', *Sowetan*, p. 4.

22 See Andile Mngxitama, 26 September 2014, 'Class theory finally decolonised', *Mail & Guardian*, http://mg.co.za/article/2014-09-26-class-theory-finally-decolonised, accessed 3 November 2014.

23 See Susan Booysen, 25 January 2015, 'The heaviness of being Julius', *The Sunday Independent*, p. 14; telephonic interview with EFF delegate to the Mangaung national people's assembly, 22 January 2015.

24 'Interview with Julius Malema by Janet Smith', in Floyd Shivambu (ed.), 2014, *The Coming Revolution*, op. cit., pp. 208–287; Julius Malema, 2 October 2014, op. cit.

25 EFF 2014 election manifesto, section 6, 'How EFF government will realise its commitments'.

26 See Khulekani Magubane, 4 March 2014, 'Malema celebrates birthday explaining policies to investors', *Business Day*, http://www.bdlive.co.za/national/politics/2014/03/04/malema-celebrates-birthday-explaining-policies-to-investors, accessed 5 March 2014.

27 Andile Mngxitama, 10 May 2015, 'How Malema sold out on land reform', *The Sunday Independent*, p. 15.

28 Controversial Kenny 'Sushi King' Kunene left/was pushed out of the EFF in August 2013. One of the reasons cited was that too many EFF supporters regarded him as *izikhotane* (people who buy expensive clothes and then burn them). See, for example, Ngwako Malatji, 25 August 2013, 'Kenny's past scuppers his leadership ambitions', *City Press*, p. 2. For a brief period he had been the EFF's head of campaigns, mobilisation and special projects.

29 Wasp was founded in March 2013, with the Democratic Socialist Movement (DSM) as a founding member. The DSM then became a Wasp affiliate. The DSM has its origins in the Trotskyist Marxist Workers Tendency (MWT); see http://workerssocialistparty.co.za/; http://www.socialistsouthafrica.co.za/, various windows, accessed 17 September 2014.

30 Wasp statement, 10 September 2013, Johannesburg, Weizmann Hamilton for the Wasp interim secretariat, http://workerssocialistparty.co.za/?p=522, accessed 13 October 2013.

31 This was a dismal result, yet there were five parties that contested at the national level and fared worse. KwaZulu-Natal and Gauteng were the two provinces with the highest number of Wasp votes; in the North West and Limpopo Wasp achieved its best provincial proportions, namely 0.07 percent in each case. Compared with the EFF's 141 000 votes in the North West, Wasp received 818. All results from www.elections.org.za, accessed 2 June 2014.

32 Sibongakonke Shoba, 11 May 2014, 'Malema quibbles but accepts poll outcome', *Sunday Times*, p. 4.

33 For example, Bongani Nkosi, 27 March 2015, 'EFF claims landslide victory over Sasco at VUT SRC', http://mg.co.za/article/2015-03-27-eff-claims-landslide-victory-over-sasco-at-vut-src?utm, accessed 28 March 2015.

34 Ipsos poll, reported in Fiona Forde, 11 May 2014, 'EFF: More than a bunch of young radicals', *The Sunday Independent*, p. 9.

35 In November 2013 Marikana lawyer Dali Mpofu left the ANC to join the EFF. Numsa's central committee, in a press statement, 2 September 2012, strongly condemned both the Lonmin mine bosses and the South African police; see http://www.politicsweb.co.za/politicsweb/view/politicsweb/en/page71654?oid=323551&sn=Detail&pid=7166, accessed 15 September 2012.

36 Julius Malema, interview with Janet Smith, in Floyd Shivambu (ed.), 2014, *The Coming Revolution*, op. cit.

37 Ibid.

38 Julius Malema, 2 October 2014, op. cit.; Julius Malema, interview with Janet Smith, in Floyd Shivambu (ed.), 2014, *The Coming Revolution*, op. cit.

39 Julius Malema, interview with Chris Barron, 25 May 2014, 'So many questions', *Sunday Times*, p. 21.

40 Andile Mngxitama, 25 July 2014, 'Parliament could kill', *City Press*, p. 3.

41 *City Press*, 21 August 2014, 'EFF's violent nature could take country backwards – ANC', http://www.citypress.co.za/politics/zizi-kodwa-effs-violent-nature-take-sa-backwards/, accessed 22 August 2014.

42 Julius Malema, quoted in George Matlala, 4 July 2014, 'We'll die for our rights, says Juju', *Sowetan*, p. 4. Also see Gareth van Onselen, 20 August 2014, 'DA misunderstands EFF's purpose', http://www.bdlive.co.za/opinion/columnists/2014/08/20/da-misunderstands-effs-purpose, accessed 22 August 2014.

43 Cited by Richard Poplak, 25 July 2014, 'Pulling no punches for a party', *The Star*, p. 9.

44 Julius Malema, interview with Janet Smith, in Floyd Shivambu (ed.), 2014, *The Coming Revolution*, op. cit.

45 Also see Fiona Forde, 2014, *Still an Inconvenient Youth*, Johannesburg: Picador Africa, pp. 161–170.

46 ANC, 25 November 2014, Media statement after the November 2014 ANC NEC meeting, Johannesburg.

47 Susan Booysen, 2013, *Twenty Years of South African Democracy: Citizen Views of Human Rights, Governance and the Political System*, research report, Johannesburg and Washington DC: Freedom House.

48 Richard Calland, 25–31 July 2014, 'Parliament gets new life in Episode 5', *Mail & Guardian*, p. 27.

49 Gareth van Onselen, 26 November 2014, 'Has the EFF sold out?' http://www.bdlive .co.za/opinion/columnists/2014/11/26/has-the-eff-sold-out, accessed 26 November 2014, also makes this point.

50 ANC, 27 November 2014, 'Sanctions against 20 EFF MPs', media statement by the office of the ANC chief whip, Parliament of South Africa.

51 Telephonic interview, former EFF official, 24 March 2015.

52 See Craig Dodds, Thabiso Thakali and Jan Cronje, 15 November 2014, *Weekend Argus*, p. 6.

53 Susan Booysen, 22 February 2015, 'Hehehe … the lessons not learnt', *The Sunday Independent*, http://www.iol.co.za/sundayindependent/hehehe-the-lessons-not-learnt-1.1821803#.VRPeqeEQvq0, accessed 26 March 2015.

54 Zizi Kodwa, 21 August 2014, statement on behalf of the ANC.

55 The FF+ had come a long way. In August 2013 it had petitioned the IEC to stop the EFF from participating in Election 2014, given the EFF leader's history of racial insults at the time. Malema had two convictions of hate speech (March 2010 and September 2011), after singing 'Dubul' iBhunu' (Shoot the Boer).

56 Msimang, former director general of the Department of Home Affairs and member of the ANC's Msimang 'line of royalty', quoted in *Mail & Guardian*, 'Zuma must pay, say ANC vets', 21–27 November 2014, p. 2. At the media briefing to the November 2014 ANC EC meeting, Secretary General Mantashe dismissed these and other comments as coming from 'private citizens expressing a view' (instead of representing voices from any of the ANC structures).

57 Quoted in Jan-Jan Joubert, 25 May 2014, 'MPs might need seat belts in new rumbustious Parliament', *Sunday Times*, p. 21; *The New Age*, 2 April 2014, 'Cosatu backs Zuma over Nkandla cash', p. 3.

58 For example, see Sibongakonke Shoba, 23 March 2014, 'Malema wants "this criminal" arrested', *Sunday Times*, p. 20.

59 Public protector, 'On the point of tenders', Report No. 10 of 2012/13, http://www. pprotect.org/library/investigation_report/2012/Final%20Report%20Signed.pdf; Public protector, '10 municipalities, 28 contracts, and a politician', http://www.ppro-tect.org/library/investigation_report/sgl%20investigation%20report.pdf, accessed 4 October 2014.

60 Zuma had the public protector report *Secure in Comfort*, March 2014, against him; see also her report on Malema, Public protector, '10 municipalities, 28 contracts, and a politician – Report on and investigation into complaints relating to the improper awarding of tenders by municipalities in the Limpopo and North West', http://www.pprotect.org/library/investigation_report/sgl%20investi gation%20report.pdf, accessed 10 July 2014; Public protector, 2013, 'On the point of tenders: Report on an investigation into allegations of impropriety and corrupt practices relating to the awarding of contracts for goods and services by the Limpopo Department of Roads and Transport', Report No. 10 of 2012/13, http:// www.pprotect.org/library/investigation_report/2012/Final%20Report%20Signed. pdf, accessed 4 October 2014.

61 The details in the rest of this section are extracted from a wide range of corroborated media reports, 2014–2015.

62 Floyd Shivambu, 30 April 2014, 'Marikana – a turning point', *The Star*, p. 15.

63 See Frank Maponya, 24 February 2010, 'Malema got tenders illegally – Moloto', *Sowetan*, p. 2.

64 See Anna Majavu, 25 March 2010, ' "I won't act on Malema" ', *Sowetan*, p. 4. The expedience for Zuma of having gone on record with this statement was that it created the opening in Zuma style to argue henceforth that he is on record for not encouraging action against Malema.

65 Blade Nzimande, 18 May 2014, in interview with Chris Barron, 'So many questions', *Sunday Times*, p. 21.

66 Interview with Janet Smith, in Floyd Shivambu (ed.), 2014, *The Coming Revolution*, op. cit.

67 *Report by the Minister of Police to Parliament on Security Upgrades at the Nkandla Private Residence of the President*, 28 May 2015, Cape Town.

68 Stephan Hofstatter, Piet Rampedi and Mzilikazi wa Africa, 26 April 2015, 'Malema: I know who gave cash to Zuma', *Sunday Times*, p. 2.

69 This might only be in April 2019. There are moves afoot in the ANC to extend Zuma's ANC term to coincide with the South African presidency. Part of the reason is that the Zuma-ists foresee 'dual centre of power' pressures for Zuma to step down in early 2018, should the ANC's December 207 conference not extend his term; interview, NEC member, 25 November 2014.

70 See, for example, EFF statement, 17 July 2015, 'EFF condemns the political violence and intolerance by ANC councillor in Rustenburg'; *The Sunday Independent*, 6 April 2014, 'ANC petrol bombs our rallies, claims EFF', p. 4; Frank Maponya, 15 May 2014, 'Mayor "attacks" EFF with bricks', *Sowetan*, p. 4.

71 See *The New Age*, 5 May 2014, 'Cronin tongue-lashes EFF', p. 5.

72 Sonti's husband was one of the 34 Lonmin mineworkers shot and killed by the SAPs in August 2012, at Wonderkop, Marikana. Peter Alexander, Thapelo Lekgowa, Botsang Mmope, Luke Sinwell and Bongani Xezwi, 2012, *Marikana: A View from the Mountain and a Case to Answer*, Auckland Park: Jacana, relate the whole massacre.

73 Several interviews with EFF politicians, November 2014, Johannesburg and Cape Town; *The Citizen*, 14 November 2014, 'Julius Malema "a liar" – disgruntled EFF member', http://citizen.co.za/275255/julius-malema-liar-disgruntled-eff-member/, accessed 14 November 2014.

74 Interview with EFF insider, granted on condition of anonymity, 20 September 2014, Cape Town.

75 Elvis Masoga, quoted in George Matlala, 4 July 2014, 'We'll die for our rights, says Juju', *Sowetan*, p. 4.

76 Julius Sello Malema, 20 January 2015, @Julius_S_Malema, 9:58 am.

77 Sabelo Ndlangisa, 4 May 2014, 'Malema: EFF is not a one-man show', *City Press*, p. 11.

78 EFF, 20 January 2015, statement by email.

79 Numsa explained: 'The United Front is a mobilising tool to organise the working class around working class issues and to build working class confidence, and working class consciousness for working class power. The United Front is not a political party but it is about demanding the implementation of the Freedom Charter'; see Karl Cloete, 20 May 2014, 'Social Movement or United Front?' posted in *NUMSA News*, http://www.numsa.org.za/article/social-movement-united-front/,

accessed 2 June 2014; United Front, 29 April 2015, 'Numsa to form workers' party', http://www.unitedfrontsa.wordpress.com/2015/04/29/numsa-to-form-workers-party/, accessed 1 June 2015.

80 Jacob Zuma, 22 March 2015, eulogy by President Jacob Zuma at the reburial of the remains of ANC struggle stalwart Mr John Beaver Marks, Ventersdorp, http://www.thepresidency.gov.za/pebble.asp?relid=19315, accessed 27 March 2015.

81 Progressive Block of Cosatu Unions, 14 July 2015, 'One battle lost, but war continues', statement.

82 See, for example, Carien du Plessis, 23 November 2010, 'Cosatu says it will back ANC in local elections', *The Star*, p. 6; George Matlala, Moffet Mofokeng and Bianca Capazorio, 11 March 2012, 'Vavi blasts Zuma', *The Sunday Independent*, p. 1.

83 To borrow a phrase from Edward S Herman and Noam Chomsky, 1988, *Manufacturing Consent: The Political Economy of the Mass Media*, New York: Pantheon Books.

84 See David Moore, 2014, 'Coercion, consent, and the construction of capitalism in Africa: Development studies, political economy, politics and the "dark continent"', *Transformation*, 84, pp. 106–131.

85 Achille Mbembe, 1–7 August 2014, 'Juju prances into the gaps left by ANC', *Mail & Guardian*, p. 20.

86 Andries Bezuidenhout, cited in Verashni Pillay, 14 November 2014, 'Numsa set to hurt ANC in 2016 polls', *Mail & Guardian*, http://mg.co.za/article/2014-11-13-numsa-set-to-hurt-anc-in-2016-polls, accessed 15 November 2014.

87 Bongani Hans, 10 March 2014, 'EFF, PAC propose post-election merger', *The Star*, p. 4.

88 Parties gain representation in, for example, Parliament if they do not have the required 0.25 percent national support to gain one seat, but fractions of other parties' votes (not enough to secure them additional seats) get added to the totals of the two or three parties just falling short of gaining seats.

89 The DLF is an anti-capitalist activist front, formed at the Conference for a Democratic Left held in Johannesburg in 2011. It has not participated in any election. This was in contrast to a series of powerful public statements that attempted to mobilise masses on this DLF platform, which would also act in unison with labour. See, for example, Statement of the DLF steering committee, 13 February 2012, 'Endorsement of Cosatu general strike: Time for poor and working people to speak out and be heard!' Also see Mazibuko Jara, 23 January 2011, 'New left seeks revamped SA', *Sunday Times*, p. 5.

90 Richard Pithouse, 9 May 2014, 'On Abahlali baseMjondolo voting for the DA in Durban', *South African Civil Society Information Service*, http://sacsis.org.za/site/article/1999, accessed 1 June 2014

91 Mmetlwe Sebei (Wasp leader), statement 11 October 2013. Also see Wasp statement, 10 September 2013, Johannesburg.

92 Blade Nzimande, 18 May 2014, op. cit., pp. 20, 21.

93 See Castro Ngobese, Numsa, 2014, 'Numsa to host International Symposium of Left Parties/Movements: 7–10 August 2014', http://www.numsa.org.za/article/numsa-host-international-symposium-left-partiesmovements-7-10-august-2014/, accessed 6 August 2014.

94 Devan Pillay, 28 February–6 March 2014, 'Is SA's left on the right road to social-
    ism?' *Mail & Guardian*, p. 25.
95 Vishwas Satgar, 22–28 August 2012, 'The "Numsa moment" leads left renewal',
    Mail & Guardian, p. 25.
96 In his Ruth First Memorial Lecture in August 2014 Numsa's Irvin Jim blamed the
    failure of the broad liberation movement to uphold the values of the Freedom
    Charter for exploitation by white monopoly capital; see *The Sunday Independent*,
    'SA off-track, ANC expired, says Numsa', 17 August 2014, p. 4.
97 See, for example, Lebogang Seale, 17 August 2014, 'Malema hits nerve on Marikana',
    The Sunday Independent, p. 7.
98 Zwelinzima Vavi, 17 August 2010, Ruth First Memorial Lecture, University of the
    Witwatersrand, http://www.cosatu.org.za/show.php?ID=3763, accessed 27 August
    2010, was a notable example of incisive critiques of the ANC being consolidated
    into an organisational base.
99 See *The Sunday Independent*, 18 March 2012, 'Simmering tensions in alliance start
    to heat up', p. 5; Moipone Malefane, 25 November 2011, 'Now Vavi dares the ANC',
    Sowetan, p. 4.
100 See Ebrahim Harvey, interview with Zwelinzima Vavi, 18 May 2014, 'Speaking
    truth to power', *City Press*, p. 11.
101 See Matuma Letsaolo, 11–16 April 2014, 'Political truce traps Vavi', *Mail &
    Guardian*, p. 2.
102 Jessie Duarte, 5 May 2014, comment on ANC intervention to retain Cosatu unity,
    Johannesburg.
103 See Sapa, 7 April 2014, 'War is not done for Vavi and allies despite court ruling',
    The Star, p. 4; Natashia Marrian, 16–21 August 2013, 'Injury time', *Financial Mail*,
    pp. 32–39.
104 See Matuma Letsaolo and Andisiwe Makinana, 26 September–2 October 2014,
    'ANC pulls out all the stops but can't heal Cosatu divide', *Mail & Guardian*, p. 8.
105 See Natashia Marrian, 31 July 2014, 'New union in ANC fold to target Numsa',
    Business Day, p. 1.
106 Stephen Grootes, 14 October 2014, 'Cosatu: Approaching Armageddon', *Daily
    Maverick*, http://www.dailymaverick.co.za/article/2014-10-14-coming-soon-cosatus-
    armageddon-button/#.VDzgOBZ6joQ, accessed 14 October 2014.
107 Andries Bezuidenhout, cited in Verashni Pillay, 14 November 2014, op. cit.
108 See Susan Booysen, 15 September 2013, 'Will a labour party split the SA vote?'
    The Sunday Independent, p. 16.

8

ANC IN THE CAULDRON OF PROTEST

ANC hegemony and dominance are constantly contested. At the beginning of its third decade in power, the range of opposition, and the hold that resistance cumulatively exercises over the ANC, make the monolith look troubled. A series of left, right and combined left-right opposition party 'sieges' in Parliament, a range of trade unions refusing to kowtow when the ANC commands, and resistance from civil society in organised and community formations signal how the intensity and diversity of opposition to the ANC have changed. This is happening gradually and in multiple ways and sites, the opposition coming from actors who diverge in political orientation, class background and organisational platform.

For a long time the ANC had prided itself on having direct bonds with the people of South Africa, and on being attentive to their voices. This connection continues but is strained by a multitude of community protests – the political-electoral bond has often remained, but under the pressure of public expression of dissatisfaction and civil disobedience, both peaceful and violent. The exchanges that emanate from community protests are often acrimonious. For example, the police are dispatched to restore order, and then retaliate. Elected representatives and state bureaucrats will be generally unavailable to give hearings to the protesters, who turn to arson and looting to escalate their voices. Councillors' houses, foreigners' shops and government buildings (municipal sites such as libraries, local police stations and home affairs offices) are common targets.

The context of protest is that incomes and standards of living in general have risen substantially in the democratic era. The black middle classes have grown, and occupy far bigger chunks of the upper living standards measure groupings. Many in the lower socioeconomic classes benefit from social grants, a social wage and temporary low-level public employment. At the same time, inequality has grown further and unemployment figures by mid-2015 were the highest in eleven years. Young people are the most likely victims of unemployment. Urbanisation rises and vast urban settlements are home to citizens who know no life but one of desperation and squalor. Community and service delivery protests are soft options next to protests of looting and destruction. Afro-foreigners who share spaces of work and residence with the poorest of South Africa are easy targets. For many of the protesters it is standard to register protest against services, living conditions and substandard political representation, and then in the next election to again endorse the governing party, overwhelmingly the ANC. My own research has indicated this relationship, with some weakening, over time.[1]

However, there are three types of exceptions to this rule: there are whole communities (even if small in number) that have swung against the ANC; election turnout has been declining and many potential voters are not interested in registering; and where protest communities continue to endorse the ANC in elections the margins by which the ANC wins are shrinking. At the same time, opposition to the ANC is widening. Civil society has become more assertive (the resistance against e-tolling is an example of a massive civil disobedience campaign). A range of civil society organisations are also ensuring that contentious issues in ANC government policy and law-making processes get challenged. The courts, in particular the high courts and Constitutional Court, have been drawn into these political processes regularly. They have come to represent a distinct – but integral and hands-on – part of government. Accountability without the engagement of the courts has become almost unimaginable.

This chapter explores two opposition modes other than formal organisations such as left parties and trade unions: community protest and 'new opposition', the latter in the form of policy-specific civil society action to oppose government policy. The new opposition alliances include civil movements and interest groups with various (or no) party political affiliations, and opposition parties. They align themselves with state institutions – such as the different divisions of the court system, and the office of the public protector – to oppose, delay and perhaps eventually obviate contested policy decisions and legislation. The chapter demonstrates how this opposition has strengthened its assault on the ANC in the time of Zuma, while community protest still coexisted largely with pro-ANC voting. It shows how protest and new opposition defied the ANC on specific policies but did not at once subvert its hegemony.

CHANGING PROTEST CULTURE

Community protest has escalated over time, on a jagged but upward curve (Table 8.1). Community protests concern getting services, or better services, or are ways to remind government and its absentee representatives that there are citizens out there who have fallen behind and suffer gross inequality, fear they may be left behind forever, are angry about their situations, and expect government to do as much for the people as it is doing for itself. New opposition expresses dissatisfaction to the point of civil disobedience, disregarding laws and snubbing government efforts to strike half-hearted compromises. New opposition resonates with a certain measure of lawlessness (both harmless and harmful) in society. Civil society has adopted a protest culture that coexists with party political and legislative opposition. Combined, these forms of protest deliver an unsurpassed wall of challenge to ANC rule.

The combination of community protest, new opposition and party political opposition tells a story of opposition amid hegemony. It is the tale of South Africans infuriated by their government but not ready to discard it or vote it out (although in Gauteng they came close in 2014). New opposition sees multiplicities of parties, interests and social movements, trade union organisations and civil society generally using public protest actions (highway blockades, marches, looting, arson, media campaigns), often along with the courts and public protector investigations, to mount challenges to specific public policies and register discontent with how the ANC government operates.

The resistance can defeat or delay government actions that lack popular legitimacy. Together these two forms of protest – one more working class or underclass, the other more middle class (but neither of them class exclusive) – aim to make the ANC state more responsive to public need and more accountable to its citizens. They could equally feed mounting resentment against, even rejection of, the ANC. A selection of protest communities has delivered such evidence.

263

Table 8.1: Rising incidence of protest action in South Africa – counts from monitors

Monitoring agency	2004	2005	2006	2007	2008	2009	2010	2011	2012	2013	2014	2015 (May)
Municipal IQ	10	34	2	32	27	107	111	82	173	155	176	–
Social Change	13	106	50	169	164	314	252	206	471	287	–	–
CLC-UWC*	–	–	–	95	120	204	130	145	150	140	218	–
SABC-Dhawraj	11	87	41	69	40	85	112	100	215	125	317	68

Source: Municipal IQ Hotspots Monitor; Social Change Research Unit; Community Law Centre, University of the Western Cape; Ronesh Dhawraj, SABC research department.

Note: * Some of these figures are approximate, deduced from bar charts.

These forms of protest gain potency in the context of an ANC hegemony that is generally post-peak. The ANC's electoral performances have been weakening; the Tripartite Alliance is disintegrating, nowadays ineffective as internal form of opposition; the ANCYL is no longer the finishing school for the next generation of respected ANC leaders. Local government is too often the dumping ground for poorly qualified cadres – or the starting point for hopeful cadres to climb the political ladder. The ANC could only hope that it would be buffered continuously by non-electoral, alternative forms of opposition rather than those challenging its hold on the state. It could only wish that the gaps in the firewall between civil society opposition and formal party political opposition politics would not close before the ANC could persuade the electorate that there is a new ANC that is sufficiently like its struggle edition.

The ANC government, however, retains agency and has been working to counter protests at its origin of community grievances. Its reaction has included (as synthesised in the discussion documents for the ANC's October 2015 National General Council meeting) Rapid Response Teams that comprise intra-state specialists. They target hot-spot municipalities and claim to have stabilised most. The same document nevertheless recognises the escalation of service delivery protests in the recent past. Leadership development programmes are also administered to political office bearers and councillors.

INTERROGATING THE DUAL REPERTOIRE OF PROTEST AND VOTING

There are gradual, piecemeal and community-specific moves away from ANC hegemony – but the emphasis is on *gradual* change that is also subject to corrective interventions by the ANC in government. The dual repertoire of protest and voting – protesting against the ANC but voting for it subsequently – continues, under strain, during Zuma's regime. Subtle changes, however, are unfolding. It is clear that there is no guarantee that the people in the longer term will continue to tolerate substandard government performance, combined with absentee representation, evidence of public sector corruption and extreme elite advancement.

Interpretations of community protest range across the spectrum of not affecting ANC support to rebellion.[2] The in-house SACP interpretation of protest is struggle for emancipatory economic transformation. At the other end of the spectrum, protest is cast as generalised rebellion, revealing signals of insurrection. There are explanations of protest as the result of the success of ANC government delivery. President Zuma offered this view, explaining that communities protest when they see that others have received more services than theirs.

While protest and ANC-supportive voting coexist generally, there is some punishment at the ballot box meted out to the ANC in other cases. The essence is that community protest largely persists as a measure of gaining government's attention, along with better representation and realisation of policies at community level. It is only infrequently that protest entails rebellion or a budding insurrection.[3] In a small way each of the protests *is* a community revolt. Yet, the protests are not at the point of becoming a generalised rejection of either the governing party or the democratic system. Instead, they are aimed largely at improving the system and bartering with the authorities for better services, conditions of life and employment. Hence, there are few severe or immediate implications for the ANC's hold on power. Protest nevertheless commonly brings evidence of the gradual erosion of ANC power, such as the outbreak of xenophobic protests: the more visible xenophobic expressions of 2008 and 2015 highlighted the extent of gross inequality and failures of government policy. These protests stressed a level of lawlessness and the existence of spaces over which the ANC state has little control.

Pre-2005 research generally surmised that community protest signals tangible dissent from the ANC and incontrovertible declines in the ANC's popular standing. Participation in protest was thus seen as a signal of problems for the governing ANC. My research[4] then indicated the dual repertoire or the fact that protest combines with pro-ANC voting. Citizens alternated ballots and bricks: one did not negate the other and communities did not feel they had to choose between the two. This was confirmed in the 2006 local government elections and, overwhelmingly, again at community level in the 2011 local elections. The ANC tended not to lose ward elections, even if there had been vehement protest in the particular community and ANC margins had started shrinking. A similar picture unfolded in 2014 – the ANC was winning even if the margins were shrinking.

The pursuit of the political meaning of community protest – more than, but often only called, 'service delivery protest' – continues. My tracking research up to May 2015 shows that most community protesters wish to improve the ANC's representation of their interests; they want more voice, service and opportunities. They revolt against the system locally. They object to, for example, the deficiencies in social services, community infrastructure and personal living conditions. The Civic Protests Barometer[5] shows that in

2007–2014, 45 per cent of protests were ascribed to grievances with municipal services, 11 per cent with services by government agencies other than municipalities, and 7 per cent due to problems with municipal governance. Around 62 per cent of protests could indeed be categorised as 'service delivery' protest. Protesters' first line of engagement is therefore to get the system to perform better for them. Protest action is a bargaining chip, an effort to be heard. Anger about conditions on the ground is commonly not transferred into electoral verdicts – at least not immediately and directly.[6]

The dual repertoire displayed how two parallel layers of democracy operate and intersect around the ANC. The essential repertoire: first vote ANC, then in between election periods protest against the ANC in government to get more attention and better action. My 2013 study of community voices on democracy and protest[7] – eight years after the original ballot-and-brick fieldwork – further confirms citizens' use of protest action as an integral part of getting representation and holding their representatives to account. These political actions still focus on getting the system to work better, rather than being a revolutionary rejection. Von Holdt further illustrates this world of protest and its use of violence, referring to violence becoming a form of agency: '[P]eople talk about violence, how it empowers them, how it gives them a sense of being able to engage the authorities.'[8] He adds that police presence often provokes community violence and more police violence itself: 'there is a pattern of police violence, the shooting of teargas and rubber bullets which then leads to running street battles…'

There is, however, also a parallel system that reveals other citizens' rejecting parts of the political system. This repertoire grows in conditions of unemployment, lack of opportunities, and ineffectual formal government. Von Holdt alludes to such a parallel system of governance.[9] There are different rules by which community politics operates, which the communities nevertheless argue are within the parameters of both the Constitution and the law. Breakdowns in the ethics and effectiveness of police and courts mean that another set of rules comes into play. Such a parallel world came to the fore in the 2008 wave of xenophobic community violence. Subaltern forces (warmongers and criminals) hijack or simply use community protest to foment their own alternative power through looting, especially of shops that belong to foreigners from Africa and southern Asia. These alternative and often criminal networks that interlink with community protest still require further research.

Abuse of the public sector supply chain management – operating via tenders and provision of inferior or price-inflated delivery – opens the gates for a further dimension of the subaltern world of deficient service delivery. In 2015 supply chain management in the public sector was set to be reformed.[10] It remained uncertain, however, to what extent and after how long the required corrections would emerge. Here is yet another type of parallel operation, in terms of governance and 'accountability' that is lodged deep within (for example) the municipal bureaucracies. Poorly qualified appointees pay their dues to the lords of the bureaucracy who gave them their jobs; as long as they pay over their dues they stay in their jobs. Performance and service to communities have nothing to do with their incumbency:

> (C)ommunities complain that there are incompetent people in charge of basic services. Why have these people been appointed if they can't do the job? And why are they so hard to shift? Two possible answers: perhaps they got the job through paying bribes. Once in the job, they will continue to pay off their patrons by funnelling government money into private accounts. Alternatively, they got the job through their political loyalty. But the result is the same: once in the job, they will pay off their political masters with government money. This has one hugely unfortunate effect: they are inviolable in their position no matter how many mistakes they make or how much money they waste, because the people they are paying off have a vested interest in keeping them there. So ... government money is being stolen AND services are being mismanaged.[11]

Updated analyses show how the dual repertoire is developing and how deviations are shaping up, even if gradually and modestly:

- A few specific communities *do* use the electoral sanction to punish the ANC for its lack of responsive and efficient representation. The question is whether systematic change is underfoot. One form in which such change has been manifested is through a protest vote for the EFF or the DA. Such instances were recorded in Election 2014 – some voting districts fell to the EFF. In other instances the EFF and the DA did not capture the voting district but substantial support was recorded.
- Protest and spectacle work well to draw attention to grievances and optimise the chance to receive better service delivery. The question, however, was whether the EFF's inherent protest-revolt character could help end the divide between citizens being angry with the ANC but not voting

against it. Could the EFF or a workers' party gain traction to bring more revolt into party politics? At least one analysis considers this possible: '[The] people in the community are aware of being used for other people's interests … but they are hoping it'll help them and open an avenue. For a lot of the communities we speak to it seems strategic: get a member of the EFF or Malema, if you can get him there, [because] the media will hopefully follow.' [12]

Gradual inroads into the ANC base

The impact of poor service delivery and deficient local governance on election results can be assessed by comparing election results in voting districts and wards in those communities that had experienced protests.[13] This is an assessment at the community level rather than individual action. One of the problems is that protesters do not always take action in their own voting districts. There is also limited evidence as to whether the protesters themselves vote or abstain. Nevertheless, such measurement reflects how citizens from particular communities experiencing certain living conditions and governance problems also keep governing parties in power.

When one looks at entire communities, election results show that opposition parties experienced limited breakthroughs. At the smaller voting district level there was more movement in opposition parties reducing ANC margins. Comparing the 2009 and 2014 election results in protest and non-protest areas it was clear that the ANC margins shrank more in the protest communities. The case of the EFF in Election 2014 illustrates these trends. The EFF parachuted campaigns into protest communities and ANC margins declined. The EFF was nevertheless the clear winner in three wards – in Rustenburg, in the Marikana area and in mining areas of the platinum belt.

The demographics of metropolitan voting trends further illustrate the complexities of the dual repertoire. There was evidence of high levels of voter alienation in South Africa's metropolitan areas, where 45 per cent of the population lives. Chapter 5 explored the ANC's declining election results in the metropolitan areas that do not incorporate substantial rural tracts. Those metropolitan areas in which the ANC in Election 2014 still fared relatively well – Mangaung, eThekwini and Buffalo City – all include traditional governance areas within their metro boundaries.[14] South Africa is increasingly urbanising, and recent internal-migrant arrivals are likely to be unemployed or underemployed, often without access to formal housing and regular services, whereas they frequently observe evidence of much higher standards of living around them. Urban and metro areas are the most likely sites for protest, given the strain on services and accumulation of un- and underemployed – and election results have already shown a drop in pro-ANC voting in these areas.

Community protest and comparative deprivation

Analyses of protest across communities and provinces show that there was hardly a question of 'no delivery' – rather, it was insufficient, compromised or mismanaged delivery. In the time of Zuma, the exercise of community protest to demand attention (or more immediate and visible action) increased. Government's 'good story' was recognised, but it also reminded citizens of how poorly their own communities measured up. At community level there had been improvements, yet there were frequent problems of consistency of supply and poor maintenance. It is often second-generation issues (including the quality and cost of the water, electricity or roads provided, or the functionality of sanitation) that differentiate otherwise similar communities and make them compare, and demand more.

Government itself used relativist language in trying to explain rising protest while the ANC in government was telling its 'good story' of transformation and democracy since 1994. In his June 2014 State of the Nation speech Zuma argued that community protest is a result of the success of ANC delivery:

> ... the protests are not simply the result of 'failures' of government but also of the success in delivering basic services ... [when 95 per cent of households have access to water, the 5 per cent who still need to be provided for felt they could not wait a moment longer]. Success is also the breeding ground of rising expectations.

Overall, it is still only a relatively small number of communities that engage in protest action – despite the rising incidence, as outlined in Table 8.1.[15] While protesting citizens are known frequently to come from communities in which poverty prevails, this should not become a generalisation. To illustrate poverty incidence, an estimated 1.6 million South African households live in informal structures;[16] just over 20 per cent of the population live in extreme poverty according to Statistics SA; seven million of the poor are in the 16–59 age band (roughly in the age group that may be available for protest action). No accurate data are available on how many South Africans have participated in community protest action, but it is only a fraction of the poor.[17]

There is a range of filter and trigger conditions, environments and expediters (Table 8.2) that will determine – variably from one potential protest locality to the next – whether widely shared delivery-deficit community situations actually trigger protests. Whether a protest happens in a particular community is determined by a complex chain of personal demographics/social-community demographics, the extent and duration of the problem, comparative experiences within municipal localities, experiences with elected representatives and officialdom, and superimposition of party political engagements combined with elite actions to get into positions of political or economic power – and expectations of reactions to the protest action. These expectations may be linked to experiences with previous protests, observation of official reactions to comparable protests, or exasperation with having exhausted the alternatives to protest. However, politicisation and political opportunity to hold government to account escalates the likelihood of community protest action while sustained problems further increase the possibility for eruptions.

Conditions vary – from communities living in immediate squalor to communities being relatively well off but not wanting to lose out on the infrastructure development that came the way of neighbouring communities. Some communities that protest, despite having received basic services, do so because of politicians' promises or constitutional guarantees that have set their expectations. In addition, rapid urbanisation adds to the numbers still without the delivery of even basic services. Many citizens are too poor to pay, even if better off than 'indigent', which would qualify them for payment exemptions (for basic amounts). Others refuse to pay because they need the money to pay for subscription television or lifestyle items.

Protests are frequently in informal settlement areas, which logically have fewer services than established residential areas. Populations are in flux, with fewer connections to the formal structures of local government, and there are fewer reasons for the local government staff to engage with them. The inhabitants, and protesters, are often relatively young, unemployed and poor, frequently existing on the margins of government and the representative system. They are often removed from the power and patronage networks that local elites mobilise to service selected and probably loyal communities.[18]

Poor quality of representation (compared with what citizens believe they are entitled to) equals and sometimes exceeds non-delivery. The first of two big

271

Table 8.2: Trajectories for the explanation of community protest

Typical sequence of filters, facilitators and triggers		Likely characteristics or contributing factors	Dynamics of determining the occurrence of protest action
SETTINGS	Personal demographics	Unemployed, youth, living in poverty, have few opportunities. Shacklords are often present; political provocateurs play factions.	Young people, amidst deprivations, are also available for protest action. Citizens in new settlements are subject to new informal power structures.
	Type of settlement, migration	Largely in urban environments, densely populated areas, often metro peripheries – mostly in informal settlements with shack housing or informal extensions.	People have been migrating to areas where they expect to have better opportunities; adverse conditions prevail but better rural areas are seen as worse.
TRIGGERS	Basic and second-generation services	Provision of basic water, sewerage and sanitation; quality and sustained provision and cost of basic services, housing and roads are the new issue.	Many services are provided, although sufficient electricity is often unaffordable, and water supply and quality of water erratic.
	Municipal governance	Officials are absent, incompetent, politically deployed, fail to do work; absorbed in own patronage employment deals.	Corrupt and/or incompetent municipal (or provincial and national, employees are accountable only to political masters.

PARTY & COUNCILLOR MODERATION / ESCALATION	Party political intermediation	Competing elites play local politics in party branches, factional battles; position for local economic advantage; channel issues through grassroots structures: street or ward committees.	Citizens observe sets of political insiders striking deals and mediating benefits; they themselves are probably outsiders; alternatively, they are oblivious to this world of party networks.
	Representation in elected and bureaucratic structures; communication	Real or attempted contact with local government politicians, struggles to enhance accountability, regular communication from political powers contributes restraining power.	Protesters battle to connect with elected representatives to deliver claims, except at election campaigns; they see well-heeled councillors, smart cars, but service and housing remain poor.
INHERENT PROTEST EXPEDITERS	Experience with previous protests	Large proportion of protests is repeat or escalated protest – marches, peaceful protests proved futile.	The more protracted the protest sequence, the more likely the community is to resort to violence.
	Police handling of protest	Police stand in for local government in engaging protesters, often poorly qualified to deal with protest.	Can act provocatively and trigger violence, fail to channel protest away from secondary protest targets such as foreigners.
	Protest, media, the power of 'spectacle' and getting attention to grievances	If frustration and insufficient delivery persist, frustrated citizens are likely to take the next step, community protest, which might incorporate violence, attract media attention and leverage action on community problems.	Protest action, especially with elements of violence/ destruction, will draw media, cause embarrassment to politicians and officials, get in higher powers like MECs, premiers and Cabinet members – increasing chances to get improved services or assurances that attention is forthcoming.

Source: Interpretation and schematic organising of protest data by Booysen.
Note: Top-end government initiatives: evidence of Department of Cooperative Governance and Traditional Affairs (Cogta) actively pursuing cleaner government and better accountability might contain rampant protest action.

problems is that councillors (and MPs and MPLs) are largely absent from the lives of the communities they were elected to serve. The second is that citizens link councillors' and municipal officials' poor performances and corruption to reductions in the quality of service. Corruption and mismanagement involve the allocation of tenders and contracts to ill-qualified service providers,[19] beside the fact that ill-considered or excessively priced contracts divert funds from actual provisioning.

Empirical tracking data reveal the confluence of procedural and substantive issues when it comes to community protests (Table 8.2).[20] There are always some substantive first- or second-generation service issues at stake. When citizens experience compromised delivery of services such as housing, water, electricity and transport, mismanagement and corruption (procedural issues) are often the causes – and many community members have personal knowledge of corruption at the point of employment, mismanagement or corruption by councillors and/or municipal officials. Second, protests are aimed at the procedural aspects of getting better representation and more ethical or democratically principled government. Municipalities frequently do not respond to memorandums and petitions, and visiting the municipality to deliver personal complaints is known not to make any difference. In many instances, councillors avoid their wards and do not engage their electorates on their delivery demands.

The ANC and ANC-in-government circa 2014–2015 were still inclined to highlight the need to communicate better with their communities, to take the communities along and let it be known what progress is being made.[21] In contrast, the emphasis for the communities was on communication with *results*. Protesters resent simply being consulted and informed about movement towards delivery at some unspecified time in the future. Increasingly they want to see the substantive results of previous consultations.[22] Communities will repeat protests when promises do not bear tangible fruit. There is also a high possibility that these protests will get more violent over time[23] – about 80 per cent of 2014 protests involved violence, compared with 50 per cent in 2007.

Protest works

Communities know that protest has an effect, especially if it also involves disruptive violence – obstruction of and damage to roads and municipal infrastructure, for example, are par for the course. As far back as community protests in Port Elizabeth's Walmer Township in 2005, communities could see the effect of protest action. In that case, the then housing minister rushed to listen to the

274

grievances. Since then, the president himself, Cabinet members, premiers, provincial executives, mayors and councillors have 'honoured' angered communities with their post-protest presences. In the immediate aftermath of the ANC's 2009 election victory communities erupted in an effort to ensure that they will not be forgotten in the anticipated post-election spate of delivery promised by the Zuma-ists in their campaign. At that stage Zuma sent in ANCYL leader Malema as mediator when communities were too angry to negotiate with premiers and provincial MECs. The communities welcomed Malema. When Malema became EFF, many communities still welcomed him. Laudable in terms of responsiveness, such engagement also shows politicians safeguarding party political interests. Richard Pithouse notes that where councillors take a visible role they 'most often function as a means of top-down social control aiming to subordinate popular politics to the party'.[24] The same trend emerged when the ANC in the 2014 election campaign engaged with protest communities to minimise damages.

In 2014–2015, protesting communities were openly talking about welcoming the EFF and Malema in solidarity because controversial leaders help them to attract further attention to their grievances. Visibility and spectacle were invaluable protest assets. As Peter Alexander and Peter Pfaffe have pointed out,[25] communities recognise that they are destroying things the community needs, but they argue that they are prepared to make the sacrifice, as Mandela had sacrificed through the years he had spent in prison. President Zuma had a different understanding, choosing to place the property of councillors (destroyed in a few protests) at the centre of his argument:

> You can't say no delivery and burn the things that have been delivered, burn the library, burn the offices. If there's a protest by people empowered by the Constitution you will find that they now break houses of poor people who might have built those houses with their own money over many years. They undermine the rights of those people to own property. At times if people are striking they go on a march and really undermine the rights of other people in the process.[26]

There are signs from government that less will be done in future (free housing will be limited); that there is not much hope for improvements in community conditions (serially ineffectual local government turnaround plans); that there are limited prospects for growth in employment (multiple government

275

schemes are not reversing labour absorption rates and national economic growth rates are not picking up). Growing urbanisation further postpones delivery dates in the areas that are likely to absorb the new arrivals.

The ANC government can gain from pre-emptively addressing problems and avoiding intractable community conflicts in the run-up to the local elections of 2016. With political management it has handled such clashes and it is possible to do a repeat act for local election 2016. Success will depend on the ANC's retaining credibility and goodwill on the ground, but as it slips in its popular standings it will also find communities less willing to give it the benefit of the doubt. As the post-liberation generation starts finding a definitive political voice, and considers it more acceptable to support opposition parties, the firewall between protest and opposition party support is likely to liquefy.

'NEW OPPOSITION' AND ANC POLICY DEFEATS[27]

As the years of ANC dominance and hegemony have extended, it has become increasingly clear that even loyal ANC supporters and voters are willing to combine voting for the ANC not just with community protest action but also with opposition in the form of civil disobedience and legal or state-procedural challenges. As in the case of protest, the period of coexisting dual repertoires of protest and electoral support remains uncertain. It could endure – or the patience with and tolerance for the ANC government may suffer erosion.

'New opposition' in the form of civil society organisations and civil society in general, along with some opposition parties and state institutions, has used the courts and legal processes and civil society mobilisation to subdue, delay or defeat undesired policy initiatives from the government of Jacob Zuma. 'New opposition' is a new construct that my analysis adds to this field of scholarship. It denotes a (nowadays) regular phenomenon that incorporates, but extends well beyond, civil society protest and social movements. Achievements of this form of opposition include the public challenge and *de facto* defeat of the Gauteng automated e-toll system and the Protection of State Information Bill, which have remained in the presidential inbox without being signed into law for a prolonged time. In some respects the resistance against President Zuma not 'paying back the Nkandla money' also equates with such 'new opposition'.

New opposition showed that the ANC, although dominant in many ways, often struggles to assert its authority and get its stances on policy and governance accepted. The ANC cannot ride roughshod over popular wishes in order to impose its own will – at least not while shifting alliances of citizens, select state institutions, some opposition parties and organised civil society join forces to oppose unpopular actions. In addition, in the times of the second Zuma administration the ANC risked losing electoral constituencies (such as important metros and their economic heartland populations) that had been mobilising on the issues that form the fulcrum of new opposition.

The new opposition actions brought messages about the future of the ANC. The anti-tolling alliances showed how it was possible, albeit with sacrifice, to take on a government that had all the required financial and legal resources and was determined to throw everything at the upstarts challenging it with a campaign of massive civil disobedience. The ANC retorted that such opposition was 'introducing interesting (though still moderate) fickleness' into South African politics.[28] Variants on this form of opposition were associated typically with opposition parties, but the actions did not depend on these parties. The DA, for example, had engaged in a long-haul legal process to gain access to the so-called spy tapes that had cleared Zuma to become president in 2009. The courts, legal process and the Constitution played substantial roles in strengthening these appeals. The activists were largely, but by far not only, middle class. The benefits of their actions spanned class interests.

Two of the best illustrations of the time of new opposition were the Protection of State Information Bill and e-tolling in Gauteng. Enactment suffered multiple delays. E-tolling was legislated and implemented, but civil disobedience and ANC election setbacks triggered reconsiderations on ANC provincial initiative, followed by sugar-coating and renewed efforts to force it in, plus expansion into the Western Cape.

Protection of State Information Bill

The Protection of State Information Bill – also dubbed the Secrecy Bill or the Media Bill[29] – was intended to replace the *ancien régime*'s Protection of Information Act of 1982. Objections to the Bill stemmed from provisions that undermine the right of access to information, as well as the rights of whistle-blowers and the media.

Section 32 of the Constitution of South Africa provides that every citizen has the right of access to any information held by the state. The Promotion of Access to Information Act 2 of 2000 (provided for in the Constitution) specifies the procedures for access to information and gives the reasons a request for information may be refused. The Promotion of Access to Information Act strikes a 'balance between the right to governmental transparency and the need to protect important countervailing interests', such as national security, defence, economic interests and the criminal justice system.[30] The Protection of State Information Bill was intended to supplement and moderate the Promotion of Access to Information Act. It came in the context of heightened ANC government sensitivity to media exposés in a time when not all was going according to plan for the ANC.

The Bill's legislative trajectory shows that the original 2008 version (the 'Kasrils Bill' in the time of Ronnie Kasrils as minister of intelligence) had provided for declassification of apartheid-era records and for records reaching the age of twenty years. It was a compromise document and was allowed to lapse with the onset of elections and the adverse political climate of Zuma's 2009 rise into state power.[31] On 22 November 2011, the National Assembly first passed the new Bill, amid concerns. Two months later, and amid much evidence of public resistance, the National Council of Provinces *ad hoc* committee hearings commenced and went around the country. The process delivered a flawed, partisan consultation process. The IFP, among others, called for the suspension of the hearings due to the events being used to mobilise ANC supporters and suppress opposition voices.[32] In an unprecedented development in 2012, state security officials appeared before the National Council of Provinces *ad hoc* committee and rejected all changes proposed by MPs, including ANC MPs.

The Department of State Security had been allowed repeatedly to make inputs into the parliamentary process. Much of this was to ensure that the Protection of State Information Bill would supersede the Promotion of Access to Information Act.[33] A few months later the National Council of Provinces passed amendments, and in April 2013 the National Assembly approved the Bill. Six months later, President Zuma invoked his powers under section 79 of the Constitution, referring the Bill back to the National Assembly. Zuma cited two sections of the Bill, namely a cross-reference in section 42 and a punctuation error in section 45, which rendered meaningless a safeguard on state powers to classify information. In October 2013 the National Assembly adopted the revised Protection of State Information Bill and again sent it to the president for his assent (the revisions included typographical corrections). In general, the Bill provides for the regulation of state information and introduces punitive measures for those who publish classified state information. Opposition parties argued that the Bill remained open to a Constitutional Court challenge. By late 2015 the Bill was still in the presidential inbox. There were ongoing calls for its withdrawal and new action to ensure that the 1982 legislation gets updated, without the Bill's errors. Some wondered whether the 2015 scandal around the leaked spy cables – the *Guardian* and Al-Jazeera had obtained hundreds of dossiers, files and cables from the world's top spy agencies to and from South Africa – would trigger a sign-off on the Protection of State Information Bill.[34] In addition, the government's embarrassments about the blocking of the mobile signal around Parliament and its resentment of assertive media houses in 2015 were also interpreted as likely reasons the ANC wanted to proceed with enactment. The state security minister confirmed that he was at an advanced stage of drafting regulations for the implementation of the Bill.[35]

The ongoing critiques of the Bill concern the stark penalties for leaking documents, with a maximum jail term of twenty-five years. The need for a 'public interest defence' also dominated the debate – such a defence would exempt individuals from prosecution should they be in possession of classified documents that reveal state ineptitude or corruption. In contrast, promoters of the Bill argue that the revised Bill criminalises the classification of documents that reveal corruption, malfeasance or wrongdoing by the state. Those actions carry a maximum sentence of fifteen years. The proponents argue that the need for a public interest defence is eclipsed since such information will no longer get classified. The revised Bill also failed to mention the role of the Media Appeals Tribunal in possible disputes.

Significant remaining problems centred on the extension and protection of state power against citizens and agencies that might reveal abuses of power:[36]

- An open-ended definition of national security, which forms the basis of all classification, opened the possibility for an inconsistent approach to what will be classified, and to the associated abuse of the law.
- Allowing for the classification of undefined 'economic and technological secrets', raising questions about state employees' proper and consistent application of the law.[37]
- Criminalising the simple possession and disclosure of classified information by members of the public. In mid-2014 the minister of justice and correctional services published amendments to the Protected Disclosures Act that included penalties for whistle-blowers disclosing false information.

279

- Lacking a public domain defence, in terms of which a citizen could claim that possession of information already in the public domain does not constitute an offence.
- Granting the minister power to extend to organs of state beyond the security cluster the authority to classify documents, largely without oversight and to a potentially limitless number of bodies.
- Keeping the classification decisions secret, posing the threat of over-classification, and maintaining the secret status of all documents classified under apartheid, with no timeline for declassification.
- The narrow 'public interest defence' in the Bill protecting disclosures in the public interest where such disclosures reveal outright criminal conduct. Disclosing shady tendering practices, improper appointments and flawed policy decisions, manifestly in the public interest, would not qualify for such protection.
- The Bill's espionage offences, which criminalise 'receiving state information unlawfully', could be used to punish researchers, activists, whistle-blowers and journalists who disclose classified information in the public interest.

A formidable anti-Protection of State Information Bill alliance coalesced over time, changing in focus and composition as the campaign unfolded. It comprised civil society advocacy organisations, local and international; the Right2Know campaign (a coalition of close to 400 civil society organisations and community groups); Cosatu, specifically the South African Democratic Teachers' Union (Sadtu) within Cosatu; Corruption Watch; the Media Institute of Southern Africa; the South Africa National Editors' Forum (Sanef); the Nelson Mandela Foundation; the Committee for the Protection of Journalists; Human Rights Watch; the Human Rights Commission; the Helen Suzman Foundation; the public protector; veteran struggle lawyer George Bizos; and others. Several opposition parties were involved. The National Council of Provinces 2012 *ad hoc* committee received approximately 260 submissions, forty-one of which were from organisations or concerned citizen groups.

Major anti-Protection of State Information Bill protest actions and developments included a September 2011 march on Parliament prompting the ANC to remove the Bill from the parliamentary programme for further public consultation. (In 2012 the Alternative Information Development Centre was removed from the National Council of Provinces *ad hoc* committee for linking

the legislation to intra-ANC developments.)[38] The ANC sent a top-level delegation to the Press Freedom Commission, arguing for the reining in of the press
through the Protection of State Information Bill and for setting up a media tribunal that would have the power to deregister or jail errant journalists. In the words
of Joe Latakgomo: 'It is the stick with which the government wants to beat the
media into submission, and having done so allow the pillaging of our resources
to flourish even as voters go hungry, are homeless, jobless...'[39] In March 2012,
opposition parties in Parliament threatened to lodge a Constitutional Court
challenge if the ANC failed to amend the Bill. Eleven opposition parties joined
forces for a joint protest rally in Khayelitsha, Cape Town; in their ranks were the
DA, Cope and the African Christian Democratic Party (ACDP). In March–April
2012, ANC MPs Ben Turok and Gloria Borman refused to vote in favour of the
Bill.[40] They were taken to an ANC disciplinary hearing but were saved when
Pallo Jordan intervened (the ANC parliamentary caucus had laid the complaint).

The heady days of counter-ANC mobilisation revealed that the ANC was
on the defensive, also suffering what the SACP's Blade Nzimande referred to
on various occasions as 'anti-majoritarian liberalism'. Parts of the Tripartite
Alliance felt that civil society, NGOs and opposition parties were combining
forces to defeat the ANC in ways that were not possible via the ballot box. It was
therefore time for the ANC to strike back. The opportunity for action on the
media and other disseminators of sensitive information came in the wake of the
racial hurt in 2012 that Brett Murray's painted depiction of Zuma as a Lenin-
like figure with exposed genitals had elicited, when the issues were resolved on
the streets, largely of Johannesburg, using marches on the Goodman Gallery
and *City Press* newspaper. The ANC's Mantashe[41] told followers: 'This is ... a
battle about domination and subjugation.' Sipho Hlongwane raised the point of
how one man's exposure had been reinterpreted to equate with the liberation of
a nation: '... something profound had just taken place ... something shifted ...
for now the ANC will retreat victorious. Why it decided to fight one man's battle
in the first place is a question it will have to answer at some point in the future.'[42]

By then it was much more than the battle for dignity versus the freedom to
express artistry. The history of past gross injustices presented the *cordon sani-
taire* for ongoing presidential protection, especially with the Mangaung conference looming at that time. The times were not right for the ANC to proceed with
the Protection of State Information Bill. For a while, political parties and the
media would also go slowly on publicising more presidential and other leader
scandals. The events of the ANC Mangaung elections, the ANC centenary, the

election campaign, the passing of Mandela and the Nkandla reports ensured that the ANC did not want to take risks with the Bill. However, as the assaults on the president and his Nkandla travails again escalated in 2015, government appeared willing to take risks and proceed.

Importantly, the Bill had been sowing internal divisions in the ANC. NEC members were reported to have been angered by being asked to endorse it without having discussed it. Their main concern was ANC factional manipulation of the Bill and factions spying on one another.[43] In 2015, President Zuma appeared to gain a round of forcefulness when he stepped into veering off-text in speeches, reprimanding and mocking the opposition, trying to turn tables on his critics. Narratives of 'enemies that are out to get us' and 'vigilance is required to protect the victories over apartheid and colonialism' helped create a bulwark that might prompt clampdowns. The NGC's October 2015 discussion documents, for example, held ample evidence of an ANC that feels besieged by hostile media.

Gauteng e-tolling

Gauteng e-tolling would divide the ANC and its support base even more deeply than the Protection of State Information Bill had managed. The trajectory that veered between legislation, implementation, reviews, amendments to the system and protest shows a complex interplay of civil society and government and was a major illustration of new opposition in the period of South Africa's third decade of democracy.[44] The campaign amounted to what was arguably the largest boycott – a few million citizens – that democratic South Africa had experienced. Many of these citizens (ANC supporters in this instance) also broke the 'electoral rule' of remaining loyal to the ANC in elections despite misgivings. E-tolls contributed to the ANC's electoral decline in Gauteng in 2014, as the ANC acknowledges in its NGC documentation.

The forty-nine gantries set up in terms of the Gauteng Freeway Improvement Project involved tolling on 185 kilometres of freeway along the N1, N3, N12 and R21 around Johannesburg and Pretoria, and became a game-changer in politics and policy. The firm Electronic Toll Collection collected e-toll fees on behalf of the South African National Roads Agency (Sanral), but by mid-2014 it was estimated that only about one-third of freeway users paid their e-tolls, and by 2015 reports revealed that the figures were dropping.[45] Some had never registered; others were de-tagging because of repeated billing errors. It had been expected that about 80 per cent of users would have been compliant at that time whereas Sanral estimated that it was only generating about a third of its projected income. E-tolling touched the pockets of all Gauteng and many other residents and affected business – and there were fears of extension into the Western and Eastern Cape provinces.

The citizens would not have been empowered to mount this resistance had it not been for the Opposition to Urban Tolling Alliance (Outa) and the network of anti-tolling interests that formed. Significant supporters of the project included the Justice Project South Africa with Howard Dembovsky leading, and Cosatu, which helped forge high-profile protests against the system. Essential spokes in the wheel were equally, and in different capacities, the courts, as well as the DA, which, for example, provided funding of R1m for Outa to continue legal challenges at a crucial stage of the campaign. The SACP urged Cabinet to take note of mass opposition to the system and instruct Sanral to abandon it,[46] also urging motorists not to register for e-tolls (at later stages it went quiet). Several church bodies, including the South African Council of Churches – in relation to the impact of e-tolling on the poor – further swelled the ranks of the alliance. The QuadPara Association of South Africa and the EFF were on board as well, the EFF threatening in its 2014 election campaign to physically remove the gantries, describing e-tolls as robbery of people who already cannot cope with the high cost of living. The Road Freight Association and the National Taxi Alliance weighed in as occasional participants, the latter because many of its taxis had not been issued with operating licences, making them liable for billing (taxis generally had already secured exemption in the pre-election time of early 2014, as millions of citizens use taxi transport daily in Gauteng). Adding to transport fares of the working classes was an impossible risk for the ANC to bear in Election 2014. The most powerful 'member' of the anti-tolling alliance was the citizenry who defied the system, and continued to do so in the face of growing obstacles and threatened penalties.

The anti-e-tolling alliance was the most formidable opposition alliance yet to emerge in post-1994 politics. It offered lessons in how ideologically diverse groupings could converge to oppose, stall and undermine (if not stop) undesirable policy. At the heart of the citizen component of this resistance project were the Gauteng freeway users – although it was illegal not to pay, Sanral refrained from pushing legal action against offenders, at least up to 2015. Outa and others had pledged legal support should anyone be formally charged; there was also a litany of road-user reports of inaccuracies and failures in the implementation of the system, cloning of vehicle registration plates being a major contributing factor to the lack of its credibility. In May 2015 Cyril Ramaphosa announced a new government compromise position, which carried the potential penalty of unpaid fees being attached to the renewal of motor vehicle licences.[47] While motorists were considering their options, the anti-tolling alliance immediately started voicing the legal pitfalls of the new penalties. The concessions that earned the label of 'lipstick on a pig' included overall lower fees, a lower cap on total monthly fees, exemption of public transport and discounts for arrears.

For a long period, Sanral had vacillated about implementation of the automated Gauteng e-toll system. It had often stalled through protracted legal challenges by organised civil society, especially Outa. First implementation would have started in February 2012. It eventually followed in December 2013, but it was partial and subject to the civil resistance. The year 2012 was high noon, with mobilisation and court challenges by Outa: as an attempted compromise national government announced in its annual budget that it would foot 25 per cent of the cost of the Gauteng Freeway Improvement Project, enabling Sanral to drop the e-toll fees. Protest grew, irrespective. Nationwide Cosatu protest against e-tolling (and labour brokers) followed. Outa filed a founding affidavit in the North Gauteng High Court, seeking an interim interdict, which was granted pending a full judicial review. In May, the Treasury filed an application to appeal the interdict in the Constitutional Court. In September, the Constitutional Court set aside the temporary interdict, enabling Sanral to proceed with e-tolling. The year ended with High Court hearings and the judgement that overruled Outa. The Gauteng e-toll process thus revealed some of the schisms in the Tripartite Alliance besides those between the ANC's national and provincial units. It also challenged Sanral to be more transparent in the details of funding mechanisms. In the Western Cape the DA took court action to force Sanral to reveal its planned tolling rates on select provincial roads. The details were only revealed once the Supreme Court of Appeal in Bloemfontein set aside a Western Cape High Court ruling that had ordered the particulars to remain secret.

An additional line of division was the national ANC and government against the Gauteng ANC and provincial government. The tolls were implemented but Gauteng baulked and reopened the issue. The dice were loaded: Gauteng voters were becoming alienated and voted against the ANC (or did not vote at all). Gauteng also became more assertive regarding the equitable distribution of state funding among provinces and the fact that Gauteng cross-subsidises other provinces' economies (countering the argument that other provinces should not be liable to help pay for Gauteng roads). Cosatu had been using this reasoning since 2012, without much effect on national government.[48]

The saga gains impetus in 2013, with Outa getting leave to appeal. By mid-year Sanral hands over contract documents to the DA, including the hitherto secret Electronic Toll Collection files. The Supreme Court hears Outa's appeal in September. In the interim, Zuma signs the Transport Laws and Related Matters Amendment Bill into law, legislation which regulates the implementation of e-tolls. The DA challenges its legality, arguing that it should have been handled as a law that affects provinces, and routed via the National Council of Provinces. In October the Supreme Court of Appeal rules against Outa.

The years 2014–2015 bring a new series of complications. A previous premier's pre-election provincial State of the Province address calls for glitches in the system to be removed. The High Court dismisses the DA's challenge to the implementation legislation. Kgalema Motlanthe defends e-tolling and urges motorists to pay. ANC Secretary General Mantashe says that Gauteng motorists should stop whining and pay – he calls the e-toll debate 'misplaced' and 'emotional', and denies that it has affected ANC 2014 electoral support. Gauteng's transport MEC notes that moves are afoot to scrap e-tolls as means to fund freeway improvement. In his State of the Province address, the next Gauteng premier, David Makhura, announces an advisory panel to 'review the impact of e-tolls'. Sanral blames Makhura for its partly failed bond option issue (Sanral depends on monthly bond options to raise operational capital). October 2014 sees the ANC Gauteng congress resolve to oppose the application of e-tolls *in its current form*, leaving the door open to a reasonable fuel levy. Gauteng ANC chairperson Paul Mashatile states that the ANC governs the country, not Sanral. A Department of Transport spokesperson retorts that it is the function of the minister of transport, and not the ANC (or the Gauteng ANC), to change policy. The Gauteng ANC provincial conference nevertheless pronounces on the issue in no uncertain terms and it is difficult for national government and Luthuli House to entirely ignore the resolution.[49] The Gauteng ANC itself presents its proposals to the panel, making it one among many; Mashatile alludes to the need for persuasion: 'I think the ANC nationally will be very happy with what we are saying … National government won't be there if they do not have the people to support them.'[50] The Gauteng review panel is, however, pressured into complying with national policy. It recommends alternative payment methods, such as increased fuel levies, and in 2015 the minister of finance flaunts further subsidies to reduce costs. By now the Gauteng ANC is more compliant and Mashatile attacks opposition party calls for an e-toll referendum, arguing that the people have already spoken through inputs into the review process.[51] Gauteng's subjugation to the national government came full circle with Ramaphosa's 2015 announcements, although the Gauteng ANC was diplomatic and pretended that its recommendations had been incorporated.

Resistance against e-tolls were driven by the pricing (substantially reduced, in several tranches) and by suspicions of corruption. Several politically connected companies were reported to be benefiting from the e-tolls contract and its multiple subcontracts. These companies were related to the ANC and Cosatu (otherwise part of the anti-tolling alliance). Cosatu's investment arm Kopano Ke Matla was revealed in 2012 to own shares in Raubex, a construction company that won a tender to build one of the freeways that were being tolled to pay for construction,[52] but no singular financial benefit relation for the ANC can be inferred. It is possible that most of the deals were above board, yet they lack transparency and some subcontracts created suspicion.[53] Pointers for further clarification included Tshebo Holdings, in which Nozala Investments and Lereko each owned 15 per cent at the time. At the head of Nozala was a trustee of the ANC's front company, Chancellor House; Lereko is owned by former Cabinet member Valli Moosa and the another Chancellor House trustee and the first ANC premier of the North West, Popo Molefe. Furthermore, Vodacom and GijimaAST would benefit, the latter 35 per cent owned by Robert Gumede, an ANC backer.

That the Gauteng ANC at first was prepared to rise in mild opposition to e-tolls, but then succumbed to the dictates of central government and top ANC structures, was a signal of what the ANC might do or not do under popular pressure – and equally an indication of how national ANC will dig in its heels in arrogant belief that it will be able to fix the damage at a later stage and through election campaigning. At first, the Gauteng ANC showed willingness to listen to its citizens, in defiance of national ANC. It could not, however, continue in its defiance. Gauteng ANC had been proudly against Zuma in campaigning for the ANC's Mangaung elective conference. It also played host to significant Zuma booing incidents – for example, at the memorial service for Nelson Mandela. However, the province's resistance against the national ANC master crumbled.

CONCLUSION: ANC COMPROMISES AND 'NEW GOVERNMENT'

The ANC's 2014 election result had briefly woken it from a contented slumber induced by a sense that it is invincible and will be in power for at least another hundred years. In the interregnum between Elections 2014 and 2016 the ANC has been jolted by reinvigorated opposition in national and provincial legislatures, but also by tenacious opposition from both organised and grassroots civil society. There was a wall of effective and policy-specific new opposition, with methods ranging from civil disobedience to violent community protests that included community justice, looting and arson. Post-election monitoring of community protest has shown a consistent stream of violence and disruption, combined with xenophobic attacks. Elements of xenophobia had been present in many of the protests for some time – it was just when these attacks spiked that they were denoted as xenophobic.

The ANC's 62 per cent electoral majority thus did not indicate that the party had been given a trusting and unconditional mandate to get on with the job of governing. Citizens handed the ANC its sizeable majority but was watching it from all sides, even protesting, to optimise chances for further policy changes. The ANC was irritated and its confidence dented at a time when it knew it was in charge of a politically controlled state with immense weaknesses. The state has huge resources but is compromised in its capacity, and hampered considerably by the superimposition of prerogatives of political loyalty to ANC's in-government operations. This ANC could obviously not assume that another election campaign like that of 2014 would sufficiently leverage the delivery of the ongoing liberation trail. Despite the liberation dividend persisting, the space to be filled by evidence of delivery (or information-propaganda that overall delivery is continuing to take shape) is growing. In lieu of delivery showing much further improvement, in crucial areas citizens will also scrutinise the extent to which protection of the president and the ANC's associated in-state games had detracted from better performance.

The ANC has worked hard to create the impression of a 'new government' and that it is as determined as the range of opposition formations. It argued in 2014 that it was now ready for *real* implementation and revealed its subscription to the consultant-driven fast-tracking Operation Phakisa for more efficient delivery.[54] Malusi Gigaba, at the time a chosen new-generation government member, argued that the ANC had learned that it needs to remain close to the people.[55] The presence of the EFF helped the ANC to sharpen its inventory. To illustrate: in October 2014 shack fires devastated the Kya Sands informal settlement, outside Johannesburg; the EFF was on site immediately to assist the community and was captured on national television. Twelve hours later, Gigaba, post-election also minister of home affairs, was on site facilitating new fee-exempted identity documents for the residents who had lost all (he also made it onto national television).

Two sets of questions in this chapter illuminate the future of the ANC beyond the time of Zuma, and its ability to regenerate its political power. The first is whether the protest action will continue to be a holding block, a cool-off capsule for discontent with the ANC – or whether protest is a signifier of pending defection from the ANC (also by young voters who have never voted ANC but were a prime catchment area). Protest incidence has grown, and protest communities are signifiers of how extreme discontent and possible alienation convert into continuous party political support, especially in elections and in relation to the ANC. The research for this study showed that while the dual repertoire persists, it *is* weakening. The study also set out a grid of protest environments, triggers, factors of representation that moderate or escalate protest, and inherent protest expediters to help elucidate sequences of causes of protest action. This helps to differentiate the levels of causes of protest. The second is whether the protest and new opposition are indicators of a broader alienation from institutional politics and less trust in the institutions of the ANC-controlled state to resolve the problems that citizens face. By the time the full impact of these events is felt, Jacob Zuma is likely to be a long-retired ex-president.

NOTES

1   Susan Booysen, 2012, 'Enduring under duress – "the ballot and the brick" amidst diversifying opposition', chapter 17 in S. Booysen (ed.), *Local Elections in South Africa: Parties, People, Politics*, Stellenbosch: SUN Press with Konrad Adenaver Foundation.

2   See Jacob Zuma, 17 June 2014, State of the Nation address by President Jacob Zuma, joint sitting of Parliament, Cape Town; Peter Alexander, 2010, 'Rebellion of the poor: South Africa's service delivery protests – a preliminary analysis', *Review of African Political Economy*, 37; Lerumo Tauyatswala, 20 February 2014, 'The anatomy of community protests in a post-apartheid South Africa', *Umsebenzi Online*, vol. 13 (7); Karen Heese and Kevin Allan, 21 February 2014, '"Victims of success" argument both true and false', http://www.bdlive.co.za/opinion/2014/02/21/victims-of-success-argument-both-true-and-false, accessed 7 October 2014; Karl von Holdt et al., 2011, *The Smoke that Calls: Insurgent Citizenship, Collective Violence and the Struggle for a Place in the New South Africa*, Johannesburg: Centre for the Study of Violence and Reconciliation. Also see Richard Pithouse, 2007, 'The University of Abahlali baseMjondolo', *Voices of Resistance from Occupied London*, 2 (October), pp. 17–20.

3   Peter Alexander and Peter Pfaffe, 2013, 'Social relationships to the means and ends of protest in South Africa's ongoing rebellion of the poor: The Balfour insurrections', *Social Movement Studies: Journal of Social, Cultural and Political Protest*, http://dx.doi.org/10.1080/14742837.2013.820904, accessed 12 March 2014.

4   Susan Booysen, 2007, 'With the ballot and the brick: The politics of service delivery in South Africa', *Progress in Development Studies*, vol. 7 (1), pp. 21–32; Susan Booysen, 2009, 'Beyond the "ballot and the brick": Continuous dual repertoires

in the politics of attaining service delivery in South Africa?' in Barry Munslow and Anne McLennan (eds), *The Politics of Service Delivery in South Africa*, Johannesburg: Wits University Press, pp. 110–142; Susan Booysen, 2012, op. cit.

5   Derek Powell, Michael O'Donovan and Jaap de Visser, 2015, Civic Protests Barometer 2007–2014, Community Law Centre, p. 11.

6   Zachary Levenson, 2014, 'Social movements in South Africa', Solidarity, Summer School 2014, http://www.solidarity-us.org/node/3677, accessed 28 July 2014, finds the same in relation to a case study of protest in Durban.

7   Susan Booysen, 2013, *Twenty Years of South African Democracy: Citizen Views of Human Rights, Governance and the Political System*, research report, Johannesburg and Washington DC: Freedom House.

8   Karl von Holdt, 2012, in P. Alexander and K. von Holdt, 'Collective violence, community protest and xenophobia', Debate, *South African Review of Sociology*, vol. 43 (2), pp. 104–111.

9   Ibid., pp. 105–106.

10 National Treasury, 2015, *2015 Public Sector Supply Chain Management Review*.

11 Niki Moore, 24 March 2015, 'The Civic Protest Barometer, episode five: So, what can be done?' *Daily Maverick*, http://www.dailymaverick.co.za/article/2015-03-24-the-civic-protest-barometer-episode-five-so-what-can-be-done/, accessed 25 March 2015.

12 Karen Runciman, quoted in Verashni Pillay, 14–20 February 2014, 'The many lives of Julius Malema', *Mail & Guardian*, p. 10.

13 Susan Booysen, Alta de Waal, Hans Ittmann and Peter Schmitz, 2014, 'Withstanding the test of time? Probing the "protest-vote ANC" dual repertoire in South Africa's Election 2014'. Workshop deliberations.

14 Point contributed by Michael Donovan, interview, 25 June 2014, Johannesburg.

15 Small number, given the large overall numbers of citizens in informal housing structures, including backyard shelters; see Housing Development Agency, 2013, *South Africa: Informal Settlements Status (2013)*, http://www.thehda.co.za/uploads/images/HDA_South_Africa_Report_lr.pdf, accessed 2 April 2014.

16 Jackie Borel-Saladin and Ivan Turok, 2013, 'Census 2011 reveals boom in backyard shacks', *Human Sciences Research Council (HSRC) Review*, http://www.hsrc.ac.za/en/review/hsrc-review-may-2013/census-2011-reveals-boom-in-backyard-shacks, accessed 1 May 2013.

17 Peter Alexander, Carin Runciman and Boitumelo Maruping, 2015, *South African Police Service Data on Crowd Incidents: A Preliminary Analysis*, Social Change Research Unit, University of Johannesburg, report on their project to start making sense of official Incident Registration Information System (IRIS).

18 See Kevin Allan and Karen Heese, 7 October 14, 'Understanding why service delivery protests take place and who is to blame', http://www.municipaliq.co.za/publications/articles/sunday_indep.pdf, accessed 9 October 2014.

19 Auditor general South Africa, 2014, *Consolidated General Report on the Audit Outcomes of Local Government: MFMA 2012–13*, http://www.agsa.co.za/Portals/0/MFMA%202012-13/2012_13_MFMA_Consolidated_general_report.pdf, accessed 27 August 2014.

20 The protest research projects at UJ and UWC are inconsistent, using disputable categorisations. For example, representation and service delivery issues are often stated side by side as reasons, along with the specification of issues.

21 See, for example, government's arguments for more of the media being vested in state hands in Mmanaledi Mataboge, 17–23 July 2015, 'State's new propaganda plan to hurt media budgets', *Mail & Guardian*, pp. 2–3.

22 Susan Booysen, 2013, op. cit.

23 Derek Powell et al., 2015, op. cit.

24 Richard Pithouse, 2007, op. cit., p. 17.

25 Peter Alexander and Peter Pfaffe, 2013, op. cit.

26 Jacob Zuma, 14 August 2014, in interview with Kevin Ritchie, 'Zuma – leaner, and confident that SA is on the right track', *Cape Times*, p. 10.

27 The details in this section are from a research project by Susan Booysen, 2011–2014, undertaken with funding from the University of the Witwatersrand. I thank Samantha Ball for research assistance on the project.

28 ANC, 2015, ANC NGC 2015, Discussion documents, *Umrabulo*, special edition; Wayne Duvenage, 5 May 2012, interview with Charl du Plessis, 'Avis man had appetite for battle', *City Press*, p. 9.

29 See Ilham Rawoot, 9–15 September 2011, 'Stories that wouldn't have been told', *Mail & Guardian*, p. 4.

30 Verne Harris, 10 October 2013, 'What is still wrong with the Protection of State Information Bill?' Research and Archive of the Nelson Mandela Centre of Memory, http://www.nelsonmandela.org/news/entry/what-is-still-wrong-with-the-protection-of-state-information-bill, accessed 4 October 2014.

31 See analysis by Dene Smuts, 18 September 2011, 'The sinister heart of the Secrecy Bill laid bare', *Sunday Times Review*, p. 5.

32 For example, *Creamer Media*, http:www.polity.org/article/if[=statement-by-the-ikatha-frrrdom-party-calling-for-a-suspension-of-the-NCOP-info-bill-hearings, accessed 27 February 2010; Glynnis Underhill and Lynley Donnelly, 23–29 September 2011, 'NEC members deny prompting halt of Secrecy Bill', *Mail & Guardian*, pp. 8–9.

33 The details are outlined in Kwanele Sosibo, 8–14 June 2012, 'MPs' input on Secrecy Bill spurned', *Mail & Guardian*, p. 8.

34 See David Smith, 24 February 2015, 'South Africa scrambles to deal with fallout from leaked spy cables', http://www.theguardian.com/world/2015/feb/24/south-africa-scrambles-to-deal-with-fallout-from-leaked-spy-cables, accessed 4 March 2015.

35 Andisiwe Makinana, 10 May 2015, 'Secrecy Bill creeps closer', *City Press*, p. 8.

36 The bullet points are derived from, among others, Vinayak Bhardwaj, 23 October 2013, 'ConCourt: Likely next step for Secrecy Bill', *Mail & Guardian*, http://mg.co.za/article/2013-10-23-concourt-likely-next-step-for-secrecy-law, accessed 1 June 2014; also see Emsie Ferreira, 11 May 2012, 'ANC relents on key parts of disputed "Secrecy Bill"', *Business Day*, p. 5.

37 Dario Milo, 11 June 2012, 'Limiting restrictions to transparency', *The Star*, p. 11.

38 See Thabo Mokone, 1 April 2012, 'MPs defend Secrecy Bill expulsion', *Sunday Times*, p. 4.

39 Joe Latakgomo, 10 February 2012, 'A stick to beat the media into submission', *Sowetan*, p. 11.

40 See Andisiwe Makinana, 15–22 December 2011, 'ANC investigates "defiant" MPs', *Mail & Guardian*, p. 5.

41 Nickolaus Bauer, 24 May 2012, 'Battle lines drawn as ANC takes "Spear" fight to the streets', *Mail & Guardian*, http://mg.co.za/article/2012-05-24-battle-lines-are-drawn-as-anc-takes-spear-fight-to-the-streets, accessed 30 July 2014.

42 Sipho Hlongwane, 30 May 2012, 'Spear march: ANC claims victory, but gallery stands its ground', *Daily Maverick*, http://www.dailymaverick.co.za/article/2012-05-30-spear-march-anc-claims-victory-but-gallery-stands-its-ground/#.VDuvXBZ6joQ, accessed 10 January 2014.

43 Moipone Malefane, 29 September 2011, 'ANC revolt blocked Secrecy Bill', *Sunday Times*, p. 2.

44 Outa, 'The court case', http://www.outa.co.za/site/the-court-case/, accessed 10 October 2014; extensive media monitoring by author.

45 Wayne Duvenage, 22 May 2015, interview SABC-SAFM.

46 SACP, 2012, 'Ban labour brokers! Stop e-toll highway robbery!' Pamphlet.

47 Cyril Ramaphosa, 20 May 2015, full text of announcement of changes to the e-tolling of Gauteng highways, http://www.rdm.co.za/politics/2015/05/20/my-new-plan-for-e-tolls, accessed 1 June 2015.

48 See Dianne Hawker and Moffet Mofokeng, 3 June 2012, 'Cosatu toll plan', *The Sunday Independent*, p. 1.

49 Ranjeni Munusamy, 'Gauteng ANC: Another twist in the e-toll', *Daily Maverick*, http://www.dailymaverick.co.za/article/2014-10-06-gauteng-anc-another-twist-in-the-e-toll/#.VDJTrxZ6joQ, accessed 6 October 2014.

50 Paul Mashatile, interview with Sakena Kamwende, SABC-SAFM, *Forum at 8*, 8 October 2014.

51 Paul Mashatile, 25 March 2015, 'E-tolls train has already left the station', http://www.iol.co.za/the-star/e-tolls-train-has-already-left-the-station-1.1837021#.VRVAJOEQvq0, accessed 27 March 2015.

52 Mandy Rossouw and Sabelo Ndlangisa, 1 April 2012, 'Tolls: Cosatu cashed in', *City Press*, p. 2.

53 Rob Rose, Mzilikazi wa Afrika and Stephan Hofstatter, 6 May 2012, 'ANC link to e-toll profits', *Sunday Times*, p. 1.

54 In 2013 Zuma was introduced to the Malaysian 'Big Fast Results Methodology', renamed Phakisa, or 'Hurry up', from the Sesotho. The government website explains that it involves setting clear plans and targets, conducting ongoing monitoring of progress and making these results public; http://www.operationphakisa.gov.za/Pages/Home.aspx, accessed 27 November 2014.

55 Malusi Gigaba, 8 May 2014, remarks to Susan Booysen, IEC Centre, Pretoria.

9

CONCLUSION – 'THE ANC IS IN TROUBLE'

The ANC's troubles started long before the tenure of Jacob Zuma as president, but reached their zenith with him at the helm. 'We admit the organisation is in trouble,' said Zuma, famously, to the ANC Youth League.[1] In this book, the phrase bears witness to the party-movement's electoral decline, organisational decay, weakened people's bond, and institutions of state and government sagging under the burden of factional-political abuse. Implicit in Zuma's statement was that much had gone right for the ANC, and because of the ANC, in its first two decades and more in power. The analysis in this book, equally, acknowledges the substantial change that took root, and specifically investigates the extent to which the ANC in the time of Zuma has been responsible for undermining itself.

Zuma's admission was an unsurpassed confession of the condition of party-and-state that came to be in his time. Contradictory behaviour was more usual – for example, to weaken the Tripartite Alliance but issue statements on how 'sacrosanct' it was, as in the mid-2015 NEC statement that 'the unity and cohesion of the Alliance is sacrosanct and … determined action should be taken to preserve, continue to build and strengthen the Alliance's capacity' to lead society'.[2] The weakness was substantially brought on by Zuma, but the president was the product of the ANC, placed in power by an ANC that re-elected him as the best person for the job. The ANC does not entirely deny the deficits and lapses under its watch, but it portrays these as externally caused, as levelled by opposition-ist, counter-revolutionary and hostile forces. The vanguard Zuma-ists, in full flight between the cover pages of the special edition of *Umrabulo*, containing the National General Council's 2015 discussion documents, write away their own cul-pability and prepare for a warlike and state-anchored offence on their attackers.

This book has synthesised those troubles, how the ANC's difficulties have expanded in the time of Zuma, roughly in the decade from 2005 to 2015 with four more Zuma years likely to follow. Zuma-ANC acolytes have assured the country that Zuma will serve out his term as president of South Africa, up to 2019. There has been a lobby to extend his term as ANC president by another two years, from 2017 (when his term as ANC president is set to end) to 2019 (to coincide with his term as president of South Africa).[3] The rationale is that this would avoid the par-ty's two-centres-of-presidential-power queries and probable pressures for Zuma to leave the country's executive position once his term as ANC president expires.

The backbone of ANC support persists, even if by now battered and, by all indications, in decline. This ANC is not in *lethal* trouble. The path of difficulties is still reversible, at least as far as the organisation and its relationship to the peo-ple are concerned. No opposition party is in touching distance. Yet, and despite Zuma's off-script ANC-in-trouble confessional, the ANC is not transmitting any signals that it is prepared to show humility, to look at the interests of the broader movement, or to consider the interests of multiparty and constitutional democ-racy rather than what is best for the Zuma corner of the ruling party.

Instead of introspectively identifying and addressing the party's prevailing troubles, the ANC inner circles, united largely around Zuma, are ruling the party with an attempted iron fist. For example, they are ensuring that the ANC in Parliament keeps opposition to heel; security and intelligence agencies (to the extent that they are functional) do what is required to enable the ANC's main body and predominant faction to rule and puts forth strident strate-gic documents to identify the hostile forces that are 'derailing the revolution'. Meanwhile the organisation tolerates public sector maladministration, legisla-ture malfunction and political class corruption because it would be politically dangerous to discipline more than a mere handful of deployees. Instead of an internal focus and reconsideration, this ANC is on mini-witch-hunts, identify-ing enemies. The ANC is a large organisation, forever sprouting factions and ambitious groupings, and could never control all that happens within, but it has been good at controlling processes where they mattered and where they helped the centre to hold.

The 'enemies' were found in the EFF, Numsa, the budding United Front and workers' party, the DA, the public protector, at times the judiciary, the media, and a host of names and faces who may have cooperated with these 'prime evils' of the Zuma era.[4] Zuma's ANC (incorporating the SACP) has become a master at the use of ideological expletives. The charges of fascists, neofascists, populists, demagogues, grey shirts, oppositionists – or even just enemies of democracy – were stacked on the heads of opponents and critics. It turned into a dangerous game for the critics of the ANC, because the 'enemies' were being framed for 'destabilising democracy' and undermining the political order. The Zuma ANC had got to the stage of pretending to see itself as personifying democracy – and anyone who did not share that view was in trouble, for those with the most power in the ruling party were willing to act forthrightly against the 'enemies' of the Zuma-ist ANC party-state.

Cosatu was being disassembled and this could well have been at the back of Zuma's mind on that November 2014 morning when he spoke the 'in trouble' words. The Cosatu split was largely instigated by the Zuma-ists, with acolytes in the Cosatu main body – overwhelmingly for the sake of containing criticism of Zuma and his ANC. Zuma was also referring to the ANC Youth League under Malema – the bottom-line reason for its exorcism was because it had criticised the leader and his influential associates. Now the former ANCYL in the form of the EFF had come to haunt the ANC, in both its previously safe territory, Parliament, and on the ground. The DA was also troubling the ANC. It had been growing steadfastly, with control in the Western Cape and inroads into the economic heartland of Gauteng. The opposition parties have become a problem for the ANC in that not only are they in a *de facto* coalition against ANC and government corruption and maladministration, but both have young black-African leaders who, in different ways, epitomise the youthful politics of a post-liberation generation.

The Zuma ANC circa 2014–2015 is under attack from the left and the right. Most significantly, President Zuma is at the heart of most of the ANC's weaknesses – and symbolises many others. Regardless, this ANC continues to be, or at least to present itself as, a believer in Zuma. The ANC is not about to suffer defeat on either flank, but is in the invidious position of having to fend off attacks on both sides. Simultaneously, it needs to get its state administration to perform better to help ensure longer-term performance amid stifling economic and fiscal conditions.

Zuma has been a strong president and leader, in a peculiar way, of the inner circles of the ANC and the ANC-infused public institutions.

Successors, both in and beyond his camp, hover but don't dare show their hands – disqualification from the presidential race is the only certain response to such 'premature' ambition. But such is Zuma's organisational power that he could slip in at a later stage a candidate of his own choice while other contenders are deferring and abiding by the apparent Zuma rules of contest. A range of these ambitions were starting to become evident in 2015, even if indirectly as a result of electoral battles in the ANC leagues and regions. Official confirmations could only follow much later. ANC deployment at top-government level extended the realms of personalised ANC rule. It was no problem for Zuma to bring the state to heel. His word, even a hint of a wish (Guptagate and Nkandla come to mind), became 'law' and the desire of the underlings. Zuma retained loyalty because those around him knew that if their last round of presidential allegiance left anything to be desired they could be demoted, discarded and disqualified.

A massive amount of power has remained vested in Zuma's hands. He has governed through the ANC, even if it is a reduced ANC, an ANC believing it could live the life of a narrow project linked to Zuma while preclaiming unfolding paper revolutions. The top level of the ANC has expanded the government project into building a middle class of which they are a part. For the millions below that status, the ANC has to keep alive the hope that tomorrow will be better than today.

TROUBLE AND REDEMPTION ACROSS THE FOUR FACES OF ANC POWER

Dominance and Decline builds on my 2011 book, *The African National Congress and the Regeneration of Political Power*, to pinpoint the four faces or pillars across which the ANC builds (and destroys) its political power. These are the ANC organisationally, the ANC in relation to the people, the ANC in elections, and the ANC in state and government.

Dominance and Decline records the changes to ANC political power in the time of Zuma. It captures inexorable decline. Zuma's presidency, supposed to have been the redeemer for an ANC that under Mbeki had increasingly disconnected from the people, has achieved the opposite. Zwelinzima Vavi had conflated his rejection of Mbeki policies with reading good leadership attributes into Zuma's political persona.[5] This well illustrates the conundrum of Zuma's rise to power. The problems did not start with Zuma, but his tenure has consolidated the ANC's trajectory of decline.

The core contradiction is how the ANC damages itself, harms constitutional democracy and undermines the democratic political order, yet retains much popular support and sufficient trust to continue being chosen in elections above other political parties. Behind this top line, however, the analysis outlines how unfolding processes weaken the ANC's hold on power. The synthesis that follows interprets the changes in each of the four pillars.[6]

The *three main sources of power* – operating across the pillars – on which the ANC draws to ensure that the process of decay is slow are the polishing of its liberation credentials; its ability as governing party to bring changes to people's lives; and its use of and influence over information to ensure the sheltering, marketing and management of public agendas and perceptions of the ANC. On this front, the ANC has leveraged powerful influence but not total control. The *greatest possible drawbacks* in the ANC's struggle to retain power include its gradual loss of credible claims as the heir to the liberation dividend; the high levels of self-embarrassment (highlighted but not caused by opposition parties) and disregard for people's insights into damage the ANC was inflicting; no apparent recanting on an ANC leadership belief that it can appropriate or abuse public resources, only correcting problems and perceptions partially at election times; annihilating state institutions in aid of the pursuit of factional interests; and using state security apparatuses for internal ANC warfare and external ANC control.

Pillar One: ANC organisationally

The organisational pillar has been subjected to the most dramatic decline of the four, yet people are also cynical about other political parties and politics generally, hardly believing that opposition parties would be an improvement and accepting the ANC's transformation to the status of a modern party that barters bourgeois patronage for working-class social wages (more under Pillar Two). Nevertheless, the decline is serious and has implications for the ANC's overall project of sustaining and regenerating its political dominance:

- The greatest internal ANC weakness comes from the tight control the Zuma grouping exercises over the organisation. Zuma is a strong leader *within the ANC*, intent on always being in strategic command and protecting leadership self-interest against being blindsided in the ANC organisationally. This being the main leader's central focus, the overall

296

organisation is impoverished. It is a fragile organisational leadership, maintaining its supremacy through suppression of dissent.

- One of the greatest injuries in the time of Zuma has been the ANC's loss of powerful leagues. The Youth League under Malema was expelled, albeit after it had become unruly and in conflict with the main body and ANC top leadership. The remainder of the ANCYL disintegrated and the attempted substitute failed to get off the ground in 2014, emerging haltingly in 2015. The EFF, by now a bigger presence than the former ANCYL, returned to haunt the main party. The Women's League continued as a hollow presence with occasional media statements, albeit bolstered by its chant of 'a woman for president'. The Veterans' League was ineffectual and divided, wracked by contentions of corruption. All three leagues nevertheless hoped to be reinvigorated through conferences and leadership elections. The 2015 NGC meeting was their deadline.

- The Tripartite Alliance under Zuma went from a powerful mobilising force to an embarrassing collapse. Where once there was a steadfast labour Alliance partner, by 2015 there were emasculated main bodies and scattered dissidents. Numsa, by now supported by Vavi and a line-up of former Cosatu unions (in some instances segments of these unions), was nurturing a rising counter-federation. What the Zuma-ists had triggered was a reduced, Zuma-loyal labour union. The SACP gave up its voice as internal sounding board. This fate was delivered by a culture intolerant of criticism, and insistence on subservience to the leader Zuma. The SACP have become Zuma's storm troopers, but accuse the EFF of being 'grey shirts'.

- The ANC's membership had grown to well over 1.2 million, and it hoped for more than two million ... while updated 2015 figures often showed declines. The ruling party had the benefit of a widely diffused branch system, which gave it strong potential to mobilise. The branches' executives played gatekeeper, alienating members, but potential and new members saw affluent insiders as role models in the branch leadership. The number of ANC branches also grew massively. It was ironic – if very accurate – that Zuma had listed gatekeeping and the influence of money among the problems in the new ANCYL, and the 2015 Alliance summit noted these as problems in the ANC main body.

- An essential element in the ANC's survival is to keep the memories of and its association with the struggle against apartheid alive. The ANC excels at this, and uses the state's cultural and communications offices to reinforce the link. Through the occurrence of continued inequality and racism the ANC could continue offering concrete grounds for mobilising against an external 'enemy force'; consequently it was easier to maintain more internal cohesion, or at least greater force in mobilisation, for ongoing hegemony. In some respects the ANC is in a no-lose situation: every incident of racism and every reminder of apartheid and colonial legacies is a motivation for the struggle to continue.

- The ANC is a well-resourced political organisation, despite occasional reports of financial 'hardship'. It continuously mobilises for donations, including from networks of those benefiting from state business. It plays cleverly with state resources; it is difficult to fault the ANC for benefiting unduly from public funds. The fusion between party and state also means that the ANC as party gets credit for the actions of the state, using public funds. Few in South Africa (and almost all who have a significant profile in the organisation) ever want to be seen to be on its wrong side. Power regenerates power.

The ANC in the time of Jacob Zuma thus appeared poised to shed several of the spokes in its organisational wheel – the Tripartite Alliance, Cosatu as a viable and unchallenged force, and the SACP as a credible concern. ANC branches across the provinces and ANC regions were increasingly corrupted when both factional warfare and branch memberships became commodities for leadership battles. Many 'little ANCs' became part of a constellation of factions – giving political identity to those who fall out with the organisation but recognise the benefits of sitting out time in offshoots. These are enclaves of ANC supporters who do not see eye to eye with the dominant ANC, but know that there are better lives for themselves if they go into political hibernation until the ANC wheel turns again.

The ANC in Luthuli House might be content about thwarting recent threats. However, the ANC's core is narrower, more contracted than ever around the Zuma grouping, and less attractive to a new generation of post-liberation citizens. It is a mass movement with growing membership (at least up to the release of formal 2014 figures), but this membership is mainly constructing a web based on mass patronage. Still, new supporters flow in – often in pursuit of transactions for jobs and tenders. As long as the state keeps functioning at levels that create opportunities and networks, this reinvented ANC – an ANC comprising members who often care neither about leadership ethics and integrity nor about the history of the organisation – will still be in the political game for the long haul.

Pillar Two: ANC in relation to the people

The ANC under Jacob Zuma did not follow through on the great Polokwane promise to reconnect with the people. Close to a decade later, the Zuma ANC was still learning the same lesson: the message that the Zuma-ists claimed to have gained from the 2014 election was that it needed to move closer to the people! (It demonstrated through delivery that it cares, but *for the time of Zuma* exact delivery details were often shrouded in silence – the preferred period of reportage was the inclusive period since 1994.) Next, the ANC claimed it needed more state-anchored media to communicate better with the people.

The people pillar remains distinct from the electoral pillar because citizens, and ANC supporters in particular, still tend to forgive at the time of elections. At other times, however, people are critical and challenging, and their behaviour often testifies to their changed relationship with the ANC. There was no sudden turning point in this relationship but during Zuma's tenure the texture changed towards more cynicism and criticism. It is also historically inevitable that the new generations will have a weaker appreciation of the ANC as liberator – although the ANC works hard to keep it alive, and holding the key to jobs and consumer-plenty helps.[7] The struggle between dominance and decline plays out through the following turns:

- The ANC retains a special bond with the people of South Africa, the liberation bond ('the ANC gave me my freedom' as per election campaign paraphernalia). However, it is counterbalanced with popular ridicule and scorn for Jacob Zuma, ranging from booing the president in stadiums to fervid attention to television broadcasts of parliamentary proceedings in which opposition members try to hold the president to account.
- In citizens' everyday thinking about their ANC there is little left of the revered former liberation movement. They no longer accept that the ANC holds the wisdom, and is right beyond criticism. Most people still reckon that they can trust the ANC to look after their interests more than they can trust the other parties, and had it not been for the people's generalised cynicism of *all* political parties the ANC would have fared much worse. The threat to the ANC in these times is that the public (and its own electoral following) will reckon that an opposition party could do a better job –

299

hence the ANC's concerted work to ensure that citizens are socialised in the belief that the struggles against racism and socioeconomic inequality have only just started.

- The intra-parliamentary left and right opposition, well supported by the people in and beyond elections, are rewriting the rules of the game and the ANC's responses are inadequate. The EFF sets new trends as a voice for angry people. The arguments raised by the opposition often echo those that the general citizenry expresses about the ANC as governing party.
- The more the ANC leadership is seen as fallible, the more it strengthens the popular hand in demanding more from the governing party. People feel entitled to good service and opportunities but are also relishing the ANC's corruption predicament: if the leaders are looking so well after themselves in becoming rich, getting into business (and especially business with the state) and finding employment for their family and associates, then the people have the right to ask the governing party to do more for them too.
- As the range of opposition parties widened during the Zuma era the people became more alert to alternatives. The scope and texture of opposition politics changed in this period, with the growth of substantial party political opposition to the left and the right of the ANC. More left opposition, especially, is taking shape and the ANC's left authenticity is challenged.
- Thus far the ANC still benefits from community protest that serves largely as a vent to let off anger with poor governance and living conditions. Protest is still used to barter for better government and a more responsive ANC. This is to the benefit of the ANC because there is less chance of the anger converting into electoral support for the opposition parties. The margins by which the ANC wins elections in protest communities, however, are decreasing. Protesters often welcome opposition party presences in their protests because this helps increase pressure on government (they do not necessarily vote for these parties). In some communities, however, protest has assumed a hostile and near-insurrectionary character (this is still the exception rather than the rule).

The ANC's relationship to the people shows slippage, but not dramatic collapse, apart from hostility in some protest communities and anti-ANC voting in Gauteng. The increased distance between the people and those in power releases more potential for future conversion into anti-ANC voting and so the ANC is working hard – low key and furtively on national radio and television – to retain its liberation link, using the state apparatus extensively to build its popular image as a party that brings change, is still occupied with the task of liberation and is working to prevent the spillover of between-election anger into electoral outcomes.

Pillar Three: ANC in elections and opposition politics

Shrinkage in the ANC's electoral majorities in the time of Zuma has played a big role in reshaping South African and ANC politics. The ANC has set the scene but the EFF and (occasionally) the DA are changing the rules of the game. Electoral regeneration of power is considered a distinct pillar, apart from 'the people', and analysed differently because elections are still the time when people relate to the ANC in a special way, remembering the struggle and the euphoria of 1994, liberation and the achievement of democracy. The ANC has also become skilled at recasting every new election as a new milestone in a liberation process that is now a much longer-term endeavour. The main acts in the ANC's struggle between dominance and decline at the electoral front are:

- The ANC in the elections under Zuma's presidency has suffered serial declines since its highs of 2004 in national and provincial elections. The decline is severe by standards of ANC hegemony, even if it retains an edge of close to forty percentage points over its closest party rival. The gap has shrunk by twenty percentage points in the last decade. The ANC's majorities in Gauteng and its metro areas have slipped into danger territory.
- The ANC nevertheless continues to notch up victories, using all possible aids to secure this standing. It has the help of a vast state apparatus to bring favourable exposure and delivery that synchronises at election times, when state departments and agencies that deal with social services come into full play. The ANC achieved its 62 per cent 2014 national result (instead of a below 60 per cent outcome) with the aid of South Africa's celebration of twenty years of democracy and the delivery cycles and events that could be orchestrated to serve its election objectives. The ANC could count on persistent support for its mantra of 'we gave South Africa its freedom'. The mass media are steered into favourable and extensive coverage – especially of the ANC government's work – at election times.
- The ANC is not about to suppress its citizens violently in order to manufacture election victories. It gives itself time and works pre-emptively. But this work is done under increasing duress. By 2015 the economy and

301

economic growth prospects remained in dire straits, while the budget deficit continued to balloon and questions were raised about the sustainability of social services (this, while public delivery was one of the ANC's most indispensable tools). Information and propaganda play a substantial part in the ANC's power repertoire.[8]

- The ANC is secure in knowing that its election results, though gradually weakening, are not collapsing. A series of three post-election Ipsos opinion polls of 2014–2015 show that the ANC is on a modest recovery track in Gauteng, and is steadying in some other provinces; its KwaZulu-Natal support pillar of 2009 and 2014, however, is slipping. The EFF and DA gained from the tide turning against the ANC. Their inroads have also been largely in urban and metropolitan areas, with the ANC hanging onto the rural vote. In this process and in the context of urbanisation trends, the ANC became more rural than before – and this was a vulnerable rural base.

- The tracks on which the key opposition parties run are not necessarily sturdier than the ANC's – and the ANC knows how to work to destabilise the likes of the EFF, as it did with Cope. By 2015 the ANC was undermining the EFF in multiple ways but by now the country is more alert to this type of interference. The EFF itself is street-smart – by members' own admission, when they were part of the ANC many of them were destabilisers of other parties. Because of its own leaders' histories, however, the EFF remains vulnerable.

- The ANC could still be severely punished for the protection it has so unreservedly extended to Zuma. On the other hand, the popular relief and gratitude towards the ANC for shedding Zuma (*once* he goes, and even if voters know that he is on a fixed term) may be so great that the ANC will gain substantial electoral rewards. Such recompenses would, however, be mediated by voter estimates of the closeness between Zuma and his successor, and by his or her political credibility.

It is only the threat of electoral defeat (in total or in strategically important sites) that will force the ANC to change its choices and behaviours. The ANC cannot dare to be seen to be falling foul of 'free and fair' elections or to refuse to accept legitimate results. However, the weakened ANC that continues to hold power is also arrogant in power. It could be argued that just as the ANC thinks it has enough control over the state to utilise it for pre-election bail-outs, the state itself may be losing many of its abilities.

Pillar Four: ANC in state and government

The state under the ANC in the time of Zuma appears decidedly weak and weakening. Illusions of policy radicalism substitute for new ideas, approaches and unambiguous implementation. The state bureaucracy at all levels lives a life of widespread adverse audit opinions, speaking of corrupt, unauthorised, indefensible and unaccountable state expenditure. The ANC majorities in the legislatures are subjugated to the executive, making a mockery of constituency and citizen representation. The president is 'king' and accountability is a foreign concept except at the nominal event level, and to a controlled extent within the ANC itself. The rule of law prevails to the extent that it does not interfere with the president and party's comfort zones: if the president wishes to escape from legal and court rulings, he will find ways to circumvent and postpone; if the ANC and president have the need to flout legal rulings, they will assert upper wisdom; if policy and governance fall short of legal and constitutional requirements, there will be historical, structural and international enemies or 'hostile forces' that will be pinpointed as the causes.

In this context the ANC state propaganda machine is gearing up, going as far as to pursue and effectively demobilise institutions such as the public protector (and on occasion the court) if they bear critiques of President Zuma, his immediate appointees, and inner circle of senior executive members. The greatest of the ironies of the ANC's coexisting dominance and decline in the time of Zuma is evident in the domain of the state:

- The ANC pretended that intractable policy problems had been solved through the NDP, before it gradually allowed NDP narratives to become subdued, but then indicated some resurrection in its NGC discussion documents. Both the plan and government action in general are labelled 'radical' to help the ANC sustain popular hope for better things to come, but in reality the ANC and its policies promote a decidedly middle-class project, supplemented with a vast social security network for the lower classes. Ironically, the new middle classes are politically divided, not returning the favour in full to the ANC, even when these classes are the products of patronage.
- Just as Zuma is not held accountable to his executive, neither does he truly hold his executive to account, apart from performance agreements linked broadly to Medium Term Strategic Framework outcomes and retribution if they fail the president in his personal pursuits. Zuma uses frequent Cabinet reshuffles (or their threat) to keep an upper hand. If underperformers and

discredited deployees remain useful to the president, they are side-shuffled rather than dismissed. Zuma restructures national government departments and further reduces accountability – new departments are frequently too new at the job to be assessed. Zuma creates interministerial committees and uses task teams as evidence of action on vexing problems of service delivery, e-tolls, Nkandla, Cosatu, labour turmoil, and buckled state-owned enterprises. There is little evidence of policy leadership by the president on the vexing issues of economic growth and employment creation.

- The ANC is fused with and entrenched in state power. Deployment of loyal cadres helps effect this control. With thorough attention to the profiling of 'good delivery news' from government, the bad news about corruption and embarrassing leaders becomes subdued. The ANC and its president refined the act of speaking out against cadre deployment (and the incompetence in performing state functions that accompanies it), and the act of promising action without following through in any significant way. The state security agencies such as the NPA, along with the core state-owned enterprises such as Eskom, Prasa and South African Airways, suffered in the time of Zuma. Damage happened often at the hands of cadres who were close to the president and in whose appointments he had had a direct hand.

- The president is personally (formally and informally) in control of the security and intelligence apparatuses. Challenges to the ANC are construed as attacks on and threats to 'democracy', even if in fact they are frequently valid and legitimate attacks on the ANC's dereliction of democratic duty. Presidential paranoia has infected the ANC and it has spread through the state apparatuses.[9]

- The ANC's apparent tolerance of corruption has demonstrated that its exercise of official power is weak. It is fragile in its deployment and retention of tainted cadres ruled neither by government nor the ANC. It displays to the people the fallibility of their own leaders.

- The ANC in state and government – also on instruction from the president and the ANC NEC – does not hesitate to try to thwart state institutions that cross swords with the president. The public protector is the foremost example.

- The ANC exercises creeping control over information – in multiple forms that are more sophisticated than outright coercion and high-level policing of the media. The ANC already has extensive influence. Some media houses are unabashedly pro-Zuma and ANC. State subsidisation comes through mass subscriptions, transfers for televised business breakfasts, and advertising. They often offer column space for senior government and ANC voices. Some purportedly independent community publications are under ANC influence or control.

- In several respects the ANC in state and government does bring improvement. Especially where it is under electoral threat, such as since 2014, the ANC has come across as a new government. There is renewed talk of accentuated initiatives in industrialisation and industrial development in Gauteng townships, infrastructure accumulation, and initiatives to develop the marine economy, or nuclear expansion. Senior ANC government functionaries (for example, the Gauteng premier), senior and top-six ANC officials, and occasionally the president himself are seen to be moving around in their communities. The media are there to bring the good news of the caring government.

State power gives access to power, and also electoral power. The South African state can still notch up the delivery records and ensure national awareness of the ANC's prowess. But how long can it so do?

TRAJECTORIES OF UNFOLDING 'TROUBLE'

Condensed scenarios for the ANC's future 'trouble trajectories' covering the period up to 2024 help to emphasise the most salient of its power-holding trends unfolding across the four pillars. Current indications are that the ANC will still be holding onto power for a considerable time, but its margins in places and at times may be minuscule. It might be moving perilously close to the end of the road of seamless power. The following lines of argument are thus based on developments in the ANC organisationally, in relation to the people, in elections in competition with other parties, and in state and government. They project 'alternative futures' that arise out of Election 2019:

- The ANC flounders further. The leagues and Tripartite Alliance continue to disintegrate. Opposition to the left of the ANC grows. The ANC is at war with itself as non-Zuma factions try to wrest control in the 2017 ANC elections, but fail. Citizen trust declines further. This is both for ANC political

305

reasons and because citizens stop believing that the economy can grow sufficiently under the ANC and that the ANC has a better ability than other parties to achieve meaningful economic growth. Opposition parties are flawed but, with the ANC failing to rebuild popular confidence, they grow in appeal, and both the DA and EFF take bigger chunks of ANC support. The ANC loses its outright national electoral majority in 2019, yet remains governing party because minor opposition parties do not align and hand the ANC control. The ANC uses its control and influence over the media to try to wrest back power. A Zuma clone who replaced Zuma as the ANC president ensures that the ANC remains *en route* to self-destruction.

- The ANC in further gradual decline. It survives Election 2019 with a new leader who came on board, although too late to engineer a turnaround or establish a post-Zuma identity for the ANC. (If the new leader rises as a result of being identified and endorsed by Zuma, much of the new hope will dissipate.) The ANC owes much of its continuing credible electoral performance to the voters' relief that the Zuma era has ended. However, state and government still suffer the aftershocks of the previous terms' leaderless regime. Too many of the former power moguls and their ambitious factotums are still hovering. The ANC continues to hang in when it comes to economic policy, and continues reinventing and supplementing the NDP. The EFF takes big forward strides and deprives the ANC of new support but shares the left territory with the workers' party. The EFF is hamstrung nevertheless by its own leadership squabbles and survives because of the support of voters who believe they have nothing to lose.

- ANC turnaround. The ANC carries out a frank internal self-reflection as to why its support and power have been slipping. It holds its 2017 national elective conference on a truly open slate, allowing new voices and credible, young leaders to emerge, so that they can bring a fresh new uprightness to Luthuli House. It facilitates open, authentic internal elections with incorruptibility, talent and dedication to shaping a new ANC as the foremost criteria for candidates. The 2019 voters reward the ANC handsomely. The ANC government does a thorough policy audit and convenes a special post-2017 election policy conference to launch a rapid process. It declares an 'emergency clean-out' of corrupt politicians and bureaucrats. Post-election, it wins back part of the EFF, with members who are satisfied that the EFF has played out its role as catalyst in exorcising Zuma and the Zuma-ists. This new ANC's focus is on correcting its own problems, rather than waging war on critics. The ANC is by now a modern post-liberation party. It continues to build national unity, but does not use liberation struggle as pardon for deficits in leadership.

The resilience and trusting forgiveness of large numbers of South Africans remain the ANC's best resource, guaranteeing that the ANC will not completely disintegrate in the short term. It is possible that the windfall of moving beyond Jacob Zuma as president would be great for the ANC, and the people would reward the party-movement for the step, forgiving many of the other shortfalls, forgetting ANC misdemeanours and other gross neglects, and steering the ANC into another cloud of optimism for renewal, and into 2019 elections that will celebrate a quarter-century of democracy. Zuma's hold over the ANC, however, has been so extensive that when he leaves the party could suffer an identity crisis in a post-Zuma void. Then would be the time for serious introspection and for a new strategy to ensure that the Zuma cult is not reinvented.

FORWARD TO THE 'THIRD LIBERATION STRUGGLE'

The ANC's 'third liberation struggle' is fought largely within itself, with the two 'personas' of the same former liberation movement battling it out. The first liberation struggle was the great emancipation that took the ANC into armed resistance, cessation, and finally the constitutional negotiations and settlement. Aided by its internal and international partners, the ANC won. The struggle for the consolidation of democracy followed, requiring demonstration that the ANC had accepted the new rules of the game and used its commanding power to bring transformation. The ANC was at the crest of its power and it was easy to play by the rules (and accept the rules as the only rules) when few threats loomed.

The third and unfolding struggle is the ANC's to win or lose. Its contours speak from the pages of this book. The ANC battles with choices between multiparty liberal democracy and invoking the great nationalistic-patriotic struggle to override constitutionalism and the rule of law – and dictating people's judgements. This third struggle sees two ANCs coexisting and contesting: one upholds constitutional state expectations and legal process and sees itself as required formally to play by the rules. The other thrives on subjugating the rules and subduing opposition and critics in the name of its electoral majority. This ANC applies state power for party-movement benefit, and specifically to promote its hold on power.

There are limits to how much the dual-character ANC can reinvent itself. The two ANCs work in conjunction to remain entrenched and, at least for the next decade – perhaps two! – will fend off growing opposition assaults. It knows that if it cedes more power electorally it runs the risk of uncontrolled domino-style slippage. One of the greatest dangers is that the ANC will interpret non-violent, institutional, robust verbal attacks in the worst possible way. Unless the ANC becomes more tolerant of criticism, it will be a 'dangerous' ANC in times to come: the defensive-manipulative ANC is likely to see many 'threats to its legitimate rule' and will use the state to minimise attacks.

The ANC's perceived 'threat' is likely to be aggravated by its constituencies' expectation for their movement to bring more evidence of completed liberation in the form of delivery and opportunities for advancement. The ANC state and government face the predicament of policies that do not go far enough. A strident patriotic bourgeoisie (also continually fostered by the ANC) are the ones who reap the benefits and whose interests articulate with those of the new ANC leadership. Where the ANC fails to deliver and transform sufficiently, its 'second-best' option is to work on how citizens perceive it. It hence needs to ensure that criticisms of the ANC either are moderated or come across as misplaced, from disloyal, misguided, hateful and dangerous enemy sources.

The details in this book demonstrate the ANC's 'impressive' repertoire for dealing with regenerating power in the time of Zuma. The party's mechanisms clearly go beyond the strictly democratic, multiparty, and free and fair kinds of political power regeneration, and into the domain of the 'second ANC'. To retain power, the party uses its control and influence over the media, state delivery cycles, and direct handouts. It also uses state institutions and resources. It makes life as difficult as possible for critical voices and opposition parties. It uses suspect and compromised appointees in senior positions to build compliance with the ANC and the president's wishes. It uses its majority in Parliament to deliver preferred political situations. When it fails to get its way, it accuses critics and opposition parties of destabilising the government and country, or of being agents of hostile foreign agencies that also use non-governmental organisations and the courts 'to undermine South African democracy'. It is a case of paranoia meets deflection.

To sustain these 'attacks in defence of democracy' the ANC needs and uses some slanted messages. ANC propaganda of the first order is on its projected self-image. Some of the rules are: Never admit that the problem is internal and inherent to the ANC's current leadership. The causes are in colonialism, capitalism, racism, the West, the EFF, Numsa, and even former ANC leaders. ANC propaganda of the second order concerns its influence and control over the media: create your own (state) media outlets, maintain ANC shareholding, or ensure there is a sympathetic ear available to media companies prepared to trade news coverage for political influence. In the case of public media, by ensuring appointments the party guarantees that there will be instructions to include sympathetic coverage.

The ANC itself defines how long the dispensation of special rights and condemnation of opposition because of the horrors of the past will last. It certainly will not in the near future stop seeing or projecting current interrogations of its operations and motives as assaults on itself as the torch-bearer of all just causes. The ANC tries to restrict opposition politics to the 'safe' chambers where it can use its majorities to determine the outcomes. Yet state intelligence and other security services are in the service of an ANC faction and even an ANC individual. Many members and leaders within the ANC find the ANC forbidding.

It is possible that South Africa has not yet seen the worst of the damage that the Zuma-ists can inflict on democracy – and on the ANC itself. In its twenty-plus years of democracy, the ANC movement could have evolved to leave more space for opposing internal and external voices. Instead, the Zuma-ANC stepped in to use internal authoritarianism – forged around a 'threatened leader' – to build a 'new frontier' against recalcitrant enemy forces, to keep the party together under a narrow, no-criticism, 'trust and follow the leader' mantle. Unfortunately the leader was deeply flawed. The ANC in the time of Zuma has become so closely questioned and so exposed for its failings that even the most positive of scenarios cannot suggest that there is a turning back and that the ANC will become stronger again.

NOTES

1   Jacob Zuma, 26 November 2014, mid-speech off-prepared-text remarks delivered at the initial consultative conference of the new ANCYL. On the eve of this conference the National Working Committee determined that it would be a consultative and not an elective conference. Zuma continued: 'There are mistakes that happened in this glorious movement since 2005 … which must not repeat themselves. We as

the leadership made a mistake by not attending to [these mistakes] ...The Youth League has been shaken and also the mother body has been shaken ...'

2   ANC, 20 June 2015, 'ANC statement on Alliance summit and ICC deliberations', Johannesburg.

3   *Mail & Guardian*, 21–27 April 2014, 'Bid to extend Zuma's term of office', pp. 2–3; Mmanaledi Mataboge, Matuma Letsoalo, Qaanitah Hunter and Thulani Gqirana, 27 March–2 April 2015, 'Bleeding ANC will still sing along with Zuma', *Mail & Guardian*, p. 8.

4   See, for example, Sarah Evans, 1 December 2014, 'Mystery document alleges Numsa is bent on regime change', *Mail & Guardian*, http://mg.co.za/article/2014-12-01-mystery-document-alleges-numsa-is-bent-on-regime-change, accessed 1 December 2014; the designation 'prime evil' is mainly associated with apartheid assassin Eugene de Kock, commanding officer of a counter-insurgency police unit that kidnapped, tortured and murdered anti-apartheid activists in the 1980s and 1990s (he was paroled in 2015).

5   Zwelinzima Vavi, 19 June 2015, interview with Power FM.

6   In typical scenario-building style each of the scenarios contains sets of variables – each linked to one of the four driving forces, for purposes of this study taken as the four pillars of ANC political power. Different combinations of the variables will produce variations on the three broad scenarios that this section outlines. See Susan Booysen, 2004, 'The scenario toolbox: Conceptual and practical tools in scenario building', Workshop on envisioning alternative futures, Nelson Mandela Metropolitan University.

7   *The African National Congress and the Regeneration of Political Power* quotes an ANC intellectual in 2011 who said: '[Electoral change] is like an ocean wave rolling towards the coast ... [the defeat of the ANC] will happen but we do not know the distance to the shore.'

8   Propaganda is defined as information of a biased or misleading nature, used to promote a political cause or point of view; see http://www.oxforddictionaries.com/definition/english/propaganda, accessed 2 October 2014.

9   For the broader theoretical context, see David Moore, "The end of the liberal attempt in Africa: The return to an authoritarian *durée*', forthcoming in *Socialist Register 2015: The Politics of the Right Today*.

SELECT BIBLIOGRAPHY

Basson, Adriaan. 2012. *Zuma Exposed*. Johannesburg: Jonathan Ball.

Booysen, Susan. 2011. *The African National Congress and the Regeneration of Political Power*. Johannesburg: Wits University Press.

Booysen, Susan. 2012. *The ANC's Battle of Mangaung*. Cape Town: Tafelberg Shorts e-Book series.

Booysen, Susan (ed.). 2012. *Local Elections in South Africa: Parties, People, Politics*. Stellenbosch: Sun Press with Konrad Adenauer Foundation.

Booysen, Susan. 2013. *Twenty Years of South African Democracy: Citizen Views of Human Rights, Governance and the Political System*. Research report. Johannesburg and Washington DC: Freedom House.

Booysen, Susan. 2015. *Youth and Political Participation in South Africa's Democracy*. Research report. Johannesburg and Washington DC: Freedom House.

Boraine, Alex. 2014. *What's Gone Wrong? On the Brink of a Failed State*. Johannesburg and Cape Town: Jonathan Ball.

Buhlungu, Sakhela and Malehoko, Tshoaedi (eds). 2013. *Cosatu's Contested Legacy: South African Trade Unions in the Second Decade of Democracy*. Leiden: Brill.

Bundy, Colin. 2014. *Short-changed? South Africa since Apartheid*. Auckland Park: Jacana.

Butler, Anthony (ed.). 2014. *Remaking the ANC: Party Change in South Africa and the Global South*. Auckland Park: Jacana.

Calland, Richard. 2013. *The Zuma Years: South Africa's Changing Face of Power*. Cape Town: Zebra Press.

Cronjé, Frans. 2014. *A Time Traveller's Guide to Our Next Ten Years*. Cape Town: Tafelberg.

Du Preez, Max. 2013. *A Rumour of Spring: South Africa After 20 Years of Democracy*. Cape Town: Zebra Press.

Forde, Fiona. 2014. *Still an Inconvenient Youth: Julius Malema Carries On*. Johannesburg: Picador Africa.

Gevisser, Mark. 2007. *Thabo Mbeki: The Dream Deferred*. Johannesburg and Cape Town: Jonathan Ball.

Gordin, Jeremy. 2008. *Zuma: A Biography*. Johannesburg and Cape Town: Jonathan Ball.

Grootes, Stephen. 2013. *S.A. Politics Unspun*. Kenilworth: Two Dogs.

Habib, Adam. 2013. *South Africa's Suspended Revolution: Hopes and Prospects*. Johannesburg: Wits University Press.

Landman, J.P. 2013. *The Long View: Getting Beyond the Drama of South Africa's Headlines*. Auckland Park: Jacana/Stonebridge.

Mangcu, Xolela. 2014. *The Arrogance of Power: South Africa's Leadership Meltdown.* Cape Town: Tafelberg.

Marais, Hein. 2001. *South Africa: Limits to Change: The Political Economy of Transition.* 2nd edition. London: Zed Books.

Mashele, Prince and Mzukisi Qobo. 2013. *The Fall of the ANC: What Next?* Johannesburg: Picador Africa.

McKaiser, Eusebius. 2013. *Could I Vote DA? A Voter's Dilemma.* Johannesburg: Bookstorm.

Meyiwa, Thenjiwe, Muxe Nkondo, Margaret Chitiga-Mabugu, Moses Sithole and Francis Nyamnjoh (eds). 2014. *State of the Nation 2014: South Africa 1994–2014: A Twenty-Year Review.* Cape Town: HSRC Press.

Murray, Martin J. 1994. *The Revolution Deferred.* London: Verso.

Ndletyana, Mcebisi (ed.). 2015. *Institutionalising Democracy: The Story of the Electoral Commission of South Africa.* Pretoria: Africa Institute of South Africa.

Odendaal, André. 2012. *The Founders: The Origins of the ANC and the Struggle for Democracy in South Africa.* Auckland Park: Jacana.

Pressly, Donwald. 2014. *Owning the Future: Lindiwe Mazibuko and the Changing Face of the DA.* Cape Town: Kwela.

Ramphele, Mamphela. 2008. *Laying Ghosts to Rest: Dilemmas of Transformation in South Africa.* Cape Town: Tafelberg.

Ranchod, Rushil. 2013. *A Kind of Magic: The Political Marketing of the ANC.* Auckland Park: Jacana.

Saul, John. 2014. *Flawed Freedom: Rethinking Southern African Liberation.* Cape Town and London: UCT Press and Pluto Press.

Schulz-Herzenberg, Collette and Roger Southall (eds). 2014. *Election 2014 South Africa: The Campaigns, Results and Future Prospects.* Auckland Park: Jacana.

Shivambu, Floyd. 2014. *The Coming Revolution: Julius Malema and the Fight for Economic Freedom.* Auckland Park: Jacana.

Siddle, Andrew and Thomas Koeble. 2012. *The Failure of Decentralisation in South African Local Government: Complexity and Unanticipated Consequences.* Cape Town: UCT Press.

Sparks, Allister. 2003. *Beyond the Miracle: Inside the New South Africa.* Johannesburg: Jonathan Ball.

Suttner, Raymond. 2015. *Recovering Democracy in South Africa.* Auckland Park: Jacana.

Turok, Ben. 2014. *With My Head Above the Parapet: An Insider Account of the ANC in Power.* Auckland Park: Jacana.

wa Africa, Mzilikazi. 2014. *Nothing Left to Steal: Jailed for Telling the Truth.* Johannesburg: Penguin.

Zegeye, Abebe and Julia Maxted. 2002. *Our Dream Deferred: The Poor in South Africa.* Pretoria: SAHO and Unisa Press.

INDEX

Page numbers in italics refer to information in illustrations.

Printed and bound by CPI Group (UK) Ltd, Croydon, CR0 4YY

09/06/2025

14685834-0003